WASSERSTROM

BIBLE AND QUR'ĀN

SBL

Society of Biblical Literature

Symposium Series

Christopher R. Matthews,
Editor

Number 24

BIBLE AND QUR'ĀN
Essays in Scriptural Intertextuality

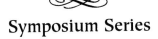

BIBLE AND QUR'ĀN

Essays in Scriptural Intertextuality

Edited by
John C. Reeves

Society of Biblical Literature
Atlanta

BIBLE AND QUR'ĀN

Essays in Scriptural Intertextuality

Cover photo of Pesher Habakkuk, Qumran, courtesy of the D. Samuel and Jeane H. Gottesman Center for Biblical Manuscripts, The Israel Museum, Jerusalem.
Cover photo of the page of Qur'an manuscript OIM A6991 containing Surahs 73:19 courtesy of the Oriental Institute of the University of Chicago.

Library of Congress Cataloging-in-Publication Data

Bible and Qur'ān : essays in scriptural intertextuality / edited by John C. Reeves.
p. cm. — (Society of Biblical Literature symposium series ; no. 24)
Includes bibliographical references and indexes.
ISBN 1-58983-064-4 (pbk.)
1. Bible—Criticism, Textual. 2. Koran—Criticism, Textual. 3. Islam—Relations—Christianity. 4. Christianity and other religions—Islam. 5. Koran—Relation to the Bible. I. Reeves, John C. II. Series: Symposium series (Society of Biblical Literature) ; no. 24.
BS471 .B492 2003
220.6—dc22 2003016705

11 10 09 08 07 06 05 04 03 5 4 3 2 1

Printed in the United States of America on acid-free, recycled paper conforming to ANSI/NISO Z39.48-1992 (R1997) and ISO 9706:1994 standards for paper permanence.

Contents

Preface

This volume owes its genesis to a series of conversations transpiring during the fall and winter months of 2001 between myself and Kent H. Richards, the executive director of the Society of Biblical Literature. Conducted under the black shadow of September 11 and distilled to their essence, our discussions centered on the disturbing lack of "official" attention granted to the biblical currents visible in the Qur'ān and its allied traditions by the Society and its constituent research, program, and publication units. Given the copious and well-attested historical, literary, and cultural linkages connecting the scriptural libraries of Judaism, Christianity, and Islam, one would anticipate encountering among the Society's proceedings a respectable number of paper proposals, article submissions, or funded research projects actively or at least tangentially exploring qur'ānic and later Islamic readings and representations of biblical characters, narratives, and themes.

We soon discovered this was not the case. There was, for example, no active program unit among those annually convened at the Society's national meetings (nor at the subsidiary regional conferences) whose defining rubric would invite such proposals.[1] A cursory search through the titles and abstracts of papers presented by Society members within these venues during the past decade uncovered almost no examples that addressed any aspect of this type of study. An inspection of the published contents of the Society's principal organ, the *Journal of Biblical Literature*, over an analogous period of time produced similar results. While the examined evidence demonstrates that many of the Society's members are heavily involved in the comparative study of biblical literature within both its ancient Near Eastern and Greco-Roman cultural contexts, it also shows that very few members today concern themselves with the Bible's (and its allied literature's) reception and reconfiguration within Islam and its world of discourse.

Things were not always this insular within the guild of biblical scholarship. Barely over a century ago, "giants" such as Goldziher, Nöldeke,

---

[1] One successful by-product of the efforts expended in producing the present volume was the formation and approval of a "Bible/Qur'ān" program unit whose initial sessions will take place at the 2003 annual meeting in Atlanta.

Wellhausen, and Robertson Smith trod the scholarly landscape, philologists and historians who were equally versatile in both biblical and Islamic studies (along with much else) and who made significant contributions to the advancement of each of these disciplines. Although uncommonly gifted and rightly celebrated for their many influential insights, these four scholars in particular were hardly unusual for their broad range of interests and abilities. To judge from a representative sampling of the articles published in some of the mainstream disciplinary journals during this era (roughly 1860–1930),[2] a significant number of their professional predecessors, peers, and successors wielded a parallel range of competencies. Largely unexceptional in this same regard were North America and its Society of Biblical Literature (founded in 1880), wherein scholars such as Richard J. H. Gottheil, Julian Morgenstern, James A. Montgomery, and C. C. Torrey exhibited a similar versatility of linguistic and critical tools.

At least two factors arguably play a role in explaining the present-day neglect of the Qur'ān and its biblical readings by most contemporary professional scholars of Bible. One is the inevitable consequence of an unfortunate institutional "reform." Since the early decades of the twentieth century, there has been a wholesale abandonment by graduate programs in biblical studies of the largely European model of a relatively lengthy comprehensive "orientalist" philological education—one that simultaneously contextualized and privileged Bible and biblically based societies among its linguistic and cultural peers, including, most importantly, Qur'ān—in favor of the largely American model of a relatively attenuated specialization in one narrowly defined discipline or even subdiscipline. Those students who today elect to pursue biblical studies in an academic setting are typically pressured both socially and economically to constrict their scholastic focus and to accelerate their graduate apprenticeship. They are often encouraged to acquire only those tools and skills minimally needed to attain a rudimentary competence and win employment within a rigidly compartmentalized and jealously competitive academic culture. Most search committees tend to view those job candidates who straddle or blur the "accepted" categorizations with perplexity, unsure where or even how to locate such versatile candidates on the map of "approved" specializations.

Another possible factor contributing to the dearth of qur'ānic studies by contemporary biblical scholars involves the general disapproval under which comparative studies have labored since the advent of the

---

[2] E.g., *Zeitschrift für die alttestamentliche Wissenschaft*, *Zeitschrift der deutschen morgenländischen Gesellschaft*, *Journal of Biblical Literature*, and *Journal of the American Oriental Society*.

postmodern critique of Western humanistic scholarship. Many such critics allege that the process of comparison itself is methodologically flawed, claiming that it necessarily and inevitably produces an evaluation involving the ultimate subjugation and diminishment of one of the compared terms in the light of and to the favor of (or privileging of) the other. There is admittedly some truth to this charge with regard to the earlier history of the comparative study of Bible and Qur'ān: one of the first examples of a supposedly "scientific" treatment of the literary relationship between these two scriptures is unabashedly devoted to exposing the latter's parasitic dependence upon Jewish traditions.[3] Nevertheless, the generic critique of comparativism as currently expressed is far too sweeping in its indictment: there are indeed legitimate means through which the comparative enterprise can be conducted that do not entail a distortion and dismissal of either pole of reference.[4] Furthermore, as noted above, biblical scholars have not heretofore displayed a particular reticence or discomfort when situating Jewish and Christian scriptures among the literary remains of nonbiblically based societies associated with the cities of Babylon, Ugarit, or Alexandria. An analogous contextualization of the contents of Bible and Qur'ān—a scripture that places itself within the biblical world of discourse—within and across their interpretative boundaries has the potential to shed an equally and mutually informative light on the compositional and hermeneutical strategies of these socially distinct yet discursively related textual communities.

In order to underscore the Society's awakened interest in and commitment to this important type of interscriptural study, I accepted its commission to identify and invite a small group of scholars whose published works already signaled an interest in the intersection of the scholarly disciplines of biblical and qur'ānic studies to prepare a set of essays that would address philological, historical, and/or cultural aspects of the textual and exegetical interfaces among the scriptures of the Abrahamic religions. For the purposes of this collaborative enterprise, the contributors were directed to construe the rubrics "Bible" and "Qur'ān" holistically and to embrace all facets of their respective exegetical embellishments: for Bible,

---

[3] See the important analysis of Susannah Heschel, *Abraham Geiger and the Jewish Jesus* (Chicago: University of Chicago Press, 1998), 50–63, as well as Reuven Firestone's discussion in this volume of Geiger's 1833 prize essay *Was hat Mohammed aus dem Judenthume aufgenommen?*

[4] See, e.g., the important recent collection of essays *A Magic Still Dwells: Comparative Religion in the Postmodern Age* (ed. K. C. Patton and B. C. Ray; Berkeley and Los Angeles: University of California Press, 2000).

this meant not only working with its "canonical" versions but also so-called "parabiblical" expressions found in classical Jewish sources,[5] apocrypha and pseudepigrapha, and early commentaries; for Qur'ān, this included considerations of the interpretive traditions found in *ḥadīth, tafsīr,* universal histories, *qiṣaṣ al-anbiyā',* and the like. The essays included in the present volume embody the response to this invitation and bear witness to a wide variety of interests and concerns. It is our collective hope that these essays will stimulate further contributions to this fascinating and exciting field of endeavor.

Citations and notational conventions generally follow the style guide of the Society of Biblical Literature and will be familiar to most students of biblical and Jewish literature.[6] Since that template does not typically incorporate notices of journal titles and standard bibliographic resources used by Islamicists, I have prepared a separate comprehensive list of abbreviations for the reader's convenience. Transliteration conventions for the various Semitic languages generally follow those suggested by the SBL style guide and the *Encyclopaedia of the Qur'ān* respectively.[7] Unless otherwise noted, references to the text of the Qur'ān use the enumeration of the standard Egyptian edition: they are indicated by the siglum Q, followed by numerical references to chapter (*sūra*) and verse (*'āya*).[8]

By way of conclusion I would like to express my deep appreciation to my collaborators for their enthusiastic response to my invitation to contribute to this volume despite the short time frame granted to them for preparation and the competing demands and pressures exerted on them by other professional obligations.

John C. Reeves
University of North Carolina at Charlotte

---

[5] I have borrowed the term "parabiblical" from a series of largely oral remarks by Robert A. Kraft regarding the difficulty of isolating a common "scripture" across the varieties of early Judaism and Christianity.

[6] *The SBL Handbook of Style for Ancient Near Eastern, Biblical, and Early Christian Studies* (ed. P. H. Alexander et al.; Peabody, Mass.: Hendrickson, 1999).

[7] *Encyclopaedia of the Qur'ān* (ed. J. D. McAuliffe; Leiden: Brill, 2001–). Two volumes (A–D; E–I) have appeared to date.

[8] E.g., Q 2:101.

Abbreviations

Primary Sources

ʾAbot R. Nat.	*ʾAbot de Rabbi Nathan*
Abr.	Philo, *De Abrahamo*
Ant.	Josephus, *Jewish Antiquities*
Apoc. Ab.	*Apocalypse of Abraham*
b.	Babylonian Talmud
B. Bat.	*Baba Batra*
Barn.	*Barnabas*
Dial.	Justin Martyr, *Dialogus cum Tryphone*
Gen. Rab.	*Genesis Rabbah*
L.A.B.	*Liber antiquitatum biblicarum* (Pseudo-Philo)
Lev. Rab.	*Leviticus Rabbah*
m.	Mishnah
Meg.	*Megillah*
Mek.	*Mekilta*
Midr. Tanḥ.	*Midrash Tanḥuma*
Midr. Teh.	*Midrash Tehillim*
Moʾed Qaṭ.	*Moʾed Qaṭan*
Naz.	*Nazir*
Ned.	*Nedarim*
Num. Rab.	*Numbers Rabbah*
Pesiq. Rab.	*Pesiqta Rabbati*
Pesiq. Rab. Kah.	*Pesiqta de Rab Kahana*
Pirqe R. El.	*Pirqe Rabbi Eliezer*
Prot. Jas.	*Protevangelium of James*
QG	Philo, *Quaestiones et solutiones in Genesin*
Šabb.	*Šabbat*
Sanh.	*Sanhedrin*
t.	Tosefta
Taʿan.	*Taʿanit*
Tanḥ	*Tanḥuma*
Tg. Neof.	*Targum Neofiti*
Tg. Ps.-J.	*Targum Pseudo-Jonathan*
Tg. Yer.	*Targum Yerušalmi*
Yal. Šim.	*Yalquot Shimoni*

Secondary Sources

ABD	*Anchor Bible Dictionary*. Edited by D. N. Freedman. 6 vols. New York: Doubleday, 1992.
ABR	*Australian Biblical Review*
AcOr	*Acta Orientalia*
AJSR	*Association for Jewish Studies Review*
AnBoll	Analecta Bollandiana
APOT	*The Apocrypha and Pseudepigrapha of the Old Testament*. Edited by R. H. Charles. 2 vols. Oxford: Oxford University Press, 1913.
BHM	*Bet ha-Midrasch*. Edited by A. Jellinek. 6 vols. Leipzig, 1853–77. Repr., Jerusalem: Bamberger & Wahrmann, 1938.
BibInt	*Biblical Interpretation*
BJRL	*Bulletin of the John Rylands University Library of Manchester*
BO	*Bibliotheca orientalis*
BSOAS	*Bulletin of the School of Oriental and African Studies*
CSCO	Corpus scriptorum christianorum orientalium
DJD	Discoveries in the Judaean Desert
DOP	*Dumbarton Oaks Papers*
EI[1]	*Encyclopaedia of Islam*. Leiden: Brill, 1913–38.
EI[2]	*Encyclopaedia of Islam*. 2d edition.Leiden: Brill. 1954–.
EncQur	*Encyclopaedia of the Qur'ān*. Edited by J. D. McAuliffe. Leiden: Brill, 2001–.
ER	*Encyclopaedia of Religion*. Edited by M. Eliade. 16 vols. New York: Macmillan, 1987.
GAS	*Geschichte des arabischen Schrifttums*. F. Sezgin. 9 vols. Leiden: Brill, 1967–84.
HUCA	*Hebrew Union College Annual*
IEJ	*Israel Exploration Journal*
IOS	*Israel Oriental Studies*
JA	*Journal asiatique*
JAOS	*Journal of the American Oriental Society*
JBL	*Journal of Biblical Literature*
JE	*The Jewish Encyclopaedia*. Edited by C. Adler et al. 12 vols. New York: Funk & Wagnalls, 1901–6.
JJS	*Journal of Jewish Studies*
JNES	*Journal of Near Eastern Studies*
JQR	*Jewish Quarterly Review*
JRAS	*Journal of the Royal Asiatic Society*
JSAI	*Jerusalem Studies in Arabic and Islam*
JSNT	*Journal for the Study of the New Testament*

JSS	*Journal of Semitic Studies*
JSSSup	Journal of Semitic Studies Supplement Series
JTS	*Journal of Theological Studies*
LCL	Loeb Classical Library
Luria	*Sefer Pirqey Rabbi Eliezer ha-Gadol*. Edited by D. Luria. Warsaw, 1852. Repr., Jerusalem: [n.p.], 1970.
Mandelbaum	*Pesiqta de Rav Kahana*. Edited by B. Mandelbaum. 2d ed. 2 vols. New York: Jewish Theological Seminary of America, 1987.
MGWJ	*Monatschrift für Geschichte und Wissenschaft des Judentums*
MIDEO	*Mélanges de l'Institut Dominicain d'études orientales du Caire*
Mus	*Le Muséon: Revue des études orientales*
MW	*The Muslim World*
NHMS	Nag Hammadi and Manichaean Studies
NTS	*New Testament Studies*
OrChr	*Oriens christianus*
OTL	Old Testament Library
OTP	*Old Testament Pseudepigrapha*. Edited by. J. H. Charlesworth. 2 vols. New York: Doubleday, 1983–85.
ParOr	*Parole de l'orient*
PEQ	*Palestine Exploration Quarterly*
Q	Qur'ān
REJ	*Revue des études juives*
RSO	*Rivista degli studi orientali*
SBLEJL	Society of Biblical Literature Early Judaism and Its Literature
SBLSymS	Society of Biblical Literature Symposium Series
Theodor-Albeck	*Midrash Bereshit Rabba*. J. Theodor and Ḥ. Albeck. 3 vols. Repr., Jerusalem: Wahrmann, 1965.
TLZ	*Theologische Literaturzeitung*
VT	*Vetus Testamentum*
WI	*Die Welt des Islams*
ZAW	*Zeitschrift für die alttestamentliche Wissenschaft*
ZDMG	*Zeitschrift der deutschen morgenländischen Gesellschaft*
ZS	*Zeitschrift für Semitistik und verwandte Gebiete*

The Qur'ān and the Bible:
Some Modern Studies of Their Relationship

Reuven Firestone
Hebrew Union College-Jewish Institute of Religion

The Institute for the Study of American Religion listed 1,667 different religious groups in the United States in 1988, 836 of them classified as "nonconventional religions," and at least 500 of this last category were founded since mid-century.[1] The United States has been a virtual breeding ground for new religious movements since its founding, but the entire world has experienced an outburst of religiosity and religious creativity in the post–World War II period that has been unprecedented, save perhaps during the Roman Empire of the first century C.E.[2] Of course, most of those ancient new religions, such as Mithraism or Hellenistic Judaism, failed. Only a few, such as Christianity and rabbinic Judaism, succeeded. The proliferation of new religious movements in the United States has, luckily, been able to serve as a laboratory for sociologists of religion, and one of the issues studied is, What makes a new religion succeed?

The work of Rodney Stark, with Laurence Iannaccone and William Simms Bainbridge, has had the greatest impact in the past two decades on this and other questions of emerging religions.[3] In order for a new religion to succeed, according to Stark, it must among other things retain a cultural continuity with the religious systems of the societies in which it appears while at the same time maintaining a certain level of tension with

---

[1] Eileen Barker, *New Religious Movements: A Perspective for Understanding Society* (London: HMSO, 1989), 148–49.

[2] Geoffrey K. Nelson, *Cults, New Religions and Religious Creativity* (London: Routledge & Kegan Paul, 1987), 1–2.

[3] The list of their individual and combined publications is huge. See Rodney Stark and William Simms Bainbridge, *The Future of Religion: Secularization, Revival, and Cult Formation* (Berkeley and Los Angeles: University of California Press, 1985); idem, *A Theory of Religion* (New Brunswick, N.J.: Rutgers University Press, 1996).

its surrounding environment.[4] One can easily observe this mimetic tension in the emergence of biblical religion and Christianity. Both retain aspects of existing contemporary religious cultures while at the same time engaging in a complicated program of re-visioning, revising, and reinterpreting them—Canaanite rituals and traditions in the case of biblical religion, and biblical and Greco-Roman religious *realia* in the case of Christianity. In order for a new religion to succeed it must be recognizable as authentic, which it typically does by incorporating recognizable *realia* of previous religions. But if it is only a copy of what already exists, it will fail to distinguish itself from other religions and therefore have no special appeal. As Stark puts it, it must be deviant, but not too deviant. It must demonstrate its authenticity through an identification with authentic religion but at the same time attract followers by establishing its positive uniqueness. Nowhere is this process seen more clearly than in the emergence of scripture, where language, narrative, theme, style, and motifs of previous religious literature(s) appear in new forms and contexts in the scriptures of emerging religions.

We can observe from our own experience that new religions emerge in a polemical environment. Establishment religions object to the threat of a new religion and try to delegitimize it, while the newly emerging religion preaches the failure of the establishment religion(s) to meet the spiritual or social needs of the new generation. In short, establishment religions can never countenance the emergence of new religious movements. They inevitably attempt to do away with them. New religious movements can only succeed when they incorporate many of the central motifs of establishment religions while preaching the failure of the very traditions from which they obtain many of their basic traits. This polemical relationship may also be observed in scripture, which inevitably records the tensions between the new religion it represents and the establishment religion(s) out of which it, directly or indirectly, evolved. The Hebrew Bible seems almost constantly to refer to the evils and the temptations of the Canaanites and their religions,[5] and the New Testament repeatedly condemns the perfidy and inadequacy of Jews and Greco-Romans and their religions.[6]

The Qur'ān exhibits the same tension described here. In fact, it contains so many parallels with the Hebrew Bible and New Testament that it

---

[4] Rodney Stark, "How New Religions Succeed: A Theoretical Model," in *The Future of New Religious Movements* (ed. D. G. Bromley and P. E. Hammond; Macon, Ga.: Mercer University Press, 1987), 13.

[5] Gen 35:2; Exod 23:23–24; Num 34:55; Deut 7:1–4; Josh 24:20; Judg 2:11–14; etc.

[6] See Matt 23; 27:25; John 8:44; Rom 2; Galatians.

could not possibly exist without its scriptural predecessors as subtexts. The Qur'ān itself recognizes this in its extremely referential nature. For example, the ubiquitous construct introducing narrative fragments, *wa'idh* "and then," has come to be understood by qur'ānic audiences as *uthkur mā kāna* "remember what occurred."[7] As in the case of the Hebrew Bible and New Testament, the argumentative nature of many intentional qur'ānic references to prior scripture reveals the polemical environment out of which Islam emerged.[8]

Moreover, as in the case of Judaism and Christianity, polemics did not cease after the establishment of the new religion. In a world in which religion defined empires and often defined national boundaries as well, and where adherents of various religions were in constant contact through geographic proximity, trade, and international politics, it was inevitable that discussion and argument continue; that discourse included critical examination of the scriptures of proximate religions.

Western thinkers[9] have responded to the striking parallels between the Qur'ān and the Bible since Islamic revelation first became known to them, but rarely until the twentieth century did their interest transcend polemics, expressing itself in anything nearing what we today would consider an objective or scientific manner (although our own generation's attempts might be similarly criticized by future scholarship). The immediate military and political success associated with Islam first shocked Christianity to its core, and it must be kept in mind that virtually all premodern intellectual endeavors in what we today casually refer to as "the West" were made by male religious thinkers who engaged in their pursuits within the framework of the church. Islam's continuing successes in the arts and sciences as well as politics and the military further threatened these leaders and colored their readings of the Qur'ān.

Western defensiveness was not merely an intellectual issue. Muslim armies threatened Europe for nearly a thousand years and from nearly all sides. The Muslim Moors of Spain represented a threat to the Holy Roman Empire of Charlemagne and his descendants despite their defeat by Charles Martel in 732. They continued to hold Narbonne, for example,

---

[7] John Penrice, *A Dictionary and Glossary of the Kor-ân* (1873; repr., London: Curzon, 1970), 4.

[8] Many of the references are not necessarily intentional.

[9] The term "West" or "Western" is fluid. Although I shall continue to refer to such readers of the Qur'ān as "Westerners," the earliest and many continuing "Western" responses to Islam derived from Byzantine Christians who lived in the Middle East. Perhaps a more accurate though more awkward term, since it would include Jews, would be "non-Muslims deriving from the Christian world."

until 759, and their growth and consolidation in North Africa and southern Italy remained a danger for centuries following. Berke Khan, the Mongol grandson of Jenghiz Khan, lord of the Golden Horde who conquered much of Russia and Eastern Europe in the thirteenth century, converted to Islam and made the Khanate into a Muslim nation. The Tatars, as the mixed Mongol and Turkish people came to be known in European chronicles, raided as far north and west as today's Poland and Lithuania. The Seljuk and then Ottoman Turks managed to wrest away the Christian heartlands of Anatolia, capturing Belgrade and Buda before Constantinople, from which they threatened Vienna itself in both 1529 and 1683. Muslim fleets operated out of various North African ports to raid Western European lands bordering the Mediterranean and fought their navies even in the Atlantic. As late as the seventeenth century, corsairs from what is today Algeria and Morocco raided southern England and Ireland and in 1627 even raided as far as Iceland.[10] It should not be surprising to observe, given the geopolitical climate, that premodern Western readings of the Qur'ān tended to be polemical.

But Europe's fear and loathing of Islam was existential as well as physical. The roots of Christianity's existential predicament had been established even before the birth of Muḥammad. Some five hundred years earlier, Christians found themselves in intense competition with Jews over the religious future of the Greco-Roman world. The old pagan religious systems were no longer adequate to fulfill the spiritual needs of the various peoples and classes in the realm; new religious movements emerged and found themselves in competition for the religious heart of the empire. The two most successful contenders were rabbinic Judaism and Christianity, but Christianity won the day and became the officially favored religion. Most other religions were then outlawed, but Judaism remained officially permitted, both for legal and religious reasons. With the emergence of the victorious religion of Christ as the official religion of the mighty Roman Empire, some of Christianity's religious thinkers and apologists saw its very victory to have proven its rightness. God was understood to have acted in history in order to prove the truth of Christianity, not only in relation to the pagan system of the old empire, but also in relation to its forebear and nemesis, Judaism. When Islam then emerged victorious over the Christian Roman Empire in the seventh century, capturing its most precious lands and holy places and threatening Constantinople itself, this doctrine of divinely ordained historical proof was shattered and its adherents badly discomfited. In fact, the identical reasoning was then applied by Muslims

10 Bernard Lewis, *Islam and the West* (New York: Oxford University Press, 1993), 11–12.

to the emerging doctrines of *Jihad*. The very victories of the Conquest were understood to prove the truth of Islam and the rightness of its ongoing campaign. Subsequently, according to the prevailing Muslim intellectual reasoning, the world was divided into two spheres: the "world of Islam," in which Islam was the ruling religiopolitical system, and the "world of war," in which Islam had not yet become the hegemonic religious system.[11]

The reaction of the Christian world to the huge success of Islam was to denigrate both the religion and its revelation. Premodern chronicles referred to Muslims in ethnic rather than religious terms—not as Muslims but rather as Saracens, Moors, Ishmaelites, Turks, Tatars, or simply as infidels[12]—in order to relieve the painful possibility that perhaps the children of God had been defeated by another faith. The Christian response was that Islam was not a true religion, Muḥammad was not a true prophet, and the Qur'ān was not a true revelation.

The general perception among Christian medieval scholars was that the Qur'ān was a haphazard collection of human documents authored by Muḥammad himself, collected after his death and proclaimed to be the word of God.[13] This view may have been influenced by the Arab Christian writer of the *Risāla*,[14] dating from the early tenth century or before, who knew of the difficulties during the earliest Islamic period in assembling a canonical text of the Qur'ān. Medieval Christian views of the Qur'ān were later influenced also by the scholastic requirement for order and a strict organizational plan for written works, a condition that clashed with the seemingly random arrangement of the Qur'ān.

Medieval and early modern Europeans tended also to view the Qur'ān through lenses that were shaped by their own personal readings of their own scriptures. Thus, the qur'ānic emphasis on a material paradise clashed with the Christian notion of a spiritual afterlife, and although they noted the many parallels between the Qur'ān and Christian scripture, they found those parallels literarily, conceptually, and theologically bizarre. Of course, the qur'ānic polemics directed against Christians (and Jews) and denigrating the extant form of prior scripture invited polemical responses. These and many other observations, such as the Qur'ān's

---

[11] Wahba Mustafa al-Zuhayli, *Athar al-Harb fil-Fiqh al-Islami* (Beirut: Dār al-Fikr, n.d.), 166–96; Majid Khadduri, *War and Peace in the Law of Islam* (Baltimore: Johns Hopkins University Press, 1955), 141–46.

[12] Lewis, *Islam and the West*, 7–8.

[13] Norman Daniel, *Islam and the West: The Making of an Image* (Edinburgh: Edinburgh University Press, 1960; repr., Oxford: Oneworld, 2000), 55–59.

[14] The name given to the author of this work is 'Abd al-Masīḥ b. Isḥāq al-Kindī, though it is undoubtedly a pseudonym (*EI*^{2} 5:120–21).

apparent internal contradictions along with its disagreements with general moral and scientific assumptions that formed the basis of medieval European life, added to the a priori condemnation of the Qur'ān by medieval Christian scholars. Most medieval Europeans were hardly curious about something as foreign and threatening as the Qur'ān. The general worldview of pre-Enlightenment Europe prevented scholars from viewing it with anything much more than hostility.

Jews had less to say about Islam or the Qur'ān than Christians. As a people lacking their own political autonomy for centuries prior to the ascendance of Islam, Jews were not nearly as threatened existentially by the Conquest as were Christians. In fact, the earliest Jewish responses to the Conquest appear as positive because they seem to have identified its military successes as a divinely ordained rectification of the injustice of Christian domination.[15] As Islamic power and its accompanying degradation replaced the earlier Christian equivalent, however, Jews also contributed to assessments of Islam and the Qur'ān that were neither complimentary nor unbiased, though because of their delicate position, Jewish writings tended to be more discreet and circumspect than those of Christians.[16]

Attempts to read the Qur'ān by applying critical but nonpolemical methods began in earnest only in the nineteenth century. A few dozen scholars writing mostly in German, French, Dutch, and English have engaged in this kind of research during the past 175 years, and virtually all found themselves working on the "biblical" material found therein. Given the number and complexity of studies and issues associated with them, this essay is limited to only a few among the more important and accessible monographs that were written or have been translated into English.

---

[15] See "Ḥizayōn 'al ha-mil–amah ha-'aḥarōnah," in *Ginzey Schechter: Genizah Studies in Memory of Solomon Schechter* (3 vols.; Texts and Studies of the Jewish Theological Seminary of America 7–9; New York: Jewish Theological Seminary of America, 1928–29), 1:310–12; English translation in Bernard Lewis, "On That Day: A Jewish Apocalyptic Poem on the Arab Conquests," in *Mélanges d'islamologie: Volume dédié à la memoire de Armand Abel par ses collègues, ses élèves et ses amis* (ed. P. Salmon; Leiden: Brill, 1974), 197–200; and "Nistarōt de-Rabbi Šim'ōn bar Yōḥay," *BHM* 3:78–82.

[16] Few were written as polemical works. See Solomon b. Abraham Adret (Rashba, 1235–1310), *Ma'amar 'al Yishma'el* (cf. J. Perles, *R. Salomo b. Abraham b. Adereth: Sein Leben und seine Schriften* [Breslau: Schletter, 1863]), a work that responds to the attacks of the eleventh-century Muslim scholar Ibn Ḥazm. Note too Simeon b. Ṣemaḥ Duran (Rashbaṣ, 1361–1444), *Qešet u-Magen,* which is mostly directed against Christianity, and also Maimonides (Rambam), *'Iggeret Teyman.*

Abraham Geiger

One of the first and certainly most revolutionary early students of the Bible and the Qur'ān was Abraham Geiger (1810–74). A Jew who had grown up with a thorough traditional religious education, Geiger was strongly influenced by the spirit of the Enlightenment and pioneered the *Wissenschaft des Judentums,* the new historically oriented study of the Jewish religion and people.[17] His interests extended beyond Judaism, however, and at the age of twenty-two he submitted a Latin entry to a contest sponsored by the Faculty of Philosophy of the University of Bonn calling for enquiries into those themes of the Qur'ān that were derived from Judaism. His entry, which he later translated into German as *Was hat Mohammed aus dem Judenthume aufgenommen?* (i.e., "What did Muḥammad borrow from Judaism?"), won the contest and was subsequently accepted as a thesis for the doctoral degree by the University of Marburg.[18] Geiger continued to engage energetically in scholarship on Judaism, but this groundbreaking monograph represents his only work dedicated to Islam.

As the title suggests, Geiger believed that the Qur'ān was a human rather than divine product and that much of it was a reshaping of Judaism. The two parts of this assumption, that the Qur'ān is not revelation but, rather, a human creation and that it is derived largely from prior monotheistic scripture and ideas, was hardly new with Geiger. But unlike his predecessors, Geiger worked with this epistemology in theoretical and scientific rather than polemical and religious terms. Although he was applauded by all of the great Arabists and Islamicists of his day (and for generations thereafter), he was criticized by some for his view that

---

[17] This approach to the study of Judaism was quite new in Geiger's day, having emerged only about a dozen years before he wrote his dissertation. It was of profound influence not only on the study of Judaism, but also on the direction of Jewish religious life. See Ismar Schorsch, *From Text to Context: The Turn to History in Modern Judaism* (Hanover, N.H.: University Press of New England, 1994), esp. 149–205; and Michael A. Meyer, "Abraham Geiger's Historical Judaism," in *New Perspectives on Abraham Geiger: An HUC-JIR Symposium* (ed. J. J. Petuchowski; Cincinnati: Hebrew Union College Press, 1975), 3–16.

[18] It was subsequently translated into English by F. M. Young in the hopes that it would draw Muslims closer to Judaism and therefore Christianity with the title *Judaism and Islam* (1898; repr., New York: Ktav, 1970). For a recent and excellent summary of Geiger's personal history and his contribution to the field of Islamic studies, see Jacob Lassner, "Abraham Geiger: A Nineteenth-Century Jewish Reformer on the Origins of Islam," in *The Jewish Discovery of Islam: Studies in Honor of Bernard Lewis* (ed. M. Kramer; Tel Aviv: Tel Aviv University, 1999), 103–35.

Muḥammad had been a sincere religious enthusiast. As Moshe Pearlman pointed out in his prolegomenon to the 1970 reprint of the English translation of Geiger's book, the renowned French Arabist Antoine Isaac Silvestre de Sacy (1758–1833) wrote that Geiger's views contrasted with his own that Muḥammad was "un imposteur adroit, préméditant toutes ses démarches, et calculant de sang-froid tout ce qui pouvait favoriser et assurer le succès de ses projets ambitieux" (a skilled imposter, premeditated in all his actions and cold-bloodedly calculating all that which favored and assured the success of his ambitious projects).[19]

Geiger's project was not intended to discredit Islam or to credit Judaism but rather to get at the "truth" (his *wissenschaftliche* scholarship on Judaism was no less critical). Yet to today's scholar he would appear somewhat naïve and judgmental as he reflected the tremendous intellectual confidence that was so much a part of his age. Geiger was unburdened with the need for religious apologetics, but he was also uninitiated into the subtleties of modern anthropological studies in orality and the transmission of tradition or modern and postmodern literary theories of composition and reading. To Geiger, the clearly observable literary, linguistic, conceptual, and ritual/legal parallels between Jewish scripture and tradition and the Qur'ān that emerged centuries later proved an obvious influence of the former on the latter. This observation also was not new; Geiger's contribution was to problematize the relationship and approach it conceptually rather than polemically, coherently rather than illogically, and systematically rather than haphazardly.

His brief introduction clearly lays out the parameters of his investigation from the outset:

> And so this treatise falls into two divisions, of which the first has to answer the following questions: Did Muhammad wish to borrow from Judaism? Could Muhammad borrow from Judaism? and if so, how was such borrowing possible for him? Was it compatible with his plan to borrow from Judaism? The second division must bring forward the facts to prove the borrowing, which has been stated on general grounds to have taken place. Only in this way can an individual proof of the kind referred to acquire scientific value, partly as throwing light upon the nature of Muhammad's plan, and partly as showing the intrinsic necessity of the fact and its actual importance by virtue of its connection with other facts of Muhammad's life and age.[20]

---

19 Moshe Pearlman, prolegomenon to the 1970 Ktav edition of *Judaism and Islam* (see preceding note), x (all subsequent references are to this edition); translated by Lassner, "Abraham Geiger," 107.

20 Geiger, *Judaism and Islam,* 2.

Geiger's method consisted of locating qur'ānic parallels with biblical and rabbinic literature that could confidently be dated prior to the seventh century C.E. Linguistic, literary, and conceptual parallels were considered proof that the later material was borrowed from the earlier. Borrowing is direct—there is rarely an assumption of intermediaries—and differences are attributed to errors, usually on the part of the receivers, though sometimes also on the part of the lenders (the uneducated Jews of Medina). He attributed some differences to purposeful distortion by the new Muslim proprietors of the religious lore/tradition.

That Muḥammad rather than the Almighty was the source of the Qur'ān is taken by Geiger as self-evident throughout his work. It is "his Qur'ān,"[21] yet Geiger credits Muḥammad with genuine religious enthusiasm. Muḥammad believed that his mission originated with God; he had no compunction about creating a scripture that could serve his Arab people as prior scriptures served earlier monotheists.[22] Geiger unselfconsciously attempts to enter the mind of this author of scriptures, and the results of this exercise anticipates the work of Stark and Bainbridge on the emergence of new religious movements: Muḥammad borrowed from Judaism in order for his new religion to be recognizable and acceptable to the inhabitants of Arabia.[23] The appearance of recognizable religious symbols and motifs provided him with the authority necessary for his project.[24] On the other hand, he could not borrow wholesale lest he be accused of failing to represent a new religious dispensation;[25] the net result of the process had to be a unique religious creation,[26] and he was obliged to denigrate the previous traditions out of which his new religion emerged. Despite the latter axiom of emerging religion, Geiger insisted (as a true representative of liberal nineteenth-century Judaism) that Muḥammad held the Jews in great respect despite his eventual enmity toward them.[27]

According to Geiger, Muḥammad did not borrow exclusively from Judaism. Pre-Islamic Arabian tradition and Christianity were additional sources for his Qur'ān, but Geiger limited himself only to the former. Certain Jewish ideas and values served Muḥammad well and were taken into Islam intact. In other cases, however, Geiger carefully noted the obvious and sometimes not-so-obvious differences in the parallels he cites. He

[21] Ibid., 21.

[22] Ibid., 25.

[23] Ibid., 4–17.

[24] Ibid., 23.

[25] Ibid., 21.

[26] Ibid., 30.

[27] Ibid., 4–17.

accounts for these differences in three ways. In some cases, Muḥammad purposefully distorted or misrepresented Jewish teachings in order to make them fit the historical, cultural, ritual, or moral-ethical contexts in which he was working.[28] In others he did not alter the information he received from his informants, but the uneducated Jewish community in Medina did not know it correctly, thereby causing the discrepancy. Finally, in some cases he recorded the information incorrectly, either because he misunderstood its meaning or because he received it in an oral rather than written form, thereby allowing for greater error.[29]

It should be noted that Geiger did not consider a simple parallel to prove the indebtedness of the Qur'ān to Judaism. He recognized that all monotheistic religions share certain common themes and therefore narrowed his search to concepts, motifs, and terms that could be studied with the philological, literary, and historical tools that he had at his disposal. In his examination of the word *tābūt,* for example, the qur'ānic term for both the ark of the tabernacle (Q 2:248) and the box in which was placed the infant Moses (Q 20:38; see Exod 2:3), he notes the nonnormative morphology of the *-ūt* ending in Arabic and attributes its origin to Jewish Aramaic, citing the parallel *têbûtâ* (תיבותא) and noting the common ending also in Christian Aramaic. Beyond the philological examination, he notes the peculiar use of the qur'ānic term for both the floating box with its biblical Hebrew cognate *tēbâ* (תבה) and the sacred ark that is rendered biblically as *ʾārôn* (ארון). In postbiblical Hebrew, however, the common term for the ark in the synagogue, itself a derivative of the ark in the tent of meeting and later the temple, is *tēbâ,* suggesting a borrowing out of a rabbinic rather than biblical Hebrew literary context.

Geiger's encyclopedic grasp of the details in Jewish literatures (prior to the emergence of good concordances, let alone computer databases) is astonishing. His approach was certainly positivistic and reductionist, but it merely reflects the intellectual fashion of his age, which was to get down to the essential textual and ideological bases upon which texts are constructed in order to uncover their sources.

Certain of Geiger's assumptions seem quite jarring to our own sensibilities today. Perhaps the most glaring is his tremendous confidence that he can unambiguously uncover the simple truth of the issue surrounding the intertextuality of Qur'ān and Bible. A second would be his view of qur'ānic authorship, which he confidently attributes entirely and directly to Muḥammad. Jacob Lassner recently noted how Geiger's method, though in many ways far ahead of his time, nevertheless rested upon two

---

[28] Ibid., 10.

[29] Ibid., 17–18.

questionable assumptions that were held by the best orientalist scholars of his day: "that the transmission of literary artifacts was consciously initiated and carefully programmed by the Muslims; and that the artifacts themselves were always discernible to the borrowers. Neither assumption reflected the complex interaction of closely linked cultures, especially in the early and fluid stages of contact."[30]

Despite its shortcomings, Geiger's work represents a new beginning for the critical comparative study of the Qur'ān and the Bible. His small but tremendously influential monograph, now nearly two centuries old, still remains a starting point for many scholars interested in probing the complex relationship between the Bible and Qur'ān.

Richard Bell

Richard Bell, a Scot, wrote his magnum opus fully one hundred years after that of Geiger, and much qur'ānic and biblical scholarship occurred in the intervening century. *The Qur'an Translated, with a critical re-arrangement of the Surahs*,[31] appeared in two volumes in the late 1930s, but because of its prohibitive price in the United States[32] and the outbreak of the Second World War, it initially did not have a great impact on the field. Now well over half a century old, Bell's method and conclusions continue to influence critical textual study of the Qur'ān, but not without some controversy (see below). He originally planned to publish the extensive notes that he accumulated in the course of writing his translation but was prevented from doing so due to the printing costs. These notes were finally released some forty years after his death in 1991 as *A Commentary on the Qur'an*.[33]

Bell's greatest contribution was his "most elaborate attempt . . . to identify and date the original units of [qur'ānic] revelation."[34] Attempts to date what would appear to be a virtually random order of the Qur'ān have been made since the earliest Islamic Qur'ān scholarship. According to al-Suyūṭi,[35]

---

[30] Lassner, "Abraham Geiger," 108.

[31] (2 vols.; Edinburgh: T&T Clark, 1937–39).

[32] Six dollars per volume due, according to John Merrill, to exorbitant U.S. customs charges (John E. Merrill, "Dr. Bell's Critical Analysis of the Qur'an," *MW* 37 [1947]: 134; reprinted in *Der Koran* [ed. R. Paret; Darmstadt: Wissenschaftliche Buchgesellschaft, 1975], 11).

[33] (2 vols.; JSS Monograph 14; ed. C. E. Bosworth and M. E. J. Richardson; Manchester: Manchester University Press, 1991). For a review, see Andrew Rippin, "Reading the Qur'ān with Richard Bell," *JAOS* 112 (1992): 639–47.

[34] Alfred T. Welch, "Al-Ḳur'ān," *EI*[2] 5:417b.

[35] Jalāl al-Dīn al-Suyūṭī, *Al-Itqān fī 'ulūm al-Qur'ān* (Beirut: n.p., n.d.), 8–18.

Muslim scholars had divided the qur'ānic chapters into Meccan and Medinan as far back as Muḥammad's cousin Ibn 'Abbās (d. 688), and that division included identifying a few verses within the Meccan *sūras* as Medinan and vice versa. But that is just about as far as it went. Western scholarship had attempted to flesh out the chronology of the *sūras* in more detail,[36] but both traditional Islamic and critical Western scholarship presumed that the *sūras* were largely intact revelations. Bell demonstrated that the *sūras* are far more complicated and that the present form of the Qur'ān is the result of the careful editing, revision, and sometimes replacement of passages. The result of his research is a published translation that is laid out on the page according to a system of columns and boxes separated by dotted lines that attempts to express something of the complex redaction process in visual form. Not only are verses (qur'ānic verses may in fact be composed of several sentences) set in relation to one another on the page, but also individual sentences or even phrases are so placed, accompanied only by a few footnotes and brief introductions to each chapter. His two-volume *Qur'an* thus represents the results of his textual study. His two-volume *Commentary* explains the meaning of his research through a detailed examination of the qur'ānic text and its complex internal textuality.

Bell identifies evidence of revision in a sudden variation in the length of verses, differences in vocabulary, abrupt changes in rhyme patterns, unwarranted shifts in personal pronouns, or a sudden discontinuity of thought.[37] The most powerful cause of these textual shifts was Muḥammad's increasing knowledge and understanding of Christianity and Judaism, which forced a reevaluation and rewriting or recontextualizing of earlier material. Muḥammad's growing awareness and understanding of prior monotheistic scriptural tradition became the major foundation around which his continuing revelation revolved. Most of the revisions were made by Muḥammad himself, though the work continued to a limited extent after his death.

Bell's claim that Muḥammad cut and pasted verses and their component parts in a process that would not be greatly different from that of Bell himself in his translation has evoked a strong response from both traditional Muslims and Western scholars, negative from the former for his audacity in manipulating the order and arrangement, and therefore the meaning, of divine revelation (as well as his assuming that Muḥammad did the same), and mixed among the latter for both his historical-methodological

---

36 See the discussion in Welch, "Al-Ḳur'ān," 5:414–19.

37 Rippin, "Reading the Qur'ān with Richard Bell," 641; Merrill, "Bell's Critical Analysis," 17–18.

assumptions and his particular results. Nevertheless, Bell's pioneering historical and form-critical work has directly or indirectly influenced virtually all critical scholarship on the Qur'ān today.

Bell's approach to the Qur'ān developed while he was preparing a series of lectures to be presented to ministers and ministerial students at the Divinity Hall of Edinburgh University in the spring of 1925. While previous studies had demonstrated the Qur'ān's close textual and linguistic affinity with Judaism, Bell felt that not enough attention had been paid to the Christian contribution to emerging Islam. His seven lectures laid out his view of the relationship between the two by exploring Christianity and its influence on Arabia prior to the birth of Muḥammad and then situating Muḥammad's prophetic career not only in relation to Arabian Judaism but also to Arabian Christianity. He revised and expanded these lectures into seven book chapters, and they were published the following year as *The Origin of Islam in Its Christian Environment*.[38]

While his original intent was to explore the nature of Muḥammad's contact with Christianity before receiving his revelations, he discovered "that the Qur'an itself contains the record of his efforts to reach a meagre knowledge of the great religion which surrounded Arabia."[39] Thus began Bell's intensive examination of the Qur'ān in relation to Christianity and within the context of the generally accepted traditional history of the origins and subsequent development of Muḥammad's prophetic mission.

Like Geiger, Bell assumes the general reliability of the traditional Islamic history of the origins and subsequent development of Muḥammad's prophetic mission; he takes issue only with the details. Bell divides Muḥammad's prophetic career into three periods.[40] The earliest represents the beginnings of his mission in Mecca. During this period, "signs" and praise of God predominate, and the revelations carry a sense of deep gratitude to the one supreme God while exhibiting no sign of any awareness of a religion called Christianity. This is not to say, however, that Christianity does not have an indirect impact on his early emerging monotheism. According to Bell, the Qur'ān reveals an awareness of Christian communities in Arabia. References to the enigmatic "Sabaeans" (*ṣābi'ūn*) refer to South Arabian Christians, in apposition to the *naṣāra* (Nazarenes?), who represent Christians or perhaps some heterodox Jewish-Christian communities to the north. The pre-Islamic "Hanifs" are

---

38 *The Origin of Islam in Its Christian Environment: The Gunning Lectures* (London: Macmillan, 1926; repr., London: Cass, 1968).

39 Ibid., vi.

40 This periodization is worked out explicitly in his later work but is evident already in *Origin*.

associated with "a dim unmoralised idea of a superior deity," and certain individuals depicted by tradition as "Hanifs" began or ended their lives as Christians (Waraqa b. Nawfal, 'Ubayd Allāh b. Jaḥsh, and Zayb b. 'Amr b. Nawfal).[41] Further, although no Christian community made its home in Mecca, Christian ideas were floating around in the town. "Will it be far wrong to surmise that Muḥammad got his information from some Christian (perhaps Abyssinian) slave in Mecca, and that he then gave the material form in his qur'āns?"[42] One example of Christian influence offered by Bell is the issue of intercession, deriving from the Christian concept of the intercession of the saints and all but nonexistent in Judaism. Muḥammad did not allow for intercession on judgment day in the Qur'ān but then added, "except that of those to whom God will give permission to intercede."[43]

Despite Muḥammad's excellent intentions, his message is rejected during this period and he is faced with continuing disbelief among the Meccan townspeople. Thus begins the second or Qur'ān period that continues until the battle of Badr in the year 2 A.H. (624 C.E.). The revelations of this period are characterized by the relatively frequent use of the term Qur'ān, although other terms such as *ṣuḥuf* ("pages") are also used. This period stresses the idea of a calamity falling upon special unbelieving peoples, the subtext of course being the unbelieving inhabitants of his own town.

Bell takes a sympathetic view of Muḥammad's prophethood, but at the same time he cannot countenance the possibility of Muḥammad receiving a truly divine revelation:

> He claimed to be an Arab prophet and he was. We shall see him consciously borrowing—he is quite frank about it. But to begin with, the materials which he uses, though they may remind us ever and again of Jewish and Christian phrases and ideas, are in reality Arab materials. They may have been originally derived from outside Arabia, but they had by Muhammad's time become part of the Arab mind.[44]

The last sentence may appear curious, particularly considering his view that Muḥammad had informants with whom he communicated directly, but Bell's intent here is not that biblical ideas had penetrated the porous

---

41 Bell, *Origin*, 57–58.

42 Ibid., 105 (parenthesis in original). Bell refers to each individual transmission of information as *qur'ān*, thus the plural form in the citation.

43 Ibid., 56.

44 Ibid., 69.

cultural boundaries of Arabia in general.[45] He meant simply that the more "primitive" (though not less intelligent) Arab mind was not capable of understanding the complexity of what might have been termed "high cultural" renderings of Christianity.

By his second period, Muḥammad had become familiar with many biblical themes, and one can observe these themes in sections that Bell classifies as Meccan. Prominent among them are the many renderings of the Moses stories, most of which he would subsequently revise and reposition during his last period in Medina.[46] To Muḥammad, his *hijra* (i.e., emigration from Mecca to Medina) was his own exodus, and his repeated reference to Moses was his way of working through his own prophetic career amidst the hostility of his enemies and opposition even from among many within the ranks (thus the telling, to cite only one example, of the story of Korah). Bell's method incorporates a psychological reconstruction of Muḥammad and the playing out of his mission, and Bell's reconstruction of the order of the Qur'ān is also a reconstruction of the order of its emergence (revelation) in relation to the life of Muḥammad.

The third period of Muḥammad's mission begins with the victory at Badr in 2 A.H.:

> Outwardly it has always been recognized that [Badr] was a turning point in Muhammad's career. It gave him prestige and established his power. Inwardly I think it was of equal consequence. The victory of the Moslems, 300 over thrice their number, was miraculous. The angels had been sent down to the assistance of the Prophet and his band. The Battle of Badr was the Calamity upon the unbelieving Meccans. It was the *Furqān,* the deliverance out of that Calamity, for the believers.... He is no longer a warner to his own city alone. He is now a warner to the world. He is the giver of laws and head of a theocratic community. He is now at last the full-fledged Prophet.[47]

Islam finally emerges in post-Badr Medina. After living among Jews for two years Muḥammad has increased his knowledge of biblical ideas and themes and has learned to differentiate between Judaism and Christianity. This is when he reaches the pinnacle of his nevertheless wanting knowledge of the Bible and of Christian theology and of the church.[48] It is also

---

[45] See Reuven Firestone, *Journeys in Holy Lands: The Evolution of the Abraham-Ishmael Legends in Islamic Exegesis* (Albany: State University of New York Press, 1990).

[46] Bell, *Origin,* 123–24; idem, *Qur'an,* 353, 373.

[47] Bell, *Origin,* 124.

[48] Ibid., 136.

when he has the resources to begin to engage in his personal editing of revelation. Indeed, he was obliged to reorder the large quantity of disparate previous revelations in order to make them consistent with the more highly developed religious system that had been emerging.

The result is the first and most important redactionary stage of a highly complex Qur'ān. Although according to Bell its redaction history is relatively simple, it is nevertheless extremely difficult to reconstruct. Muḥammad as primary editor formulated the many disparate revelations, already existing in written form, into the *sūras*, but he and later redactors had to work with a very difficult situation:

> All the possibilities of confusion in written documents have had to be considered—corrections, interlinear additions, additions on the margin, deletions and substitutions, pieces cut off from a passage and wrongly placed, passages written on the back of others and then read continuously, front and back following each. It is to this, rather than to textual defects, or to confusion in Muhammad's own thought and style that the dreary welter of the Qur'ān so often deplored by Western writers is due.[49]

Bell, then, was the first to engage in a radical rethinking of the redaction history and process established by Islamic religious tradition, and his result was a significantly different ordering of revelation. Yet as he did so, he never questioned the general schema of the traditional Islamic biography of Muḥammad, which is authenticated by, if not based upon, qur'ānic revelation. Bell never recognized "the circularity in such a process, using the Qur'ān especially in the Meccan period to deduce historical progression in order to be able to reformulate the Qur'ān into a historical order."[50] But no one at his time questioned the general historical context of emerging Islam; they were only beginning to question the Bible's story of its own genesis as scripture.

John Wansbrough

Western scholars of Islam have always assumed, in agreement with Islamic tradition, that the Qur'ān emerged in relation to the history of Muḥammad and therefore represents, in at least a vague way, real history. But like the scriptures of Judaism and Christianity, Islamic scripture emerged in what could be described, for all intents and purposes, as a historical vacuum. It is true that writing, and even the writing of history, certainly existed at least during the emergence of the New Testament and

---

49 Bell, *Qur'an,* vi.

50 Rippin, "Reading the Qur'ān with Richard Bell," 640.

the Qur'ān (and writing, by definition, certainly existed during the emergence of a written Hebrew Bible), but no extant contemporary writings seem to express an interest in any of these revelations. Later writings relate to them within the contexts of the religions themselves by applying subsequent perspectives onto the earlier material. This methodology is repeated so often that religious sources establish a powerful institution of "sacred history" that is difficult to get around in order to uncover a neutral historical record unencumbered by theological constructs or other religious needs.

Sacred history in the religious context[51] is a construct applied to a canon of texts that represents a worldview constructed from theology, law, ethics, and the particularist element of election. The neutral historicity of Moses or Jesus or Muḥammad is irrelevant to religious sensibility unless it supports or confirms the worldview of the believer (or better, perhaps, the religious institution). Traditional religious scholarship always presumes and never challenges the sacred history of tradition, and that sacred history becomes such a part of the general intellectual milieu that it is difficult even for critical scholars to transcend completely. This has clearly been the case with biblical scholarship and remains so to this day. According to John Wansbrough, the problem may be said to be compounded with qur'ānic scholarship for a variety of reasons that cannot be examined in any detail here. In short, according to Wansbrough and those who have been strongly influenced by his bold ideas, Western scholarship on the Qur'ān has been blessed with exceptional philology but simplistic or wanting literary and historical methodology.[52] It has not succeeded in extricating itself from the historical presuppositions of Islamic tradition, therefore failing to advance the critical historical study of the Qur'ān (and Islamic tradition) much beyond that of traditional Islamic scholarship.

John Wansbrough avoids the historical conundrum by reading the Qur'ān not as existing in a historical context but rather as existing in a literary context, that is, by reading the Qur'ān entirely literarily and refusing to read it historically. Others from Theodor Nöldeke onward have read the Qur'ān in a literary as well as historical manner, but Wansbrough's understanding of qur'ānic history is that it is entirely "salvation history," a sacred

---

[51] At least in the religious context of the traditional monotheisms exhibited by varieties of Judaism, Christianity, and Islam.

[52] Andrew Rippin attributes this to intellectual laziness, the desire to produce positive results, and an "irenic approach" that avoids hard questions in its desire to understand and relate to Islamic religiosity. See his "Literary Analysis of *Qur'ān, Tafsīr,* and *Sīra:* The Methodologies of John Wansbrough," in *Approaches to Islam in Religious Studies* (ed. R. C. Martin; Tucson: University of Arizona Press, 1985), 156–59.

history written in literary form in order to demonstrate God's unique relationship with his prophet Muḥammad and, therefore, his newly elected people and religion in Muslims and Islam. Reading the Qur'ān can tell us nothing of the early seventh century, when, according to Islamic tradition, it emerged as a text revealed to God's prophet and subsequently recited publicly by him. It cannot tell us about a historical Muḥammad. It can only tell us about those who were responsible for its emergence as the text we know today.

Wansbrough's literary reading ends up, finally, with a historicization of the Qur'ān by reconstructing a literary history of the text that places it in ninth-century Iraq. Arabic literature only emerges at this time, and the famous habit of early religious writers to cite earlier authorities in a chain of tradition leading all the way back to the generation of Muḥammad can as easily be an arbitrary construct of back-projection as a depiction of historical reality. Wansbrough argues that there is no authentic literary material before the late eighth century to the early ninth century. His study and conclusions are indeed radical, but he states at the outset and repeats not infrequently that his efforts are tentative and conjectural.[53] One of the extraordinary aspects of his contribution is his boldness, not out of disrespect to the Qur'ān and Islamic tradition, but rather out of intellectual and scholarly integrity in applying methodologies to qur'ānic studies that were never fully carried through before him.

Wansbrough's *Quranic Studies,* written between 1968 and 1972, was published in 1977, and his second and closely related monograph, *The Sectarian Milieu,* which was written between 1973 and 1977, was published in 1978. The two works fit together logically, and their serial release was probably not unintentional.[54] The first, which is the subject for discussion here, concentrates on the formation of the Qur'ān along with those early exegetical writings (*tafsīr*) that witness that formation, while the latter study examines the continuing evolution of early Islam through the traditional biographies (*sīra*) of Muḥammad and beyond. Wansbrough's method, but much more so his conclusions, have been severely criticized by Western as well as traditional Islamic scholars. The pros and cons need not be rehearsed here.[55] The truism that method influences results is no

---

53 John Wansbrough, *Quranic Studies: Sources and Methods of Scriptural Interpretation* (Oxford: Oxford University Press, 1977), xi, 119, 138, etc. See also idem, *The Sectarian Milieu: Content and Composition of Islamic Salvation History* (Oxford: Oxford University Press, 1978).

54 Rippin, "Methodologies," 153.

55 For reviews of *Quranic Studies,* see Josef van Ess, *BO* 35 (1978): 349–53; Edward Ullendorf, *BSOAS* 40 (1977): 609–12; Rudi Paret, *Der Islam* 55 (1978):

more relevant than in the case of Wansbrough versus his critics, yet despite criticism and condemnation, the jury still cannot reach a verdict. We are less interested here with his conclusions than we are with his method, particularly in his first essay in *Qur'anic Studies,* which is highly comparative and contextualized literarily in biblical and postbiblical Jewish tradition.

Wansbrough's analysis begins and ends within a context of scripture and interpretation in general. He examines how qur'ānic words, phrases, symbols, and ideas fit into the unfolding of generic scripture. His models are drawn mostly from the Bible and rabbinic tradition (and it should be noted here in support of Wansbrough's thesis, though he does not, that the latter in the form of the Talmud functions in rabbinic Judaism also as scripture). His goal is not to show, as was Geiger's and Bell's, that Muḥammad received much of his scriptural information directly or indirectly from Jewish or Christian informants but rather to demonstrate how the Qur'ān developed organically within a sectarian biblical/rabbinic milieu. The so-called "biblical" materials that are found in the Qur'ān "are not so much reformulated as merely referred to."[56] That is, the Qur'ān is a highly referential text that establishes its relevance and authority by situating itself fully within the context of generic scripture. A great deal of earlier scholarship tried to prove the biblical origin of much of the Qur'ān but was then perplexed by the nature and consistency of the sometimes strange divergences from biblical texts. Wansbrough observes the Qur'ān emerging in "a strongly sectarian atmosphere, in which a corpus of familiar scripture was being pressed [through reference, not through citation] into the service of as yet unfamiliar [that is, emerging] doctrine."[57] The narrative material finding biblical parallels he calls *exempla* because they are not, strictly speaking, narrative at all. They are, rather, allusive references to illustrative situations that may have evolved out of material originating essentially for homiletical purposes.

The Qur'ān is full of biblical imagery, but the imagery is not limited to the *exempla.* The imagery of divine retribution, for example, is expressed through what Wansbrough calls the "substantives" of *umma* (nation), *awwalīn* (predecessors), *qarn* (generation), and *qarya* (abode). The key here is imagery and not cognate or linguistic parallels. A whole series of key Arabic lexicographical usages that may or may not find linguistic parallels with Hebrew or Aramaic are used to express the imagery. Other such

---

354–56; William A. Graham, *JAOS* 100 (1980): 137–41; Leon Nemoy, *JQR* 68 (1978): 182–84; R. B. Serjeant, *JRAS* (1978): 76–78; Issa J. Boullata, *MW* 47 (1977): 306–7; Ewald Wagner, *ZDMG* 128 (1978): 411; and Kurt Rudolph, *TLZ* 105 (1980): 1–19.

56 Wansbrough, *Quranic Studies,* 20.

57 Ibid., bracketed comments added.

images include "sign" (*āya/ōt*), "exile" or displacement (expressed often by the stem *hjr*), and covenant (usually *mithāq/'ahd*), and Wansbrough stresses that the means of expressing these images is not rigid; they may employ other terminology and phraseology. These images situate the Qur'ān within the context of scripture; they are not intended as reproductions of biblical institutions.

The Qur'ān, like all scripture, must conform to recognizable patterns of human utterances, and the Qur'ān indeed contains imagery according to established literary types known from the Bible. In the case of the Qur'ān and the Bible, the phenomenon is mimetic. This differs from the relationship between the New Testament and the Hebrew Bible, where figural interpretation establishes a claim of fulfillment by the former over the latter. Qur'ānic allusions to biblical themes mostly reflect rather than develop biblical themes, but they are not merely calques of earlier, fixed forms.[58] They represent a historiography that conveys a new dispensation in the revelation of the Qur'ān, and that very revelation reveals its polemical environment in, for example, its record of argument regarding the modes of revelation: Jewish and pagan demands for Muḥammad to produce a scripture according to biblical paradigms.[59] That new dispensation is burdened, however, by its relationship to Jewish scripture and must therefore be differentiated by the text itself, by its own polemic, and by its early interpretation.[60]

Wansbrough has been criticized for placing the emergence of the Qur'ān in a narrowly Judaized environment,[61] and it is true that his analytical vocabulary as well as his parallel citations are taken almost entirely from biblical or rabbinic sources. In Wansbrough's case, however, his methodology does not reveal an ideological bias, as had those of previous orientalists. His inclination toward the use of Jewish paradigms is acknowledged at the outset as an experimental means of deriving intertextual meaning from the Qur'ān. He correctly notes the much greater overlap with Jewish scriptural rather than Christian scriptural references,[62] an observation that had been explained previously by Islamic tradition through the history of Muḥammad's interaction with the Jews of

58 Wansbrough, *Quranic Studies,* 33.

59 Wansbrough suggests that the pagans are retrojected into the polemic. Many negatives associated with pagans originated within a polemical environment as anti-Jewish but were later retrojected to Arabian pagans. This will be treated below.

60 Wansbrough, *Quranic Studies,* 43.

61 Graham, review of Wansbrough, *JAOS* 100 (1980): 140.

62 That would include, for example, references to those parts of the Hebrew Bible that are more regularly cited in Jewish than in Christian interpretation.

Yathrib/Medina.[63] By dehistoricizing the Qur'ān, he is forced to limit his analysis to a purely literary investigation of the relationship.

Wansbrough's refusal to accept the reliability of Arabic literature to provide any accurate information about early Islam echoes the work of Joseph Schacht and has been echoed further by other scholars in the past two decades.[64] Most scholars of early Islam, however, while still questioning that literature's reliability, do not take such a radical stand. To dismiss such a comprehensive and complex literary structure with its intricate record of traditionists through many generations, and representing many communities transmitting pieces of internally corroborated (if not always consistent) information, has struck many in the scholarly community as unnecessarily reductionist. On the other hand, Wansbrough's arguments are always impressive even if not always convincing. They should tug at one's conscience and force responsible scholars to take great care in their reading of the literature.

Wansbrough is a difficult read, partly because of his convoluted syntax and liberal use of untranslated Latin terminology for easily rendered English equivalents, and partly for his unsystematic use of Arabic (and Hebrew and Aramaic), sometimes in original orthography and sometimes transliterated, but in either case more often than not untranslated. It is worthwhile, nonetheless, to plow through his work and especially his first essay, "Revelation and Canon." His notations of ideational, thematic, interpretive, and semantic parallels are tremendously instructive, as are his comments regarding earlier work on the same and related topics. The bottom line of his view of Qur'ān-Bible intertextuality is that the former emerged out of a corpus of what he terms "prophetic *logia*"[65] that existed, so to speak, in the "public domain." What became the Qur'ān was eventually separated out of this

---

63 "A single reference to a Christian covenant (Q 5:14), like inclusion of Jesus in Q 33:7 (above), represents chronological extension, not historical development" (Wansbrough, *Quranic Studies,* 11). See also ibid., 39–42, where the story from the *Sīra* about Ja'far and other Muslims interacting with the Ethiopian *negus* parallels Christian prescriptions of essentials for faith (Acts 15:20, 28–29), though this may have been necessary because in the story, Ja'far was trying to prove to the *negus* that he was not simply attesting a newly made-up religion.

64 Joseph Schacht, *An Introduction to Islamic Law* (Oxford: Clarendon, 1964). See especially Patricia Crone and Michael Cook, *Hagarism: The Making of the Islamic World* (Cambridge: Cambridge University Press, 1977).

65 From Greek *logion* (λόγιον), a saying or oracle, defined by *Webster's Third New International Dictionary* (1981) as "a short pointed pregnant saying or observation, esp. of a religious teacher." This would be similar to *memra* in traditional Jewish terminology, but I understand Wansbrough's use of the term to refer to a somewhat larger literary structure.

mass and built into an independent literary source. The formulation of the Qur'ān involved considerable literary technique, but the end result nevertheless contained a rather erratic distribution of obviously related pericopes. These *logia* or pericopes were probably the intellectual property of various communities, perhaps representing different regions or differentiated in other ways. The *logia* were sometimes contradictory and most likely derive from a polemical environment, possibly in eighth–ninth century Mesopotamia (Jewish *Bavel*), as what became Islam emerged out of a heterodox environment of polemics and debate among a variety of groups associated or conversant with rabbinic Judaism. The process of canonization was protracted and should be seen as part of the process of community formation. That is, the coalescence of the Qur'ān occurred simultaneously with the coalescence of its community of readers/hearers. Ultimately the collection of prophetic *logia* required a prophet to authenticate it. This prophet was found or produced in the Arabian Ḥijāz through a process of back-projection.[66]

Wansbrough's greatest contribution is perhaps his breaking through the ice of rigid historicizing of the Qur'ān. While his critique of the reliability of Arabic literature for the construction of early Islamic history is more convincing than his own rehistoricization, his refusal to be complacent has opened up the field and invites others to engage in similar bold scholarship. He recognizes the extreme complexity of intertextuality in scriptural studies and points the way to future scholarship. Perhaps what seems to have vexed his scholarly contemporaries the most is the truly postmodern aspect of his project. In a field that is positivist and notoriously modern, and despite Wansbrough's attempts, as everybody's in the field to produce a hermeneutically closed system, he proves that there is no final reading of qur'ānic intertextuality. It stands ever ready for another interpretive pass.

---

66 Wansbrough, *Quranic Studies*, 48–52.

A Prolegomenon to the Relation of the Qur'ān and the Bible

Vernon K. Robbins and Gordon D. Newby
Emory University

When an interpreter approaches the Holy Qur'ān from a perspective informed by a history of the world's major religions, this canonical collection of 114 *sūras* or "chapters" has the nature of a third canonical collection among the People of the Book. Traditional interpretation argues that around 90 C.E. rabbis at Jamnia (Jabneh or Yavneh) established the twenty-four books of the Tanak[1] (Hebrew Bible) as canonical[2] Holy Scripture for Jewish people.[3] By approximately 110 C.E. Christians had written additional letters, narratives, and the like containing a dynamic relation to the Jewish Tanak,[4] and by 200 C.E. most early Christians began to refer to a selection of these writings as New Testament (or New Covenant) alongside the Tanak as Old Testament (or Old Covenant).[5] Shortly after the death of Muḥammad in 632 C.E., the Qur'ān emerged as a canonical recital of God's Holy Word that reconfigured aspects of both Hebrew Bible and New Testament discourse in a context of Jewish, Christian, and Muslim interaction. Building on this insight, the

---

1 Judaism regularly refers to the Hebrew Bible as the Tanak (also Tanakh or Tanach), which is an acronym created from the first Hebrew letters of *Torah, Neviim* (Prophets), and *Ketuvim* (Writings).

2 For the concept of canon, see James A. Sanders and Harry Y. Gamble, "Canon," *ABD* 1:837–61.

3 See Jack P. Lewis, "Jamnia (Jabneh), Council of," *ABD* 3:634–37.

4 The Christian Old Testament contains the same writings as the Tanak. However, it divides the twenty-four books into thirty-nine, making some into "first" and "second," like 1 Samuel and 2 Samuel. Also, after the first five books of the Torah (or Pentateuch), the Christian Old Testament gives some of the books a different location than they have in the Hebrew Bible.

5 See Harry Y. Gamble, "Canon: New Testament," *ABD* 1:853–61; Jack R. Lundbom, "New Covenant," *ABD* 4:1088–94.

authors of this essay probe the relation of the Qur'ān to the Bible from the perspective of the relation among the Tanak, the New Testament, and the Holy Qur'ān.

Early Muslims perceived that there was a close relationship between the Qur'ān and antecedent biblical texts and figures. In the first Islamic century, Muslim exegetes sought Jewish and Christian texts that would explain the qur'ānic biblical references, enhance a broad understanding of the history of revelation in general, and show in particular how the Qur'ān stood at the end of a series of revelations from God to humankind. The texts that came into the purview of the Muslim exegetes comprised more than just the biblical texts of Hebrew Bible and New Testament. Apocryphal and pseudepigraphical texts were used as well as midrashic and homiletic writings, often with uncertain understanding about their relationship to the accepted canons of scripture in Judaism and Christianity. The result was the introduction into the Muslim understanding of the Qur'ān of a vast body of material generally termed *Isrā'īlīyāt*. By the end of the second and into the third Islamic centuries, the general Muslim attitude viewed the *Isrā'īlīyāt* material at first with suspicion and then with hostility. In the face of polemics with Jews and Christians, who argued that the Qur'ān was merely derivative from the Bible, Muslims argued for the unique and inimitable nature of the Qur'ān. Any relationship between biblical figures and themes found in the Qur'ān was held to be the result of God's previous revelation to humankind, and any differences were the result of Jews and Christians corrupting that revelation. The Qur'ān was not regarded as an imitation of the Bible. Rather, the biblical figures of the Qur'ān were thought to be incomplete foreshadows of Muḥammad, who was the Seal of the Prophets and the culminating recipient of God's Word.[6]

The modern history of Western scholarship about the relationship of the Qur'ān to the Bible begins in earnest with Abraham Geiger's *Was hat Mohammad aus dem Judenthume aufgennomen?*[7] His insights were a product of the Enlightenment and nourished by the development of the perspectives of scientific inquiry developing in the nineteenth century. For Geiger, the "scientific"[8] approach required a search for Ur-texts, paralleling the search for Mesopotamian and Egyptian Ur-texts for the Hebrew Bible.

---

6 For a discussion of this period with relevant bibliography, see Gordon D. Newby, *The Making of the Last Prophet: A Reconstruction of the Earliest Biography of Muhammad* (Columbia: University of South Carolina Press, 1989), 10–12.

7 Abraham Geiger, *Was hat Mohammed aus dem Judenthume aufgenommen? Eine von der Königl. Preussischen Rheinuniversität gekrönte Preisschrift* (Bonn: Baaden, 1833).

8 That is, *wissenschaftlich* or scientific in the broadest sense.

Subsequent Western scholarship in this vein came to regard the Qur'ān as somehow inferior to antecedent scripture precisely because it was derivative, and considerable effort was spent explicitly or implicitly attempting to demonstrate that the biblical ideas and figures in the Qur'ān were "borrowed" from Judaism or Christianity.[9] Because scholarship of this sort was tied to various colonial enterprises, few Muslims pursued this line of inquiry, even when they acknowledged that there was some kind of relationship between the Bible and the Qur'ān.[10]

In the last third of the twentieth century, some scholars began a thoroughgoing exploration of the relationship between Judaism, Christianity, and Islam in the formative period of Islam. This included a renewed look at the relationship between the qur'ānic text and the biblical texts, including many of the noncanonical works. It became clear that the relationship between any particular qur'ānic text and its biblical referent was the product of complex interactions among different readers of the texts, who were reading for different reasons and ends. The tools of historical philology that had dominated Orientalism were augmented by the techniques of literary criticism that were being applied to biblical texts. It became clear to some that the Qur'ān could be viewed as a product of the coparticipation of reading God's Holy Word by Jews, Christians, and Muslims.[11] From this perspective, the polemical interpretations of the "borrowing/lending" metaphor as well as the reductionist search for the Ur-text could be

---

[9] Of the many articles and monographs, the following give a representative sample of this type of approach to the relationship of the Qur'ān and the Bible: Tor Andrae, *Der Ursprung des Islams und das Christentum* (Uppsala: Almqvist & Wicksells, 1926); Richard Bell, *The Origin of Islam in Its Christian Environment* (London: Cass, 1926); idem, "Muhammad and Previous Messengers," *MW* 24 (1934): 330–40; S. D. Goitein, "Muhammad's Inspiration by Judaism," *JJS* 9 (1958): 149–62; Bernard Heller, "La legende biblique dans l'Islam," *REJ* 98 (1934): 1–18; H. Hirschfeld, *Jüdische Elemente im Korân: Ein Beitrag zur Korânforschung* (Berlin: self-published, 1878); J. Horovitz, "Jewish Proper Names and Derivatives in the Koran," *HUCA* 2 (1925): 145–227; Arthur Jeffery, *The Foreign Vocabulary of the Qur'ān* (Baroda: Oriental Institute, 1938); M. Lidzbarski, *De propheticis, quae dicuntur, legendis arabicis: Prolegomena* (Lipsiae: Drugulini, 1893); Y. Moubarac, *Abraham dans le Coran* (Paris: Vrin, 1958); G. Parrinder, *Jesus in the Qur'ān* (New York: Barnes & Noble, 1965); W. Rudolph, *Die Abhängigkeit des Qorans von Judentum und Christentum* (Stuttgart: Kohlhammer, 1922); I. Schapiro, *Die haggadischen Elemente im erzählenden Teil des Korans* (Leipzig: Fock, 1907).

[10] For a seminal critique of Orientalist scholarship and its relationship to colonialism, see Edward W. Said, *Orientalism* (New York: Pantheon, 1978).

[11] See Newby, *Making,* 21–25 for a discussion and some relevant bibliography.

replaced by the more generative method of analyzing the rhetorical structures of the Qur'ān's readings of God's Holy Word.

Literary Poetics As a Step toward Renewed Interest in the Relation of the Qur'ān to the Bible

Work on the literary nature of the Bible during the final quarter of the twentieth century brought new insights into the study of the Tanak and the New Testament. These insights began a transitional stage that can guide a renewed investigation of the relation of the Qur'ān to the Bible. William A. Beardslee's *Literary Criticism of the New Testament* reveals Amos Wilder's influence on literary interpretation of the New Testament as early as 1970.[12] Robert Alter's *The Art of Biblical Narrative*[13] and *The Art of Biblical Poetry*[14] exhibit a shift of interest to the literary poetics of the Tanak by the 1980s. In 1985, Meir Sternberg's *The Poetics of Biblical Narrative* focused on the ideological and dramatic nature of biblical narrative.[15] By 1987, Robert Alter and Frank Kermode had assembled essays on the writings of the Hebrew Bible and the New Testament under the title of *The Literary Guide to the Bible*.[16] During the same period of time, Michael Fishbane's *Biblical Interpretation in Ancient Israel* focused on innerbiblical exegesis, exhibiting dynamics of legal, haggadic, and mantological exegesis in the Hebrew Bible.[17] Then in 1988, a collection of essays appeared entitled *Mikra: Text, Translation, Reading and Interpretation of the Hebrew Bible in Ancient Judaism and Early Christianity*.[18] By the 1990s, the interplay of literary, innerbiblical, and ideological interpretation of the Hebrew Bible and the New Testament began to reach a significantly advanced stage. Commentaries guided by modern literary insights into biblical literature began to appear on individual writings, and investigations of

---

[12] William A. Beardslee, *Literary Criticism of the New Testament* (Philadelphia: Fortress, 1970).

[13] Robert Alter, *The Art of Biblical Narrative* (New York: Basic Books, 1981).

[14] Robert Alter, *The Art of Biblical Poetry* (New York: Basic Books, 1985).

[15] Meir Sternberg, *The Poetics of Biblical Narrative: Ideological Literature and the Drama of Reading* (Bloomington: Indiana University Press, 1985).

[16] Robert Alter and Frank Kermode, eds., *The Literary Guide to the Bible* (Cambridge: Harvard University Press, 1987).

[17] Michael Fishbane, *Biblical Interpretation in Ancient Israel* (Oxford: Clarendon, 1985).

[18] Martin Jan Mulder, ed., *Mikra: Text, Translation, Reading and Interpretation of the Hebrew Bible in Ancient Judaism and Early Christianity* (Assen: Van Gorcum; Philadelphia: Fortress, 1988).

portions of biblical discourse from the Hebrew Bible to Islamic tradition began to emerge.[19]

In the midst of the new interest in the literary poetics of the Bible, Paul Ricoeur gave us, with his essay in 1980 entitled "Toward a Hermeneutic of the Idea of Revelation,"[20] an especially good place to begin a renewed investigation of the relation of the Qur'ān to the Bible. In this essay, he discusses five discourses in the Tanak: prophetic, narrative, prescriptive, wisdom, and hymnic discourse.[21] This means, for Ricoeur, that there are five distinctive "literary poetics" in the context of Torah, Prophets, and Writings. In each instance, there are two or more entire books in the Hebrew Bible that contain a particular kind of literary poetics. Ricoeur does not list them, but it is easy to see the literary home of prophetic poetics in those books called the Major and Minor Prophets in higher biblical criticism; the literary home of narrative poetics in Genesis through Exod 19, Joshua through 2 Kings, Ezra-Nehemiah through 1–2 Chronicles, and perhaps Ruth; the literary home of prescriptive poetics in Exod 20–40, Leviticus, and Deuteronomy; the literary home of wisdom poetics in Proverbs, Ecclesiastes, and Job; and the literary home of hymnic poetics in Psalms and Songs of Songs. This was an important advance in biblical interpretation, because it called attention to the power of biblical literature to evoke poetic modes that call forth imaginative, creative images of human life and its responsibilities in the world.

When an interpreter moves to the Christian New Testament, it is obvious that there is no book of Psalms and no book of prophetic oracles in it. This means, following Ricoeur's perspective, that there is no entire book containing hymnic or prophetic discourse. Also, there is no entire book containing extended prescriptive discourse like Exod 20–40, Leviticus, or Deuteronomy. In addition, there is no book of Proverbs in the

---

[19] E.g., Shalom Goldman, *The Wiles of Women/The Wiles of Men: Joseph and Potiphar's Wife in Ancient Near Eastern, Jewish, and Islamic Folklore* (Albany: State University of New York Press, 1995).

[20] Paul Ricoeur, *Essays on Biblical Interpretation* (Philadelphia: Fortress, 1980), 75–85. Subsequently, David Tracy built on Ricoeur's insights in *Plurality and Ambiguity: Hermeneutics, Religion, Hope* (San Francisco: Harper & Row, 1987). Also see Gerald O. West, *Biblical Hermeneutics of Liberation: Modes of Reading the Bible in the South African Context* (2d ed.; Maryknoll, N.Y.: Orbis, 1995).

[21] Ricoeur does not give substantive consideration to apocalyptic discourse but refers to it simply as "subsequently grafted on to the prophetic trunk" (77). His lack of attention results, of course, from his focus on the Tanak, where there is so much prophetic literature and the earliest images of destruction during the "last days" occur in this literature. Nevertheless, his typology of five kinds of discourses is a good place to begin in an assessment of discourses in the New Testament.

New Testament. But this does not mean there is no entire book containing wisdom discourse in the New Testament, since the Epistle of James is regularly considered to be wisdom discourse. The epistle is different in many ways from Proverbs, Ecclesiastes, and Job in the Hebrew Bible, but it has important relationships with Sirach and Wisdom of Solomon in the Old Testament Apocrypha. There are five biographical-historiographies in the New Testament: the four Gospels and the Acts of the Apostles. In Ricoeur's terminology, all of these books are some kind of "narrative." After the five biographical-historiographies, a reader finds twenty-one letters or epistles in the New Testament, with "letter" referring to writings interpreters think actually were sent to early Christian communities to be read to them[22] and "epistle" referring to more formal treatises that early Christians over time referred to as letters.[23] Then, the New Testament ends with an apocalypse, a form embedded in Daniel in the Tanak[24] and on the horizons of the Old Testament Apocrypha with *4 Ezra* and among the Jewish pseudepigrapha with *1 Enoch, 2 Baruch,* and other writings.

In many ways, what one might call the invasion of epistolary poetics into scripture becomes most noticeable in the New Testament. Twenty-one of the twenty-seven writings that constitute the New Testament are called epistles. In addition, there are two letters in the Acts of the Apostles (15:22–29; 23:25–30)[25] and seven in the Apocalypse of John. In fact, the nature of the opening and closing of the Apocalypse of John gives it the framework of an ancient letter.[26] In the New Testament, then, twenty-one writings that exhibit an "epistolary poetic" are a medium of revelation in the context of five biographical histories (four Gospels and the Acts of the Apostles) and one apocalypse (Apocalypse of John).

If the relation of the five poetic discourses in the Hebrew Bible (prophetic, narrative, prescriptive, wisdom, and hymnic) to the three in the New Testament (biographical-historiography, epistle, and apocalyptic) demonstrates a substantive reconfiguration of canonical discourse, the Qur'ān represents an even more substantive reconfiguration with its recital of rhyming prose.[27] Some of the *sūras* that contain rhyming prose

---

22 Such as Paul's 1 Thessalonians, 1–2 Corinthians, Galatians, Philippians, and Philemon.

23 Such as the Epistle to the Hebrews and 2 Peter.

24 Dan 7–12.

25 Roman Christians report in Acts 28:21 that they have received no letters from Judea about Paul.

26 Adela Yarbro Collins, "Revelation, Book of," *ABD* 5:696–99.

27 Devin J. Stewart, "Saj' in the Qur'ān: Prosody and Structure," *Journal of Arabic Literature* 21 (1990): 101–39.

are similar to what Ricoeur called "hymnic discourse," some of the *sūras* contain what one might call "prayer discourse," and still other parts of it are like "hymnic narration." Overall, however, a literary poetic approach to the relation of the Hebrew Bible, the New Testament, and the Qur'ān is not a very promising approach.

From Literary Poetics to Social Rhetorics in the Bible

During the 1990s, rhetorical interpreters of the Bible moved beyond the literary poetics to the social rhetorics of biblical literature. The goal has been not only to claim more fully the power of biblical discourse but to claim its power in social, cultural, and ideological contexts. The current essay builds on advances made during the 1990s by merging insights into rhetorics with insights into social, cultural, and ideological discourse.

Social Rhetorics in the Hebrew Bible

Recently, Walter Brueggemann's *Theology of the Old Testament: Testimony, Dispute, Advocacy*[28] has moved analysis and interpretation of the Tanak beyond its literary poetics into its "rhetorics."[29] This is a very significant move, since it shifts the focus beyond the literary poetics of the Tanak to its oral power (its rhetorics) to effect change within human community. It is well known that throughout Mediterranean antiquity people did not regularly read texts individually, as we do today. Rather, people experienced written text as a flow of sounds in a context where someone performed the text orally. Biblical text, then, was first and foremost an oral performance for people.[30] During and after the fourth

---

[28] Walter Brueggemann, *Theology of the Old Testament: Testimony, Dispute, Advocacy* (Minneapolis: Fortress, 1997).

[29] For the importance of the term and concept of *rhetorics,* see Wilhelm Wuellner, "Hermeneutics and Rhetorics: From 'Truth and Method' to 'Truth and Power,'" *Scriptura* special issue 3 (1989): 1–54; see also Vernon K. Robbins, "Where Is Wuellner's Anti-Hermeneutical Hermeneutic Taking Us? From Schleiermacher to Thistleton and Beyond" (forthcoming).

[30] See John Miles Foley, *The Theory of Oral Composition: History and Methodology* (Bloomington: Indiana University Press, 1988); idem, *The Singer of Tales in Performance* (Bloomington: Indiana University Press, 1995); Werner H. Kelber, *The Oral and Written Gospel* (Philadelphia: Fortress, 1983); idem, "Jesus and Tradition: Words in Time, Words in Space," *Semeia* 65 (1994): 139–47; Vernon K. Robbins, "Oral, Rhetorical, and Literary Cultures: A Response," *Semeia* 65 (1994): 75–91; Bernard Brandon Scott and Margaret E. Dean, "A Sound Mapping of the Sermon on the Mount," in *Treasures New and Old: Recent Contributions to Matthean Studies* (ed. D. R. Baur and M. A. Powell; SBLSymS 1; Atlanta: Scholars Press, 1996),

century C.E., certain people began to read the Bible individually. Still to our present day, however, many people experience the Bible primarily through oral performance of it in public settings.

Brueggemann's analysis and interpretation of the Hebrew Bible brings to life the multiple rhetorics of testimony to God in four kinds of testimony: (1) core testimony; (2) countertestimony; (3) unsolicited testimony; and (4) embodied testimony. The core testimony of Israel features: (a) verbal sentences;[31] (b) adjectives;[32] (c) nouns;[33] and (d) Yahweh fully uttered.[34] The countertestimony of Israel features: (a) cross-examining Israel's core testimony;[35] (b) the hiddenness of Yahweh;[36] (c) ambiguity and the character of Yahweh;[37] and (d) Yahweh and negativity.[38] The unsolicited testimony of Israel features: (a) Israel as Yahweh's partner;[39] (b) the human person as Yahweh's partner;[40] (c) the nations as Yahweh's partner;[41] and (d) creation as Yahweh's partner.[42] The embodied testimony of Israel features: (a) the Torah as mediator;[43] (b) the king as mediator;[44] (c) the prophet as mediator;[45] and (d) the sage as mediator.[46] This is a rhetorical theology of the Hebrew Bible that contributes directly to sociorhetorical analysis and interpretation of early Christian and qur'ānic discourse. The first question for us is how first-century Christians appropriated and reconfigured conventional

---

311–78; Margaret E. Dean, "The Grammar of Sound in Greek Texts: Toward a Method for Mapping the Echoes of Speech in Writing," *ABR* 44 (1996): 53–70; Richard A. Horsley and Jonathan A. Draper, *Whoever Hears You Hears Me: Prophets, Performance, and Tradition in Q* (Harrisburg, Pa.: Trinity Press International, 1999).

31 Brueggemann, *Theology*, 145–212.

32 Characteristic markings of Yahweh (ibid., 213–28).

33 Yahweh as constant (ibid., 229–66).

34 Ibid., 267–303.

35 Ibid., 317–32.

36 Ibid., 333–58.

37 Ibid., 359–72.

38 Ibid., 373–99.

39 Ibid., 413–49.

40 Ibid., 450–91.

41 Ibid., 492–527.

42 Ibid., 528–51.

43 Ibid., 578–99.

44 Ibid., 600–621.

45 Ibid., 622–79.

46 Ibid., 680–94.

rhetorics in the Mediterranean world, which included the rhetorics in the Hebrew Bible.

SOCIAL RHETORICS IN THE NEW TESTAMENT

With the aid of three major literary modes—biographical-historiography (Gospels and Acts); epistles; and apocalypse—first-century Christians interwove six sociorhetorical modes of discourse—wisdom, miracle, prophetic, suffering-death, apocalyptic, and precreation discourse—into a distinctive, dynamic, and multivalent mode of discourse that became canonical for Christians in the Mediterranean world. In sociorhetorical interpretation, the technical term for each mode of discourse is *rhetorolect*.[47]

> A rhetorolect is a form of language variety or discourse identifiable on the basis of a distinctive configuration of themes, topics, reasonings, and argumentations. By their nature, rhetorolects interpenetrate one another and interact with one another like dialects do when people from different dialectical areas converse with one another. The interaction of rhetorolects in early Christianity created new configurations of speech as the movement grew. Every early Christian writing contains a configuration of rhetorolects that is somewhat different from every other writing. These differences, interacting with one another, create the overall rhetorical environment properly called early Christian discourse.[48]

In order to understand each rhetorolect, it is necessary to understand the nature of rhetorical discourse. A beginning place is to understand that rhetorical discourse elaborates *topoi*. In Carolyn Miller's terms:

> The *topos* is a conceptual space without fully specified or specifiable contents; it is a region of productive uncertainty. It is a "problem space," but rather than circumscribing or delimiting the problem, rather than being a closed space or container *within* which one searches, it is a space, or a located perspective, *from* which one searches. I am thinking here of the linguistic notion of "semantic space." ... Such semantic

[47] For a discussion of the term *rhetorolect,* see Vernon K. Robbins, "The Dialectical Nature of Early Christian Discourse," *Scriptura* 59 (1996): 353–62; also available online at http://www.emory.edu/COLLEGE/RELIGION/faculty/robbins/dialect/dialect353.html. For the argumentative nature of each rhetorolect, see Vernon K. Robbins, "Argumentative Textures in Socio-Rhetorical Interpretation," in *Rhetorical Argumentation in Biblical Texts* (ed. A. Eriksson et al.; Harrisburg, Pa.: Trinity Press International, 2002), 27–65.

[48] Robbins, "Dialectical Nature," 356.

> networks may be conditioned both by the peculiarities of community history and by apparently logical relationships (like opposition and inclusion).[49]

For rhetorical analysis and interpretation, it is important to understand that "Once a topical pattern has developed into common use, it will be used over and over in various manifestations and will be effective by virtue of its recognizability."[50] This recognizability sometimes is distinctive of a particular kind of culture in a particular region of the world. Wilhelm Wuellner has taught us, basing his insights on ancient rhetorical treatises and Curtius's interpretation of them, that rhetorical discourse elaborates *topoi* in two ways: amplificatory-descriptive, and argumentative-enthymematic.[51] Thus, a major presupposition for sociorhetorical interpretation is that each rhetorolect in the New Testament uses social, political, cultural, and religious locations of thought, practice, and argumentation as resources for elaboration and argumentation. One of the keys is to identify locations that function in a primary way in one or another rhetorolect. For example, one primary location for the *topoi* in New Testament wisdom discourse is the household, for miracle discourse a major location is the intersubjective body of individuals, for prophetic discourse the kingdom is a major location of thought, for suffering-death discourse the *polis,* and for apocalyptic and precreation discourse the empire is a major location of thought.

Social Rhetorics in the Qur'ān

The Qur'ān contains substantive miracle, wisdom, prophetic, and apocalyptic discourse. Precreation discourse is implicit rather than explicit in the Qur'ān. In the decades after the death of the prophet Muḥammad, the Qur'ān itself became a dynamic subject of precreation discourse, in particular in the controversy about whether the Qur'ān was created or uncreated. In a context where Christians were arguing that Jesus existed with God

---

49 Carolyn R. Miller, "The Aristotelian *Topos:* Hunting for Novelty," in *Rereading Aristotle's Rhetoric* (ed. A. G. Gross and A. E. Walzer; Carbondale: Southern Illinois University Press, 2000), 141.

50 Barbara Warnick, "Two Systems of Invention: The Topics in *Rhetoric* and *The New Rhetoric,*" in Gross and Walzer, *Rereading Aristotle's Rhetoric,* 110.

51 Wilhelm H. Wuellner, "Toposforschung und Torahinterpretation bei Paulus und Jesus," *NTS* 24 (1978): 467: "eine zweifache Funktion: eine argumentativ-enthymematische und eine amplifikatorisch-darstellerische Funktion." See also Walter J. Ong, *Orality and Literacy: The Technologizing of the Word* (New York: Routledge, 1988), 110–11. See the less explicitly rhetorical approach to "motifs" in F. Gerald Downing, "Words As Deeds and Deeds As Words," *BibInt* 3 (1995): 129–43.

prior to creation as the Logos and Jesus was never created, many Muslims argued that the Qur'ān existed with God prior to creation and was never created. In turn, Jewish tradition in contemporaneous midrashic works, for example, *Pirqe Rabbi Eliezer*, argued that seven things existed with God prior to creation: Torah, Gehinnom, the garden of Eden, the throne of glory, the temple, repentance, and the name of the messiah. The Qur'ān does not develop suffering-death discourse characteristic of Christianity. Six verses in the Qur'ān assert that the prophets were wrongfully slain,[52] but opposition to the belief that Jesus was slain is so strong that suffering-death discourse is not prominent in qur'ānic discourse.

Miracle Discourse in the Qur'ān

Miracle discourse is prominent in the Qur'ān. Thirty-six times in the Qur'ān the clause "Allah is (Thou art/He is) able to do all things" occurs.[53] In addition, ten verses refer to Allah as "Almighty,"[54] and forty-eight verses refer to Allah as "Mighty."[55] In qur'ānic discourse, the miraculous power of Allah is grounded in Allah's creation of the heavens and the earth. As Q 50:38 says: "And verily We created the heavens and the earth, and all that is between them, in six days, and naught of weariness touched Us."[56] Since Allah produced all creation originally, Allah has the power to reproduce it.[57] Indeed, God's ability to produce and reproduce creation is easy,[58] and people can easily see the evidence that God produced it by "traveling in the land" (Q 29:20). In addition, God has no difficulty giving life to humans and resurrecting them to new life, since humans are one of God's creations out of dust. As Q 64:7 says: "Those who disbelieve assert that they will not be raised again. Say (unto them, O Muḥammad): Yea, verily, by my Lord! ye will be raised again and then ye will be informed of what ye did; and that is easy for Allah."[59] The

---

[52] Q 2:61, 91; 3:21, 112, 181; 4:155.

[53] Q 2:20, 106, 109, 148, 259, 284; 3:26, 29, 165, 189; 5:17, 19, 40, 120; 6:17; 8:41; 9:39; 11:4; 16:77; 18:46 [45]; 22:6; 24:45; 29:20; 30:50; 33:27; 35:1; 41:39; 42:9; 46:33; 48:21; 57:2; 59:6; 64:1; 65:12; 66:8; 67:1.

[54] Q 3:6, 18; 12:39; 13:16; 14:48; 22:40, 74; 40:16; 57:25; 58:21.

[55] 2:129, 209, 220, 228, 240, 260; 3:62, 126; 4:56, 157, 165; 5:38, 118; 6:96; 8:10, 49, 63, 67; 9:40, 71; 14:4; 16:60; 27:9, 78; 29:16, 42; 30:27; 31:9, 27; 34:27; 35:2, 44; 36:38; 39:1; 40:8; 45:2, 37; 46:2; 48:7, 18; 57:1; 59:1, 24; 60:5; 61:1; 62:1, 3; 64:18; 67:2.

[56] See also Q 7:54; 10:3; 11:7; 25:59; 32:4; 57:4.

[57] Q 10:3–4, 34; 27:64; 30:11, 19; 50:11; 85:13.

[58] Q 29:19; 30:27.

[59] See also Q 2:73, 260; 3:27; 6:35, 95, 111; 7:57; 10:31; 21:21; 22:6; 25:3; 30:50; 36:12, 33; 41:39; 42:9; 50:3, 11, 43.

emphasis on humans as made of earth occurs clearly in Q 30:19: "He brings forth the living from the dead, and He brings forth the dead from the living, and He revives the earth after her death. And even so will you be brought forth."

In the Hebrew Bible, narratives about Moses, Elijah, and Elisha describe scenes with dramatic miracle discourse. The Qur'ān refers to Moses more than any other person in the Bible or anywhere in the world[60] (137 times), and there are a significant number of words in the context of these references that qualify as miracle discourse. In the context of nine references to Moses, there is explicit mention of clear proofs or miracles,[61] a term that occurs fifty times in the Qur'ān.[62] There are seventy-four references to Pharaoh in the Qur'ān, and most of these references recount, speak directly about, or evoke dynamics of Moses' confrontations with Pharaoh. A number of these verses use constructions such as "when we did deliver you" (2:49), "we rescued you" (2:50), "and we drowned the folk of Pharaoh" (2:50) to communicate God's miraculous activity of leading the people of Israel out of Egypt. Q 7:133 refers to the flood, locusts, vermin, frogs, and blood as a succession of clear signs or miracles that Pharaoh and his people did not heed.

The Qur'ān articulates no discourse with an emphasis on miracle either for Elijah or Elisha. Reference to Elisha occurs only twice in qur'ānic discourse: once he is listed with Ishmael, Jonah, and Lot as people whom God preferred among God's creatures (6:86 [87]); and once he is listed with Ishmael and Dhu'l Kifl as of the chosen (38:48). There is no emphasis on miracle in either context referring to Elijah or Elisha.

The Qur'ān refers to Elijah three times. Q 6:85 (86) lists Elijah along with Zechariah (father of John the Baptist), John (the Baptist), and Jesus as among the righteous. While there is no emphasis on miracle in this context, qur'ānic discourse about Zechariah and Jesus includes an emphasis on miracle, and John's birth is miraculous. Thus, in an implicit manner the grouping of Elijah with Zechariah, John, and Jesus may be perceived

---

60 One might think the Qur'ān would refer to Muḥammad more times than anyone else. Since many verses in the Qur'ān address Muḥammad directly, Pickthall's English version adds Muḥammad's name in parentheses so often that a concordance search exhibits 272 occurrences of his name. However, the name Muḥammad occurs only four times in the Arabic text of the Qur'ān (3:144; 33:40; 47:2; 48:29).

61 Q 2:92; 4:153; 7:85, 104–105; 11:17; 17:101; 20:70–72; 29:39; 40:28.

62 In addition to the references in note 49, Q 2:87, 185, 209, 213, 253; 3:86, 105, 183, 184; 5:32, 110; 6:57, 157; 7:101; 8:42 (bis); 9:70; 10:13, 74; 11:28, 53, 63, 88; 14:9; 16:44; 20:133; 30:9; 35:25, 40; 40:22, 34, 50, 66, 83; 43:63; 47:14; 57:25; 61:6; 64:6; 98:1, 4.

to evoke an image of righteous people around whom God's miraculous powers were at work in a special way. One should mention again, however, that the emphasis in the context is on these men as "of the righteous," without any reference to God's miraculous work in the world. The other two references to Elijah occur in Q 37:123, 130, where the discourse attributes speech to Elijah as one who was sent to warn. Since the content of Elijah's speech is apocalyptic in tone, discussion of these references is present in the section below on apocalyptic discourse.

Unlike the Qur'ān's reference to Elijah only three times, the New Testament refers to Elijah twenty-nine times,[63] in comparison to sixty-six references to Elijah in the Hebrew Bible. Luke 4:25–26 and Jas 5:16–17 summarize episodes in which God's miraculous power worked through Elijah, and Jesus' raising of the son of the widow of Nain from death in Luke 7:11–17 is a reconfiguration of Elijah's raising of the son of the widow of Zarephath in 1 Kgs 17:17–24.[64] In addition, the Elijah-Elisha stories in the Hebrew Bible functioned for early Christians as a prefiguration of Jesus' miracles and played a highly formative role in the narrative portrayal of those activities in the Gospels of Mark and Luke.[65] Moreover, the one explicit reference to Elisha in the New Testament (Luke 4:27) focuses on his healing of Naaman the Syrian from his leprosy.[66]

There are seventy-nine references to Moses in the New Testament.[67] Only Rev 15:3, however, comes close to associating Moses with miraculous discourse when the song of Moses and the Lamb begins with "Great and amazing are your deeds." John 6:32 refers to Moses' giving of the bread out of heaven to the people, but it is doubtful that there is any emphasis on the miraculous in the assertion. In contrast, the miracle is "the true bread from heaven that the Father gives." One could almost say, then, that the New Testament and the Qur'ān exhibit a reversal of emphasis on miracle in the context of Elijah and Moses. For the New Testament, Elijah is the prominent miracle prophet in the story of Israel, and Elisha is

---

[63] Matt 11:14; 16:14; 17:3, 4, 10, 11, 12; 27:47, 49; Mark 6:15; 8:28; 9:4, 5, 11, 12, 13; 15:35, 36; Luke 1:17; 4:25, 26; 9:8, 19, 30, 33; John 1:21, 25; Rom 11:2; Jas 5:17.

[64] A similar story is recounted of Elisha in 2 Kgs 4:32–37.

[65] Wolfgang Roth, *Hebrew Gospel: Cracking the Code of Mark* (Oak Park, Ill.: Meyer-Stone, 1988); Thomas L. Brodie, *The Crucial Bridge: The Elijah-Elisha Narrative As an Interpretive Synthesis of Genesis-Kings and a Literary Model for the Gospels* (Collegeville, Minn.: Liturgical Press, 2000).

[66] The Hebrew Bible contains eighty-six references to Elisha, in comparison with sixty-six references to Elijah.

[67] The Hebrew Bible refers to Moses more than seven hundred times.

included in this emphasis; for the Qur'ān, Moses is the prominent miracle prophet in the story of Israel rather than Elijah and Elisha.

The other person whom qur'ānic discourse associates explicitly with miracles is Jesus, son of Mary. Q 2:87 emphasizes that Jesus followed after Moses with "clear proofs," and God supported Jesus with the holy spirit.[68] Once the Qur'ān clearly groups Moses and Jesus together (2:136), and once Moses and Jesus are grouped together at the end of a list of four prophets including Noah and Abraham (33:7). Jesus is the only one in the Qur'ān, besides God himself, who is given the power to raise the dead. Jesus raises the dead with God's permission (3:49; 5:110) alongside of his creating a live bird out of clay, healing the blind, and healing the leper. Qur'ānic discourse refers to these activities respectively as Jesus' coming with a sign (3:49) and with clear proofs (5:110).

The Qur'ān refers to Jesus twenty-five times,[69] exactly the same number of times it refers to Adam.[70] No miracles are attributed to Adam, but the Qur'ān asserts that "the likeness of Jesus with God is as the likeness of Adam. He created him of dust, then He said unto him: Be! and he is" (Q 3:59). Like Adam, Jesus was human; but also like Adam, God created Jesus simply by saying, "Be!" As the angel explained to Mary, "So (it will be). God creates what He will. If He decrees a thing, He says unto it only; 'Be!' and it is" (Q 3:47).

Wisdom Discourse in the Qur'ān

Since "God creates what He will" (5:17) and is able to do all things, there could be great difficulty if Allah's will were arbitrary. To the good fortune of all, Allah's power and will are grounded in wisdom, which includes mercy and forgiveness. Forty-eight times the Qur'ān refers to Allah as "(Al)mighty, Wise"[71] and seven times as "Knower, Powerful" or "Mighty, Knower."[72] In the Qur'ān, God's knowledge is fully as great as God's power. Words referring to knowing, knowledge, and knower occur, on the basis of Pickthall's version, 692 times in the Qur'ān. Thirty-two times the

---

68 See also Q 2:92, 253.

69 Q 2:87, 136, 253; 3:45, 52, 55, 59, 84; 4:157, 163, 171; 5:46, 78, 110, 112, 114, 116; 6:85; 19:34; 33:7; 42:13; 43:63; 57:27; 61:6, 14.

70 Q 2:31, 33, 34, 35, 37; 3:33, 59; 5:27; 7:11, 19, 26, 27, 31, 35, 172; 17:61, 70; 18:50; 19:58; 20:115, 116, 117, 120, 121; 36:60.

71 Q 2:129, 209, 220, 228, 240, 260; 3:6, 18, 62, 126; 4:56, 158, 165; 5:38, 118; 6:96; 8:10, 49, 63, 67; 9:40, 71; 14:4; 16:60; 27:9, 78; 29:26, 42; 30:27; 31:9, 27; 34:27; 35:2, 44; 36:38; 39:1; 40:8; 45:2, 37; 46:2; 48:7, 19; 57:1; 59:1, 24; 60:5; 61:1; 62:1, 3; 64:18; see also 42:51 (Exalted, Wise); 41:42 (Wise, Owner of Praise).

72 Q 16:70; 30:54; 40:2; 41:12: 42:3, 50; 43:9.

Qur'ān refers to God as "Knower, Wise."[73] Thirteen times the Qur'ān says that God is "the Knower of all things."[74] God knows the invisible and the visible,[75] the things hidden,[76] the unseen.[77] God knows what is in the breasts of people,[78] and God knows sins.[79]

The Qur'ān also refers to God in a manner Pickthall rendered as "Aware." God is aware of "all who are in the heavens and the earth" (17:55). Indeed, God is "Aware of all things."[80] The Qur'ān refers to God six times as "Wise, Aware,"[81] four times as "Knower, Aware,"[82] four times as "Subtle, Aware,"[83] and twice as "Responsive, Aware."[84] God is aware of what all people do:[85] both the good things of those who go aright[86] and those who do evil or wrong.[87] God is aware of all that is hidden in human breasts.[88]

God is aware of all these things and knows them because God both hears and sees all things. God is the Hearer, Knower.[89] As part of this, of course, God is the Hearer of Prayer.[90] In addition, God sees all things

---

[73] Q 2:32; 4:11, 17, 24, 26, 92, 104, 111, 170; 6:18; 8:71; 9:15, 28, 60, 97, 106, 110; 12:6, 83, 100; 22:52; 24:18, 58, 59; 33:1; 43:84; 48:4; 49:8; 51:30; 60:10; 66:2; 76:30.

[74] Q 2:29, 282; 4:32, 176; 5:97; 8:75; 24:35, 64; 33:54; 42:12: 57:3; 58:7; 64:11; see also 4:70 (Knower); 36:79 (Knower of every creation); 15:86 (all-wise Creator); 4:12; 22:59 (Knower, Indulgent).

[75] Q 6:73; 9:105; 19:9; 23:92; 32:6; 39:46; 59:22; 62:8; 64:18; cf. 18:26.

[76] Q 5:109; 9:78; 34:48.

[77] Q 34:3; 35:38; 72:26; see also 6:50.

[78] Q 3:29, 119, 154; 5:7; 8:43; 11:5; 28:69; 31:23; 35:38; 39:7; 42:24; 64:4; 67:13.

[79] Q 17:17; 15:58.

[80] Q 2:231; 6:101; 9:115; 21:81; 29:62; 33:40; 48:26; 49:16; see also 35:14.

[81] Q 6:73, 83, 128, 139; 15:25; 27:6; 34:1; cf. 11:1 (Wise, Informed); 24:10 (Clement, Wise).

[82] Q 4:35; 31:34; 49:13; 66:3.

[83] Q 6:103; 22:63; 31:16; 33:34; 67:14; see also 4:39 (ever Aware).

[84] Q 2:158; 4:147.

[85] Q 2:283; 13:33; 17:54; 22:68; 23:51; 48:11; 58:13; 63:11; 64:8.

[86] Q 2:215; 3:92, 115; 4:127; 6:53; 9:44; 16:125; 17:84; 24:30, 41; 28:56; 39:70; 53:30, 32.

[87] Q 2:95, 187, 246; 3:63; 6:58, 119; 9:47; 10:36, 40; 12:19; 19:70; 20:104; 23:96; 26:188; 28:85; 35:8; 39:70; 46:8; 53:30; 62:7; 68:7.

[88] Q 3:119, 154, 169; 11:5; 29:10; 31:23; 35:38; 42:24; 64:4; see also 60:1.

[89] Q 2:127, 137, 181, 224, 227, 244, 256; 3:34, 35, 121; 4:148; 5:76; 6:13, 115; 7:200; 8:17, 42, 53, 61; 9:98, 103; 10:65; 12:34; 21:4; 24:21, 60; 29:5, 60; 31:28; 41:36; 44:6; 49:1; 58:1; see also 34:50 (Hearer, Nigh).

[90] Q 3:38; 14:39; 37:75.

(67:19). God is the "Hearer, Seer."[91] God sees "what you [pl.] do"[92] and "what they do."[93]

In the Qur'ān, Joseph, son of Jacob, and the qur'ānic personage Luqmān are the people most closely associated with wisdom, with Solomon and David also included. Joseph received wisdom and knowledge (12:22) from God for his task on earth. This made Joseph a lord of knowledge (12:76). In turn, Joseph is called "the truthful one" (12:46: *ayyuha*). This wisdom even enables Joseph to make his father Jacob a wise seer who can say: "Said I not unto you that I know from Allah that which ye know not" (12:96). In the *sūra* titled Luqmān, God is "the True" (31:30), and there is an emphasis that God gave Luqmān wisdom (31:12). In the context of Joseph and Luqmān, there is an emphasis on God as true. In turn, God gave David and Solomon wisdom (judgment and knowledge). This made them wise in judgment and understanding (21:78–79).

The Qur'ān does not contain a separate "wisdom" section but rather embeds wisdom, attributed to God, throughout many of the *sūras*. The wise, who submit to God's will, who become Muslim, are those who see the wisdom within the qur'ānic discourse itself.

Prophetic Discourse in the Qur'ān

Everyone knows there is prophetic discourse in the Qur'ān, since Muslim tradition emphasizes that Muḥammad is the final, most authoritative prophet. Readers of the Qur'ān will know, however, that the word messenger (*rasūl*) is even more frequent than the word prophet (*nabī*) and that Muslims refer first and foremost to Muḥammad as The Messenger. The Qur'ān refers a total of seventy-eight times to a prophet.[94] The New Testament refers to a prophet 150 times,[95] which is almost twice as many times as the Qur'ān. In contrast, the word "messenger" occurs 368 times in the Qur'ān (Pickthall: 243 times in the singular and 125 times in the plural). This is almost two and one-half times as often as the word "prophet" occurs in the New Testament and almost four and three-fourths times more than the word "prophet" occurs in the Qur'ān.

---

91 Q 4:58, 134; 17:1; 22:61, 75; 40:20, 56; 42:11; see also 17:96 (Knower, Seer); 18:26 (clear of sight, keen of hearing).

92 Q 2:110, 232, 237, 265; 3:156, 163; 11:112; 33:9; 34:11; 41:40; 48:24; 49:18; 57:4; 60:3; 64:2; see also Knower of what you used to do (16:28); Seer of his bondsmen (3:15, 20; 42:27); and Seer of his slaves (35:31, 45).

93 Q 2:96; 5:71; 8:39, 72.

94 Fifty-seven times in the singular; twenty-one times in the plural.

95 Sixty-four times in the singular; eighty-six times in the plural.

The remarkable frequency of the word *messenger* in the Qur'ān indicates that, for this revelatory discourse, God sent messengers at various times to people with various combinations of abilities.[96] They are sent as miracle workers; as people who transmitted God's wisdom, knowledge, and truth; as people who announced God's good news; and as special warners of the terrible things that will happen to disbelievers. The concept of prophet is closely related to messenger, since God sends prophets. In qur'ānic discourse, however, God sends all kinds of messengers, and only certain ones are regularly referred to as prophets. God sends only certain messengers with miracles to confirm what they do. There are signs that accompany all of God's messengers, since God's creation presents signs of God's powerful activity every day. These signs function only for believers as portents that reveal the remarkable beneficence and mercy of God, of course. For unbelievers, these signs are simply natural functions of the universe and not anything that especially reveals the nature and magnificence of God.

Sūra 21, entitled The Prophets (*al-Anbiyā'*), recounts circumstances around eleven Hebrew Bible people (Noah, Abraham, Lot, Ishmael, Isaac, Jacob, Moses, Aaron, David, Solomon, Job), one New Testament person (Zechariah, father of John the Baptist), and three other prophets (Idrīs, Dhu'l-Kifl, Dhū'l-Nūn). In addition to *Sūra* 21, which is devoted entirely to prophets, there are lists of prophets in various verses in the Qur'ān. Jesus is most noticeably absent from *Sūra* 21, since he is included in lists of prophets among Abraham, Ishmael, Isaac, Jacob, and Moses in 2:136; 3:84; 4:163–164 and among Noah, Abraham, and Moses in 33:7. It is also surprising that Jonah does not appear in *Sūra* 21. Jonah appears only once in a list of prophets (4:163–164), but he has wonderful company there: Noah, Abraham, Ishmael, Isaac, Jacob, Moses, Aaron, David, Solomon, Job, and Jesus. In addition, Jonah appears among Ishmael, Elisha, and Lot in 6:86; receives special recognition in 37:139–148 after Noah (37:75–82), Abraham (37:83–111), Isaac (37:112–113), Moses and Aaron (37:114–122), Elijah (37:123–132), and Lot (37:133–138); and there is a *sūra* named Jonah (Q 10 *Yūnus*).

The term *prophethood* and the singular or plural of *prophet* occurs eighty-three times in the Qur'ān. There is no verb that Pickthall interprets in English as "to prophesy." God promises 117 times. Prophets transmit God's knowledge, wisdom, truth, and good news; and they warn. Prophets in the Qur'ān do not prophesy. Thus, the Qur'ān makes no references to prophecies, and it does not describe anyone as prophesying. Both God and Satan promise (2:268). This would seem to fit the Islamic contention that Muḥammad ends prophecy.

---

[96] A current web site offers an article arguing for the introduction of twenty scriptures by twenty successive prophets: http://www.submission.org/Quran-19.html.

Apocalyptic Discourse in the Qur'ān

Apocalyptic discourse is highly present in the Qur'ān. References to the day of judgment occur fourteen times,[97] to those who believe in God and the last day twenty-seven times,[98] and things that will happen on the day of resurrection seventy-one times.[99] Norman O. Brown, following the lead of Louis Massignon, has called *Sūra* 18 the "Apocalypse of Islam." "Surah 18," he says, "is the apocalypse of Islam: the heart of its message, not displayed on the surface, is the distinction between surface and substance, between *Zahir* and *bâtin*."[100] What Brown asserts about *Sūra* 18 is true for most of the Qur'ān. Almost the entire presentation of themes in the Qur'ān involves either an implicit or explicit reference to the eschaton. As we have indicated elsewhere, the very presentation of time is focused on a compression of the period from creation to the last day, with a resulting emphasis of making all temporal events affected by a sense of the end.[101] In this context, one of the tasks of God's messengers is to warn people about the rewards of belief and the consequences of disbelief.

Apocalyptic discourse in the Qur'ān sets up the alternative of gardens and paradise for believers and fire for disbelievers. The gardens and paradise as humans' reward for good action are mentioned 130 times.[102] These gardens, modeled on the garden of Eden in Gen 2–3, have much

---

[97] Q 1:4; 15:35; 26:82; 37:20; 38:78; 51:12; 56:56; 68:39; 70:26; 74:46; 82:15, 17, 18; 83:11.

[98] Q 2:8, 62, 126, 177, 228, 232, 264; 3:114; 4:38, 39, 59, 136, 162; 5:69; 7:45; 9:18, 19, 29, 44, 45, 99; 24:2; 29:36; 33:21; 58:22; 60:6; 65:2.

[99] Q 2:85, 113, 174; 3:55, 77, 161, 180, 185, 194; 4:87, 109, 141, 159; 5:14, 36, 64; 6:12; 7:32, 167, 172; 10:60, 93; 11:60, 98, 99; 16:25, 27, 92, 124; 17:13, 58, 62, 97; 18:105; 19:95; 20:100, 101, 124; 21:47; 22:9, 17, 69; 23:16; 25:47, 69; 28:41, 42, 61, 71, 72; 29:13, 25; 30:56; 32:25; 35:14; 39:15, 24, 31, 47, 60, 67; 41:40; 42:45; 45:17, 26; 46:5; 58:7; 60:3; 75:1; 75:6.

[100] Norman Oliver Brown, *Apocalypse and/or Metamorphosis* (Berkeley and Los Angeles: University of California Press, 1991), 81.

[101] Gordon D. Newby, "Quranic Texture: A Review of Vernon Robbins' *The Tapestry of Early Christian Discourse* and *Exploring the Texture of Texts*," *JSNT* 70 (1998): 93–100.

[102] Q 2:25, 82, 221, 266; 3:15, 136, 195, 198; 4:13, 57, 122; 5:12, 65, 85, 119; 6:99; 7:40, 42, 43, 44, 46, 49, 50; 9:21, 72, 89, 100, 111; 10:9, 26; 11:23, 108; 13:23, 35; 14:23; 15:45; 16:31, 32; 17:91; 18:31–34, 40; 19:61, 63; 20:76; 22:56; 23:19; 25:15, 24; 26:85, 90; 29:58; 30:15; 31:8; 32:19; 34:15–16; 35:33; 36:34; 37:43; 38:50; 39:73–74; 40:8, 40; 42:7, 22; 43:70, 72; 44:25, 52; 46:14, 16; 47:6, 15; 48:5, 17; 50:9, 31; 51:15; 52:17; 53:13; 54:54; 55:46, 54, 62; 56:12, 89; 57:12, 21; 58:22; 59:20; 61:12; 64:9; 65:11; 66:8, 11; 68:17, 34; 69:22; 70:35, 38; 71:12; 74:40; 76:12; 78:16, 32; 79:41; 80:30; 81:13; 85:11; 88:10; 89:30; 98:8.

in common with the heavenly garden-city as it is depected in Rev 22:1–5. Fire, the reward of those who sin, is mentioned 148 times,[103] and there are 103 references to hell.[104] This means that sixty-one *sūras* refer explicitly to the fire, with one more implying it (Q 42). Fifty-two *sūras* appear not to contain a reference to the fire for unbelievers or allude to it.[105] *Sūra* 2: *al-Baqarah*, the longest *sūra* in the Qur'ān, has fourteen or fifteen references to the fire, more references than any other *sūra*. *Sūra* 3: *Āl-'Imrān*, has eleven references to the fire. *Sūra* 101: *al-Qāri'ah* ends with the words "raging fire." It is unusual that the phrase "the fire of God" appears only once in the Qur'ān (104:6), since fire is intimately associated with the nature of God in the Bible.[106] The Qur'ān appears to present fire much more like the Revelation to John, where fire is explicitly an instrument of God but not identified so intimately with the internal nature of God.[107]

In a context where people face an alternative between the raging fire and gardens of delight on the basis of belief or disbelief, a major task of God's messengers is to warn people about the rewards of belief and the consequences of disbelief. It was noted above in the section on miraculous discourse how the Qur'ān emphasizes the role of Elijah as warner about the consequences of disbelief, rather than as agent of God's miraculous

---

[103] Q 2:24, 39, 80, 81, 119, 126, 167, 174, 201, 217, 221, 257, 266, 275; 3:10, 16, 24, 103, 116, 131, 151, 162, 185, 191, 192; 4:10, 14, 30, 56, 145; 5:29, 27, 72, 86; 6:27, 128; 7:36, 44, 47, 50; 8:14; 9:17, 35, 63, 68, 81, 109, 113; 10:8, 27; 11:16, 17, 83, 98, 106, 113; 13:5, 35; 14:30, 50; 16:62; 18:29, 53; 21:39; 22:19, 51, 72; 23:104; 24:57; 27:90; 28:41; 29:24; 32:20; 33:64, 66; 34:12, 42; 35:6, 36; 38:27, 59, 61, 64; 39:8, 16, 19; 40:6, 41, 43, 46, 47, 49, 72; 41:19, 24, 28, 40; (42:45); 45:34; 46:20, 34; 47:12, 15; 51:13; 52:13, 14, 18, 27; 54:48; 55:35; 56:94; 57:15, 19; 58:17; 59:3, 17, 20; 64:10; 66:6, 10; 69:31; 70:15; 71:25; 72:15, 23; 73:12; 74:31; 76:4; 84:12; 85:5; 87:12; 88:4; 90:20; 92:14; 98:6; 100:2; 101:11; 102:6; 104:6; 111:3.

[104] Q 2:119, 206; 3:12, 197; 4:55, 93, 97, 115, 121, 140, 169; 5:10, 86; 7:18, 41, 179; 8:16, 36–37; 9:35, 49, 63, 68, 73, 81, 95, 109, 113; 11:119; 13:18; 14:16, 29; 15:43; 16:29; 17:8, 18, 39, 63, 97; 18:100, 102, 106; 19:68, 86; 20:74; 21:29, 98; 23:103; 25:34, 65; 26:91; 29:54, 68; 32:13; 35:36; 36:63; 37:23, 55, 64, 68, 163; 38:56, 85; 39:32, 60, 71–72; 40:7, 49, 60, 76; 43:74; 44:47, 56; 45:10; 48:6; 50:24, 30; 52:13, 18; 54:48; 55:43; 56:94; 57:19; 58:8; 66:9; 67:6; 69:31; 70:15; 72:15, 23; 78:21; 79:36, 39; 81:12; 82:14; 83:16; 85:10; 89:23; 96:18; 98:6; 102:6.

[105] 1, 12, 15, 17, 19–20, 25–26, 30–31, 36–37, 43–44, 48–50, 53, 60–63, 65, 67–68, 75, 77–83, 86, 89, 91, 93–97, 99, 103, 105–110, 112–114.

[106] E.g., Num 16:35; Deut 4:24, 33, 36; 5:4, 5, 22, 24, 26; 9:3; 18:16; 32:22; 1 Kgs 18:24, 38; 2 Kgs 1:10; Job 1:16; Pss 18:8; 29:7; 50:3; 78:21; 79:5; 89:46; 97:3.

[107] Rev 1:14; 2:18; 3:18; 4:5; 8:5, 7, 8; 9:17, 18; 10:1; 11:5; 13:13; 14:10, 18; 15:2; 16:8; 17:16; 18:8; 19:12, 20; 20:9, 10, 14, 15; 21:8.

power. Q 37:123–132 evokes Elijah's confrontation with the worshipers of Baal with reference to the doom that awaits them, rather than with reference to the manifestation of God's power in fire that came down and consumed the offerings (1 Kgs 18:36–39; see also 2 Kgs 1:10).

In addition, a number of *sūras* in the Qur'ān vividly present details of the day of judgment in a manner reminiscent of Mark 13, Matt 24, Luke 21, and Rev 20–21 in the New Testament. *Sūra* 82 ("The Cleaving" [*al-Infiṭār*]) presents in only nineteen verses the splitting of the heavens, the dispersing of the planets, the raging of the seas, and the overturning of the graves that will occur on the day of judgment. *Sūra* 75 ("The Rising of the Dead" [*al-Qiyāmah*]) presents in detail the sequence of events at the end, including the darkening of the sun and moon (see Mark 13:24 and its parallels), when the righteous will be resurrected.

Noah and Jonah are apocalyptic prophets. In many ways, their discourse brings coherence to all of qur'ānic discourse, which, as we mentioned above, seems apocalyptic in its overall nature, while at the same time using a variety of discourses.

Conclusion

In this prolegomenon, we have tried to indicate a new direction for qur'ānic study that places the Qur'ān within the same discourse environment as Hebrew and Christian Scriptures. Through the use of social and rhetorical analysis, the three scriptures and their related interpretive writings can be treated as commensurable without being reductionist or assuming a discourse of "borrowing/lending," which always privileges the antecedent tradition. Our efforts are already generating new arenas of investigation for us. One, mentioned above, is the pervasive apocalyptic nature of the Qur'ān. Another is how closely the Qur'ān is in conversation with the Gospel of Luke and its subsequent heritage in Christian tradition. Space in this essay has not allowed us to demonstrate these directions, but we hope to publish studies on these topics in the near future. In the meantime, it is our hope that other scholars will see the utility of the method we have outlined here and help us with our project of analyzing just how the Qur'ān is the third partner in this conversation about God's Word.

Some Explorations of the Intertwining of Bible and Qur'ān

John C. Reeves
University of North Carolina at Charlotte

> "a palimpsest, layer upon layer, tradition upon tradition, intertwined to the extent that one cannot really grasp one without the other, certainly not the later without the earlier, *but often also not the earlier without considering the shapes it took later.*"[1]

Many contemporary biblical scholars are aware that Bible and Qur'ān share and exploit a common layer of discourse consisting of a number of stories and themes featuring and drawing on certain paradigmatic characters, such as Noah, Abraham, and Moses. Most, however, do not pursue the literary ramifications of this nexus, and hence they remain remarkably oblivious to the rich reservoirs of traditional lore tapped and channeled by the Qur'ān and its expounders.[2] The intent of the present essay is to suggest that a careful reading of the Qur'ān in tandem with the interpretive traditions available in ancillary Muslim literature such as *ḥadīth,* classical commentaries, antiquarian histories, and the collections of so-called

---

* An earlier version of a portion of this essay was published electronically as "Toward a Rapprochement between Bible and Qur'ān," *Religious Studies News—SBL Edition* 2.9 (December 2001), which is accessible at http://www.sbl-site.org/Newsletter/12_2001/ReevesFull.htm.

[1] H. Lazarus-Yafeh, *Intertwined Worlds: Medieval Islam and Bible Criticism* (Princeton: Princeton University Press, 1992), 4, emphasis added.

[2] A particularly valuable survey of this labyrinthine corpus, supplemented with copious bibliographical references, is H. Schwarzbaum, *Biblical and Extra-Biblical Legends in Islamic Folk-Literature* (Beiträge zur Sprach- und Kulturgeschichte des Orients 30; Walldorf-Hessen: Verlag für Orientkunde Dr. H. Vorndran, 1982). See also C. Adang, *Muslim Writers on Judaism and the Hebrew Bible: From Ibn Rabban to Ibn Hazm* (Leiden: Brill, 1996), 1–22.

"prophetic legends" (*qiṣaṣ al-anbiyā'*)[3] can shed a startling light on the structure and content of certain stories found in Bible and its associated literatures (such as Jewish pseudepigrapha and rabbinic midrash). Indeed, the results of this type of study imply that the Qur'ān and the other early Muslim biblically allied traditions must be taken much more seriously as witnesses to "versions of Bible" than has heretofore been the case.[4]

Let us consider three examples of how a careful reading of Qur'ān and other early Muslim authorities sheds some valuable interpretive light on the shaping and refraction of Jewish and Christian scriptural traditions from the early centuries of the Common Era.

Idrīs "Is" Enoch

During a qur'ānic rehearsal of the careers of a series of biblical figures to whom Islam accords the status of "prophet" (*nabī*),[5] we encounter the

---

[3] For guidance pertaining to this latter literary genre, see especially Schwarzbaum, *Legends*, 46–75; J. Pauliny, "Some Remarks on the *Qiṣaṣ al-Anbiyā'* Works in Arabic Literature," in *The Qur'an: Formative Interpretation* (ed. A. Rippin; Aldershot: Ashgate, 1999), 313–26.

[4] Not all these "versions" of Bible exist (or even once existed) in written form, just as the Qur'ān itself as revelatory locus resists confinement to the bounds of a physical text. The former point emerges from a consideration of the abundant evidence collected by James L. Kugel, *The Bible As It Was* (Cambridge: Harvard University Press, 1997); the latter from D. A. Madigan, *The Qur'ân's Self-Image: Writing and Authority in Islam's Scripture* (Princeton: Princeton University Press, 2001). For some exemplary approaches to the comparative study of biblical and qur'ānic traditions, note James L. Kugel, *In Potiphar's House: The Interpretive Life of Biblical Texts* (San Francisco: HarperCollins, 1990), 28–65; M. R. Waldman, "New Approaches to 'Biblical' Materials in the Qur'ān," *MW* 75 (1985): 1–16; N. Calder, "From Midrash to Scripture: The Sacrifice of Abraham in Early Islamic Tradition," *Mus* 101 (1988): 375–402; D. J. Halperin, "The Hidden Made Manifest: Muslim Traditions and the 'Latent Content' of Biblical and Rabbinic Stories," in *Pomegranates and Golden Bells: Studies in Biblical, Jewish, and Near Eastern Ritual, Law, and Literature in Honor of Jacob Milgrom* (ed. D. P. Wright et al.; Winona Lake, Ind.: Eisenbrauns, 1995), 581–94. See now the truly groundbreaking study of R. Firestone, "Comparative Studies in Bible and Qur'ān: A Fresh Look at Genesis 22 in Light of Sura 37," in *Judaism and Islam: Boundaries, Communication and Interaction: Essays in Honor of William M. Brinner* (ed. B. H. Hary et al.; Leiden: Brill, 2000), 169–84.

[5] A convenient listing of the qur'ānic "prophets" is available in T. P. Hughes, *Dictionary of Islam* (1885; repr., New Delhi: Cosmo Publications, 1977), 475–76. For more nuanced discussions of this office and its occupants, see U. Rubin, "Prophets and Progenitors in the Early Shī'a Tradition," *JSAI* 1 (1979): 41–65; G. D. Newby,

following enigmatic statement: "Mention in the book Idrīs, for he was a truthful one, a prophet; and We raised him to a lofty place" (Q 19:56–57). Given the clear biblical provenance of the names appearing in these verses' immediate environment—such as those of Moses, Abraham, and Noah—one might legitimately expect Idrīs to be a biblical character as well. However, neither the name Idrīs nor any plausible permutation thereof figures in either the Hebrew or Christian Bibles. Some Western scholars have sought to resolve this identity crisis by positing a corruption in the transmission of the qur'ānic name, but their suggestions are not very compelling.[6] On the other hand, the postqur'ānic Muslim interpretive tradition, as mediated by the standard commentaries and histories, avers that the prophet Idrīs is in fact identical with the biblical antediluvian forefather Enoch (Gen 5:21–24).[7]

In spite of this important testimony—one that appears early and recurs repeatedly throughout Muslim literature—some modern scholars continue to harbor doubts. In a recent study P. S. Alexander writes: "Now it seems abundantly clear that although the identification of Idrīs with Enoch is standard in the Tafsīr literature ... the Qur'ān was not, in fact, referring to Enoch. The name Idrīs is nothing like the name Enoch, and no convincing link between the two has ever been suggested."[8] This is, however, not a particularly compelling argument. If Alexander's proffered criterion for equivalence—presumably a discernable phonetic correspondence between the names Idrīs and Enoch—should be admitted as a cogent objection, then one would be forced to discard a number of other hitherto undisputed

---

The Making of the Last Prophet: A Reconstruction of the Earliest Biography of Muhammad (Columbia: University of South Carolina Press, 1989), 18–24; M. R. Waldman, "Nubuwa," *ER* 11:1–7.

6 The most important suggestions are summarized by P. Casanova, "Idrîs et 'Ouzaïr," *JA* 205 (1924): 357–58; G. Vajda, "Idrīs," *EI*² 3:1030–31; see also Y. Erder, "The Origin of the Name Idrīs in the Qur'ān: A Study of the Influence of Qumran Literature on Early Islam," *JNES* 49 (1990): 339–50, esp. 340–41; idem, " Idrīs," *EncQur* 2:484–86.

7 A convenient anthology of such traditions, although mediated through a Shī'a perspective, is available in Sayyid Ni'mat Allāh al-Jazā'irī, *Qiṣaṣ al-anbiyā'* (ed. H. M. 'Aqil; Beirut: Dār al-Balāgha, 1991), 81–89. Jazā'irī's collection was abstracted in turn from the massive *Biḥār al-anwār* of Majlisī, a magisterial library of Shiite lore compiled in the seventeenth century (110 vols.; Tehran: Dār al-Kutub al-Islāmīyah, 1957–), 11:270–84.

8 P. S. Alexander, "Jewish Tradition in Early Islam: The Case of Enoch/Idrīs," in *Studies in Islamic and Middle Eastern Texts and Traditions in Memory of Norman Calder* (ed. G. R. Hawting et al.; JSSSup 12; Oxford: Oxford University Press, 2000), 23.

equivalencies linking qur'ānic and extraqur'ānic characters. For example, the Babylonian angels Hārūt and Mārūt (Q 2:102) are most certainly reflexes of the disgraced heavenly Watchers Shemhazai and 'Azael, whose corruptive activities are extensively profiled in Jewish pseudepigraphic lore.[9] This is true despite the absence of any common elements among their respective names. Nor does any modern scholar seriously dispute the identification of the enigmatic Dhū'l-Qarnayn "the two-horned one" (Q 18:83–98) with Alexander the Great,[10] even though again there is no similarity between the spelling of these names. Hence the lack of a consonantal overlap between the names Idrīs and Enoch is hardly a conclusive factor for dismissing their narratological equivalence.

There is, however, one important clue already within the qur'ānic verses that fosters an identification of Idrīs with Enoch, namely, their suggestive reference to the apparent supernatural removal of Enoch from human society: "We raised him [i.e., Idrīs] to a lofty place."[11] Although the Hebrew Bible (Gen 5:22–24) is strikingly reticent on Enoch's fate, remarking only that he consorted with divine beings and turned up missing because "God took him,"[12] the rich legendary circle of traditions surrounding this character as found in "books" allegedly authored by Enoch and in other various derivative literatures produced over the course of the first millennium of the Common Era furnish a multitude of details about his journey(s) to the supernal realm and eventual installation among the angelic beings in heaven or, alternatively, his divinely supervised sequestration

---

[9] M. Grünbaum, "Beiträge zur vergleichenden Mythologie aus der Hagada," in idem, *Gesammelte Aufsätze zur Sprach- und Sagenkunde* (ed. F. Perles; Berlin: Calvary, 1901), 59–75; B. Heller, "La chute des anges: Schemhazai, Ouzza et Azaël," *REJ* 60 (1910): 202–12; G. Vajda, "Hārūt wa-Mārūt," *EI*[2] 3:236–37. The present author is currently preparing a new comparative study of these materials.

[10] Thereby sidestepping mystical exegesis, such as that of Ibn al-'Arabī. See W. M. Watt, "Iskandar," *EI*[2] 4:127; J. Renard, "Alexander," *EncQur* 1:61–62.

[11] While it is true that some commentators (and hence Qur'ān translations) interpret the phrase "lofty place" to refer to a change in status rather than of cosmic locale, most of the legendary embellishments tied to this verse understand its import to connote Idrīs's physical ascent to heaven.

[12] Gen 5:24: ויתהלך חנוך את האלהים ואיננו כי לקח אתו אלהים, a passage wherein James C. VanderKam rightly calls attention to the missing definite article on the final Hebrew word and suggests "the priestly writer meant to distinguish between the *ha-'elohîm* [Reeves: "divine beings, angels"] with whom Enoch had ongoing fellowship and the deity [*'elohîm*] who removed him after 365 years" (*Enoch: A Man for All Generations* [Studies on Personalities of the Old Testament; Columbia: University of South Carolina Press, 1995], 13). Note also *Jub.* 4:21 and D. Dimant, "The Biography of Enoch and the Books of Enoch," *VT* 33 (1983): 21.

from mortal society within a celestial garden of Eden. One of these latter sources (*Jub.* 4:23) expresses Enoch's removal from human society in these terms: "And he was taken up from among humankind, and we brought him into the Garden of Eden (so as) to honor and glorify (him)."[13] This statement is intriguingly congruous with the qur'ānic "We raised him to a lofty place," even when one disregards the interesting parallel usage of the first-person plural pronoun to reference their respective angelic interlocutors.[14] Recalling that there is a persistent tradition within early eastern Christendom that situates Eden at the top of a cosmic mountain,[15] one begins to realize that there may be further "subtextual" linkages between these two texts. One might compare Enoch's first-person description of his removal from earth as portrayed in the so-called Animal Apocalypse of *1 Enoch:* "and those three [heavenly beings] that had last come forth grasped me by my hand and took me up, away from the generations of the earth, and raised me up to a lofty place" (*1 En.* 87:3).[16] It is almost as if the Qur'ān has paraphrased this latter clause from *1 Enoch* in its description of the fate of Idrīs. These intriguing intertextual strands that subtly join Genesis, *Jubilees, 1 Enoch,* and Qur'ān reunite in Saadia Gaon's tenth-century Arabic translation of Gen 5:22–24 wherein distinctive verbal elements of Q 19:56–57 are incorporated.[17]

---

[13] Translated from R. H. Charles, *Maṣḥafa Kufālē, or the Ethiopic Version of the Hebrew Book of Jubilees* (Anecdota Oxoniensia; Oxford: Clarendon, 1895), 17.

[14] The same first-person style (i.e., the angels referenced as "we") is found in 4Q227 (4QpsJub^{c}) frag. 2; see the edition of James C. VanderKam and J. T. Milik in *Qumran Cave 4,* vol. 8, *Parabiblical Texts, Part 1* (ed. H. Attridge et al.; DJD 13; Oxford: Clarendon, 1994), 171–75 and pl. XII (PAM 43.238).

[15] See N. Séd, "Les hymnes sur le Paradis de Saint Ephrem et les traditions juives," *Mus* 81 (1968): 459; R. Murray, *Symbols of Church and Kingdom: A Study in Early Syriac Tradition* (Cambridge: Cambridge University Press, 1975), 306–10; G. Widengren, *Muhammad, the Apostle of God, and His Ascension* (Uppsala: A.-B. Lundequistska Bokhandeln, 1955), 208–9. Note Ezek 28:12–18; Isa 14:12–15; *1 En.* 18:6; 24:3–25:7; 32:3–6; Ephrem, *Hymnen de Paradiso* 1.4 (cited by Séd, "Les hymnes," 474).

[16] Ethiopic *makān nawwāx* (መካን ነዋኅ) for "lofty place." Ethiopic text cited from *Das Buch Henoch: Äthiopischer Text* (ed. J. Flemming; Leipzig: Hinrichs, 1902), 120; translation cited from that of R. H. Charles, *APOT* 2:251.

[17] Even though Saadia actually argues—in agreement with *Targum Onqelos*—that Enoch died. Saadia's *Tafsīr* to Genesis was reproduced by P. A. de Lagarde, *Materialien zur Kritik und Geschichte des Pentateuchs* (2 vols.; Leipzig: Teubner, 1867), 1:6. See also the important remarks of M. Zucker, *Saadya's Commentary on Genesis* (New York: Jewish Theological Seminary of America, 1984), 328–29 n. *203.

A suggestive junction of Jewish (also Christian) Enoch and Muslim Idrīs attributes is also visible within the ninth-century Muslim chronicler Ya'qūbī's treatment of this biblical character in his summary of antediluvian "history" in his *Ta'rīkh*. It is often remarked that the standard appellation for Enoch in extant Enochic and cognate literatures is the epithet "righteous" (Greek δίκαιος; Hebrew צדיק; Aramaic קשיט; etc.) and its various permutations.[18] Rabbinic literature critically underscores this apparently popular assessment of Enoch's piety when it rejoins, for example, that "he [i.e., Enoch] is not inscribed within the book of the righteous but instead the book of the wicked" (*Gen. Rab.* 25:1).[19] Ya'qūbī preserves echoes of this distinctive theme and cements the identification of Enoch with Idrīs by creatively fusing the relevant qur'ānic and biblical verses: "Idrīs enjoined his offspring to be faithful in the worship of God and to practice righteousness and true religion. Then God raised him after three hundred years had passed."[20]

But why the peculiar name "Idrīs"? Muslim interpreters agree that the designation is not Arabic, a concession that fueled repeated attempts by Western commentators to see in the name the remaining fragments of a name such as Andreas, Esdras, or even Poimandres.[21] Nevertheless, earlier traditional scholars do provide a type of "midrashic" explanation for the name Idrīs that achieves broad recognition within the rich treasuries of exegetical and antiquarian lore compiled and transmitted by early Muslim exegetes, historians, and collectors of biblical folklore. One of the earliest contributors to this kind of study was the ninth-century scholar Ibn Qutayba,[22] wherein we read:

> To Seth was born Enosh, as well as (other) sons and daughters, and to Enosh was born Kenan, and to Kenan was born Mahalalel, and to Mahalalel was born Yared, and to Yared was born Enoch, and he is Idrīs.... He bore the name Idrīs on account of the quantity of knowledge and religious practices which he learned [*darasa*] from the Scripture of God Most Exalted. God Most Exalted revealed to him thirty scrolls. He was the first

---

18 See the discussion in John C. Reeves, *Heralds of That Good Realm: Syro-Mesopotamian Gnosis and Jewish Traditions* (NHMS 41; Leiden: Brill, 1996), 184–85.

19 So R. Ḥama in the name of R. Hosh'aya (ed. Theodor-Albeck 1:238).

20 *Ibn Wādih qui dicitur al-Ja'qubi historiae* (ed. M. T. Houtsma; 2 vols.; Leiden: Brill, 1883), 1:8–9. The final sentence is based upon Gen 5:21–22. This edition will henceforth be cited as Ya'qūbī, *Ta'rīkh*.

21 See especially Erder, "Origin of the Name," 340–41.

22 For information on this figure and his significance, see G. Lecomte, "Ibn Ḳutayba," *EI*[2] 3:844–46; Lazarus-Yafeh, *Intertwined Worlds*, 172 *s.v.* Ibn Qutayba; Adang, *Muslim Writers*, 30–36.

> to write with a pen.... He was the great-grandfather of Noah. He was raised up at the age of 365 years.[23]

In other words, the name Idrīs reflects a wordplay on the verbal root *darasa,* which is in turn connected with the acquisition and promulgation of knowledge.[24] Enoch becomes Idrīs to mark that character's distinction in academic pursuits. Unsurprisingly, this is precisely the type of *curriculum vita* exhibited by the character Enoch within Jewish and Christian pseudepigraphic sources: he is the first to write, he becomes proficient in astronomical and calendrical lore, and he admonishes his contemporaries—the infamous *dōr ha-mabbūl*—to practice righteousness and true piety.[25] These same collections of traditions often supply a series of reasons why Enoch deserved this boon, most of which revolve around his scholastic attainments and exemplary piety. Given his scholastic and moral attainments, and the well-attested intercultural popularity of the figure of Enoch as celestial voyager and purveyor of supernatural secrets, it should occasion little surprise that the Qur'ān and its early exegetes likewise signal a familiarity with these influential literary traditions.

Idrīs "As" Enoch

Consider now the following tradition found in the ninth-century Muslim historian Ya'qūbī amidst his summary rehearsal of the career of the prophet Idrīs, whom, as we have seen, is most often identified with the biblical forefather Enoch. Ya'qūbī recounts:

> When he [i.e., Enoch/Idrīs] was 65 years old, he fathered Methuselah.[26] He admonished the descendants of Seth, together with their wives and

---

[23] Ibn Qutayba, *Kitāb al-ma'ārif* (ed. Th. 'Ukkāsha; 2d ed.; Cairo: Dār al-Ma'ārif, 1969), 20–21.

[24] Also emphasized by Erder, "Origin of the Name," 341–42.

[25] Note *1 En.* 12:3–4; 81:1–82:3; *Jub.* 4:16–25; 4Q227 (4QpsJub^{c}) frag. 2; Michael Syrus, *Chronicle* 1.5 (see *Chronique de Michel le Syrien, patriarche jacobite d'Antioche, 1166–1199* [ed. J.-B. Chabot; 4 vols.; repr., Brussels: Culture et Civilisation, 1963], 4:4 [text]); *Chronicon ad annum Christi 1234,* 1:39.1–8 (see *Anonymi auctoris Chronicon ad annum Christi 1234 pertinens* [ed. J.-B. Chabot; 2 vols.; CSCO 81–82; Paris: Reipublicae, 1916–20]); Bar Hebraeus, *Chronicon Syriacum* (ed. P. Bedjan; Paris: Maisonneuve, 1890), 5.10–6.18.

[26] Essentially a translation of Gen 5:21: ויהי חנוך חמש וששים שנה ויולד את מתושלח "Enoch lived for sixty-five years and then fathered Methuselah." It should be noted that the Syriac testimonia to the life of Enoch sometime follow the Septuagintal chronology for Enoch's life, wherein his age is 165 when he fathers Methuselah.

> children, about descending (from the mountain), for this (possibility) distressed Enoch. He summoned his offspring—Methuselah, Lamech, and Noah—and said to them: "I know that God will inflict a great merciless punishment on this generation!"[27]

Several things are worthy of note in this short extract. Perhaps most noticeable is Ya'qūbī's obvious reliance upon the Christian *Cave of Treasures* legendary cycle for the basic narrative thread of his own "biblical history."[28] His dependence is instanced in the present citation by its presumption that the descendants of Seth inhabit the slopes of a mountain, which mountain we learn from the *Cave* cycle is the one at whose summit is paradise.[29] Their place of dwelling contrasts with that of the wicked progeny of Cain, a group who indulge in all manner of debauchery and who inhabit the plain below.[30] Much of the narrative tension in the initial chapters of the *Cave of Treasures* revolves around the corruptive danger posed to the line of Seth (who here play the role of the "sons of God" signaled in Gen 6:2) by the degenerate offspring of Cain (the "mortal women" of the same verse).[31]

Equally intriguing are the words spoken by Enoch in this story. Direct discourse in Ya'qūbī's "biblical history" is sometimes tied to "quotations"

---

27 Ya'qūbī, *Ta'rīkh* (ed. Houtsma), 1:8.

28 Explored in a preliminary fashion by A. Götze, "Die Nachwirkung der Schatzhöhle," *ZS* 3 (1925): 60–71; N. Abbott, *Studies in Arabic Literary Papyri I,* vol. 1, *Historical Texts* (Chicago: University of Chicago Press, 1957), 46–50. Important textual resources for studying the *Cave of Treasures* cycle include S.-M. Ri, *La Caverne des Trésors: Les deux recensions syriaques* (CSCO 486, scrip. syri t. 207; Louvain: Peeters, 1987); A. Battista and B. Bagatti, *La Caverna dei Tesori: Testo arabo con traduzione italiana e commento* (Jerusalem: Franciscan Printing Press, 1980), 1–56 (text), wherein the *Kitāb majāll* (i.e., Book of Scrolls) first published by M. D. Gibson is reprinted; and C. Bezold, *Die Schatzhöhle »Mĕʿārath Gazzē«* (Leipzig, 1883–88; repr., Amsterdam: Philo, 1981).

29 Interestingly this motif reenters Jewish lore in the medieval Jewish *Yerahme'el* manuscript collection of exegetical traditions. Therein it states: בני שת היו יושבים בהרים אצל גן עדן. Text cited from *Sefer Zikkronot hu' Divrey ha-Yamim le-Yeraḥme'el* (ed. E. Yassif; Tel Aviv: Tel Aviv University Press, 2001), 115.

30 Yerahme'el: וקין היה יושב בשדה דמשק אשר שם הבל נהרג. The underlined term stems from Gen 4:8.

31 Such a reading of the primary actors of Gen 6:1–4 narratologically emerges from the immediately precedent juxtaposition of the Cainite (4:17–24) and Sethian (5:1–32) genealogies. For a summary sketch of the history of this interpretation, see John C. Reeves, *Jewish Lore in Manichaean Cosmogony: Studies in the Book of Giants Traditions* (Cincinnati: Hebrew Union College Press, 1992), 186–87 and 199 nn. 2–3.

from written revelatory discourse of various types, such as in order to situate a qur'ānic declaration or pronouncement within a narrative setting.[32] In other words, biblical characters may sometimes "speak" words that are associated with them as authors or actors in other scriptural sources. Enoch, as we have seen above, enjoys a reputation for literary production, and the so-called *Ethiopic Enoch* (or *1 Enoch*) and *Slavonic Enoch* (or *2 Enoch*) survive today as important ancient witnesses to the types of literature associated with his name. Hence, when Enoch "speaks," as he does in this pericope, one must be attuned to the possibility that the author may be quoting from an allegedly Enochic scripture.

"He summoned his offspring—Methuselah, Lamech, and Noah—and said to them: 'I know that God will inflict a great merciless punishment on this generation!'" Compare this Enochic oracle with the first statement attributed directly to Enoch that is recorded in the initial chapter of our present *1 Enoch:* "not to this generation, but rather to a distant generation do I speak" (1:2).[33] This latter authentic Enochic citation explicitly associates the proper target audience for the contents of *1 Enoch* with a generation who lives near the anticipated eschaton or end of days, not, it explicitly emphasizes, Enoch's antediluvian contemporaries. The Ya'qūbī citation, by contrast, reverses this dichotomy and identifies Enoch's message in this instance as being directed not to future worthies (as in *1 En.* 1:2) but instead specifically to "this generation," namely, his peers. The this generation/distant generation interplay between these two widely disparate literary sources seems deliberate. The problem comes in analyzing its import. Is it simply a matter of signaling the author's awareness that a prophet's primary mission is to convey warnings to his own people during his lifetime and that Enoch, given his status as prophet, must have had some message for his contemporaries? Might the author be consciously tweaking the rhetorical structure of *1 En.* 1:2, in which case one must concede the intriguing likelihood that some form of *1 Enoch* would have been known to either Ya'qūbī or his source? Or might the author be informing us that there is in fact another "book of Enoch"—still awaiting

---

[32] For example, Iblīs (i.e., Satan) weeps before Adam and Eve in the garden. When they inquire about the reason for his grief, he responds: 'Because *Your Lord has forbidden you this tree only to prevent you from becoming angels or from becoming immortal! He swore to them: Most truly I am giving you good advice!*' The italicized words reproduce Q 7:20–21, now situated within a narrative context. Citation from Ya'qūbī, *Ta'rīkh* (ed. Houtsma), 1:2.

[33] I render the fragmentary Aramaic Ur-text of *1 En.* 1:2 as preserved in 4Q201 (4QEn[a] ar) I 4: לא להדי[ן דרה להן לד[ר ר]חיק אנה ממ]לל. The Greek version is similar: καὶ οὐκ εἰς τὴν νῦν γενεὰν διενεούμην, ἀλλὰ ἐπὶ πόρρω οὖσαν ἐγὼ λαλῶ. See Reeves, *Heralds of That Good Realm,* 24 n. 45.

modern discovery—that featured oracles and visions pertinent to "this generation, rather than a distant one"? In that vein, persistent reports within Muslim authorities regarding the existence of numerous works allegedly authored by Enoch assume a greater significance.[34]

Q 2:30 AND ITS "BIBLICAL" ROOTS

Q 2:30 reads: "And when your Lord said to the angels, 'I am putting a deputy on the earth!,' they responded: 'Would You put on it one who will corrupt it and shed blood? We (by contrast) extol Your praise(s) and sanctify You!'" We learn from the following verse that this "deputy" (*calīph*) is in fact Adam,[35] the first human being, and God goes on to create him despite these angelic objections. Once Adam has been created, God immediately challenges the reproving angels to measure their mental acumen against that of the new creature by "coining names for everything" (2:31). Predictably, the angels fail this test miserably, whereas Adam experiences no difficulties whatsoever in assigning names to the various creatures. His triumph, however, is somewhat tarnished, since the text also notes that Adam had been previously coached for this contest by God (2:31)![36]

Earlier scholars rightly acknowledge a close structural and dialogical affinity between what the Qur'ān reports here about a heavenly consultation concerning the fabrication of humanity and a parallel cycle of legends surrounding the creation of Adam found in rabbinic literature.[37] In that latter corpus of Jewish texts, the scene is usually constructed as follows:

---

[34] See, for example, the testimony of the tenth-century historian Mas'ūdī: "Thirty scrolls were revealed to him [i.e., Enoch], just as before him twenty-one scrolls were revealed to Adam and twenty-nine scrolls were revealed to Seth. Within them [Enoch's scrolls] were psalms of praise and hymns." Passage cited from Mas'ūdī, *Murūj al-dhahab wa-ma'ādin al-jawhar: Les prairies d'or* (ed. C. Barbier de Meynard and P. de Courteille; 9 vols.; Paris: Imprimerie impériale, 1861–77), 1:73.

[35] For brief discussions regarding the possible meanings of this word in relation to the creation of Adam, see C. Schöck, "Adam and Eve," *EncQur* 1:22–26, esp. 23; W. Kadi, "Caliph," *EncQur* 1:276–78. A more comprehensive treatment is provided by M. J. Kister, "Ādam: A Study of Some Legends in *Tafsīr* and *Ḥadīṯ* Literature," in idem, *Concepts and Ideas at the Dawn of Islam* (Aldershot: Ashgate/Variorum, 1997), 113–74, esp. 115–32.

[36] One might compare a cognate tale about the humiliation of Satan found in the rich medieval collection of Jewish legends transmitted by R. Mosheh ha-Darshan in *Bereshit Rabbati;* see the appendix to the present article.

[37] Abraham Geiger, *Judaism and Islam* (1898; repr., New York: Ktav, 1970), 75–77; H. Speyer, *Die biblischen Erzählungen im Qoran* (repr., Hildesheim: Olms, 1988), 51–54.

a. God resolves to create Adam.
b. The angels object to God's plan
c. usually due to allegations of Adam's inherent uselessness or weakness.
d. God goes ahead and creates Adam anyway,
e. sometimes declaring the superiority of human wisdom to that of the angels,
f. which is often "proven" by an animal-naming contest,
g. which the angels lose
h. but which Adam wins.

There are a number of variant versions of this distinctive tale-type,[38] whose precise details may change from source to source but whose general outline remains fairly constant.[39] Of especial interest for our present purposes are the unusually specific reasons advanced by the angels for refraining from Adam's creation. Within the rabbinic material, the typical response by the angels to God's announcement about his intention to create Adam is to exclaim Pss 8:5 or 144:3–4,[40] both of which stress the inherent uselessness or weakness of mortals, but neither of which specify any particular failings or crimes. By contrast, Q 2:30 departs significantly from this standard template when it portrays the angels saying, "Would You put on it one *who will corrupt it and shed blood*?" Were this verse to figure in a completely unique narrative scenario, it would probably attract little attention. But since it occurs within what is otherwise a relatively

[38] More precisely, a "motif" in the "tale-type" concerned with the "Creation of humanity," namely, A1217.1 "Rebel angels object to creation of man," in S. Thompson, *Motif-Index of Folk-Literature* (6 vols.; Bloomington: Indiana University Press, 1932–36), 1:203. I use the term *tale-type* here for what L. Dégh terms a "master story"; see her *Legend and Belief: Dialectics of a Folklore Genre* (Bloomington: Indiana University Press, 2001), 49.

[39] See *Gen. Rab.* 17:4; *b. Sanh.* 38b; *Pesiq. Rab Kah.* 4.3 (ed. Mandelbaum 1:60–61); *Pirqe R. El.* §13; *Num. Rab.* 19:3; Zohar 3.207b. These examples can easily be multiplied. Christian and Muslim versions of this tale often embellish it with either a parallel or supplemental account of the "fall of Satan": note *Vita Adae et Evae* 12–17; *Cave of Treasures* §§2–3 (ed. Ri); Q 2:30–37; 15:28–38; 38:71–81.

[40] Ps 8:5 (Eng. 8:4) asks: "What is man that you are mindful of him, mortal man that you take note of him?" Similarly Ps 144:3 queries: "O LORD, what is man [Adam] that you should care about him, mortal man that you should think of him?" The use of psalmic "quotations" need not necessarily imply that the biblical book of Psalms had a premundane existence; rather, rabbinic midrash often narratively contextualizes the unattributed declarations, queries, and exclamations frequently found in canonical works such as Psalms or Job.

stable narrative setting whose elemental components do not significantly vary for over one thousand years of literary history, it becomes positively arresting. A major question generated by this formulation of the text is whether the Qur'ān envisions a specific narrative event or sequence of such events when it represents the angels condemning humanity for its impending "corruption of the earth" and the "shedding of blood."[41]

Antediluvian biblical narrative, an integrated sequence of stories embraced by both the Qur'ān and its interpretive community as a normative portrayal of early human history, immediately suggests one possible candidate for the referent of the angels' accusation. The infamous "generation of the flood" (דור המבול) explicitly "corrupted the earth" (Gen 6:11–12) and "engaged in violence" (6:11–13), therein an undifferentiated mayhem, but which we learn from the parallel accounts in *1 Enoch* and *Jubilees* involved the "shedding of blood."[42] After the flood, when God reestablishes his covenant with Noah, the flood hero receives some detailed instructions pertaining to the proper handling of "blood," some of which focus upon the grievous consequences that befall one who "sheds human blood" (Gen 9:2–6; *Jub.* 6:6–8, 12–13; 7:27–33). The attention devoted to this topic within the "biblical" templates suggests that an improper handling of blood—including that of humans—is somehow implicated in those events that "corrupt the earth" and precipitate the universal deluge.[43]

A better candidate, however, may be the earlier story of Cain and Abel (Gen 4:1–16), some echoes of which also appear in the Qur'ān (5:27–32).[44]

---

41 "How could the angels say to their Lord, when He told them that He was placing a viceregent on earth: 'Will You place thereon one who will work corruption there, and shed blood?,' when Adam had not yet been created, let alone his offspring, so that the angels could have known through the evidence of their eyes what they would do? Did they have knowledge of the unperceivable ... that they could say this? Or did they say what they said through conjecture?" Ṭabarī goes on to relate a number of opinions regarding the possible resolution of this seeming foreknowledge. Quotation cited from Abū Ja'far Muḥammad b. Jarīr al- Ṭabarī, *The Commentary on the Qur'ān: Being an Abridged Translation of Jāmi' al-bayān 'an ta'wīl āy al-Qur'ān* (ed. J. Cooper et al.; Oxford: Oxford University Press, 1987), 1:211. See also M. Ayoub, *The Qur'an and Its Interpreters* (2 vols.; Albany: State University of New York Press, 1984–), 1:73–93.

42 *Jub.* 5:2–4 (?); 7:21–26; 1 *En.* 7:4–6; 9:1, 9.

43 This point is explicitly emphasized in *Jub.* 7:25 (*APOT* 2:24): "And the Lord destroyed everything from off the face of the earth; because of the wickedness of their deeds, and because of the blood which they had shed in the midst of the earth He destroyed everything."

44 While the basic story is recounted here, the names of the feuding brothers are conspicuously absent in the qur'ānic version. Later tradition supplies the assonant

Many modern students of Bible fail to discern the pivotal significance that this tale actually plays in the present narrative structure of Genesis due to the enormous theological weight with which ancient, medieval, and modern Christian interpreters have invested the immediately preceding story of Adam and Eve's misadventure in the garden (Gen 2:25–3:24). The subsequent Cain and Abel affair, having been ideologically overshadowed by the account of the primal couple's hubris and disobedience to their Creator, is in effect often reduced to an appendix serving to reinforce the Christian dogma of the fall.[45] While admittedly the episode of disobedience in the Garden was not a good thing, the story of Cain and Abel introduces something foreign into the created order, namely, the "corruption" and "bloodshed" of which the qur'ānic angels speak. It represents a critical turning point in antediluvian narrative history and is (from the point of view of the final redactor of Genesis) the key crime that leads ineluctably to the flood.

Evidence supporting these points can be gathered from both a structural and exegetical scrutiny of the Masoretic Text of Genesis. A structural examination swiftly reveals that the stories of Adam and Eve in the garden (Gen 2:4b–3:24) and of Cain and Abel (Gen 4:1–16) form almost perfect mirror images:

Gen 2:4b–3:24	**Gen 4:1–16**
Adam: "worker" of אדמה	Cain: "worker" of אדמה
within Eden	outside of Eden
admonished to avoid a type of action	admonished to avoid a type of action
does the action anyway	does the action anyway
in association with a woman	[possibly over a woman][46]

sobriquets Qābīl and Hābīl. For illuminating presentations of the textual interfaces among the Jewish, Christian, and Muslim interpretations of this story, see Geiger, *Judaism and Islam,* 80–82; Speyer, *Erzählung,* 84–88; N. A. Stillman, "The Story of Cain and Abel in the Qur'an and the Muslim Commentators: Some Observations," *JSS* 19 (1974): 231–39; H. Busse, "Cain and Abel," *EncQur* 1:270–72.

45 E.g., "The narrator [of Gen 4:1–16] shows what happened to mankind *when once it had fallen from disobedience to God.* This is actually the first picture of man *after he was expelled from Paradise,* and the picture is a terrible one. Sin has grown like an avalanche. It has taken total possession of the man who associated with it, for *this man outside Paradise* is a fratricide from the beginning." Quotation taken from G. von Rad, *Genesis: A Commentary* (rev. ed.; Philadelphia: Westminster, 1973), 108, emphases added.

46 *1 En.* 85:3; *Jub.* 4:1, 9 already know this tradition about the brothers' rivalry over their potential bride, as does the Syriac *Cave of Treasures* and the Muslim compilations of "biblical lore" ultimately indebted to it. L. Ginzberg, *The Legends of the Jews* (7 vols.; Philadelphia: Jewish Publication Society, 1909–38), 5:138–39

question-response sequence
result: death (mortality)
plus curses (including אדמה)
expulsion

question-response sequence
result: death (murder)
plus curses (more than אדמה)
expulsion

While both stories result in the manifestation of "death," the deaths depicted are in no way equivalent.[47] The death that results from Adam's disobedience may be a misfortune, but it is presented as a universal, natural, and even inevitable event that will eventually and inexorably lay claim to all organic life. The pertinent point of the garden story, when cast in this light, is not so much about detailing the consequences of human rebellion and corruption as it is about exposing human stupidity in their forfeiture of immortality. By contrast, the death introduced by Cain's homicide marks a qualitatively different type of demise: it is individually plotted and targeted, and it represents a premature and illicit termination of a divinely ordained determination of life span.

If its primary motifs have been coherently reconstructed, the narrative logic of the structural juxtaposition demands that the murder of Abel should function as the first fatal shedding of blood in the course of antediluvian "history." Does this exegetical conclusion withstand a narratological scrutiny? Two possible interpretive problems emerge here: (1) the "garments of skin" (כתנות עור) mentioned in Gen 3:21 ("and the LORD God fashioned garments of skin for Adam and his wife, and he clothed them"); and (2) Abel's sacrificial offering from his flock in Gen 4:4a ("and moreover Abel brought from the firstborn of his flock and from their fats").

A simple (*peshat*) reading indicates that a slaughter of animals, and hence a fatal shedding of blood, might be presupposed for both texts. However, a canvassing of the exegetical tradition surrounding each of these verses reveals that neither passage *necessarily* involves the violent death of animals. With regard to the "garments of skin,"[48] some interpreters

---

n. 17 accumulates abundant references to this motif in rabbinic, Christian, and Muslim sources.

47 Such emerges from a contextual reading of Gen 2:17b ("for on the day you eat from it you will certainly die").

48 Also relevant here would be the extremely popular exegetical option that interprets the "garments of skin" as the stretching of the epidermis over the human body in order to replace the original "garments of glory" forfeited as a result of the primal couple's expulsion from Eden. For a masterful examination of this specific theme, see Gary A. Anderson, "The Garments of Skin in Apocryphal Narrative and Biblical Commentary," in *Studies in Ancient Midrash* (ed. J. L. Kugel; Cambridge: Harvard University Center for Jewish Studies, 2001), 101–43.

opine that the skin employed was that previously sloughed by the serpent.[49] Others note that since fur and wool grow out from the skin, they also can be considered part of a single substance, namely, "skin," and that God simply collected and wove together the bits of fur pulled off mammals by briars and thorns as they passed through the thickets of Eden.[50] With regard to Abel's offering, there is a recurring tradition that no blood was spilled by the officiant during its presentation: "How did he do it? R. Yose b. Hanina said, Whole, with their skin (intact), without flaying or dismembering."[51] Other sources read the term "firstborn" (בכורות) as if it signified "firstfruits" (בכורים), thereby transforming the ceremony from one involving the terminal slaughter of animals to one involving the solemn presentation of substances produced by living animals, such as dairy products and wool. In fact, one popular explanation grounds the later *shaatnez* taboo—the biblical prohibition against blending wool and linen in the manufacture of cloth (Deut 22:11; Lev 19:19)—in this particular offering, explaining that Cain offered flax seed and Abel wool: God thoughtfully rejected the offering of Cain in order to prevent this forbidden combination of items.[52] Another tactic utilized for defusing the scene's potential for violence is to read the phrase "from their fats" (only one word in Hebrew מחלבהן) as "from their milk," an interpretive option that involves no emendation of the consonantal text.[53] The very existence of such reading strategies for these potentially problematic verses prior to

---

49 *Tg. Ps-J.* Gen 3:21; *Pirqe R. El.* §20 (ed. Luria 46a; note especially his commentary); *Midr. Teh.* 92:6. Note Abraham ibn Ezra *ad* Gen 3:21: "others say there was an animal who was of anthropoid form, and God issued a command and it (the animal) shed its skin."

50 *Gen. Rab.* 20:12 (ed. Theodor-Albeck 1:196–97): "R. Samuel b. Nahman (said), Camel-wool and rabbit-fur are 'garments of skin,' for they grow from the skin." Note Rashi *ad* Gen 3:21: "Some say (from) material which comes from skin, like rabbit-fur which is soft and warm, and He made garments for them from it."

51 *Gen. Rab.* 22:5 (ed. Theodor-Albeck 1:208). Note Radaq *ad* Gen 4:4: "it seems to me that he (Abel) did not slaughter the offering, but left it tethered alive at that place which was fixed for it, so that fire from heaven could descend to consume it, just as occurred for the offering(s) of his father. They (i.e., Adam, Cain, Abel, etc.) did not slaughter because (at that time) they did not eat meat." Regarding the last point, see Gen 1:29 and *b. Sanh.* 59b.

52 *Tanḥ., Bereshit* §9; *Pirqe R. El.* §21 (ed. Luria 48b–49a).

53 So apparently Josephus, *Ant.* 1.54: Ἄβελος δὲ γάλα καὶ τὰ πρωτότοκα τῶν βοσκημάτων "Abel (came) with milk and the firstlings of his flocks." Text and translation cited from H. St. J. Thackeray, *Josephus: Jewish Antiquities, Books I–IV* (LCL 242; Cambridge: Harvard University Press; London: Heinemann, 1930), 24–25 and Thackeray's note f.

Abel's murder serves to validate our above suspicion about the climactic enormity of that crime. Nothing remotely like it had ever happened before, and once the murder is committed, its effect is to unleash a pent-up wave of bloodthirsty violence (Gen 4:14) that wends its way through Lamech (Gen 4:23–24) and the generation of the flood.

Fatal "shedding of blood" would then appear to be a crucial motif for understanding the narrative logic of Gen 2–9 in its canonical form. Does not Q 2:30 explicitly confirm the validity of such a *biblical* reading when the angels presciently condemn humanity as "a shedder of blood"? Does it not illuminate and even justify the prominent role played by "bloodshed" in the extrabiblical accounts of the predeluge generations? In other words, Qur'ān and its interpretive tradition arguably function here as valuable witnesses to the crucial nature of this theme in early Jewish narrative, a theme whose centrality within the first few chapters of Genesis has been obscured and then largely ignored by postbiblical Christian commentators.

Appendix: The Humiliation of Satan Legend from *Bereshit Rabbati*[54]

"And all the years of Adam—those which he lived—were 930 years" (Gen 5:5). Three people cheated the Angel of Death out of gaining power over their souls, and they were Adam the protoplast, Jacob our ancestor, and Moses our teacher.

(How did) Adam the protoplast (do so)? The day when he was endowed with his knowledge, the Holy One, blessed be He, commanded the ministering angels: "Enter and bow down to him!"[55] The ministering angels entered to perform the will of the Holy One, blessed be He. (However,) Satan, who was the mightiest of all the angels in heaven, said to the Holy One, blessed be He, "Master of the universe! You created us from the Divine Glory, and now You say to us, 'Bow yourselves down!' before one whom You created from the dirt of the earth??!?"[56] The Holy One, blessed

54 *Midrash Bereshit Rabbati* (ed. Ḥ. Albeck; Jerusalem: Mekize Nirdamim, 1940), 24.21–25.18.

55 According to Latin *L.A.E.* 14:1–2, it is the archangel Michael who commands the angels and Satan to "worship the image of the Lord God, just as the Lord God has commanded." The Armenian version (ibid.) represents Michael as summoning the angels, to whom then God says: "Come, bow down to god whom I made." Translations cited from *A Synopsis of the Books of Adam and Eve: Second Revised Edition* (ed. G. A. Anderson and M. E. Stone; SBLEJL 17; Atlanta: Scholars Press, 1999), 16E.

56 Latin *L.A.E.* 14:3: "I will not worship him who is lower and later than me. I am prior to that creature. Before he was made, I had already been made. He ought

be He, answered him: "This one who originates (from) the dirt of the earth possesses some wisdom and intelligence which is not in you!"[57] Satan responded, "Try me!", and so He put him to the test.

The Holy One, blessed be He, said to him: "Behold, I have created cattle, creeping things, wild beasts, and birds on the earth. Descend so that you might arrange them in front of yourself and in front of him (Adam). If you can give names to all of them, I will command Adam to bow down to you, and I will install you beneath the presence of My Glory indefinitely. However, if Adam can give them the names which correspond to their names which are with Me,[58] you must bow down to Adam, and Adam will be in My garden to serve and to protect."[59] The Holy One, blessed be He, descended to the Garden of Eden, as Scripture affirms: "My Beloved has descended to his garden" (Cant 6:2), and Satan also descended.

When Adam noticed that Satan [*sic*][60] had descended, he stood up and told his wife: "Come, let us bow down before the Holy One, blessed be He, Who created us!", as it is written, "Come and let us worship and bow down before His footstool, and let us praise the Lord our Maker!" (Ps 95:6). At that time the Holy One, blessed be He, asked Satan, "Will you begin giving names to the cattle, or will Adam?" Satan answered Him, "I will go first!" The Holy One, blessed be He, brought a bull and a cow and stood them before Satan. He said to him, "What are the names of these?" He did not know. He removed them from before him and brought a camel, and

---

to worship me." Translation from Anderson and Stone, *Synopsis,* 17E. Note also Q 38:76: "I [Iblīs] am superior to him [Adam]. You created me from fire, whereas You created him from clay."

[57] Compare Q 2:31–33.

[58] I.e., a thing's "name" as a perfect expression of its "essence" or "nature."

[50] Note that nothing is said about Satan losing his heavenly position. Contrast Latin *L.A.E.* 15:3–16:1: "I (Satan) said: 'If he (God) grows angry with me, I will place my seat above the stars of heaven and I will be like the Most High.' Then the Lord God grew angry with me and sent me forth with my angels from our glory. On account of you (Adam) we were expelled from our dwelling into this world and cast out upon the earth." Translation from Anderson and Stone, *Synopsis,* 17E. Note too the early application of Isa 14:13–14 to Satan by the author of *L.A.E.* See also *2 En.* 29:4–5 (long): "And one [Satanail] from out [of] the order of angels, having turned away with the order that was under him, conceived an impossible thought, to place his throne higher than the clouds above the earth, that he might become equal in rank to my power. And I threw him out from the height with his angels, and he was flying in the air continuously above the bottomless." Translation cited from *APOT* 2:447.

[60] Perhaps, as Albeck suggests, we should read instead "the Holy One, blessed be He."

asked him, "What is its name?" He did not know. He removed that one and brought a donkey, but he did not know (its name).[61]

Now the Holy One, blessed be He, had endowed Adam with mental organization via wisdom, and a voice with which to speak and respond, as it is written: "Adam possessed mental plans" (Prov 16:1). He brought the cattle before him, and the Holy One, blessed be He, said to him: "What shall the name of this one be called?" Since He began (his question) with the letter *beth,* he answered Him, "*baqar*" (cattle). He then stood the camel before him and asked, "And this one too, what is its name?" Since He began (his question) with the letter *gimel,* he said "*gamal*" (camel). He stood the donkey before him, and asked, "This animal, what is its name?" Since He began (his question) with the letter *ḥeth,* he said, "*ḥamor*" (donkey).

When Satan realized that the Holy One, blessed be He, had endowed Adam with wisdom,[62] he let out a great cry and ascended back to heaven. The Eternal One said to him, "Why did you cry out?" He responded, "And why shouldn't I cry out! You created me from Your Own Presence and created Adam from the dirt of the earth, yet you have granted to him wisdom and intelligence!" The Holy One, blessed be He, said to him: "Satan, O Destroyer, why are you surprised?"[63]

---

61 Compare *Gen. Rab.* 17:4 (ed. Theodor-Albeck 1:155–56); *Pesiq. Rab Kah.* 4.3 (ed. Mandelbaum 1:60–61); *Pesiq. Rab.* §14; *Num. Rab.* 19:3, where the ministering angels (מלאכי השרת) collectively are incapable of providing names for the animals.

62 Or: "when Satan realized that the Holy One, blessed be He, had given Adam insight," perhaps a better rendering in this context of God's hint-giving.

63 A new and unrelated legend now follows, and eventually the story about how Adam attempts to cheat the Angel of Death. The denouement of the "fall of Satan" episode is lacking in *Bereshit Rabbati.*

Israel and the Torah of Muḥammad

Brannon M. Wheeler
University of Washington

In his exegesis of Q 3:93, Abū al-Qāsim Maḥmūd b. ʿUmar al-Zamakhsharī (467–538) states that God revealed the Torah, specifically prohibiting certain foods, because of the Israelites' disobedience. He explains this in the context of the revelation of Q 4:160 and 6:146, with specific reference to the Jews' claim, in the time of the Prophet Muḥam-mad, that these food prohibitions went back to the time of Abraham and Noah.

> The word of God (Q 3:93): "All food was allowed for the Israelites except that which Israel prohibited himself before the revelation of the Torah. Say: Bring the Torah and recite from it if you are truthful."
>
> It (Q 3:93) was a rebuke of the Jews and their lying when they wanted their innocence recognized concerning that about which God had denounced them in his word: "On account of the iniquity of those who are Jews, we forbade them the good things which were allowed for them" (Q 4:160), to the word of God: "a painful chastisement" (Q 4:18), and in the word of God: "For those who are Jews we forbade everything with claws and from cattle and sheep we forbade the fat.... this was their punishment on account of their disobedience" (Q 6:146).
>
> They (Jews) detested the denial of what angered them and were resentful of that which was articulated in the Qur'ān regarding the prohibitions of good things on account of their disobedience and wickedness, so they said: "We are not the first for which it has been prohibited. This is but an ancient prohibition, a prohibition incumbent upon Noah, Abraham, and those Israelites who came after him and so on, so that the prohibition ended up incumbent upon us. Therefore what is prohibited for us is just as what was prohibited for those who were before us."[1]

There are separate but related claims made in this exegesis of Q 3:93 that require further explanation. Here the Jews object to the accusations of Q

[1] Al-Zamakhsharī, *al-Kashshāf ʿan ḥaqāʾiq ghawāmiḍ al-tanzīl wa ʿuyūn al-aqāwīl fī wujūh al-taʾwīl* (Beirut: Dār al-Kutub al-ʿIlmīyah, 1415), 1:377, *s.v.* Q 3:93–94.

4:160 and 6:146 that certain foods were prohibited to them on account of their disobedience. This response is also an objection to the implicit claim of the Prophet Muḥammad that since the laws found in the Torah were revealed as a punishment for the Israelites only, therefore these same laws are no longer in effect. In other contexts, as is here only suggested, the Jews' objection is made directly to the prophet's claim, found in Q 3:95, that he is following the religion of Abraham.

This exegetical linkage of Q 3:93 to 6:146 asserts an interpretation with problematic implications for the early Islamic understanding of the relation between the Qur'ān and the Torah. Al-Zamakhsharī's exegesis recognizes that there were certain food prohibitions given by God to the Jews, prohibitions not found in the Qur'ān nor incumbent upon Muslims. The mention of the Torah twice in Q 3:93, once apparently as a challenge to the Jews to disprove the first part of Q 3:93, suggests to some exegetes that additional food prohibitions, including those mentioned in Q 6:146, are to be found in the Torah. Such an explanation eschews the argument that the Jews altered the Torah by physically removing or adding certain verses to the text (*taḥrīf*). If additional food prohibitions were found in the Torah, the implication of Q 6:146 is that the discrepancy between the food prohibitions in the Torah and the Qur'ān are to be understood as the result of a revelation aimed specifically at the Israelites because of their disobedience.

By itself, Q 3:93 does not refer to the reason for the addition of food prohibitions in the Torah; rather, the verse was interpreted as a statement concerning the nondivine origins of all food prohibitions before the revelation of the Torah. Q 6:146 does not specify the disobedience as a punishment for which the food prohibitions were revealed, but the link to Q 3:93 suggests that the disobedience is related to the food prohibitions that Israel/Jacob imposed upon himself and that were subsequently followed by his descendants. The link between Q 3:93 and 6:146 also depends on how early exegesis identified which food Israel/Jacob prohibited and which verses in the Torah Q 3:93 references. An examination of these issues shows that what is at issue is the Jews' claim that their food prohibitions originated as revelation. The Prophet Muḥammad's claim, reflected in Q 3:93, is that these prohibitions were imposed upon the Israelites only after they took them upon themselves, thus falsely attributing divine origins to their own self-imposed regulations.

Genesis 32:33

To understand how the challenge to produce and read from the Torah, mentioned in the second part of Q 3:93, was thought to be a refutation of the Jews' objection to the Prophet Muḥammad, it is important to determine what food Jacob is thought to have prohibited and how this relates to the

Torah. The exegesis of Q 3:93 presents two separate explanations: Jacob prohibited sinews or he prohibited camel meat and milk. ʻImād al-Din Ismāʻīl b. Kathīr (d. 774), in his exegesis of Q 3:93, reports, on the authority of Ibn ʻAbbās, that Jacob forbade the eating of sinews.

> Ibn ʻAbbās said: Israel—that is, Jacob—was afflicted with sciatica in the night. It would disturb him and wake him from his sleep but it would go away in the morning. So he made a vow to God that if God cured him he would not eat sinews, and the offspring of his house would not eat sinews. This is what al-Ḍaḥḥāk and al-Suddī said also.
>
> It is also reported by Ibn Jarīr [al-Ṭabarī] in his commentary. He also relates that his sons followed him in prohibiting this, following his example.[2]

Although this account contains no direct link to Q 3:93, it includes the basic elements common to most of the exegesis that associates Jacob's food prohibition in Q 3:93 with sinews. Jacob prohibits sinews because he is afflicted with sciatica. The affliction is severe during the night but subsides during the day. It is also reported that Jacob's descendants followed his example in prohibiting the eating of sinews.

Note also that Ibn Kathīr does not provide the context for this report, the context in which Ibn ʻAbbās provided this information, or an explanation of how Ibn ʻAbbās knew that the prohibition of sinews was to be understood as the reference in Q 3:93. Nor is there further indication of this context in the two accounts attributed to Ibn ʻAbbās in the early exegesis of Abū Jaʻfar Muḥammad b. Jarīr al-Ṭabarī (d. 310) cited by Ibn Kathīr as his source.

> Ibn ʻAbbās said: Israel was afflicted with sciatica and would spend his nights screaming, so he made a vow that if God cured him he would not eat sinews. So God revealed: "all food was allowed for the Israelites except that which Israel prohibited himself."
>
> Ibn ʻAbbās said: "All food was allowed for the Israelites except that which Israel prohibited himself before the revelation of the Torah." He said: Israel was afflicted with sciatica and would spend his nights screaming, so he prohibited himself to eat sinews.[3]

Neither of these reports state that Ibn ʻAbbās heard this information from the Prophet Muḥammad or another source, nor do they explain

---

[2] Ibn Kathīr, *Tafsīr al-Qur'ān al-aẓīm* (Beirut: Dār al-Jīl, n.d.), 1:361, *s.v.* Q 3:93.

[3] Al-Ṭabarī, *Jāmiʻ al-bayān fī tafsīr al-Qur'ān* (Beirut: Dār al-Kutub al-ʻIlmīyah, 1412), 3:351, *s.v.* Q 3:93. This account is also found in Fakhr al-Dīn al-Rāzī, *Mafātīḥ al-ghayb* (Beirut: Dār al-Kutub al-ʻIlmīyah, 1411), *s.v.* Q 3:93.

the circumstances in which Ibn 'Abbās gave his interpretation of Q 3:93. In the second of the two reports, Ibn 'Abbās does not state that Jacob made a vow with God, only that he prohibited sinews because of his affliction. Neither of the reports indicate, as Ibn Kathīr added, that the Israelites followed this prohibition after Jacob.

In his exegesis of Q 3:93, al-Ṭabarī provides two similar reports, given on the authority of Qatādah, identifying sinews with the prohibited food.

> Qatādah said: It was mentioned to us that the food which Israel prohibited himself was because he was afflicted with sciatica during the night so that he was not able to sleep. So he made a promise that if God cured him he would not eat nerves ever again. His children followed after this removing the sinews from meat.
>
> Qatādah added: He made a promise that if God cured him he would not eat sinews ever again. So his children promised to follow him in removing sinews from meat. What he prohibited himself before the revelation of the Torah was sinews.[4]

Qatādah's reports do not cite Q 3:93 directly, as do the reports of Ibn 'Abbās, but they are phrased as though in response to the question of what Jacob prohibited in the verse. Both of these reports also add the significant detail that Jacob's descendants followed him in prohibiting the eating of sinews. Neither of these reports, like those of Ibn 'Abbās, provide a context for the information, except for Qatādah's claim in the first report that the information was conveyed to him by an unidentified source.

There is another account in al-Ṭabarī, preserved in two similar reports, that provides more of a context for the information about Jacob prohibiting sinews. Both of the reports feature Ibn 'Abbās rather than being related on his authority.

> A Bedouin came to Ibn 'Abbās and said that he made his wife forbidden for himself. Ibn 'Abbās said: "She is not forbidden to you." The Bedouin said: "Why? For God said in his book: all food was allowed for the Israelites except that which Israel prohibited himself." Ibn 'Abbās laughed and said: "What do you know about what Israel prohibited himself?" Then he went to the people and reported to them. He said: "Israel became afflicted with sciatica and he made incumbent upon himself that if God cured him from this he would not eat sinews. For this reason, the Jews remove the sinews from meat."[5]

---

[4] Al-Ṭabarī, 3:350–51, *s.v.* Q 3:93.

[5] Ibid., 3:350, *s.v.* Q 3:93.

This account appears to be a play on words at the expense of the Bedouin's understanding of Q 3:93. The Bedouin does not recognize the word for "sciatic vein" (*nasā*) and so apparently confuses it with "women" (*nisā'*). The same point is made in the second report,[6] indicating that the identification of Jacob's prohibition with sinews or the sciatic vein may have presented some linguistic difficulties and suggesting that the accounts using this word had their basis in a particular context.[7]

It is evident from these reports that some of the exegesis of Q 3:93 understood Jacob's prohibition in relation to the reference in Gen 32:33 to the Israelites not eating the sinew or sciatic nerve: "Therefore the Israelites do not eat the sciatic nerve that is on the socket of the thigh until this day, for he (the angel) had touched the socket of Jacob's thigh at the sciatic nerve." It is striking that none of these reports identifying sinews as the food Jacob prohibited indicate that this interpretation of Q 3:93 was linked to the Prophet Muḥammad or information derived from him. There is also a discrepancy between the reports—which have Jacob making the prohibition—and Gen 32:33, in which Jacob apparently plays no role in initiating the prohibition observed by the Israelites. The link between Q 3:93 and Gen 32:33 is even more evident in the account of Jacob's prohibition found in the exegesis of Abū 'Abdallāh Muḥammad b. Aḥmad al-Qurṭubī (d. 671). This account is given on the authority of Ibn 'Abbās, Mujāhid, Qatādah, and al-Suddī, though it is not found in earlier exegetical reports associated with these names.

> Jacob was returning from Harran, heading toward Jersualem, at the time he was fleeing from his brother Esau. He was a strong man, and on the way he met an angel, and Jacob thought that he was a robber, so he wrestled with him. The angel injured Jacob's thigh and then ascended into the sky. Jacob looked at it and his sciatic sinew was inflamed. In consequence of this, there was great pain. He could not sleep the night from the pain, and he passed the night screaming. So Jacob swore that if God cured him he would not eat sinews, and would not eat food in which there were sinews. He prohibited it himself. Following him, his children removed the sinews from meat.[8]

---

[6] See al-Ṭabarī, 3:350, *s.v.* Q 3:93.

[7] This linguistic difficulty is also suggested by two reports, given on the authority of "a man from the Anṣār" (a follower who joined the Prophet Muḥammad when he arrived in Medina), that the Prophet Muḥammad described the meaning of "sciatic vein" in Aḥmad b. Ḥanbal, *Musnad* (ed. Samīr Ṭāha al-Jazūb; Beirut: al-Maktab al-Islāmī, 1413), 5:107, *s.v.* # 20693–20694. This seems to be the only preserved prophetic reference to *nasā* in the authoritative *ḥadīth* collections.

[8] Al-Qurṭubī, *al-Jāmi' li-aḥkām al-Qur'ān* (Beirut: Dār Iḥyā' al-Turāth al-'Arabī, 1405), 4:134–35, *s.v.* Q 3:93. See Mahmoud Ayoub, *The Qur'ān and Its Interpreters: The House of 'Imrān* (Albany: State University of New York Press, 1992), 252.

In this more detailed account, the cause of Jacob's affliction is said to be the wrestling between him and the angel, closely paralleling the larger narrative of Gen 32:23–33.

Although the other accounts do not mention how Jacob became afflicted with sciatica, it is possible that this wrestling incident is presumed or is the unspoken cause in other reports. Note, however, that Jacob is not sick but rather injured and that it was his injury that leads him to the prohibition of sinews. In al-Qurṭubī's account, Jacob is afflicted with pain and screams only during the same night on which the attack of the angel takes place, not over a long period of nights. Jacob seems to have been cured this same night after making his vow prohibiting the eating of sinews, though the mention in other reports of the sciatica afflicting Jacob every night and subsiding in the mornings may also be a reference to this original injury.

The account in al-Qurṭubī might also help to explain the discrepancy between Gen 32:33 and the statement found in Q 3:93 and its exegesis that it was Jacob's own prohibition that led to the later Israelite prohibition of sinews. According to a report provided in al-Qurṭubī, on the authority of al-Ḍaḥḥāk, the angel attacked Jacob in the first place because Jacob had not fulfilled an earlier vow he had made with God: "The reason for the angel injuring Jacob was that Jacob had vowed that if God gave him twelve sons and he reached Jerusalem safely, that he would sacrifice the last of his sons. This was an exemption from his vow."[9] Taken by itself, this account presents a different understanding of the link between Jacob's sinew injury and his vow. Rather than vowing to prohibit sinews because of his injury, Jacob is injured by the angel because he has already made a vow to sacrifice his son. Jacob does not directly prohibit sinews, but by not fulfilling his original vow Jacob brings the attack of the angel, his injury, and the eventual prohibition of sinews followed by his descendants. It is possible that other reports attributing to Jacob a vow to prohibit sinews are an adaptation of this account of his breaking of a vow resulting in the prohibition. Other reports may have eschewed the more involved story to avoid questions about Jacob's status as a prophet yet breaking a vow and fighting with an angel.

This last account, given on the authority of al-Ḍaḥḥāk, may preserve an interpretation of the reasons for the angel's attack of Jacob in the biblical context of Gen 32, and explain something of the origins of Jacob's food prohibition in the exegesis of Q 3:93. In Gen 28:20–22, Jacob makes a vow with God.

> Jacob made a vow saying: If God will be with me and watch over me on this way that I go, and will give me food to eat and a garment to wear,

---

[9] Al-Qurṭubī, 4:135, *s.v.* Q 3:93. See Ayoub, *The Qur'ān and Its Interpreters,* 252.

> and if I return safely to my father's house, then the Lord shall be my God. This stone which I have set up as a pillar will become a house of God and everything that you give me I shall tithe, tithe it to you.

Although Jacob does not explicitly vow to sacrifice his son in this account, he does vow to give God a tithe of everything God gives him if God returns him safely to his father. Tithing is not revealed to Jacob as a law but is something Jacob makes incumbent upon himself with his vow. In the course of Gen 29–32, Jacob acquires both livestock and sons through the intervention of God, though there is no indication that he tithes any of this to God.

Rabbinic exegesis of Gen 32:23–33 also interprets the attack upon Jacob as due to Jacob's not fulfilling his vow to make a tithe to God of his livestock and sons. In *Pirqe Rabbi Eliezer,* the angel stops Jacob and demands that he tithe his livestock and sons. *Targum Yerušalmi* of Gen 32:25 also states that the angel appeared to Jacob in the shape of a man and reminded him that he had promised to tithe what he obtained from God, including his sons.[10] One account in *Pirqe Rabbi Eliezer* states that Jacob tithed his livestock but upon counting his sons, excluded the first-born children of the four mothers, and ended up with only eight sons, not enough to require a tithe.[11]

Genesis 32:15–22 and 33:1–11 recount how Jacob does not make a tithe to God as he crosses the river and thus returns safely to the land of his father as he mentioned as part of his vow in Gen 28:20–22, but instead Jacob gives a gift of his livestock to his brother Esau. In *Midrash Tanḥuma* and *Midrash Rabbah* on Gen 32:21, it is stressed that Jacob is sending to Esau the tithe he should be giving to God. In Gen 32:19, Jacob refers to Esau as "his lord," though he had promised to call Yahweh his God in Gen 28:20–22. In his exegesis of Gen 32:21, Ramban states that Jacob sent the gift to Esau as a ransom to appease his older brother for when he gained his birthright. This showed that Jacob did not trust God's earlier promises, including God's protection in bringing him back safely to his father.[12]

---

[10] Citations from *Targum Yerušalmi* are taken from the *Miqra'ot Gedalot.*

[11] See *Midrash Pirke de Rabbi Eliezer* (trans. Gerald Friedlander; 1916; repr., New York: Sepher-Hermon, 1981), 284.

[12] A similar theme is reflected in some of the accounts that, building on the mention that Jacob was afraid of his older brother, state that the angel attacked Jacob in order to help prepare him for his encounter with Esau. See Abkir in *Yal. Šim.* §132 (*Yalqut Shimoni* [ed. D. Hayman and Y. Shiloni; 2 vols.; Jerusalem: Mosad ha-Rav Kook, 1984], 1:132, 181). Other accounts mention that the blessing that Jacob demanded of the angel was a confirmation of his birthright over Esau; see, e.g., Zohar 3.45a.

Pirqe Rabbi Eliezer states specifically that Jacob took a "tithe" of his possessions and sent it to Esau, at which time God rebuked Jacob and modified his promise of Gen 25:33 that the older Esau would serve the younger Jacob, so that Esau would rule over Jacob until the end of this world.[13]

It is interesting to note that there is some disagreement concerning which son Jacob was supposed to tithe to God. One account in *Pirqe Rabbi Eliezer,* echoing *Jub.* 32:3, states that Levi was counted as the tenth son and was dedicated to the service of God in the priesthood.[14] Exodus 13:11–16 contains the law of the firstborn, stated again in Exod 28:28–29 and 34:19–20, mentioning the sacrifice of the firstborn son, though Levi was the third son born to Jacob and Leah.[15] In the account of al-Ḍaḥḥāk, Jacob is said to have promised to tithe the last of his sons, which at that time would have been Joseph, because Rachel had not yet given birth to Benjamin. Although not the first son born to Jacob, Joseph was the firstborn of Rachel for whom Jacob had originally contracted marriage with Laban. As Jon Levenson has pointed out, the story of Joseph is the loss and return of Jacob's beloved son, analogous to other Israelite rituals that substitute for the literal sacrifice of the firstborn son: "the father's choicest son receives his life anew, and the man who, one way or another, gave him up or should have done so, gets back the offspring who had been marked for death."[16] The report of al-Ḍaḥḥāk connecting Jacob's vow to sacrifice his son Joseph with the attack of the angel further emphasizes the expiatory nature of the link between Jacob's injury and the prohibition of sinews. In al-Ḍaḥḥāk's account, Jacob is attacked not because he is trying to save himself from his brother, because he gave God's tithe of

---

13 See *Midrash Pirke de Rabbi Eliezer* (trans. Friedlander), 285–86. A similar stress upon Jacob's mistake and God's modification of his promise is found in *Gen. Rab.* 76:2–3, 11. See also Gerson D. Cohen, "Esau As Symbol in Early Medieval Thought," in idem, *Studies in the Variety of Rabbinic Cultures* (Philadelphia: Jewish Publication Society, 1991), 243–69.

14 *Midrash Pirke de Rabbi Eliezer* (trans. Friedlander), 285.

15 On the issue of child sacrifice in the Bible and Israelite religion, see Jon D. Levenson, *The Death and Resurrection of the Beloved Son: The Transformation of Child Sacrifice in Judaism and Christianity* (New Haven: Yale University Press, 1993), esp. 113 on Gen 32:33.

16 Ibid., ix. Levinson also cites other examples of child sacrifice found in the Hebrew Bible that are not necessarily interpreted as expiatory. See Judg 11:29–40 and 2 Kgs 3:26–27. *Gen. Rab.* 60.3 sees Jephthah's sacrifice of his daughter in Judg 11:29–40 as a punishment for his making the vow in the first place. For further discussion of this case, see David Marcus, *Jephthah and His Vow* (Lubbock: Texas Tech University Press, 1986).

the livestock to Esau, but rather because Jacob is trying to save his son from being given to God.

There is a related incident found in Exod 4:24–26 where Moses is attacked by God, also apparently on account of his firstborn son Gershom:

> Now it was on the journey, at the night-camp, that the Lord encountered him and sought to make him die. Zipporah took a flint and cut off her son's foreskin, she touched it to his legs and said: "Indeed a bridegroom of blood are you to me." Thereupon he released him. When he let him alone, she said: "a bridegroom of blood" because of the circumcision.

The exegesis of these enigmatic verses is plentiful, but it seems that the attack on Moses, like that on Jacob, is linked to his son. God's attack on Moses is stopped only once his son has been circumcised, indicating that the circumcision substitutes for the life of Moses.[17] This is similar to al-Ḍaḥḥāk's account of the attack on Jacob. The close connection between circumcision and sacrifice in rabbinic exegesis also supports the interpretation of the son's circumcision here as a substitute for or symbolic of his sacrifice.[18] Moses is attacked because he has not circumcised his son and, in some accounts, because he himself has not been circumcised, an obligation enjoined since the time of Abraham. The release of Moses comes only after the circumcision is performed. Jacob is also attacked because he has not carried out his obligation to sacrifice his son, but instead of making the sacrifice, Jacob is injured. This injury, as expiation for not sacrificing his son, then results in the prohibition of sinews among his descendants.

The exegetical claim that Q 3:93 refers to God's imposition of food regulations as a punishment is evident given the account, attributed to al-Ḍaḥḥāk, that Jacob was injured because he did not fulfill his vow to tithe his son. In several instances, rabbinic exegesis explains that the children of Jacob prohibited sinews because they were the cause of Jacob's injury.[19] The prohibition as a commemoration of Jacob's injury is also indicated in

---

[17] This interpretation is propounded in Levenson, *Death and Resurrection*, 50–51. See also the discussion and bibliography in Brevard S. Childs, *The Book of Exodus: A Critical, Theological Commentary* (OTL; Philadelphia: Westminster, 1974), 95–101.

[18] See the discussion in Howard Eilberg-Schwartz, "The Fruitful Cut: Circumcision and Israel's Symbolic Language of Fertility, Descent, and Gender," in idem, *The Savage in Judaism: An Anthropology of Israelite Religion and Ancient Judaism* (Bloomington: Indiana University Press, 1990), 141–76.

[19] See, for example, Zohar 1.170b–171a; *Midrash ha-Gadol* 1:513–14. *Gen. Rab.* 78:6 states that although God permitted the eating of sinews, the Israelites prohibited them anyhow. Linked to Gen 32:33, this act of piety seems to be a commemoration of Jacob's injury.

Rashi's exegesis of Gen 32:33 and the discussion of the term "sciatic sinew" in tractate *Ḥullin*.[20] Quoting Jer 51:30 and Gen 41:51, both Rashi and *Ḥullin* link the terminology used to describe the injury to the notion of the injury as delivering Jacob from fulfilling his vow. The prohibition against eating sinews was because of Jacob's injury, which al-Ḍaḥḥāk attributes to Jacob not fulfilling his vow. Jacob does not fulfill his self-imposed vow but instead is punished by God with an injury that results in the Israelites not eating sinews. From this perspective, the imposition of the prohibition of sinews is as a punishment that Jacob brought upon himself and followed by his descendants after him.

GENESIS 9:3

Although the explanation that Jacob prohibited the eating of sinews fits well with Gen 32:33, there are a number of accounts that state that it was camel meat and milk rather than sinews that Jacob is said to have prohibited in Q 3:93. These accounts share some features with the sinew explanations, but the reference to the Torah in the last part of the verse seems to be directed toward Gen 9:3 rather than 32:33. The call to produce the Torah in the second part of Q 3:93 is understood, in these accounts, as a reference to the Jews whose challenge to the prophet is considered to be the reason for the revelation of Q 3:93. An example of this is found in al-Ṭabarī's exegesis of Q 3:93:

> A group of Jews came to the Apostle of God and said: "Oh Abū al-Qāsim, tell us what food Israel prohibited for himself before the revelation of the Torah." The Apostle of God said: "I entreat you by the one who revealed the Torah to Moses, do you know that Israel-Jacob was very sick for a long time, so he made a vow to God that if God would cure him from this disease then he would prohibit his favorite food and drink. His favorite food was the meat of camel and his favorite drink was camel's milk." The Jews said: "By God, yes."[21]

In this account, it is specified that Jacob was sick for a long time rather than being injured and that he prohibited camel meat and milk because it was his favorite food and drink.

Unlike the accounts involving sinews, this account in al-Ṭabarī is linked back to the Prophet Muḥammad and is set in the context of the Jews

---

[20] See Rashi to Gen 32:33; also the lemma "*gid ha-nasheh*" in *Ḥiddushey Yitzḥaq be-R. Avraham mi-Narbonna: 'Al hilkhot ha-Rif mi-masekhet Ḥullin* (Jerusalem: Makon Yerushalayim, 1988/89).

[21] al-Ṭabarī, 3:352, *s.v.* Q 3:93. See Ayoub, *The Qur'ān and Its Interpreters*, 251.

challenging his authority. This explanation for the revelation of a particular verse, especially the *miḥan al-yahūd* or "tests of the Jews," is well known in the exegesis of verses relating to the Torah or stories of the Israelites.[22] In al-Ṭabarī's account, though, the revelation of Q 3:93 does not answer the Jews' question, but rather the Jews' question seems to presuppose the revelation of Q 3:93. The Jews ask the Prophet Muḥammad to explain what food is meant in Q 3:93, the correct answer presumably demonstrating his prophethood. Whether the answer is derived from revelation is not stated, nor is the answer explaining the food Jacob prohibited provided in the text of the Qur'ān.

The Jews' question concerning Jacob's prohibition is also found in Ibn Kathīr's exegesis of Q 3:93, linking it also to the revelation of Q 2:97–98:

> Ibn 'Abbās said: A group of Jews went to the Apostle of God and they said: "Oh Abū al-Qāsim, we will ask about five things. If you tell us about them we will know that you are a prophet and follow you." He made them take an oath like Israel took from his sons when he said: "God is witness to what we say." He said: "Go ahead."
>
> They said: "Tell us, what is the mark of the prophet?" He said: "His eyes sleep but his heart does not sleep." They said: "Tell us, how does a woman produce both males and females?" He said: "The two semens meet. When the semen of the man is predominant, then it is a boy. When the semen of the woman is predominant, then it is a girl."
>
> They said: "Tell us, what did Israel prohibit for himself?" He said: "He was afflicted with sciatica and he could not become better except by the milk of such and such"—(Aḥmad said: some say "camel")—"so he prohibited its meat." They said: "You are right."
>
> They said: "What is thunder?" He said: "One of the angels of God responsible for the clouds with his hand, or his hands, breaking from light which the clouds hold back when God commands." They said: "What is the sound that is heard?" He said: "Its sound."
>
> They said: "You are right and only one thing remains and it is that which if you tell us it we will follow you: There is no prophet to whom an angel has not come with the message. Tell us who is your companion?" He said: "Gabriel." They said: "This Gabriel descends in war and battle and is an enemy of ours. If only you had said Michael who descends in mercy and help. So God revealed: "Say: who is an enemy to

---

22 For an overview of this genre of explanation, see Jalāl al-Dīn al-Suyūṭī, *al-Itqān fī 'ulūm al-Qur'ān* (ed. Muṣṭafā Dīb al-Bughā; Damascus: Dār Ibn Kathīr, 1416), ch. 9; Badr al-Dīn al-Zarkashī, *al-Burhān fī 'ulūm al-Qur'ān* (ed. Yusūf 'Abd al-Raḥmān al-Mar'ashlī et al.; Beirut: Dār al-Ma'arifah, 1415), ch. 1 (note the many bibliographic references on pp. 115–16).

> Gabriel? It is he who brought it down to your heart by the permission of God, confirming that which was between his hands, a guidance [*hadā*] and good news [*bushrā*] to the believers." (Q 2:97)[23]

Like the account in al-Ṭabarī, this account does not specify that the information about camel meat and milk is directly related to the revelation of Q 3:93. The whole series of questions seem to hinge on the revelation of Q 2:97 in response to the Jews' denial of the Prophet Muḥammad's answer to their last question. Note also that in Ibn Kathīr's account Jacob prohibits camel meat though it is camel milk that eases his sciatica. In addition, the specification of "camel" is added only by the transmitter cited by Ibn Kathīr.

Neither al-Ṭabarī nor Ibn Kathīr's account mention Jacob's wrestling with the angel, but in his exegesis of Q 3:93, al-Qurṭubī mentions two related reports, cited by al-Tirmidhī, that suggest connections to still other verses:

> In al-Tirmidhī, it is reported on the authority of Ibn 'Abbās that the Jews said to the Prophet: "Tell us what did Israel forbid himself?" He said: "He used to live as a nomad, and his sciatic sinew became afflicted, and he found nothing that would ease his pain except for camel meat and milk, so this he prohibited." They said: "You are right."
>
> He mentioned the report: It is said that he made a vow that if he was cured of it, he would renounce the food and drink he loved best, and the food and drink he loved best was camel meat and milk.[24]

Here, al-Qurṭubī gives two different reasons for Jacob's prohibition of camel meat and milk, yet he retains the mention of Jacob's sickness being caused by sciatica, attributing this to Jacob's nomadic lifestyle. The first account makes no mention of a vow but agrees with the accounts of al-Ṭabarī and Ibn Kathīr, adding that Jacob renounced the only food that would ease his pain. This detail also allows al-Qurṭubī to combine the identification of sciatica as Jacob's affliction with his prohibition of camel meat and milk, leaving the more intuitive explanation that sinews were prohibited because Jacob's sciatic sinew was the cause of his suffering.

---

23 Ibn Kathīr, 1:361, *s.v.* Q 3:93. There is another version of this story in Ibn Hishām, *al-Sīrah al-nabawīyah* (Cairo: Dār al-Kutub, 1355), 375–76; see Alfred Guillaume, *The Life of Muhammad: A Translation of Ibn Isḥāq's Sīrat Rasūl Allāh* (Oxford: Oxford University Press, 1955; repr., Karachi: Oxford University Press, 1967), 255.

24 Al-Qurṭubī, 4:134, *s.v.* Q 3:93.

The second account in al-Qurṭubī indicates that Jacob renounced his partaking of camel in the context of a vow, presumably with God, to be cured of the sciatica. There is no mention in the second account of the Jews, though the emphasis of camel meat and milk as Jacob's beloved food instead indicates a link between Q 3:93 and Q 4:160: "On account of the iniquity of those who are Jews, we prohibited for them the good things which had been allowed for them, on account of their blocking many from the way of God." In both of al-Qurṭubī's accounts, stress is placed on the fact that the food prohibited was originally intended to be a good thing, and was only prohibited by Jacob in the context of his vow, but not otherwise meant to be prohibited. This link to Q 4:160, cited by al-Zamakhsharī, shifts the exegesis away from Jacob and the Israelites and toward the Jews challenging the Prophet Muḥammad's claim that it was Jacob who first prohibited camel meat and milk.

Although al-Ṭabarī, Ibn Kathīr, and al-Qurṭubī relate these accounts to the revelation of Q 3:93, probably because they help to identify the food Jacob prohibited, the accounts themselves do not explain the reason for the revelation of Q 3:93 in the first place. Abū al-Ḥasan 'Alī b. Aḥmad al-Wāḥidī (d. 468) gives a more direct explanation for the revelation of Q 3:93. In his exegesis of this verse, al-Wāḥidī reports that the Jews objected to the Prophet Muḥammad's claim to be following the religion of Abraham:

> The word of God: "All food was allowed for the Israelites."
>
> This was revealed when the Prophet said that he was following the religion of Abraham. The Jews objected: "How can this be when you eat the flesh of camels and drink their milk?" The Prophet said: "This was lawful for Abraham, and is also lawful for us." The Jews said: "Everything we now consider unlawful was unlawful for both Noah and Abraham, and has thus come down to us." Then God revealed this verse (Q 3:93).[25]

This account is also closely related to al-Zamakhsharī's linking of Q 3:93 and Q 4:160, in which the Jews object that the food prohibition (unidentified in al-Zamakhsharī) originated not with Jacob but with Abraham and Noah. It is striking that in al-Wāḥidī the Jews allegedly deny the same information (viz., that Jacob prohibited camel meat and milk) that the accounts of al-Ṭabarī and Ibn Kathīr have the Jews affirming. In the exegesis of al-Wāḥidī and al-Zamakhsharī, the context is shifted away from Jacob and his vow precisely by the Jews' claim that their current food

---

[25] Al-Wāḥidī, *Asbāb al-nuzūl* (Beirut: al-Maktabah al-Thaqāfīyah, 1410), 61, *s.v.* Q 3:93. This is also found in Ayoub, *The Qur'ān and Its Interpreters,* 250, *s.v.* Q 3:93. A similar account is found in al-Rāzī, , 8:120, *s.v.* Q 3:93.

prohibitions predated Jacob and were in effect for Noah and Abraham. According to al-Wāḥidī, Q 3:93 was not revealed in response to the Jews' question about Jacob's prohibition but rather in objection to the Prophet Muḥammad's claim to follow the religion of Abraham. This claim is not made in Q 3:93, but the religion of Abraham is discussed throughout Q 3:65–97 with specific references in verses 68 and 95. The theme of the Jews "blocking many from the way of God" mentioned in Q 4:160 is also found in Q 3:98–102 following the verses on the religion of Abraham. In al-Wāḥidī's exegesis, the more specific explanation of the reason for Jacob's prohibition relating to his sciatica is dropped, as is mention of Jacob altogether.

According to Fakhr al-Dīn al-Rāzī (fl. 544–604), the Jews' claim that their current food prohibitions go back to the time of Noah is related to the mention of the Torah in the second part of Q 3:93:

> The Jews said to the Prophet: "You claim that you are from the community of Abraham. If this is the case, then how can it be that you consume camel meat and its milk when this is prohibited in the religion of Abraham?" Thus they made these words like a defaming stab into the truth of his claim.
>
> The Prophet responded to this attack by saying: "This was allowed to Abraham, Ishmael, Isaac, and Jacob, except what Jacob forbade himself for a certain reason. This prohibition remained with his children."
>
> The Jews denied this, so the Apostle ordered them to bring the Torah and requested that they find in it a verse which indicated that camel meat and its milk were forbidden to Abraham. They were incapable of doing this and were discredited. This was revealed to show that they were liars about the claim of these things being prohibited to Abraham.[26]

Q 3:93 challenges the Jews to produce the Torah and admit that there is nothing in the text that indicates that camel meat and milk was prohibited to Abraham. It is the absence of a verse prohibiting camel that is here explicitly linked to the claim of whether or not certain foods were prohibited before the time of Jacob. From the perspective of al-Rāzī, the question of what Jacob prohibited is irrelevant because the issue here is that the Prophet Muḥammad claims there were no food prohibitions prior to Jacob, whereas the Jews claim that their food prohibitions go back to the time of Noah and Abraham.

It would be difficult to show that the second part of Q 3:93 should be understood as a challenge for the Jews to disprove the Prophet Muḥammad's

---

26 Fakhr al-Dīn al-Rāzī, 8:120, *s.v.* Q 3:93. Also see Ayoub, *The Qur'ān and Its Interpreters*, 253–54.

statement that Jacob prohibited for himself camel meat and milk. The accounts found in al-Ṭabarī and Ibn Kathīr in which the Jews ask the Prophet Muḥammad to identify the food Jacob prohibited seem unrelated to the challenge to produce the Torah. If the reference to the Torah is understood in relation to Jacob's prohibition of sinews, then the existence of Gen 32:33 would confirm the first part of Q 3:93 that all food was allowed except that which Jacob prohibited himself. The accounts in al-Ṭabarī and Ibn Kathīr do not provide the reason for the revelation of Q 3:93. In each of these accounts, the Jews assent that the Prophet Muḥammad answers their question correctly. Further, this information about Jacob's prohibition of camel meat and milk is not to be found in the Torah, and if it had been in the Torah then the Jews' question would not have been a real test of Muḥammad's prophethood. All of the questions asked of the Prophet Muḥammad by the Jews in the account of Ibn Kathīr are designed to be answered correctly only by a prophet and not someone learned in the Torah. These accounts in al-Ṭabarī and Ibn Kathīr seem only to demonstrate the prophethood of Muḥammad, that his knowledge is derived from revelation.

If the mention of the Torah at the end of Q 3:93 was to be understood as a challenge for the Jews to show evidence only that there were food prohibitions given before the time of Jacob, the Jews could have cited an explicit case from the time of Noah to support their claim. Genesis 9:3–4 contains an account of food laws given to Noah:

> Every living and crawling thing shall provide food for you, no less than the foliage of plants. I give you everything, with this exception: you must not eat flesh with life, that is to say blood, in it.

Genesis 9:4 could be used to invalidate the general sense of Q 3:93 that there were no food prohibitions before the time of Jacob. This reference is well known in rabbinic exegesis in the discussion of the so-called Noahide laws that were given to Noah and that are thus incumbent upon all people. The Babylonian Talmud includes a long discussion of the seven precepts given to Noah:

> Our Rabbis taught: Seven precepts were the sons of Noah commanded: social laws, to refrain from blasphemy, idolatry, adultery, bloodshed, robbery, and eating flesh cut from a living animal. R. Ḥanania b. Gamaliel said: Also not to partake of the blood drawn from a living animal."[27]

[27] See *b. Sanh.* 56b.

According to R. Huna, R. Judah, and all the disciples of Rab, execution is specified as the punishment for anyone, Jew or non-Jew, who breaks one of these laws.[28] These precepts are considered to be revealed laws, lacking only three additional precepts (keeping Sabbath, honoring parents, and social laws) to be revealed specifically to the Jews at Marah.

By identifying the food prohibition of Q 3:93 as camel, the exegetes precluded the use of Gen 9:3–4 to impugn Q 3:93. Instead of the Jews making the case that the Prophet Muḥammad was not following the religion of Abraham by eating camel, the Prophet Muḥammad uses the Torah to verify his claim and to show that the Jews' food prohibitions abrogate the food laws originally revealed to Noah and Abraham. This is made explicit in Fakhr al-Dīn al-Rāzī's exegesis:

> A number of proofs for the prophethood of Muhammad were indicated by this. The first is that the Jews were unable to deny this issue of abrogation. Second, their lies became apparent because they attributed things to the Torah which were not in it and denied things from it which were in it. Third, the Apostle was an illiterate man who could not read nor write and was thus prevented from knowing these heavenly secrets from the sciences of the Torah except by information from heaven.[29]

The claim is that the Jews attempted to hide or deny the existence of Gen 9:3 because it would confirm Q 3:93 and the authority of the Prophet Muḥammad. Genesis 9:3 corresponds closely to the first part of Q 3:93 and thus supports the claim that all food was allowed for the Israelites. Genesis 9:4 also explicitly states that the only exception to the general rule allowing the meat of all animals is that it not have blood in it. This corresponds to other verses in the Qur'ān such as the first two food prohibitions mentioned in Q 6:145, said to represent all that which is found in what was revealed to Muḥammad concerning food, and a similar list of food injunctions found in Q 5:3.

It is possible, with the reference to food prohibitions at the time of Noah, that the Jews are portrayed here as making the argument that Noah had knowledge of the Torah and its food prohibitions in particular. There are two verses in Genesis that indicate that the food laws concerning clean and unclean animals were known to Noah. In Gen 7:2, God instructs Noah to take upon the ark seven pairs of clean animals but only two pairs of unclean animals. Genesis 8:20 also states that Noah made a sacrifice to God of the clean animals and birds. Rashi seems to suggest

---

[28] See *b. Sanh.* 57a.

[29] Fakhr al-Dīn al-Rāzī, 8:120, *s.v.* Q 3:93. See Ayoub, *The Qur'ān and Its Interpreters,* 253–54.

this, interpreting Gen 7:2 as an indication that Noah knew the Torah.[30] Yet he goes on to conclude, especially in his exegesis of Gen 8:20, that Noah did not know the Torah: "Noah said: God commanded me to take (into the ark) from these (clean animals) seven by seven only in order to make an offering from them." God ordered Noah to take seven clean animals in Gen 7:2 only so that an offering could be made of them in Gen 8:20.[31] The *Midrash Rabbah* to Gen 8:20 likewise states that Noah deduced which animals to sacrifice on the basis that God had commanded him to bring extra exemplars of certain species. Furthermore, if Noah knew the laws of the Torah, then why did he make a sacrifice from all the clean animals, including those that the Torah forbids as offerings?[32] Neither Gen 7:2 nor 8:20 refers to using these animals as food, nor does either verse specify that the clean and unclean categories conform to the lists found in Lev 11 and Deut 14:3–21.

There are other problems associated with the notion that Noah knew the laws of the Torah. According to some strands of rabbinic exegesis, Noah did not actually perform the sacrifice mentioned in Gen 8:20. *Midrash Tanḥuma* states that Noah had been attacked and maimed by a lion on the ark, and consequently his son Shem performed the sacrifice.[33] Zohar Ḥadash recounts a tradition that Shem received knowledge of the Torah from Enoch, who had received it from Seth, and Seth from Adam. From Shem, knowledge of the Torah passes to Japhet and eventually reaches Abraham. Knowledge of the Torah specifically skips Noah, and it is further stated that after the flood God decided all of the Torah was too much, so he gave only the seven Noahide precepts while waiting for the time of Abraham to impose the whole of the Torah.[34]

Other Jewish and Christian exegeses understand Gen 9:3 as an easing of the earlier food prohibitions imposed upon Adam in Gen 3:18–19.

---

30 Compare with *Gen. Rab.* 34:9 and *Midr. Tanḥ.* Va-yakhel §6.

31 Note that Rashi seems to suggest that Noah was commanded to take seven clean animals, consisting of three pairs and one extra animal, and not seven pairs of clean animals. The odd clean animal was the one to be sacrificed after the subsiding of the flood.

32 See *Gen. Rab.* 34:9.

33 See *Midr. Tanḥ.*, Noaḥ §9; *Midr. Tanḥ.* (Buber) Wa-etḥanan §1; as well as the other references cited by Louis Ginzberg, *The Legends of the Jews* (7 vols.; Philadelphia: Jewish Publication Society, 1909–38), 5:187–88 nn.51–52.

34 See Zohar Ḥadash, Midrash Ha-Ne'elam, Noaḥ 29. Note the account in Fakhr al-Dīn al-Rāzī in his exegesis of Q 3:93 that the Jews claimed that the prohibition of camel had been in effect since the time of Adam (8:119–120); see Ayoub, *The Qur'ān and Its Interpreters*, 2:253–54.

Midrash Rabbah on Gen 9:3 explains that Adam was not permitted to eat meat but only the foliage of plants mentioned again in Gen 9:3.[35] Echoing the reference to the forbidding of "good things" in Q 4:160, Adam's punishment centers specifically on the prohibition of the good foods that were previously allowed for him.[36] Genesis 3:18–19 contains food laws given to Adam as punishment for his sin of eating from the forbidden tree in the garden of Eden. These food laws are seen as a substitute for Adam's earlier access to the tree of life.[37]

The exegetical claim that Q 3:93 refers to the prohibition of camel, especially as a response to the claim that these food prohibitions went back to Noah, resonates with the larger rabbinic understanding of Gen 9:3 and its relation to the progressive revelation of food prohibitions. The Noahide laws are universal precepts that relax the more stringent food requirements imposed on Adam. Although Gen 17 records the additional requirement of circumcision, in terms of food prohibitions there are no further indications until 32:33, which may be connected with Jacob's vow in 28:20–22. Just as Adam's sin of eating from the forbidden tree results in the food prohibition of 3:18–19, Jacob's breaking of his vow results in the prohibition of sinews. The next food prohibitions come in the Torah revealed to Moses, which, al-Zamakhsharī states, is also imposed as a punishment for the disobedience of the Israelites. Challenging the Jews to find evidence for the prohibition of camel before the time of Jacob and Moses, the exegesis of Q 3:93 uses the Torah and its interpretation to demonstrate the authority of the Prophet Muḥammad's claim to be following the religion of Abraham.

Conclusions

The various accounts associated with the exegesis of Q 3:93 may or may not represent historical encounters between the Prophet Muḥammad

---

35 *Gen. Rab.* 34:13. See also Origen's homily on Genesis (1:17), where he states that to Adam God permitted the eating of vegetables and fruits but eating meat is only later allowed after the covenant made with Noah. See *Origen: Homilies on Genesis and Exodus* (trans. R. E. Heine; Washington, D.C.: Catholic University of America Press, 1982), 69–70. A similar interpretation is given by Philo; see his *QG* 2.57 on Gen 9:3 (Philo, *Questions and Answers on Genesis* [trans. R. Marcus; LCL 380; Cambridge: Harvard University Press, 1953], 143).

36 See *ʾAbot R. Nat.* B §42 on the prohibition of good foods and the substitution of agriculture for the fruits in the garden of Eden.

37 In *Midrash ha-Gadol* on Gen 3:24, it is said that the Torah replaces the tree of life for Adam as punishment for his sin. In his interpretation of Gen 3:24, Philo states that Adam could always look back to the garden and remember his expulsion. See *QG* 1.57 (trans. Marcus, 35); also note the excursus in *Tg. Yer.* Gen 3:24.

and the Jews of Medina. What they do reflect is an exegetical dialogue and polemic between Muslims and Jews regarding the status of the Qur'ān vis-à-vis the Torah regarded as another revealed text. The challenge to the Jews to produce and read from the Torah in Q 3:93 produces different results depending upon how the food prohibition mentioned in Q 3:93 is related to Genesis. In relation to Gen 32:33, Q 3:93 emphasizes that the prohibition of sinews originated not as divine revelation but as a result of Jacob's vow. The reference to Gen 9:3 highlights a more general pattern of laws, specifically food prohibitions, imposed upon the Israelites for their disobedience to God. At issue is not the revelatory status of the Torah or the accusation that the text of the Torah has been altered. On the contrary, the exegesis of Q 3:93 depends on the Torah to make its case. The Torah, like the Qur'ān, is a revealed text, but unlike the Qur'ān, the Torah was revealed as a punishment specifically for the Israelites. With the revelation of the Qur'ān and its revival of the universal religion of Abraham, the Torah is no longer considered canonical.

The crux in the interpretation of Q 3:93 is that the Israelites instituted their own laws but attributed these laws to God. In his exegesis of the verse, al-Ṭabarī explains in his own words the reason for the revelation of Q 3:93:

> By this (Q 3:93) God meant that he had not prohibited any food before the revelation of the Torah to the Israelites—the Israelites being the descendents of Jacob, son of Isaac, son of Abraham the friend of God. Rather, all of this was allowed for them except what Jacob had prohibited to himself. His descendents prohibited it introducing a customary practice [*istinana*] on the authority of their father Jacob without God's prohibiting this to them by inspiration, revelation, or from the word of his prophet to them, before the revelation of the Torah.[38]

What is at issue in this verse is not whether it was sinews or camel that Jacob prohibited. Rather, the issue is that the Jews are making a false claim that their food prohibitions go back before the time of Jacob. Note also, reflecting Gen 32:33, that it is the descendants of Jacob who introduce the practice and then attribute it to Jacob without his consent. The Jews' claim that these prohibitions predated Jacob also involves the denial of the Israelites' having imposed the prohibitions upon themselves and the false attribution of the origins of the food prohibitions to God:

> Others say: There was nothing from that (food) prohibited for them nor did God prohibit it in the Torah, but it is something they prohibited themselves following their father. Then they attributed its prohibition to God.

---

[38] al-Ṭabarī, 3:348, *s.v.* Q 3:93.

> Thereby they lied about God in attributing this to him. God said to our Prophet Muhammad: "Say to them, Muhammad: If you are truthful, bring the Torah and recite so that we will see whether this is in it or not."[39]

The last part of Q 3:93 is mentioned here and expanded to include the reason for the Jews' being challenged to produce and read from the Torah. Whether this is taken as a reference to Gen 9:3 or 32:33, it entails that the Jews would be forced to admit that their claim is false and that the Prophet Muḥammad and the Qur'ān are right.

This argument against the claim of the Jews also highlights the implication of Q 3:93 that these food prohibitions were later revealed in the Torah. In his exegesis linking Q 3:93 to Q 4:160, al-Ṭabarī stresses that after the Israelites had falsely attributed the origin of these food prohibitions to Jacob and to God, these food prohibitions were imposed on the Israelites and required by God as a punishment:

> The Jews said: "We only prohibit that which Israel prohibited himself, and Israel prohibited sinews for he was afflicted with sciatica, afflicting him in the night but leaving him in the morning. Therefore he swore that if God cured him from it he would not eat sinews ever again." Subsequently God prohibited it for the Jews. Then he said: "Say: Bring the Torah and recite it if you are truthful"—this was not prohibited to you except by your own injustice. Likewise the word of God: "On account of the injustice of those who are Jews we prohibited for them good things which were allowed for them" (Q 4:160).
>
> God prohibited for the Israelites in the Torah that which Israel had prohibited himself, on account of their rebellion against themselves and their injustice to the Torah. Say Muhammad: "Jews, come and deny that this is in the Torah, recite it if you are truthful, that God did not prohibit this for you in the Torah, but that you prohibited it on the basis of Israel's prohibition of it on himself.[40]

The statement that God later made incumbent Jacob's prohibition on the Israelites in the Torah could, in this case, be a reference to the prohibition of camel in Lev 11:14 and Deut 14:7. Here, as in the exegesis of al-Zamakhsharī, the challenge to produce the Torah is linked to Q 4:160, the implication being that the evidence of the Torah would compel the Jews to admit that these food prohibitions were revealed not in the time of Jacob or earlier but only later to Moses.

In his exegesis, Ibn Kathīr focuses on Q 3:93 as one of many examples in the Torah that demonstrate that God did impose different laws at

---

[39] al-Ṭabarī, 3:348, *s.v.* Q 3:93.

[40] al-Ṭabarī, 3:348, *s.v.* Q 3:93.

different times and that the Torah in particular imposed prohibitions that were not in effect before its revelation:

> God showed that abrogation [*naskh*], the occurrence of which they denied, was possible and had taken place. God had written in their book, the Torah, that when Noah left the ark God permitted for him to eat from all the animals of the earth. Then after that, Israel forbid himself the meat of camel and its milk, and his sons followed him in this. The Torah came forbidding this and other things in addition to this.
>
> God allowed Adam to marry his sons to his daughters, and then this was prohibited after that. To take a concubine as a wife was permitted in the revealed law [*sharī'ah*] of Abraham, as Abraham did with Hagar when he took her as a concubine along with Sarah. God made this likewise prohibited in the Torah for the Jews. Likewise, marriage to two sisters at the same time was allowed just as Jacob did marrying two sisters. Then God prohibited this for the Jews in the Torah.
>
> All of this was written for them in the Torah which they have. This is precisely abrogation. Of a similar nature is what God legislated for Jesus in his allowing some of what was forbidden in the Torah. Why did the Jews not follow him but instead lie about him and oppose him? Of similar nature is that which God sent with Muhammad from the religion of the upright and straight path, the community of Abraham. Why did they not believe?[41]

Ibn Kathīr reiterates that the dispute behind Q 3:93 was about the Jews' refusal to admit the authority of the Prophet Muḥammad. The issue is not whether the Jews claimed the laws of the Torah were always in effect since the time of Adam. Ibn Kathīr stresses the parallel between the Israelites who refused to acknowledge that they imposed upon themselves the prohibition of camel and the Jews who objected to the Prophet Muḥammad's claim that he was reviving the religion of Abraham. As al-Zamakhsharī notes, in objecting to the Prophet Muḥammad's claim the Jews denied that the Torah had been revealed as a punishment. The Prophet Muḥammad's use of "abrogation" is a return to the original covenant made with Abraham, a covenant that had been displaced by the Torah which was revealed specifically and only to the Israelites as a punishment.

This approach to the exegesis of Q 3:93 resonates with some early Christian views of the Torah as a revealed but no longer canonical text. Romans 4 makes the case that it is following the religion of Abraham applicable to all his descendants, not the Mosaic law of the Torah applicable only to the Israelites, for the former allows all people to inherit the promise made to Abraham in Gen 17:4–8. Galatians 3, drawing upon

---

41 Ibn Kathīr, 1:361, *s.v.* Q 3:93. See Ayoub, *The Qur'ān and Its Interpreters*, 2:251–52.

Deut 27:26 and 21:23, further refers to the Torah as a curse, a temporary suspension of the promise made to Abraham.[42] Some Christian exegesis of these and related passages concludes that this meant the Torah was revealed only as a punishment for the Jews. For some exegetes, such as the author of the *Epistle of Barnabas,* the Torah was to be disregarded altogether because it was imposed only as a punishment for the Israelites' worship of the golden calf.[43]

Other Christian exegetes focus specifically on the revelation of food prohibitions in the Torah. In his *Dialogue with Trypho,* Justin Martyr states that God prohibited the Israelites from eating certain foods. Justin first cites Gen 9:3 as evidence that all food was allowed to the Israelites and then states that the food prohibitions came in the Torah:

> Then God, through Moses, ordered you (Jews) to abstain from all unclean, harmful, and violent animals, because after you had eaten the manna in the desert and had seen all the miracles God wrought for your sake, you did not hesitate to make and adore the golden calf.[44]

In another passage, Justin says that God imposed these food prohibitions, as well as other laws in the Torah, so that the Jews would be reminded of God and not again forget him to serve other gods.[45] In his *Demonstrations,* Aphrahat also cites Gen 9:3 to show that all types of food were allowed to the Israelites until God prohibited certain types specifically to punish the Israelites for worshiping the gods of the Egyptians, including the golden calf.[46] In his treatise *Against the Jews,* Tertullian uses Gen 25:23 and Rom

---

[42] For an overview of these ideas, see James L. Kugel and Rowan Greer, *Early Biblical Interpretation* (Philadelphia: Westminster, 1986), 126–54, esp. 142–45.

[43] On the views of Barnabas, see Pierre Prigent, *Les testimonia dans le christianisme primitif: L'Épître de Barnabé I–XVI et ses sources* (Paris: Gabalda, 1961); L. W. Barnard, *Studies in the Apostolic Fathers and Their Background* (Oxford: Blackwell, 1966), ch. 9; Klaus Wengst, *Tradition und Theologie des Barnabasbriefes* (Berlin: de Gruyter, 1971). For an overview of the golden calf episode in the biblical context, see George W. Coats, *Rebellion in the Wilderness* (Nashville: Abingdon, 1968); as well as I. Lewy, "The Story of the Golden Calf Reanalyzed," *VT* 9 (1959): 318–22.

[44] Justin Martyr, *Dial.* 20, in *Saint Justin Martyr* (trans. T. B. Falls; New York: Christian Heritage, 1888), 178.

[45] See Justin Martyr, *Dial.* 46. A similar argument is made for the practice of keeping the Sabbath (29).

[46] Aphrahat, *Demonstration* 15, in Jacob Neusner, *Aphrahat and Judaism: The Christian-Jewish Argument in Fourth-Century Iran* (Leiden: Brill, 1971), ch. 5, esp. pp. 53–54.

9:12 to link Israel's loss of favor to the time of the revelation of the Torah. According to Tertullian, God's promise that Esau (Israel) would serve Jacob (the church) took effect when the Israelites asked Aaron to make the golden calf.[47]

It is also evident that the rabbis recognized the significance of the episode of the golden calf and the implications it had for the Israelites receiving the promises made to Abraham. For example, *m. Meg.* 4:10 states that the second part of the golden calf account in Exod 32:21–25 is to be read but not translated. A similar injunction appears in the margins of *Targum Neofiti* to these verses.[48] In his *Jewish Antiquities,* Josephus omits the entire episode of the golden calf.[49] Several rabbinic sources also mention the diseases contracted by the Israelites and their loss of signs and sacerdotal privileges as being the result of the Israelites' disobedience with the golden calf.[50] The link between the Israelites' sin and the promise made to Abraham in Gen 17:8 is sometimes stressed.[51] Because of their disobedience, the Israelites are condemned to wander in the desert, thus delaying their reception of the promise made to Abraham in Gen 17:8.

The revelation of the Torah as punishment entails two separate consequences for the Israelites and Jews. On the one hand, the laws of the Torah are revealed as a punishment. Linking Q 3:93 to Q 4:160, Muslim exegesis holds that the Torah reminds Jews of God by prohibiting good things, such as camel meat and milk, which should otherwise be enjoyed. Christian exegetes likewise focus on food prohibitions, Sabbath observance, and sacrifices as obligations imposed upon the Israelites and the Jews, restricting them from enjoying things allowed to the generations

---

[47] Tertullian, *Against the Jews* 1.6–7, in Corpus Christianorum 2, 1340. For a brief discussion of this remark, see Pier Cesare Bori, *The Golden Calf and the Origins of the Anti-Jewish Controversy* (trans. D. Ward; Atlanta: Scholars Press, 1990), 15. On Tertullian's views of the Torah, see C. Aziza, *Tertullien et le judaïsme* (Paris: Belles Lettres, 1977).

[48] These points are mentioned in Bori, *Golden Calf,* 13.

[49] See Josephus, *Ant.* 3.95–101; Bori, *Golden Calf,* 13.

[50] On the diseases, see *Sipre* Num §1 *(Siphre d'be Rab Fasciculus primus: Siphre ad Numeros adjecto Siphre Zutta* [ed. H. S. Horovitz; repr., Jerusalem: Wahrmann, 1966], 4); *Lev. Rab.* 16:1 (ed. Margulies 1:347); *Num. Rab.* 7:2 and 7:4. On the loss of signs and sacerdotal privileges, see *Mek.*, Baḥodeš §2 (*Mekilta de-Rabbi Ishmael* [ed. J. Z. Lauterbach; 3 vols.; 1933–35; repr., Philadelphia: Jewish Publication Society, 1976], 2:205). For an overview of this discussion, see Bori, *Golden Calf,* 12–13; L. Smolar and M. Aberbach, "The Golden Calf Episode in Postbiblical Literature," *HUCA* 39 (1968): 91–116.

[51] See Bori, *Golden Calf,* 13.

before Moses.[52] On the other hand, the revelation of the Torah, in light of the golden calf episode, is also seen as a revocation or suspension of the covenant made with Abraham. Developing the implications of Gal 3, Barnabas claims that when Moses broke the first set of tablets, God withdrew his covenant from the Israelites.[53] A similar claim is found in al-Ṭabarī, from Ibn Isḥāq:

> God had written on tablets for Moses encouragement and details of everything, as well as right guidance and mercy. When he (Moses) threw them down, God withdrew [*rafa'a*] six of the seven parts and left the seventh saying: "In their inscription there is guidance and mercy for all those who fear their Lord."[54]

There is another reference to the withdrawal of the Torah from the Israelites, on account of their worshiping of idols, found in al-Ṭabarī 's exegesis of Q 2:246. Because of their disobedience, the Israelites forfeit the promise made to Abraham and receive stricter laws reminding them of their transgression.

The exegesis of Q 3:93 does accuse the Jews of distorting the revelation, but not by physically altering the text of the Torah. Instead, the Israelites, because of their disobedience, are the cause of the Torah being revealed as it was. The Torah did not enjoin the same laws as those enjoined upon Abraham, nor is the revelation it contains in agreement with the revelation contained in the text of the Qur'ān. That the Torah contained certain laws, here food prohibitions, that were not found in the Qur'ān and were therefore considered to have been abrogated is evident from the exegesis of Q 3:93, 4:160, and 6:146, among other verses. In his exegesis of Q 6:146, Ibn al-'Arabī makes this explicit:

---

[52] See, for example, Justin, *Dial.* 29 (Sabbath), 46 (food prohibitions); Aphrahat, *Demonstrations* 12 (paschal sacrifice), 13 (Sabbath), 15 (food prohibitions); Cyprian, *Testament* 1.1 (Corpus Christianorum 3:6). Justin's views are discussed briefly in Kugel and Greer, *Early Biblical Interpretation,* 142–45.

[53] See *Barn.* 14:1–5; 4:6–8. In his analysis of this point in *Barnabas,* Greer points out that while the first set of tablets was inscribed by the finger of God (Exod 31:18), the second set is written by Moses himself (Exod 34:28). See Kugel and Greer, *Early Biblical Interpretation,* 141–42.

[54] This is taken from al-Ṭabarī, *Ta'rīkh al-rusul wa al-mulūk,* 495. The passage can also be found translated in Gordon D. Newby, *The Making of the Last Prophet: A Reconstruction of the Earliest Biography of Muḥammad* (Columbia: University of South Carolina Press, 1989), 134. The verse quoted at the end of the passage is Q 7:154, which is taken as a reference to the tablets of Moses. For references to rabbinic sources in which it is stressed that God replaced the tablets Moses broke, see Smolar and Aberbach, "Golden Calf Episode."

> God states that he wrote for them the prohibition of this in the Torah, but God abrogated all of this with the law [*sharī'ah*] of Muhammad. He caused to be allowed for them what used to be forbidden for them as a punishment by means of hardening their burden with great prohibitions. The prohibition ceases with Muhammad and his community. Incumbent upon all of creation is the religion of Islam, what it allows, what it prohibits, what it commands, and what it forbids.[55]

The claim of the exegetes is not that the Qur'ān abrogates the Torah by implementing a new revelation. Rather, the revelation received by the Prophet Muḥammad revives the original covenant revealed to Abraham but that was distorted and lost by the Israelites and later the Jews. The revealed laws of Islam and the promises that accompany them are considered to apply to all people because, unlike the Torah but like the Noahide laws, the revelation of the Qur'ān and the Prophet Muḥammad's implementation of the religion of Abraham are meant for the Gentiles.[56]

---

[55] Ibn al-'Arabī, 2:296, *s.v.* Q 6:146.

[56] Ibn Ḥazm states that the Islamic *sharī'ah* applies to all people, Muslim and non-Muslim alike. See his *al-Iḥkām fī uṣūl al-aḥkām* (Beirut: Dār al-Kutub al-'Ilmīyah, n.d.), ch. 30, 2:103–114. Note, however, especially as evinced in the legal exegesis surrounding Q 5:41–45, that Ibn Ḥazm's claim is not without some disagreement. Ḥanafī scholars, for example, allow Jews and Christians to treat wine and pigs as property. Abū Ḥanīfah and Muḥammad al-Shaybānī also allow Jews, Christians, and Magians to regulate themselves in marriage according to their own laws. See Abū Bakr al-Jaṣṣāṣ, *Aḥkām al-Qur'ān* (Beirut: Dār al-Kitāb al-'Arabī, n.d.), 2:234–237, *s.v.* Q 5:42. For further discussion of the application of marriage laws, see al-Ṭaḥāwī, *Sharḥ ma'ānī al-āthār,* 4:143.

On the Early Life of Abraham: Biblical and Qur'ānic Intertextuality and the Anticipation of Muḥammad

Brian M. Hauglid
Brigham Young University

Abraham's early life, as presented in both qur'ānic and extraqur'ānic tradition, finds some notable points of contact with biblical tradition as well as departing from it in significant ways. In his *Journeys in Holy Lands*,[1] Reuven Firestone focuses on Abraham's emigration to Mecca and his near sacrifice of his son and explores the relationship that developed between the biblical, pre-Islamic Arab, and Islamic traditions. One of the chief lessons of Firestone's study of biblical and Islamic intertextual tradition is that rather than viewing these traditions strictly in terms of dependence and expansion or cause and effect, it is more fruitful to analyze the role of biblically related materials in early Islam as part of a creative effort to produce an Islamic literature that is as unique as the antecedents from which it initially came forth. A study of this type may, in addition, shed more light on the development of early biblical literature. For instance, nonbiblical tradition such as we find in Islam may retain certain biblical elements Jews or early Christians did not choose to emphasize.

Using Firestone's intertextual approach I will first examine Abraham's life from his birth to his rescue from a fire from the biblical perspective and then from the qur'ānic point of view. This type of study will provide an opportunity to examine the intertextuality that took place between the biblical and qur'ānic environments. Finally, I will analyze the Islamic reorientation of biblically related literature to demonstrate how the Islamicized interpretations of events of the early life of Abraham, from the early period of Islam, anticipate the coming of the Prophet Muḥammad.

---

[1] Reuven Firestone, *Journeys in Holy Lands: The Evolution of the Abraham-Ishmael Legends in Islamic Exegesis* (Albany: State University of New York Press, 1990).

Biblically Related Interpretations on the Early Life of Abraham

Biblical passages provide little information on the early life of Abraham. For instance, Genesis records virtually nothing about the circumstances of Abraham's birth (11:27) and scant information is given of his years in Ur of the Chaldees (11:28–31). However, from a very early period (perhaps the third to the second centuries B.C.E.), biblical interpreters identified certain motifs concerning Abraham's early life from a few select Bible verses. For instance, Josh 24:2–3 supplies information missing in Genesis and perhaps explains why Gen 12 begins with Abraham being told to leave his homeland: "And Joshua said unto all the people, Thus saith the Lord God of Israel, Your fathers dwelt on the other side of the flood in old time, even Terah, the father of Abraham, and the father of Nachor: and they served other gods. And I took your father Abraham from the other side of the flood, and led him throughout all the land of Canaan." James Kugel points out, "Who 'they' refers to is not clear; but if Abraham is singled out in virtually the next breath, 'Then I took your father Abraham,' it seemed that the reason must be that 'they' refers to Terah and Nahor and the others, *but not to Abraham!* They served other gods, but Abraham did not, and for that reason 'Then I took your father Abraham.'"[2] Bolstering Josh 24:2–3 is Isa 51:2: "Look unto Abraham your father, and unto Sarah that bare you: for I called him *alone* and blessed him, and increased him." Kugel notes, "If God called Abraham alone, is this not another way of saying that Abraham was quite unique among his family members? He—and not his father, Terah, or his brother, Nahor—was summoned personally to God's service."[3] Kugel identifies the following motifs from early biblical literature that build upon the notion in Josh 24:2–3 and Gen 12:1–2 that Abraham had to leave idolatrous Ur:

1. Abraham the monotheist: interpreting Josh 24:2 "other gods" (Jdt 5:6–9; *Jub.* 11:16–17, 12:2, 6–7; Philo, *Abr.* 71; *L.A.B.* 23:5; Josephus, *Ant.* 1:154–57).

2. Terah, priest of idolatry: interpreting Josh 24:2 "They [i.e., Terah, Nahor] served other gods" (*Jub.* 11:16, 12:1–3, 6–7; *Apoc. Ab.* 1, 3; *Gen. Rab.* 38:13).

3. Abraham the astronomer: Chaldea was famous for astronomy and astrology (the pseudo-Orphica cited by Clement of Alexandria; the fragments of Eupolemus and Artapanus cited by Eusebius; Josephus, etc.).

---

2 James L. Kugel, *Traditions of the Bible: A Guide to the Bible As It Was at the Start of the Common Era* (Cambridge: Harvard University Press, 1998), 245, emphasis original.

3 Ibid., emphasis original.

4. Tipped off by the stars: Abraham's knowledge of astronomy led him to discover that there was only one God (*Jub.* 12:17–18; Philo, *Abr.* 69–71; Josephus, *Ant.* 1.167–168).

5. Abraham rescued from Chaldea: Isa 29:22 "redeemed" can also mean "rescued" (Jdt 5:8–9; *Jub.* 12:6–7; Josephus, *Ant.* 1:157, etc.).

6. Abraham saved from the fire: "I am the Lord that brought thee out of Ur (interpreted anciently as fire) of the Chaldees" (Gen 15:7) (*Apoc. Ab.* 8:1–6; *Tg. Neof.* Gen 11:31, 15:7; *Gen. Rab.* 38:13; *L.A.B.* 6:4–5; 23:5).[4]

Both Jewish and Islamic legends are replete with stories containing these motifs surrounding Abraham's years in Ur of the Chaldees. Jewish legends originated more directly from the biblical base in passages such as Josh 24, Gen 12, and Isa 29; later interpreters added variations on these. However, Islamic lore, although related to these biblical motifs indirectly, is reinterpreted according to the Qur'ān to give ultimately a new context from which meaning may be derived within an Islamic framework. Firestone has astutely observed, "Part of the sublimity of the Qur'ān was its success in rendering Biblicist traditions that had found their way into Arabia meaningful to the indigenous non-Biblicist Arab population—to provide the framework for successful diffusion."[5]

Qur'ānic Interpretations on the Early Life of Abraham

As with earlier biblical prophets, the story of Abraham is not presented in a narrative form in the Qur'ān. In fact, the Qur'ān provides only an array of unconnected verses that presuppose a certain amount of background information on the part of the reader. However, when select verses (e.g., Q 6:74–82; 19:41–50; 21:51–71; 37:83–98) related to Abraham are viewed together, a few motifs quickly emerge, such as Abraham arguing with his father and the people about idolatry and Abraham being cast into a fire. Moreover, like the biblical text, the Qur'ān does not address Abraham's birth or formative years in Ur of the Chaldees. For this information extraqur'ānic sources such as *Tafsīr* (qur'ānic exegesis), *Ta'rīkh* (historical chronology), and the *Qiṣaṣ al-anbiyā'* (tales of the prophets) provide reports (*ḥadīth*) that generally fill in information where the Qur'ān is silent. This exegetical material is biblically related even when not found in the Bible proper, for it is related to Jewish midrash or, in some instances, Christian sources that interpret biblical passages.[6] In

---

[4] Ibid., 245–54.

[5] Firestone, *Journeys in Holy Lands,* 156.

[6] Camilla Adang, *Muslim Writers on Judaism and the Hebrew Bible: From Ibn Rabban to Ibn Hazm* (Leiden: Brill, 1996), 4–5. For a discussion of Christians

other ways these sources are reminiscent of a pre-Islamic environment, and, more commonly, they describe or demonstrate the development of the Islamic identity as a restored religion through the instrumentation of Muḥammad. These sources supplement the qur'ānic account and provide a way for the Qur'ān to give the story its unity and Islamic meaning.[7]

In the Islamic context, Abraham's birth and early life revolve around the apostate and idolatrous conditions of his time. Abraham's story is dispensational, like that of the earlier prophets such as Adam, Enoch, and Noah. (A dispensation, in general, is a cyclical period wherein a prophet is born at a wicked and sinful time in history; he seeks to overthrow the idolatry of his time and is successful to some degree but ultimately fails and is followed by another prophet who again attempts to restore what had been lost in the previous dispensation.) The Islamic Abraham narrative opens with the idolatrous world he is born into. Jewish and Christian texts give more information than Islamic sources about the beginnings of this idolatry. Most suggest that it took place during the time of Serug, Abraham's great-grandfather (Gen 11:22–23). One Christian text, the *Cave of Treasures*, composed in the fourth to sixth centuries C.E., explains that "in the days of Serug the worship of idols entered the world. And in his days the children of men began to make themselves graven images, and it was at this time that the introduction of idols into the world took place."[8] After Abraham learns of the wicked practices of his day, he makes every effort to rid his family and people of idol worship, but like his predecessors, Abraham ultimately fails to bring about the total destruction of idolatry.

This cyclical dispensational pattern begins with Adam and ends with Muḥammad, who is considered the last (or seal) of the prophets. Of course, qur'ānic exegetical literature views the biblically related literature prior to Muḥammad as corrupt and attempts to correct it through

---

quoting biblical passages in the Qur'ān, see Sidney H. Griffith, "The Qur'ān in Arab Christian Texts; The Development of an Apologetical Argument: Abū Qurrah in the Mağlis of al-Ma'mūn," *ParOr* 24 (1999): 203–33.

[7] Firestone, *Journeys in Holy Lands*, 20, 158.

[8] E. A. Wallis Budge's translation as found in *Traditions about the Early Life of Abraham* (ed. J. A. Tvedtnes et al.; Provo, Utah: Foundation for Ancient Research and Mormon Studies and Brigham Young University, 2001), 189–90 (hereafter referred to as Budge). See also Jewish commentary on Gen 11:1–4 in *Targum Pseudo-Jonathan and Targum Neofiti*, which specify that the tower built to reach heaven was to have an idol placed at its top (Budge, 65–66, 68). Verse 4 reads "let us make a name," which is interpreted in *Midrash Rabbah* as meaning "nought else but an idol" (Budge, 91).

the retelling of stories of earlier prophets, such as Abraham, within a qur'ānic context.[9]

EARLY ISLAMIC NARRATIVES ON THE EARLY LIFE OF ABRAHAM

Islamic sources cite fairly early transmitters through whom the Abraham narrative emerges. Schützinger used two main versions of the narrative, Al-Suddī (d. 745) and Ibn Isḥāq (d. 767) as found in Ṭabarī's famous *History* and commentary (*Jāmi'*), to compare and contrast the early part of the narrative in his study of Abraham's dealings with the legendary Nimrod.[10] Here I will examine a number of Islamic exegetical texts (i.e., *Tafsīr, Ta'rīkh, Qiṣaṣ al-anbiyā'*) that give a narrative report or comment on biblically related motifs concerning the early life of Abraham.[11] These texts provide close to one hundred traditions that designate a particular traditionist (*isnād*), the majority divided among four noted traditionists.

---

9 For a Christian discussion of the Qur'ān as flawed scripture, see Griffith, "The Qur'ān in Arab Christian Texts," 205–6.

10 Heinrich Schützinger, *Ursprung und Entwicklung der arabischen Abraham-Nimrod Legende* (Bonn: Rheinische Friedrich-Wilhelms-Universität, 1961).

11 The following can serve as a sampling of sources: Ka'b al-Aḥbār (d. 652, see n. 12 above); Isḥāq Abū Ḥudhayfa b. Bishr al-Qurayshī (d. 821), *Mubtada' al-dunyā wa-qiṣaṣ al-anbiyā'*, MS Huntington 388 (Oxford Bodleian), folios 160b–170b (an English translation by the present author and an Arabic transcription of the manuscript can be found in Budge, 310–26, 515–19, respectively); Abū Ja'far Muḥammad b. Jarīr al-Ṭabarī (d. 923), *Ta'rīkh al-rusūl wa-al-mulūk* (12 vols.; Misr: Muḥammad 'Abd al-Lateef al-Khatib, 1905); *The History of al-Tabari*, vol. 2, *Prophets and Patriarchs* (trans. W. M. Brinner; Albany: State University of New York Press, 1987); Abū al-Ḥasan 'Alī b. Ibrāhīm b. Hāshim b. Mūsā b. Bābawayhī Al-Qummī (d. 939), *Tafsīr al-Qummī* (2 vols.; 1387/1967); Abū Isḥāq Aḥmad b. Muḥammad b. Ibrāhīm al-Tha'labī al-Nīsābūrī (d. 1036), *Qiṣaṣ al-anbiyā'* (Beirut: Dār al-Kutub 'Ilmiyya, 1414/1994); Abū 'Abd Allāh Muḥammad b. Aḥmad b. Muṭarrif al-Kinānī al-Ṭarafī (1065), *Qiṣaṣ al-anbiyā'*, English excerpt in Budge, 370–80; Radī al-Dīn Abū 'Alī al-Fadl b. al-Ḥasan Amīn al-Dīn al-Ṭabarsī (d. 1153), *Majma' al-bayān fī tafsīr al-Qur'ān* (30 parts, 8 vols.; Syria: 1354/1935); Qutub al-Dīn Sa'yud b. Hibat Allāh al-Rāwandī (d. 1177), *Qiṣaṣ al-anbiyā'* (Beirut: Mu'asaset al-Mufid, 1409/1989); 'Abd al-Raḥmān b. 'Alī b. Muḥammad Abū al-Farash b. al-Jawzī (d. 1200), *Zād al-masīr fī 'ilm al-tafsīr* (8 vols.; Beirut: Dār al-Kutub al-'Ilmiyya, 1994); 'Izz al-Dīn Abū al-Ḥasan 'Alī b. al-Athīr (d. 1233), *Al-Kāmil fī-al-ta'rīkh* (12 vols.; Beirut: Dār Ṣadir and Dār Bayrūt, 1385/1965); 'Abd Allāh b. 'Umar b. Muḥammad b. 'Alī Abū al-Khayr Nāṣir al-Dīn al-Baiḍāwī (d. 1286), *Anwār al-tanzīl wa-asrār al-ta'wīl* (n.p., 1899–1902); 'Imād al-Dīn Ismā'īl b. 'Umar b. Kathīr (d. 1373), *Qiṣaṣ al-anbiyā'* (Cairo: Dār al-'Ulūm al-'Arabiyya, 1418/1998); *Mukhtaṣar tafsīr Ibn Kathīr* (2 vols.; Beirut: Dār el-Marefah, 1420/1999).

Eight incomplete narratives are attributed to Ka'b al-Aḥbār (d. 652),[12] twenty to Ibn 'Abbās (d. 767),[13] thirteen to al-Suddī,[14] and sixteen to Ibn Isḥāq.[15] In addition, I will refer to other early sources not identifying a transmitter, such as al-Ya'qūbī, al-Mas'ūdī, al-Maqdisī, and al-Zamakhsharī,[16] to demonstrate the widespread unity of interpretation, particularly in the beginning period of Islamic development.

In general, the early life of Abraham consists of the following motifs. Usually a tyrannical king, commonly identified as Nimrod, is the ruler at the time of Abraham's birth. Either a new star appears or Nimrod reports seeing a star, sometimes in a dream, and is told by his prognosticators that the star represents Abraham, who will somehow overturn Nimrod and his idolatrous people. Of course this news frightens Nimrod, so he issues an edict of slaughter for all male infants born in his kingdom. Despite Nimrod's best efforts to kill Abraham, he is born in a cave and emerges as a formidable opponent to Nimrod. Abraham first identifies the idolatrous environment of his father and the people through seeing heavenly bodies (Q 6:76–78), and later he mocks the ineffectual nature of the idols. Abraham also argues with his father and mocks his idols (Q 6:42), sometimes he decries idol worship in the presence of worshipers (Q 29:16–24), and

---

12 Ka'b al-Aḥbār's narrative derives from an Arabic manuscript written in Hebrew script and published in Constantinople in 1718. A French translation is in Bernard Chapira, "Légendes bibliques attribuées à Ka'b al-Ahbar," *REJ* 69 (1919): 86–107; 70 (1920): 37–43. An English translation of the French (taken from Budge, 298–302) will be used in this study.

13 Isḥāq ibn Bishr, *Mubtada'*, fol. 162b, lines 12–13, 15–17; 165b, lines 7–15; 168b, line 15; 169a, line 1 (Budge, 313–14, 318, 323; [text] 517, 519); Ṭabarī, *Ta'rīkh*, 1:121, 124 (trans. Brinner, 53–54, 54–55, 59–60); Tha'labī, 73–74, 78; Ṭarafī (see Budge, 378); Ṭabarsī, 4:55; Ibn al-Jawzī, 3:55–56, 5:270; Baiḍāwī, 2:433, 4:258–59; Ibn Kathīr, 150–51.

14 Ṭabarī, *Ta'rīkh*, 1:122, 123–24 (Brinner 56, 59); Tha'labī, 73, 73, 74, 76; 78, 78; Ṭarafī (see Budge, 373); Ṭabarsī, 54–55; Ibn al-Jawzī, 270, 270; Baiḍāwī, 2:432–33.

15 Ṭabarī, *Ta'rīkh*, 1:119, 122, 122, 123, 124, 125 (Brinner, 50–52, 56, 56, 58, 60–61, 61); Tha'labī, 73, 74, 74, 77, 78, 78; Ibn al-Athīr, 1:94–100; Baiḍāwī, 432, 433, 433ff.

16 Aḥmad b. Abī Ya'qūb b. Waḍiḥ al-Ya'qūbī (d. 897), *Ta'rīkh al-Ya'qūbī* (Beirut: 1379/1960); Abū al-Ḥasan 'Alī b. al-Ḥusayn al-Mas'ūdī (d. 956); *Murūj al-dhahab wa ma'adin al-jawāhir* (see Budge, 351–53); Al-Muṭahhar b. Ṭāhir al-Maqdisī (fl. 966), *Kitāb al-Bad' wa-al-ta'rīkh* (see Budge, 354–56); Abū al-Qāsim Maḥmūd b. 'Umar b. Aḥmad al-Zamakhsharī, *Al-Kashshāf ḥaqā'iq al-tanzīl wa 'uyūn al-aqāwīl fī wujūh al-ta'wīl* (4 vols.; Cairo: Muṣṭafā al-Bābī al-Ḥalabī, 1966–68), 2:576, 578.

he even destroys some of them (Q 21:58). Abraham's fame increases, and Nimrod sentences him, with the approbation of his people, to a fiery death (21:68). Abraham, however, is saved by God's command to the fire to be "cool and safe upon" him (21:69). Afterwards, Nimrod offers sacrifice to Abraham's God but does not cease his idolatry, and from that time forth he stays away from Abraham.

In two of the earliest versions of the young life of Abraham, those of Ka'b al-Aḥbār (d. 652), a Yemenite Jewish convert to Islam, and Ibn 'Abbās (d. 687), the above-mentioned general outline is presented with few variations. Almost the entire Ka'b al-Aḥbār narrative used in the present analysis comes from the French translation of Bernard Chapira in his article, "Légendes bibliques attribuées à Ka'b al-Ahbar" (see note 12 above). It is difficult to ascertain the origin and veracity of this source, which makes it suspect; however, this text provides useful information for the study of the Abraham narrative and possible linkages between the biblical tradition and early Islam in its developmental period.

Chapira's translation, then, provides the majority of this narrative. Six other exegetical sources give eight additional reports of Ka'b al-Aḥbār and are noted in the following reconstruction.

A. Ka'b al-Aḥbār 's Version

1. Abraham converses about idols with an old woman, and she is converted to Islam.
2. Nimrod hears about Abraham and sends an army after him. But Gabriel places a veil between Abraham and soldiers to protect Abraham. The soldiers flee.
3. Abraham is transported by Gabriel to Iraq, whence Nimrod has fled, and preaches monotheism.
4. Nimrod orders that Abraham be cast into the fire.
5. Abraham is encouraged by his mother to obey Nimrod, but instead Abraham's mother learns about the true God.
6. Abraham is placed on a catapult (*al-manjanīq*) and propelled into the fire. No one could use any fire at the time of Abraham's fire (Tha'labī, Ibn Kathīr).[17] Everything, except the lizard, tried to put out the fire of Abraham (Baiḍāwī).[18]
7. Gabriel offers to help Abraham, and it is refused.
8. God makes the fire cold, and the fire becomes a garden of paradise, or the fire only burns the fetters of Abraham (Tha'labī, Ṭarafī, Ṭabarsī, Ibn

[17] Tha'labī, 78; Ibn Kathīr, *Qiṣaṣ*, 151.

[18] Baiḍāwī, 4:258.

al-Jawzī, Baiḍāwī, Ibn Kathīr).[19] Abraham remains in the fire for seven days (Ibn al-Jawzī, Baiḍāwī).[20]

9. Nimrod worries that people may convert, so he confronts Abraham.

10. The giving of life and death exchange confounds Nimrod. (Q 2:258).[21]

This version gives no information surrounding the circumstances of Abraham's birth and the earliest period of his youth because the manuscript is incomplete and begins in the middle of Abraham's discussion with the old woman, suggesting the likelihood, of course, that this manuscript at one time did begin with the birth of Abraham and his earlier life. However, if the transmitter of this report is Ka'b al-Aḥbār (which is questionable),[22] it would be among the earliest extant Islamic reports about Abraham.

Motifs 1, 2, and 3 are unique to this narrative, and motifs 5 and 9 are otherwise rare in Islamic exegetical literature. Although not found in Islamic literature, motifs 1, 2, and 3 are attested in Jewish midrashic sources, a circumstance perhaps indicative of some early intertextual points of contact and discussion of biblically related materials and their place in Islamic exegesis. As an example of motif 1, *Seder Eliyahu Zuta* recounts a story about two men, one thirty years old and the other fifty, who are chided by Abraham because they worship what had been made that day.[23] In the *Midrash Rabbah*, a late fourth- or early fifth-century text, we see again both men, but in this account a woman approaches Abraham and asks if he would make an offering of her flour, or meal, to the idols. Abraham offers the meal to these gods mockingly and breaks them with a stick.[24] Motif 1 shows a possible intertextual contact, since the later Islamic reports also speak of the old woman who approaches Abraham to have him offer her meal to the idol gods. However, Ka'b al-Aḥbār rephrases this motif to set up Abraham's eventual encounter with Nimrod, who has Abraham thrown into a fire. Motif 2 is striking in that it is not well attested in Jewish and even less often in Christian texts. In a legend contained in Jellinek's *Bet ha-Midrash*, Nimrod is said to have sent an army after Abraham and is thwarted by a cloud

---

[19] See also, Tha'labī, 78; Ṭarafī (see Budge, 379); Ṭabarsī, 4:55; Ibn al-Jawzī, 5:270 (citing Ka'b and Wahb b. Munabbih also); Baiḍāwī, 4:259; Ibn Kathīr, *Qiṣaṣ*, 151.

[20] Ibn al-Jawzī, 5:270; Baiḍāwī, 4:259.

[21] See also Deut 32:39. See John Wansbrough, *Quranic Studies: Sources and Methods of Scriptural Interpretation* (Oxford: Oxford University Press, 1977), 31.

[22] See Firestone, *Journeys in Holy Lands*, 196 n. 55.

[23] See H. Speyer, *Die biblischen Erzählungen im Qoran* (repr., Hildesheim: Olms, 1988), 136–38.

[24] *Gen. Rab.* 38:19, conveniently reproduced by Speyer, *Erzählungen*, 135–36.

and mist,[25] but Jellinek suggested from internal evidence that this Abraham narrative may have come from Arabic into Hebrew and therefore may be dated much later.[26] Motif 3 is not attested in Jewish or Christian texts, which may either indicate a unique Islamic creation or something that was lost from the biblically related literature. Finally, motif 10 is well attested in Jewish literature, which stresses Abraham's constant struggle against the idolatrous practices of his day.[27]

B. Ibn 'Abbās's Version

The following is a reconstruction of the Abraham narrative based on seventeen reports of Ibn 'Abbās that come from eight exegetical works. Of these seventeen reports, one is based on the authority of Ibn Ma'sūd and the companions of the Prophet.

1a. Nimrod sees a star that blots out the light of moon and sun. Nimrod becomes frightened and summons his magicians, soothsayers, astrologers, and priests, who predict that there would be one born who would overthrow idol worship and his kingdom. Nimrod moves to another town, taking all the men but leaving all the women behind. Nimrod gives an order for all male infants to be slain (Ṭabarī).[28]

1b. When Abraham is conceived, the priests say to Nimrod that Abraham was conceived that very night (or would be conceived soon). Nimrod separates the men from the women (Ibn al-Jawzī).[29] Nimrod orders a slaughter of the infants. The mother of Abraham flees for safety. After the birth, Abraham's mother places him in a field. Āzar (Abraham's father; see Q 6:74) later digs a hole near a river. He barricades the door so wild beasts cannot get to Abraham (Tha'labī, Ibn al-Jawzī, al-Baiḍāwī).[30]

2. Nimrod gives Āzar an assignment that will require him to go to the city. Nimrod commands Āzar not to have intercourse with his wife. Āzar cannot control himself and his wife conceives, so he hides his pregnant wife in a cave (Ṭabarī).[31]

---

[25] A. Jellinek, *Bet ha-Midrasch* (6 vols.; repr., Jerusalem: Bamberger & Wahrmann, 1938), 1:25–34; Abraham's escape from Nimrod's army is recounted on p. 28.

[26] Ibid., 1:xvi; 2:xxxii.

[27] Abraham I. Katsh, *Judaism in Islam: Biblical and Talmudic Backgrounds of the Koran and Its Commentaries* (2d ed.; New York: Barnes, 1962), 175–76.

[28] Based on the authority of Ma'sūd and the companions of the Prophet. See Ṭabarī, *Ta'rīkh*, 1:121 (Brinner, 53).

[29] Ibn al-Jawzī, 3:55.

[30] Tha'labī, 73–74; Ibn al-Jawzī, 3:55–56; Baiḍāwī, 2:433.

[31] Ṭabarī, *Ta'rīkh*, 1:121 (Brinner, 53).

3. Not aware of Āzar's wife's pregnancy and the long lapse of time since the prophecy, Nimrod begins to doubt the prediction of his priests and soothsayers. Soon after, Abraham is born (Ṭabarī).[32]

4. In the cave Abraham grows in a day as if it were a week, a week as if a month, and a month as if a year (Ibn Bishr, Ṭabarī).[33] Abraham receives milk and honey through sucking his thumb (Ibn Bishr).[34] Meanwhile, Nimrod forgets the whole matter (Ṭabarī).[35]

5. When Abraham comes out of the cave, he learns from his father about animals because he only knew about his parents and had never before left the cave and knew of no other living things (Ṭabarī).[36]

6. Abraham questions his parents about who his Lord is (Q 19:46–48; Ibn al-Jawzī).[37] He sees the sun, moon, and stars and learns of the true God (Q 6:76–79; Ṭabarī).[38]

7. Abraham's father makes his living manufacturing idols (Ibn Bishr, Ṭabarī).[39] He employs his sons (Ṭabarī),[40] including Abraham, in selling these idols (Ibn Bishr, Ṭabarī). Unlike his brothers (Ṭabarī), Abraham returns home not having sold a single idol (Ibn Bishr, Ṭabarī). Abraham's sales pitch: "Who would buy what harms and is of no use?" (Ibn Bishr, Ṭabarī).[41] Abraham argues with his father about the powerlessness of the idols (Q 6:74; Ṭabarī).[42]

8. Abraham takes idols to the river and mocks them; news of Abraham reaches Nimrod (Ibn Bishr).[43]

9. Āzar invites Abraham to a festival for the idols. Abraham complains of foot pain to stay back (Q 37:88–89; 21:57). While the people are away, Abraham destroys idols at the house of the gods. When the people return, they suspect Abraham (Ṭabarī).[44]

---

32 Ibid.

33 Ibid.; Ibn Bishr, fol. 162b, lines 12–13 (see Budge, 313–14).

34 Ibn Bishr, fol. 162b, lines 15–17 (see Budge, 314).

35 Ṭabarī, *Ta'rīkh*, 1:121 (Brinner, 53).

36 Ibid. (Brinner, 53–54).

37 Ibn al-Jawzī, 3:56. For a discussion of this motif as imagery of exile, see Wansbrough, *Quranic Studies*, 7.

38 Ṭabarī, *Ta'rīkh*, 1:121 (Brinner, 54).

39 Ibn Bishr, fol. 165b, line 7 (Budge, 318); Ṭabarī, *Ta'rīkh*, 1:121 (Brinner, 54).

40 Ṭabarī, *Ta'rīkh*, 1:121 (Brinner, 54).

41 Ibn Bishr, fol. 165b, lines 8–9 (Budge, 318); Ṭabarī, *Ta'rīkh*, 1:121 (Brinner, 54).

42 Ṭabarī, *Ta'rīkh*, 1:121 (Brinner, 55).

43 Ibn Bishr, fol. 165b, lines 10–14 (Budge, 318).

44 Ṭabarī, *Ta'rīkh*, 1:121–22 (Brinner, 55).

10. Abraham's mother has a dream wherein she sees Abraham in the fire surrounded by a green garden and the fire did not harm him (Ibn Bishr).[45]

11. God pronounces that the fire be cool and safe upon Abraham (Q 21:69). If the cold had not been followed by peace, Abraham would have died of the cold (Ṭabarī, Tha'labī, Ṭarafī, Ibn al-Jawzī, Baiḍāwī, Ibn Kathīr).[46] Another man (the Angel of Shade) is seen with Abraham in the fire (Ṭabarī).[47] Abraham trusts in God's protection (Baiḍāwī, Ibn Kathīr).[48] God subdues Nimrod, who is plagued by an insect that enters his brain (Ṭabarsī).[49]

As far as the early life of the Abraham narrative is concerned, even the later transmitters, such as al-Suddī and Ibn Isḥāq, have followed Ibn 'Abbās quite closely (aside from a few minor variations). Commonly referred to as the father of Islamic exegesis, Ibn 'Abbās was an excellent commentator on the Qur'ān and was well acquainted with Jewish and Christian legendary traditions. Ibn 'Abbās therefore seems a likely candidate for one who was instrumental in bridging biblically related materials and qur'ānic-based texts. In addition to its intertextuality, the Abraham narrative can also be interpreted typologically as prefiguring the birth of Muḥammad and his own conflict with idolatry, as the following analysis will demonstrate.

Typological Anticipation of Muḥammad

From as early as the beginning of the nineteenth century, it has been recognized by Western scholarship that, in the Islamic world, the life of Abraham is typologically connected to that of Muḥammad. Abraham Geiger notes that, according to Muḥammad, "Abraham was his great prototype, the man of whom he thought most highly, and the one with whom he liked best to compare himself in opinion."[50] In Y. Moubarac's study of

---

45 Ibn Bishr, fol. 168b line 15–169a line 1 (Budge, 318).

46 Ṭabarī, *Ta'rīkh*, 1:124 (Brinner, 59); Tha'labī, 78; Ṭarafī (see Budge, 378); Ibn al-Jawzī, 5:270; Baiḍāwī, 4:259; Ibn Kathīr, *Qiṣaṣ*, 151. Ibn Sa'd records a report from Ibn 'Abbās that the fire into which Abraham was thrown occurred in Kuthā (*Al-Ṭabaqāt al-kabīr* [8 vols.; Beirut: 1380/1960], 1:46).

47 Ṭabarī, *Ta'rīkh*, 1:124 (Brinner, 60).

48 Baiḍāwī, 4:258; Ibn Kathīr, *Qiṣaṣ*, 150; *Mukhtaṣar*, 2:68.

49 Ṭabarsī, 4:55.

50 Abraham Geiger, *Judaism and Islam* (repr., New York: Ktav, 1970), 95. One explanation for this asserts that Muḥammad tried to "strengthen his position against

the figure of Abraham in the Qur'ān, it is also concluded that Abraham is the perfect religious model for the subsequent entrance of Muḥammad into Islam through divine election.[51] Moreover, Arthur Jeffery has paid particular attention to Muḥammad and Islam as a restoration of the religion of Abraham.[52] According to motif 1a, the astrologers of Nimrod informed him that a boy would be born who would change the religion of the people and destroy Nimrod's kingdom. One evening while Nimrod slept, he dreamed he saw a star that took the light away from the sun and the moon until no light remained in either of them. Nimrod inquired of his priests and prognosticators to ascertain the meaning of the dream and was told that the star represented the newborn boy who would destroy his kingdom. Hence, Nimrod issued an edict to slaughter all the male newborns in his kingdom under the age of two years.[53] This motif suggests the general feeling of anticipation that prevailed just prior to the birth of Abraham. In Islamic tradition, the time period prior to Muḥammad's birth was also one of anticipation. According to Ibn Isḥāq, Muḥammad's father was proposed to by another woman prior to marrying Amina, the mother of the Prophet. He asked this woman why she had not insisted on marriage, and she replied that her brother, Waraqa b. Nawfal, who was a Christian and had studied the scriptures, prophesied that a prophet would

---

Jewish opponents in Medina" and therefore "made out of Abraham the most prominent figure in premohammedan religious history." For the arguments that lead to this conclusion, see R. Gottheil, "Abraham," *JE* 1:87–88. See Rudi Paret, "Ibrāhīm," *EI*² 3:980–81. In one Islamic tradition Muḥammad said, "If you want to see Abraham, then look at your companion (i.e., the Prophet)." Implied in this statement is the argument that Muḥammad considered himself as looking like Abraham (see Bukhārī, *Ṣaḥīḥ* (9 vols.; [New Delhi: Kitab Bhavan, 1987], 4:367). According to the *Sīra*, after Muḥammad's ascent to heaven "the Apostle described to his companions Abraham, Moses, and Jesus, as he saw them that night, saying: 'I have never seen a man more like myself than Abraham'" (Ibn Hishām, *Sīrat al-Nabī* [Cairo: Maktabāt al-Jumhūrīya, 1971], 183).

[51] Y. Moubarac, *Abraham dans le Coran* (Paris: Vrin, 1958), 59 (and note also 15, 25, 54–55). For Abraham as the object of divine election prior to Moses, see John Wansbrough, *The Sectarian Milieu: Content and Composition of Islamic Salvation History* (Oxford: Oxford University Press, 1978), 42, 101–2.

[52] Arthur Jeffery, *The Qur'ān As Scripture* (New York: Books for Libraries, 1980), 76–78.

[53] Ibid. Joseph Campbell has studied this theme in the cultural context of many other ancient civilizations; see his *The Masks of God* (4 vols.; repr., New York: Arkana, 1991), 3:339–50. In *The Book of Jasher* (Salt Lake City: Parry, 1973), 8:13, 17 (see J. Dan, *Sefer ha-Yashar* [Jerusalem: Mosad Bialik, 1986], 65), only Terah's son is sought for slaughter.

be born among the people.[54] In addition, a star appeared indicating the birth of the Prophet.[55]

The Ibn 'Abbās account of Abraham's birth is, of course, set in an entirely different time period than Muḥammad's, and therefore many details differ, but the general ideas of anticipation and the appearance of the star are common to both stories. Essentially, Ibn 'Abbās has integrated these aspects of the haggadic story of Abraham and reoriented them to Islam. Regarding the star, motif 1a indicates that Nimrod saw in a dream a star that outshone the sun and the moon. This is most likely a reinterpreted version of a Jewish story concerning the astrologers of Nimrod who, "when they left the house, they lifted up their eyes toward heaven to look at the stars," and "one great star came from the east and ran athwart the heavens and swallowed up the four stars at the four corners."[56] Christians, of course, also accept the appearance of a star at the birth of Christ.[57] Later Muslim commentators who do not base their report on Ibn 'Abbās have also adopted the idea of a star appearing to Nimrod in a dream before the birth of Abraham.[58] This may indicate that the star motif was a widespread

---

[54] Alfred Guillaume, *The Life of Muhammad: A Translation of Ibn Isḥāq's Sīrat Rasūl Allāh* (Oxford: Oxford University Press, 1955), 68–69. Arabic text in *Sīrat al-Nabī* (1971), 61.

[55] Ibid., 70; Arabic text in Ibn Hishām, *Sīrat al-Nabī* (1971), 166.

[56] Louis Ginzberg, *The Legends of the Jews* (7 vols; Philadelphia: Jewish Publication Society, 1909–38; repr., Baltimore: Johns Hopkins University Press, 1998), 1:207; *The Book of Jasher*, 8:10, 17 (Dan, *Sefer ha-Yashar*, 64–65). Patai and Graves similarly note that at Abraham's birth "an enormous comet coursed around the horizon from the east, and swallowed four stars each fixed in a different quarter of heaven" (Robert Graves and Raphael Patai, *Hebrew Myths: The Book of Genesis* [Garden City, N.Y.: Doubleday, 1964], 134). See also D. Sidersky, *Les origines des légendes musulmanes dans le Coran et dans les vies des prophètes* (Paris: Librairie Orientaliste Paul Geuthner, 1933), 31, and Schützinger, *Ursprung und Entwicklung*, 142, who also identify Jewish legends of a star. It should again be noted that it is not possible to determine the precise direction of influence. One scholar has observed that the material in the *qiṣaṣ* tradition "is in part borrowed from Jewish sources.... In some cases the Islamic legend of Abraham has even influenced the later Jewish tradition" (Paret, "Ibrāhīm," *EI*^{2} 3:980). Hence, there may be some Islamic influence on later Jewish tradition. However, an attempt to show direction of influence would be laborious and ultimately speculative at best; the assumption taken in this study is that, for the most part, the Jewish traditions precede the Islamic traditions. In any event, the question of direction does not pose a major problem for an Islamic typological unity.

[57] See Matt 2 and Luke 2.

[58] Baiḍāwī also notes that Nimrod sees a star in his sleep; see *Anwār al-tanzīl*, 2:432. See also Kisā'ī's version of this legend in Wheeler M. Thackston Jr., *The Tales*

part of the belief structures of both the Jews and the Christians before and after the period of Ibn 'Abbās. The Islamic adoption of the star motif anticipating Abraham's birth and connecting it with the same motif prior to Muḥammad's birth reinforces the Muslim view of Islam as a restored religion within the otherwise polluted environment of the Jews and the Christians. In essence, the star of Abraham can be viewed as a prototype of the star of Muḥammad.

Ibn 'Abbās places the birth of Abraham in a cave (see motif 4). During this period Abraham miraculously grows and receives nourishment from sucking his fingers. Jewish tradition also places Abraham in a cave at birth. In one of these traditions God opens two windows in the cave: one puts forth oil and the other a fine flour.[59] In another "Abram, lying alone in the cave without food, began to weep: but God sent the archangel Gabriel to give him milk, which flowed from the finger of his right hand—so the child was suckled."[60] The motif of a cave and miracle feedings can also be found in the Christian tradition in which angels bring sustenance to saints in need.[61] Although this tradition is not in the Qur'ān, some Muslim commentators have transmitted this tradition along with Ibn 'Abbās.[62] In

of the Prophets of al-Kisa'i (Chicago: Great Books of the Islamic World, 1997), 137; Ibn al-Athīr, 1:94; Ṭabarsī, *Majma' al-bayān fī tafsīr al-Qur'ān* (30 vols; Iran, 1983), 7:325.

59 Schützinger, *Ursprung und Entwicklung,* 143.

60 Graves and Patai, *Hebrew Myths,* 136. Ginzberg notes that Abraham sucked milk from the little finger of his right hand until he was ten days old (*Legends of the Jews,* 1:189). See also ibid., 5:210 n. 14, in which two sprouts spring up in the cave, one flowing with honey, the other with milk. See also Jellinek, *Bet ha-Midrasch,* 1:26 (Hebrew text).

61 Note *Prot. Jas.* 8:1: "And Mary was in the temple of the Lord as a dove that is nurtured: and received food from the hand of an angel" (*The Apocryphal New Testament* [trans. M. R. James; Oxford, 1924; repr., Oxford: Clarendon, 1975], 42). Perhaps the *Protoevangelium of James* provided some of the material about the childhood of Mary in Q 3:37. See also Ginzberg, *Legends of the Jews,* 5:212, n. 29. Christian tradition has also placed the birth of Jesus in a cave (*Prot. Jas.* 18:1; 19:2 [James, *Apocryphal New Testament,* 46]). See also Joseph Campbell, *The Hero with a Thousand Faces* (New York: Pantheon, 1949; repr., Princeton: Princeton University Press, 1972), 323–25.

62 Ṭabarī, of course, relates a similar account. However, instead of Abraham sucking several fingers, he sucks sustenance only out of his thumb (*Ta'rīkh,* 1:51). Kisā'ī records that the breasts of Abraham's mother flowed with milk and honey; this is in addition to Abraham having access to honey in his thumb, wine in his index finger, milk in his middle finger, cream in his ring finger, and water in his little finger (Thackston, *Tales,* 138). See also al-Maqdisī, 3:54; Baiḍāwī, 2:433;

addition, the tradition of Abraham miraculously growing in a cave can also be found in Jewish haggadic as well as in Muslim traditions.[63] No story of miraculous growth exists in the traditions surrounding Muḥammad's birth, but there is a tradition of a miraculous feeding. As the story goes, Ḥalīma, a wet nurse, goes to Mecca to look for foster children, but because of the rough ride and sleeplessness she cannot produce any milk; even the camel cannot produce milk. Upon arriving in Mecca, only the orphaned Muḥammad was available for adoption. Ḥalīma takes him, and miraculously her breasts fill with milk. Likewise, the camel is able to give milk again. Thus all are able to drink to their satisfaction.[64] Again, the miraculous feeding of Abraham, although not qur'ānic, typologically anticipates Muḥammad.

According to Ibn al-Jawzī (see motif 7), Ibn 'Abbās reports that when Abraham leaves the cave he asks his mother who his Lord is. She replies, "I am." He asks, "Who is your Lord?" She says, "Your father." He asks, "Who is my father's Lord?" She answers, "Nimrod!" Abraham asks who is Nimrod's Lord and is told to be silent. Later Abraham approaches his father Āzar and asks him the same questions and angers his father.[65] Most Islamic commentators usually insert the "Who is my Lord?" motif just prior to Abraham's seeing the heavenly bodies experience described in Q 6:76–79:

> When the night descended upon Abraham, he saw a star and exclaimed: "This is my Lord!" When the star had set down, Abraham said, "I love not those that set." But when he saw the moon rising in splendor, he exclaimed: "This is my Lord!" But when it set he said, "Unless my Lord guide me, I shall be as those who have gone astray." When he saw the sun rising in splendor, he exclaimed: "This is my Lord! This is the greatest of

---

al-Rabghūzī, *The Stories of the Prophets: Qiṣaṣ al-Anbiyā': An Eastern Turkish Version* (trans. H. E. Boeschoten and M. Vandamme; 2 vols.; Leiden: Brill, 1995), 1:94.

[63] For the Jewish traditions see Ginzberg, *Legends of the Jews*, 1:190–91; Graves and Patai, *Hebrew Myths*, 136–37. Ginzberg also argues that there are Christian traditions of this motif (*Legends of the Jews*, 5:210 n. 15). In *The Book of Jasher*, 8:36, Abraham lives in the cave for ten years (Dan, *Sefer ha-Yashar*, 67). Note that Schützinger refers to a tradition that has Abraham in a cave for three years (*Ursprung und Entwicklung*, 143). See also al-Rabghūzī, *Stories of the Prophets*, 1:94; Ibn al-Athīr, 1:95; Baiḍāwī, 2:433. For a variation on this tradition, see Kisā'ī (Thackston, *Tales*, 138), wherein it is implied that Abraham lived in the cave for four years.

[64] Ibn Hishām, *The Life of Muhammad*, 70–71; *Sīrat al-Nabī* (Beirut: Dār Rākyanī, 1965), 64–65.

[65] Tha'labī, 74. *The Book of Jasher* has Abraham and Terah holding an extended conversation about the worship of idols; see 11:16–22 (Dan, *Sefer ha-Yashar*, 75–77).

> them!" But when it set he said, "O people, I am indeed free from your (guilt) of giving partners to God. I turn my face to the One who created the heavens and the earth. And never shall I give partners to God."[66]

While this motif certainly underscores the call of Abraham by referring to this *sūra,* the call of Abraham is also parallel to a similar account in Jewish literature. According to this tradition:

> When the sun sank, and the stars came forth, he said, "These are the gods!" But the dawn came, and the stars could be seen no longer, and then he said, "I will not pay worship to these, for they are no gods." Thereupon the sun came forth, and he spoke, "This is my God, him will I extol." But again the sun set, and he said, "He is no god," and beholding the moon, he called her his god to whom he would pay Divine homage. Then the moon was obscured, and he cried out: "This, too, is no God! There is one who sets them all in motion."[67]

Another connection to this heavenly event occurs just after Gabriel visits Muḥammad for the first time. According to this tradition, Muḥammad prepares to climb a mountain and throw himself down to his death. When he is halfway up the mountain, Gabriel appears and says: "O Muḥammad! Thou art the apostle of God and I am Gabriel." Muḥammad raises his head

---

66 There is much discussion of these verses in the Muslim histories and commentaries. See Ṭabarī, *Ta'rīkh,* 1:51; idem, *Jāmi' al-bayān 'an ta'wīl al-Qur'ān* (30 vols.; Cairo: Muṣṭafī al-Bābī al-Ḥalabī, 1968), 7:247–52; Ibn Isḥāq in Gordon D. Newby, *The Making of the Last Prophet: A Reconstruction of the Earliest Biography of Muhammad* (Columbia: University of South Carolina Press, 1989), 68; Kisā'ī in Thackston, *Tales,* 138; al-Rabghūzī, *Stories of the Prophets,* 1:94–96; Ibn al-Athīr, 1:95; al-Maqdisī, 3:49–50. Baiḍāwī also records Abraham questioning his mother concerning his Lord before his call (*Anwār al-tanzīl,* 2:433). See also Qurṭubī, *al-Jāmi' al-aḥkām al-Qur'ān* (Egypt: Dār al-Kitāb al-Misriyya, 1966), 7:25–28; Ibn Kathīr, *Tafsīr,* 3:52–57; Ibn al-Jawzī, 3:55–59; Nasafī, *Tafsīr al-Qur'ān al-Jalīl* (3 vols; Cairo: al-Matba'a al-Amiriyya bi-Būlāq, 1936), 1:482; Zamakhsharī, 2:30–31; Ṭabarsī (1983), 7:322–25.

67 Ginzberg, *Legends of the Jews,* 1:189. According to Ginzberg, in another tradition Gabriel comes to Abraham after this episode and teaches him (*Legends of the Jews,* 5:210 n. 16). For variations of this event, see also *The Book of Jasher,* 9:13–19, 20; Graves and Patai, *Hebrew Myths,* 136; *Apoc. Ab.* 19:1–9 (see Charlesworth, *OTP,* 1:698–99); Sidersky, *Les origines,* 35–36. According to Haim Schwarzbaum, this episode "belongs to the cumulative pattern of folktales.... This Quranic story is also derived from Jewish sources"; cited from his *Biblical and Extra-Biblical Legends in Islamic Folk-Literature* (Walldorf-Hessen: Verlag für Orientkunde Dr. H. Vorndran, 1982), 11.

toward heaven and sees Gabriel, but when he turns his head the other way he can still see him in the heavens. Any direction he turns his head, Gabriel is there.[68] It can be argued that this particular vision is a counterpart to Abraham's. Both events operate as defining calls to monotheism, and both deal with heavenly objects (sun, stars, and moon for Abraham; Gabriel for Muḥammad). Abraham's rejection of the heavenly objects is counter-balanced by Muḥammad's acceptance of the heavenly Gabriel, but both receive reinforcement of their respective divine calls.

Ibn 'Abbās reports in motif 7 that Āzar/Terah,[69] Abraham's idolatrous father, was a manufacturer and seller of idols who also employed Abraham in his business. This is another Jewish theme[70] that provides a degree of typological anticipation of Muḥammad. Just as Abraham received resistance and persecution from someone within his family, so also did Muḥammad receive persecution in the form of harassment by the Quraysh. Two other themes (motifs 9 and 11) that typify Muḥammad also present themselves during this period of Abraham's life, according to Ibn 'Abbās: the breaking of the idol gods and the encounter with Nimrod. It will be recalled that in motif 7, while in his father's employ, Abraham would often ask people why they would buy a god that cannot hear, see, or move and thus arouses the suspicions of the people. One day as the people leave to go to a feast, Abraham feigns a sickness in order to stay back, goes to the "hall of the gods," and with an axe destroys all of the idol gods except the largest one. Abraham then places the axe in the hands of the largest god.

---

68 Ibn Hishām, *The Life of Muhammad*, 106. See also *Sīrat* (1965), 102.

69 For discussion of the name Āzar/Terah among Muslims, see Ṭabarī, *Jāmi'*, 7:242–244, who seems to examine most aspects of both names. See also Nasafī, 1:481, who argues that Āzar is a surname. Ibn Kathīr says Āzar means "the idol" (*Tafsīr*, 3:53). Zamakhsharī proposes that Āzar was the name of an idol (*Kashshāf*, 2:29–30). See also Baiḍāwī, 2:430; Qurṭubī, 2:22–23; Ibn al-Jawzī, 3:54–55.

70 See Schützinger, *Ursprung und Entwicklung*, 141. Muslim sources suggest that on the day of resurrection Āzar will unsuccessfully seek forgiveness from God. See al-Kinānī, *Kitāb al-Ḥaydah* (Damascus: n.p., 1964), 176–79. Bukhārī notes the Prophet said: "On the Day of Resurrection Abraham will meet his father Āzar, whose face will be dark and covered with dust. (The Prophet) Abraham will say (to him): 'Didn't I tell you not to disobey me?' His father will reply: 'Today I will not disobey you.' Abraham will say: 'O Lord! You promised me not to disgrace me on the Day of Resurrection; and what will be more disgraceful to me than cursing and dishonoring my father?' Then God will say (to him): 'I have forbidden Paradise for the disbelievers.' Then he will be addressed: 'O Abraham! Look! What is beneath your feet?' He will look and there he will see … (an animal), blood stained, which will be caught by the legs and thrown in (hell) fire." Āzar here is turned into an animal and thrown into hell (*Ṣaḥīḥ*, 4:365).

When the people return and see the gods destroyed, they become concerned and question Abraham. Abraham says, "The biggest one did it" and almost convinces the people of the error of worshiping these man-made idols. However, Nimrod, who plays the chief adversary of Abraham, has the people build a large fire, erect a catapult, and toss Abraham into the fire. Abraham is not harmed by the fire but remains in it for seven days and is kept company by the angel Gabriel.[71] Both the idol-smashing and Nimrod themes are well founded in Jewish literature,[72] and it is moreover commented upon by many Muslims as this motif is also in the Qur'ān.[73] However, as Abraham Geiger observed, the Jewish legend has the dialogue and destruction of the idols occur only between Abraham and his father, whereas the Ibn 'Abbās account situates the encounter between Abraham and Nimrod and his people. According to Geiger, this can be "explained by the fact that Abraham is intended to be a type of Muhammad, and so it is necessary that he should be represented as a public preacher."[74] It can also be argued that Muḥammad dealt with both the idolatry and Nimrod motifs. Ibn Iṣhāq in *The Life of Muhammad* notes that idolatry was also pervasive prior to and during the time of the Prophet.[75] In addition, he also develops a Nimrod-type arch rival to Muḥammad in the person of Abu Jahl, who constantly attempts to thwart Muḥammad at every

---

71 Tha'labī, *Qiṣaṣ*, 52–54.

72 For the idol-smashing and Nimrod motifs, see Sidersky, *Les origines*, 36–38; Schützinger, *Ursprung und Entwicklung*, 145–50, 152–54; Ginzberg, *Legends of the Jews*, 1:197–203, 5:212 n. 33, 5:215 n. 40; Graves and Patai, *Hebrew Myths*, 140–42; *The Book of Jasher*, chs. 11–12 (pp. 24–33); *Apoc. Ab.* 1–3 (*apud* Charlesworth, *OTP*, 1:689–90). According to Schwarzbaum, "the satirical vein exhibited in the story is derived from Talmudic-Midrashic sources, where it is also emphasized that Abraham placed in the hand of the biggest idol a hatchet" (*Biblical and Extra-Biblical Legends*, 11).

73 Q 21:68–69. The idolatry motif in the story of Abraham is discussed extensively among Muslims. See al-Rabghūzī, 1:96–99; Kisā'ī in Thackston, *Tales*, 140–41, 146–47; Ibn Isḥāq in Newby, *Last Prophet*, 68–69. See also Ṭabarī, *Ta'rīkh* (Brinner, 1:52–57); idem, *Jāmi'*, 7:242–244; Ibn Kathīr, *Tafsīr*, 3:53; Baiḍāwī, 2:430; Zamakhsharī, 2:29–30; Ṭabarsī, (1983), 7:321–22; Ibn al-Jawzī, 3:54; Qurṭubī, 7:22–23; Ibn al-Athīr, 1:96. Nimrod and the fire of Abraham is also a theme commonly treated by Muslims. See Ibn Isḥāq in Newby, *Last Prophet*, 70–71; Ṭabarī, *Ta'rīkh* (Brinner, 1:58–61); idem, *Jāmi'*, 15:43–45; al-Rabghūzī, 1:100–105; Ibn al-Athīr, 1:99–100; Baiḍāwī, 4:258–59; Zamakhsharī, 2:578; Ibn Kathīr, *Tafsīr*, 4:572–73; Nasafī, 2:409; Ṭabarsī (1983), 17:54; Qurṭubī, 11:304; Ibn al-Jawzī, 5:270.

74 Geiger, *Judaism and Islam*, 99.

75 *The Book of Idols: Being a Translation from the Arabic of the Kitāb al-Aṣnām by Hishām Ibn al-Kalbī* (trans. N. A. Faris; Princeton: Princeton University Press,

turn.[76] Muḥammad's life, therefore, has many of the same motifs that are found in the Abraham narrative.

Conclusion

Especially during the eighth to tenth centuries C.E., a lively textual interchange existed between Jews, Christians, and Muslims. Contacts between these religious groups provided the impetus to reorient biblical materials to give meaning to their particular belief structures and scriptural texts. For example, early Jewish interpreters had deduced the idolatrous world of Abraham based on comparisons of biblical passages such as Josh 24 and Gen 12. Some of the Abraham motifs that Jewish and Christian interpreters brought into biblically related texts are also alluded to in the Qur'ān. Even more of these interpretations are present in the Islamic exegetical texts of *Tafsīr*, *Ta'rīkh*, and *Qiṣaṣ al-anbiyā'*, based on reports (*ḥadīth*) stemming from early transmitters such as Ka'b al-Aḥbār and Ibn 'Abbās. However, Islamic exegetes did not just parrot Jewish or Christian themes but Islamicized them and reoriented them to anticipate Muḥammad. This created a novel body of literature quite unique in its own right and worthy of attention from scholars examining the textual interplay of Jews, Christians, and Muslims from the eighth century and beyond.

1952), 4–7. Note pp. 35–39 in Guillaume's translation of the *Sīra* for a good review of idol worship among the Arabs.

[76] Note, for example, pp. 119–20, 160–62, 177–79, 283–84 in Guillaume's translation of the *Sīra*.

The Prediction and Prefiguration of Muḥammad

Jane Dammen McAuliffe
Georgetown University

If read as documentary attestation for the thought world of nascent Islam, the Qur'ān presents us with a scripturally aware society and itself manifests a high degree of scriptural self-consciousness. It represents itself as belonging to the category of encoded divine revelation, a category constructed both chronologically and thematically.[1] Self-referential designations of its status as recitation (*qur'ān*),[2] revelation (*waḥy, tanzīl*), book (*kitāb*), and criterion or proof (*furqān*) combine with self-descriptions as "an Arabic recitation" (*qur'ānan 'arabiyyan,* Q 12:12; 20:113; 39:28; 41:3; 42:7; 43:3), "a clear recitation" (*qur'ān mubīn,* Q 15:1), "the clear book" (*al-kitāb al-mubīn,* Q 12:1; 26:2; 27:1; 28:2; 43:2; 44:2), with "verifying verses" (*āyāt bayyināt,* Q 22:16; 29:49; 57:9). Situating itself within a progressive conception of "salvation history," the Qur'ān recognizes, represents, and evaluates earlier scriptural entrants. Terms found in the Qur'ān reflect this awareness: Torah (*Tawrāt*), Gospel (*Injīl*), and Psalms (*Zabūr*)—to use the most common English translations—are presented as the revelatory heritage of other religious groups, just as the Qur'ān itself suffices "as a guidance and a mercy and a good tiding for all those who submit themselves to God" (Q 16:89, *wa-hudan wa-raḥmatan wa-bushrā lil-muslimīn*).

---

[1] Further to this see Stefan Wild, "The Self-Referentiality of the Qur'ān: Sūra 3:7 As an Exegetical Challenge," in *With Reverence for the Word: Medieval Scriptural Exegesis in Judaism, Christianity, and Islam* (ed. J. D. McAuliffe et al.; Oxford: Oxford University Press, 2003), 422–36; Angelika Neuwirth, "From the Sacred Mosque to the Remote Temple: Sūrat al-Isrā' between Text and Commentary," in McAuliffe, *With Reverence for the Word,* 376–407; and Jane Dammen McAuliffe, "Text and Textuality: Q 3:7 As a Point of Intersection," in *Literary Structures of Religious Meaning in the Qur'ān* (ed. I. J. Boullata; London: Curzon, 2000), 56–76.

[2] Transliteration of Arabic terminology follows the system of the *Encyclopaedia of the Qur'ān* (ed. J. D. McAuliffe; Leiden: Brill, 2001–), with some slight modifications.

Explicit mention of previous scriptures and the Qur'ān's own self-consciousness as a scripture offer but one aspect of a biblical-qur'ānic connection, but it is a foundational one. From it spring the many questions and concerns that have preoccupied Muslim and non-Muslim scholars, both ancient and modern. Chief among these concerns—and a prime candidate for polemical and apologetic exchange through the centuries—has been the theological dilemma posed by questions about biblical "influences" on the Qur'ān, or qur'ānic "borrowings" from the Bible.

From the position of normative Muslim teaching, the matter is quite simple. While acknowledging a connection with earlier revelations, the Qur'ān understands itself to be a direct disclosure from God to the last of God's prophets. The doctrinal mandate, then, is divine dictation, not verbal inspiration. The linguistic medium itself, Arabic, is sacralized by divine usage to such a degree that translations of the Qur'ān into other languages forfeit any status as scripture. Consequently, the "stream of revelation," as conceptualized within a Muslim perspective, is not a continuous and cumulative process. God has revealed his guidance to many messengers and prophets, but each instance is best understood as a re-presentation of the same message in a medium and a manner specifically suited to its intended recipients. Theoretically, at least, there can be no discrepancy in the content of these revelations because they all proceed from the same source. Since the human mediator of God's message is not so much a composer as a conduit and since, in the developed Islamic doctrine of prophethood, that mediator is deemed to be sinless, divergence among the received revelations could only be the result of corruption introduced by the processes of reception and transmission.

Commonalities between the Qur'ān and previous scriptures must therefore be viewed as divinely intended, not the consequence of human compositional or redactional efforts. The concerns of historical and philological criticism remain irrelevant to most Muslims.[3] Yet to speak only of the divinely sanctioned continuity of scriptural revelation does not express the full qur'ānic understanding of this process because it ignores temporal considerations. Muslims understand the Qur'ān to be not only the continuation of a long series of divine disclosures but also their culmination. As expressed in passages such as Q 46:12, the Qur'ān confirms and completes

---

[3] This statement must be qualified with reference to the work of a number of Muslim scholars who have adopted and promoted a more contextually sensitive understanding of the Qur'ān's revelations. See, e.g., Fazlur Rahman, *Major Themes of the Qur'ān* (Minneapolis: Bibliotheca Islamica, 1980), a contemporary classic, and Mohammed Arkoun's recently released *The Unthought in Contemporary Islamic Thought* (London: Saqi, 2002).

all previous revelations: "Before it was the book of Moses as a guide [*imām*] and a mercy. This is a confirming book [*kitābun muṣaddiqun*] in an Arabic tongue to warn those who do evil and good tidings for those who do good."[4] These notions of completion and confirmation are reinforced with references to Muḥammad as the "seal of the prophets" (Q 33:40).

But beyond the Muslim theological discomfort with discussions of influences and borrowings stands a deeper judgment. It would be a mistake to understand the Islamic sense of scriptural culmination as a strictly linear progression. While the Qur'ān recognizes the supersessionist claims that Christianity makes against Judaism, the Islamic tradition does not relate itself to previous "People of the Book" in precisely the same fashion. Building upon a core insight that submission to God—the basic sense of the word *islām*—is the fundamental human-divine relation, Islam is more profoundly a religion of restoration than a new dispensation. The classically developed conception of the Qur'ān as the eternal, uncreated speech of God views it as proceeding from a preexistent archetype, variously termed "the well-guarded tablet" *(al-lawḥ al-maḥfūz)* or "the mother of the book" (*umm al-kitāb*). As God's final act of revelation, the Qur'ān effectively abrogates all previous revelations or renders them otiose but does so by reclaiming, recovering, and restoring the primordial divine message.[5] An oscillation between the perfected and the primordial is a defining feature of qur'ānic self-understanding.

Given this conception of the Qur'ān's status, where do the Hebrew Bible and the New Testament stand? Or to use qur'ānic terminology, do the Tawrāt and the Injīl retain any continuing value in the eyes of Muslim believers? As I have explained at length in an earlier article, trying to answer this question surfaces an abiding tension within classical Muslim scholarship.[6] There is a long history of polemical discourse, subsumed under the technical term "alteration" (*taḥrīf*) that stresses the corrupted nature of existing versions of the Jewish and Christian scriptures. The qur'ānic grounds for these assertions can be found in a collection of verses that lodge various charges against the continuing reliability of earlier revelations. The accusations and their developed exegesis span the

---

[4] Q 46:30, "They said: O our people! We have listened to a book revealed after Mūsā verifying that which is before it, guiding to the truth and to a right path"; and Q 3:3, "They said: O our people! We have listened to a book revealed after Mūsā verifying that which is before it, guiding to the truth and to a right path."

[5] See Jane Dammen McAuliffe, "The Abrogation of Judaism and Christianity in Islam: A Christian Perspective," *Concilium* (1994/3): 154–63.

[6] See Jane Dammen McAuliffe, "The Qur'ānic Context of Muslim Biblical Scholarship," *Islam and Christian-Muslim Relations* 7 (1996): 141–58.

expanse from deliberate alteration and concealment to inadvertent confusion and neglect.

Concurrent with this discourse of distrust another scholarly trajectory evolved, that of using previous scriptures for their probative value. As will shortly be discussed, the Qur'ān contains several passages that came to be interpreted as evidence that Muḥammad's coming had been announced by earlier prophets and scriptures. These verses prompted an investigation of the biblical books to determine, if possible, the precise points of reference. In a common apologetic move, however, Muslim biblical scholarship ranged well beyond this motivating impulse and discovered other texts, such as those that could easily be construed to predict the triumph of Islam in its community and its conquests.

Despite the efforts of those medieval authors whom I would term "Muslim biblical scholars," an ambivalent attitude toward the earlier scriptures, and their narrative and exegetical elaboration, has long dominated Muslim estimations of the Bible and continues to do so. The great mass of material, eventually dubbed "Isrā'īliyyāt," that the Islamic tradition absorbed from the Banū Isrā'īl, the "Children of Israel," became an object of concern and critical assessment.[7] In a process of evolving self-definition, the Muslim scholarly community began consciously to mark narrative material as "within" or "beyond" those boundaries that it claimed for itself. Debates about the reliability of stories associated with the Jews and the Christians, whether biblical or extrabiblical, drove some Muslim scholars to question the utility of their inclusion within Islamic literature, broadly conceived, even for purposes of popular religious oratory and moral exhortation.

This brief summation of the conceptual framework within which Muslim biblical scholarship has operated and of the theological tensions that surround any assessment of the biblical-qur'ānic connection provides the context for taking a closer look at a specific scholar and a specific subject. The scholar is Abū Ja'far Muḥammad ibn Jarīr al-Ṭabarī, the medieval Qur'ān commentator and historian who set these two disciplines on their classical course, and the subject is prediction and prefiguration, topics that offer rich possibilities for this kind of cross-tradition and intertextual analysis.

Within the comparative study of religious traditions, prediction and prefiguration motifs abound. The prior, often scriptural, annunciation of prophets, founder-figures, and other such charismatic individuals is a

---

[7] See Jane Dammen McAuliffe, "Assessing the Isrā'īliyyāt: An Exegetical Conundrum," in *Story-Telling in the Framework of Non-fictional Arabic Literature* (ed. S. Leder; Wiesbaden: Harrassowitz, 1998), 345–69.

common *topos* in most of the world's literate religions. Not infrequently it forms a canonical point of connection between an earlier tradition and that which followed it. Buddhist biographical literature, for example, creates lineage links between Gautama and those who are seen as his previous embodiments or forerunners. Classical Christian biblical interpretation is replete with typological and prophetical identification. As has already been indicated, the Islamic tradition employs this *topos,* and early Muslim literature attests to its prevalence and popularity. A prominent instance may be found in the work of the tenth-century historian and exegete Abū Ja'far Muḥammad ibn Jarīr al-Ṭabarī, who treats the scriptural prediction and prefiguration of Muḥammad in both of his major works.

In the late ninth and early tenth century Abū Ja'far Muḥammad ibn Jarīr produced two of the most enduring works of medieval Islamic learning.[8] One was a complete commentary on the Qur'ān, and the other was a universal history. Both were written in Arabic, and together their most commonly available editions comprise at least fifty volumes. Al-Ṭabarī, however, was probably not an Arab. His name reflects his birth area of Ṭabaristān, and his first language was Persian. He was born in 839 in Āmul, a city near the southern shore of the Caspian Sea that now lies within the boundaries of the Iranian province of Mazandaran. As a very young child he began his education in the Qur'ān and, according to his biographers, had memorized its text by age seven, a feat not uncommon among precocious Muslim youth. Like most scholars of the medieval Islamic world, in early adulthood he began the educational forays that would carry him far distances. While Baghdād eventually became his permanent home, he is reported to have spent time in the southern Iraq cities of Baṣra and Kūfa, as well as in Palestine, Syria, and Egypt. His life in Baghdād was that of a scholar and teacher, and he concentrated his efforts and his output in four areas: traditions (*ḥadīth*), jurisprudence, qur'ānic exegesis, and history. His legal teachings, in particular, were not without controversial consequences, and the standard medieval biographies of al-Ṭabarī refer to rioting mobs who surrounded his house. He lived a full life, however, dying in 923 at the age of eighty-four.

---

[8] For a brief biographical sketch of al-Ṭabarī, see Jane Dammen McAuliffe, *Qur'ānic Christians: An Analysis of Classical and Modern Exegesis* (New York: Cambridge University Press, 1991), 38–45; and C. E. Bosworth, "al-Ṭabarī," *EI*² 10:11–15. The most extensive treatment in English of al-Ṭabarī's life and works is by Franz Rosenthal, *The History of al-Ṭabarī,* vol. 1, *General Introduction and From the Creation to the Flood* (trans. F. Rosenthal; Albany: State University of New York Press, 1989), 5–134. This can very usefully be supplemented with reference to Claude Gilliot, *Exégèse, langue, et théologie en Islam: L'exégèse coranique de Tabari (m. 310/923)* (Paris: Vrin, 1990), 19–68.

As was the practice of this period, al-Ṭabarī's writings were the result of multiple stages of production, beginning with dictated lectures that were then copied and circulated in sections. Subsequent changes and additions to these segments would eventually be collated in the final compilation of the work. With al-Ṭabarī's *Tafsīr* (commentary) and his *Ta'rīkh* (history), compilation and collation also define his operative methodology. Each is a summative archive of the most important scholarly efforts in these respective fields for the preceding two centuries. The full title of the commentary is "The Comprehensive Clarification of the Interpretation of the Verses of the Qur'ān" (*Jāmi' al-bayān 'an ta'wīl āy al-Qur'ān*), and there is textual evidence that it precedes the history, at least in its initial formulation, because it is mentioned in the latter.[9] It is a full-scale, "linked" (*musalsal*) commentary; that is, it comments upon each verse of the Qur'ān in textual succession. Al-Ṭabarī's *Jāmi' al-bayān* set the pattern and, to a considerable extent, the contents of most of the classical commentaries to follow. Several editions are still in print—it can be found in Muslim bookstores everywhere—and it remains a basic tool for any exegetical study of the Qur'ān.

Al-Ṭabarī's second major work, his universal history, commonly bears the title "The History of Messengers and Kings" (*Ta'rīkh al-rusul wa-l-mulūk*), although some manuscripts carry variations of this.[10] Just as the commentary is ordinarily referred to only as the *Tafsīr*, the ordinary Arabic word for exegesis or interpretation, the history is usually called simply the *Ta'rīkh*. Unlike the *Tafsīr*, however, the *Ta'rīkh* has recently been translated into English by a large team of scholars. Glancing through the contents pages of the thirty-nine volumes that constitute this translation is a good way to capture both the coverage and the areas of primary concentration for this work.[11] Beginning with the creation and the flood, the first six volumes of this translated edition of the *Ta'rīkh* cover such qur'ānic (and biblical) figures as Abraham, Ishmael and Isaac, Joseph, Moses, David, Solomon, and Jesus, as well as individuals and episodes from the

---

9 Muḥammad ibn Jarīr al-Ṭabarī, *Jāmi' al-bayān 'an ta'wīl āy al-Qur'ān* (ed. Maḥmūd Muḥammad Shākir et al.; Cairo: Dār al-Ma'ārif, 1374–/1954–). This richly annotated edition has never been completed and must, therefore, be supplemented with that edited by Aḥmad Sā'īd 'Alī et al. (Cairo, 1954–57; repr., Beirut: Dār al-Fikr, 1984).

10 Abū Ja'far Muḥammad ibn Jarīr al-Ṭabarī, *Ta'rīkh al-rusul wa-l-mulūk* (ed. M. J. de Goeje et al.; 15 vols.; Leiden: Brill, 1879–1901). See also the edition edited by Muḥammad Abū l-Faḍl Ibrāhīm (10 vols.; Cairo: Dār al-Ma'ārif, 1960–69).

11 Ehsan Yarshater, ed., *The History of al-Ṭabarī* (39 vols.; Albany: State University of New York Press, 1987–98).

pre-Islamic history of the Arabs, the Persians and the Byzantines. Starting with the fifth volume, however, and the life of Muḥammad, the *Ta'rīkh*'s focus contracts sharply, and subsequent volumes closely follow the unfolding fortunes of the early caliphate and the Umayyad and ʿAbbāsid dynasties.

The two works are, of course, very different genres. As just described, the *Tafsīr* is an exegetical source structured as a *musalsal* commentary, while the later *Ta'rīkh* adopts an annalistic framework commencing with the world's creation. Although in many respects these two works are incommensurate, a host of commonly held, underlying assumptions connects them both, assumptions that surface as they treat the prediction and prefiguration of Muḥammad, albeit in quite different ways.

Abraham, Moses, and Jesus Predict Muḥammad

In three well-known verses Muslims have long found their principal qur'ānic evidence for the biblical annunciation of Muḥammad .[12] Taken together these passages have provided a scriptural mandate for the forms of intellectual investigation that I have called Muslim biblical scholarship. They also present this mandate in connection with the three principal biblical prototypes to Muḥammad's prophethood, namely, Abraham, Moses and Jesus. As we look at these three verses through the lens of al-Ṭabarī's *Tafsīr*, we will do so in the order in which they emerge in the text of the Qur'ān itself. This bypasses, of course, all of the efforts made by both Muslim and non-Muslim scholars to establish the chronology of this text, but it respects the centuries-old practice of the exegetical tradition that deals sequentially with the codified structure of the Qur'ān.

Abraham steps to the fore in the first passage to be discussed, Q 2:127–129:

> When Abraham and Ishmael were raising the foundations of the House, [they prayed]
> "Our Lord, accept from us [this prayer].
> Truly you are the Hearer, the Knower. (127)
> Our Lord, make us submissive [*muslimayn*] to you and from our seed [bring forth] a community submissive [*ummatun muslimatun*] to you. Show us your places of ceremony [*manāsikanā*]. Forgive us.
> Truly you are the Forgiver, the Merciful. (128)

---

12 These are by no means the only qur'ānic loci that have motivated Muslim scholarship on the Bible. For example, Jacob Lassner has presented Ibn Isḥāq's interpretation of Q 3:81, *wa-idh akhadha llāhu mīthāqa l-nabiyyīn,* in the *Sīra* as a primordial mandate for the prophetic annunciation of Muḥammad; see his "The Covenant of the Prophets: Muslim Texts, Jewish Subtext," *AJSR* 15 (1990): 207–38.

Our Lord, send them a messenger from among them [*rasūlan minhum*] who will recite your verses/signs for them and who will teach them the book and the wisdom [*al-kitāb wa-l-ḥikma*] and who will purify them/cause them to increase.

Truly you are the Mighty, the Wise." (129)

This pericope is clearly an antiphonal prayer formula, and I have laid it out so that the alternating intercessions and doxologies can be clearly distinguished. Abraham's intercessions, which form the basic structure of these verses, embrace both present and future and include both himself and his son, as well as succeeding generations. The threefold supplication, presaged in the first verse by the request for "a community submissive to you," is replicated in al-Ṭabarī's treatment of this passage. His exegetical analysis reflects the three different parts of this prayer. It is the final part, a request for a "messenger from among them" (*rasūlan minhum*) that is particularly pertinent to the present subject. This is where the first prediction motif emerges, prompting the exegete to engage retrospectively the chronology of "salvation history" that culminated in the prophet Muḥammad. To identify the divinely requested messenger, al-Ṭabarī cites a prophetic *ḥadīth* that explicitly links his exegesis of this passage with that of the third to be discussed here, that is, Q 61:6. Two early biographers of Muḥammad, Ibn Isḥāq (d. 150/767) and Ibn Sa'd (d. 230/845), are his source. From the latter he draws, by three different chains of transmission (*isnād*), on the version that is traced to the Syrian tradent 'Irbāḍ ibn Sāriyya al-Sulamī[13] (d. ca. 75/694): "I heard the Messenger of God say, 'I was with God in the mother of the book[14] as the seal of the prophets when Adam was still imbedded/inearthed in his clay [*la-munjadilun fī ṭīnatihi*].[15] [Furthermore] I will inform you of the interpretation [*ta'wīl*] of

---

13 Muḥammad ibn Aḥmad al-Dhahabī, *Siyar a'lām al-nubalā'* (ed. Shu'ayb al-Arna'ūṭ et al.; Beirut: Mu'assasat al-Risāla, 1981–), 3:419–22. This *isnād*: 'Imrān ibn Bakkār al-Kalā'ī—Abū l-Yamān—Abū Kurayb—Ibn Abī Maryam—Sa'īd ibn Suwayd—al-'Irbāḍ ibn Sāriyya al-Sulamī.

14 Ibn Sa'd's rendition in his *Ṭabaqāt* (*Al-Ṭabaqāt al-kubrā* [ed. Iḥsān 'Abbās; Beirut: Dār Ṣadir, 1960], 1:149) varies somewhat, including the substitution here of *innī 'abdu llāhi wa-khātamu l-nabiyyīn.*

15 Ibn Manẓūr, *Lisān al-'arab* (Beirut: Dār Ṣadir, 1955–60), 11:104, gives *munjadilun* as one who falls or is thrown on the ground. He offers a variant of this *ḥadīth* (but cf. *anā khātamu l-nabiyyīna fī ummi l-kitāb* etc.) as a *locus classicus* for this word. Other versions of this in Ibn Sa'd, *Ṭabaqāt,* 1:148–59 read *idh Ādamu bayna l-rūhi wa-l-jasadi.* Uri Rubin renders it as "when Adam was still rolling in his clay" or "was still just clay." See his *The Eye of the Beholder: The Life of Muḥammad As Viewed by the Early Muslims* (Princeton: Darwin, 1995), 38; and

that: I am [the answer to] the prayer of my father Abraham, the good news [*bishāra*] of Jesus to his people, and the dream of my mother.'"[16] Another variant that Ibn Sa'd presents, but one that al-Ṭabarī does not repeat, emphasizes both the exegetical function of this *ḥadīth,* and its specific connection with Q 2:129, by cutting the Prophet's statement at Abraham, that is, dropping the mention of Jesus and following it with the citation of the verse phrase "Our Lord, send them a messenger from among them" (*rabbanā wa-bʿath fīhim rasūlan minhum*).[17]

Whereas al-Ṭabarī drew these variants from the section in Ibn Sa'd's *Ṭabaqāt* on "The Prophethood of God's Messenger," what he took from Ibn Isḥāq occurs in a quite different context. Here the setting is the narrative account in his biography of Muḥammad (*Sīra*) about the angelic cleansing of Muḥammad's heart, a setting that actually foregrounds a section of the full *ḥadīth* that al-Ṭabarī drops from his citation in the exegesis of Q 2:129.[18] In Ibn Isḥāq, and in al-Ṭabarī's analogous use of this *ḥadīth* in his *Ta'rīkh,*[19] the key phrase "I am the prayer of my father Abraham and the good news of Jesus" is followed by "And when my mother was pregnant with me, there went out from her a light which illuminated the Syrian fortresses of Buṣrā for her."[20] Beyond his use of this *ḥadīth* to identify "a messenger from among them" (*rasūlan minhum*), al-Ṭabarī does little more than provide glosses for the constituent phrases of this verse. The only point upon which he makes an exegetical adjudication is the significance of the term *ḥikma,* a word that is frequently translated as "wisdom."[21]

---

his "Pre-existence and Light: Aspects of the Concept of Nūr Muḥammad," *IOS* 5 (1975): 88, respectively.

16 Al-Ṭabarī, *Jāmiʿ al-bayān* (ed. M. Shākir), 3:83.

17 Ibn Sa'd, *Ṭabaqāt,* 1:149.

18 Al-Ṭabarī, *Jāmiʿ al-bayān* (ed. M. Shākir), 1:82. *Isnād:* Ibn Ḥumayd—Salama—Muḥammad ibn Isḥāq—Thawr ibn Yazīd—Khālid ibn Maʿdān al-Kalāʿī.

19 Al-Ṭabarī, *Ta'rīkh,* 1:979.

20 ʿAbd al-Malik ibn Hishām's recension of Muḥammad ibn Isḥāq, *Sīrat rasūl Allāh* (ed. F. Wüstenfeld; 2 vols. in 3; Göttingen: Dieterichesche Universitäts-Buchhandlung, 1858–60), 1:106, with the *isnād:* Thawr ibn Yazīd—Khālid ibn Maʿdān al-Kalāʿī. The *topos* of wombs or vaginas emitting predictive light arises in connection with subsequent figures, such as Shabīb ibn Yazīd, the Khārijī rebel (al-Ṭabarī, *Ta'rīkh,* 2:977).

21 As this is the first qur'ānic mention of the term, al-Ṭabarī groups the various views into two categories. The only citation for the first is Qatāda's (d. 118/736) identification of *ḥikma* as the *sunna.* The second group includes those who associate the term with *dīn,* specifically adherence to its *fiqh* aspect. For this al-Ṭabarī offers, on the authority of ʿAbd al-Rahmān ibn Zayd (d. 182/798), three qur'ānic references and a concluding definition of *ḥikma* as "something which God places in

The next passage, which is from the seventh *sūra,* requires some words of introduction. Q 7:157 occurs within a long narrative section on the prophet Moses, a section preceded by a series of "punishment stories" involving both biblical (Noah and Lot) and nonbiblical ('Ād, Ṣāliḥ, and Shuʿayb) figures. This qur'ānic account of Moses includes his dialogues with Pharaoh, the duel with Pharaoh's sorcerers, the plagues visited upon his people, the deliverance of the Israelites, the events at Mount Sinai, and the episode of the golden calf. The immediate context of the verse under discussion, Q 7:157, is the divine response to Moses' plea for the forgiveness of his people in the aftermath of the golden calf episode. God promises that his mercy will extend to those who fear him, who give alms, who believe in his signs, and[22]

> who follow the Messenger, the *ummī* [unlettered or "unscriptured" or gentile] prophet whom they find written with them in the Tawrāt and the Injīl; he orders them to do right and forbids them from doing wrong. He makes good things lawful for them and makes foul things prohibited to them. He rids them of their burden [*iṣr*] and the fetters [*aghlāl*] which were on them. Those who believe in him and honor and help him and follow the light which is sent down with him, those are the fortunate [*mufliḥūn*].

In a fashion similar to that of the first pericope, Q 2:127–129, this verse moves in two directions. The first and last phrases present the divine prediction of that believing community (cf. the *ummatun muslimatun* of Q 2:127–129) from whom the promised messenger will spring (*rasūlan minhum*). The inner section of this verse offers a depiction of that messenger in terms of his annunciation and identification, his defining characteristics, and his liberating actions. He is announced and identified in the Jewish and Christian scriptures (Tawrāt and Injīl). He is defined as a messenger, a prophet to the "unscriptured" (*al-nabiyya al-ummiyya*)[23] and as having

---

the heart and by which He enlightens it." Al-Ṭabarī sides with this latter, defining *ḥikma* as the knowledge of God's prescriptive and proscriptive revelations (*aḥkām*) that can only be attained through the exposition of His messenger (*Jāmi' al-bayān* [ed. M. Shākir], 3:87). On the full phrase *al-kitāb wa-l-ḥikma,* see Daniel A. Madigan, *The Qur'ān's Self-Image: Writing and Authority in Islam's Scripture* (Princeton: Princeton University Press, 2001), 93–96.

22 The syntactic connection between the two verses, which is often blurred in translation, is clearly evident in Arabic: *fa-sa'aktubuhā li-lladhīna yattaqūna wa-yu 'tūna l-zakāta wa-lladhīna hum bi-āyātinā yu'minūna* (156) *lladhīna yattabi'ūna l-rasūla l-nabiyya l-ummiyya* etc.

23 This translation represents a highly contested understanding of the Arabic phrase. Muslim translations would be "an unlettered or illiterate prophet," which

been predicted or "written" (*maktūb*) in earlier scriptures. Muḥammad's prophetic office will be exercised by (1) ordering the right and forbidding the wrong, (2) making lawful and prohibiting, and (3) ridding his community of "their burden and the fetters which were upon them." In this verse, defining characteristics are also applied to Muḥammad's community: they are identified as those who believe, honor, help, and follow the light and who, as a consequence of these states and actions, can rightly be called fortunate (*mufliḥūn*).

As he begins his commentary on Q 7:157, al-Ṭabarī makes its connection (*nasab*) with the preceding verses quite explicit. On the authority of such well-known early exegetes as Ibn 'Abbās, Sa'īd ibn Jubayr, al-Suddī, and Qatāda, he cites seven variants of a *ḥadīth* that associates mention of the "godfearing" in the immediately previous verse with the identification in this verse of the "community" (*umma*) of Muḥammad. Interestingly, however, in the midst of this catalogue, he interjects a *ḥadīth*, by three quite different chains of transmission, from Nawf al-Ḥimyarī al-Bikālī (d. ca. 95/712) a prominent Syrian source of Isrā'īliyyāt.[24] Both its placement and content make it worth quoting:

> When "Moses chose of his people seventy men"[25] for the rendezvous with his Lord, God said to Moses, "I will make the earth a place of worship [*masjid*] for you and a means of cleansing [*ṭahūr*].[26] I will place the Sakīna with you in your houses. I will make you [able to] recite the Tawrāt from memory [*'an ẓahri qulūbikum*]. Man and woman, freeborn and slave, young and old will recite it." Moses said to his people, "Truly God will make for you the earth clean and a place of worship." They said, "We want to pray only in churches [*kanā'is*]." Moses said, "He will place the

---

forms the basis of a theological assertion mentioned earlier that is fundamental to the Muslim attitude to the Bible, i.e., that Muḥammad's knowledge of earlier prophets and peoples and of their scriptures was the result of divine revelation rather than his literate acquaintance with these texts. For the connection of this term with Gen 17:20 and other biblical *goy* passages, see Rubin, *Eye of the Beholder*, 22–30, which cites earlier scholarship on this phrase. Sebastian Günther seeks to harmonize competing interpretations of *al-nabiyya al-ummiyya* by reading it as an indication of both "the 'origin' (national-Arab) and the 'originality' of the Prophet of Islam—who was not influenced, taught or pre-educated by reading any previous sacred scripture"; quoted from his article "Illiteracy," *EncQur* 2:499.

[24] Nawf al-Ḥimyarī, who is traditionally identified as the son of Ka'b al-Aḥbār's wife, was a transmitter of *ḥadīth* and popular narrative (*qāṣṣ*). See Khayr al-Dīn al-Ziriklī, *A'lām* (Beirut: Dār al-'Ilm lil-Malāyīn, 1992), 8:54.

[25] Q 7:155.

[26] There are only two qur'ānic instances of *ṭahūr*: Q 25:48 and Q 76:21. This term can also refer to the use of dust as an ablution agent.

> Sakīna with you in your houses." The people replied, "We only want it to be as it was in the Ark [*al-tābūt*]." He said, "He will make you [able to] recite the Tawrāt from memory. Man and woman, freeborn and slave, young and old will [be able to] recite it." They said, "We only want to recite it looking at it." So God said, "I will ordain it for those who are god-fearing, etc. They are the *mufliḥūn*."[27]

When faced with the phrase "whom they find written near them in the Tawrāt and the Injīl" (*alladhī yajidūnahu maktūban 'indahum fī l-tawrāti wa-l-injīl*), al-Ṭabarī presents a well-known description on the immediate authority of 'Abdallāh ibn 'Amr al-'Āṣ (d. ca. 42/663), as transmitted by 'Aṭā' ibn Yasār (d. 103/722), with secondary attestation from Ka'b al-Aḥbār (d. ca. 32/652–53).[28] Several variations of this may be found in the section of Ibn Sa'd's *Ṭabaqāt* entitled "The Description [*ṣifa*] of God's Messenger in the Torah and the Gospel."[29] Commencing with a qur'ānic description, a quote from Q 33:45—"O Prophet, truly We have sent you as a witness, an announcer of good tidings and a warner"—al-Ṭabarī's account continues:

> In the Tawrāt it is, "O Prophet, We have sent you as a witness, an announcer of good tidings and a warner and as a refuge [*ḥirz*] for the *ummiyyīn*.[30] You are My servant and My messenger. I have called you *al-mutawakkil* [i.e., the one who trusts in God]. He is not crude, nor uncouth, nor clamorous in the markets; (one who) does not repay evil with evil but forgives and pardons. We will not grasp him (in death) until through him We make the crooked religion [*milla*] straight, so that they say 'There is no god but God.' By him We will open hardened hearts [*qulūban ghulfan*], deaf ears [*ādhānan ṣumman*] and blind eyes [*a'yunan 'umyan*]."

'Aṭā' continues: "Then I met Ka'b [al-Aḥbār] and I asked him about that. The two (accounts) did not disagree by so much as a letter except that Ka'b spoke in his dialect '*qulūban ghulūfīyan, ādhān ṣumūmīyan,* and *a'yun 'umūmīyan.*'"[31] Both Hava Lazarus-Yafeh and Uri Rubin, following Josef

---

27 Al-Ṭabarī, *Jāmi' al-bayān* (ed. M. Shākir), 13:161–62.

28 A Yemenī Jewish convert to Islam who is frequently cited as a source of Jewish lore.

29 Ibn Sa'd, *Ṭabaqāt,* 1:360–63.

30 See n. 23 above.

31 Al-Ṭabarī, *Jāmi' al-bayān* (ed. M. Shākir), 13:164–65. The *sīra* recension of Ibn Bukayr provides a variant of this, also attributed to Ka'b, and another on the authority of 'Ā'isha, which situate the description not in the Tawrāt but the Injīl. Both may be found in the section on the conversion of Abū Dharr; see Muḥammad ibn Isḥāq, *Kitāb al-siyar wa-l-maghāzī* (ed. Suhayl Zakkar; Beirut: Dār al-Fikr, 1398/1978), 141–42. An unidentified fragment (*laysa bi-faẓẓin wa-lā ghalīẓ*)

Horovitz,[32] have recently found here an echo of the Servant Songs in Second Isaiah, particularly Isa 42:2.[33]

While the phrase "He makes good things lawful for them and makes foul things prohibited to them" prompts nothing more than the expected reference to dietary permissions and proscriptions, the mention of "burden" (*iṣr*) and "fetters" (*aghlāl*) elicits a direct exegetical judgment from al-Ṭabarī.[34] The issue here is whether the "burden" should be construed as God's covenant (*'ahd* and *mīthāq*) with the Banū Isrā'īl, as expressed in the Torah injunctions, or as a general harshness and strictness (*tashdīd*) in Jewish religious life.[35] (Incidentally, one of the *ḥadīth* brought in support of the first view contains al-Ṭabarī's only mention of the Injīl in reference to this passage.) Al-Ṭabarī's adjudication is actually a harmonization of these two glosses.

The third text to be discussed, Q 61:6, brings these prediction passages forward in time to Jesus, a figure viewed by Muslim sources as the penultimate prophet before Muḥammad. In this passage from the sixty-first *sūra* (*sūrat al-ṣaff*) can be found a frequently cited instance of both scriptural

---

appears—this time in connection with Q 61:6—in Abū Rifā'a 'Umāra ibn Wathīma al-Fārisī's (d. 289/902) *Kitāb bad' al-khalq wa-qiṣaṣ al-anbiyā'*; see R. G. Khoury, *Les légendes prophétiques dans l'Islam depuis le Ier jusqu'au IIIe siècle de l'Hégire* (Wiesbaden: Harrassowitz, 1978), 330 [Arabic text].

32 *EI*[1], *s.v.* Tawrāt.

33 "Not crying out, not shouting, not making his voice heard in the street." Further in the same chapter of Isaiah occur references to blind eyes and to deaf ears. See Hava Lazarus-Yafeh, *Intertwined Worlds: Medieval Islam and Bible Criticism* (Princeton: Princeton University Press, 1992), 78; see also her mention (p. 109) of Abū Nu'aym al-Iṣfahānī's citation of Isa 42:7 in his *Dalā'il al-nubuwwa.* Note also Rubin, *Eye of the Beholder*, 30.

34 The commentaries on this verse generate a catalogue of prescriptions and proscriptions that cluster largely around the categories of forbidden/permitted food and of pure/impure status. See al-Ṭabarī, *Jāmi' al-bayān* (ed. M. Shākir), 13:166–68; al-Qummī, *Tafsīr al-Qummī* (Qumm: Mu'assasat Dār al-Kitāb lil-Ṭibā'a wa-l-Nashr, 1984), 2:242; al-Ṭūsī, *al-Tibyān fī tafsīr al-Qur'ān* (Beirut: Dār Iḥyā' al-Turāth al-ʿArabī, n.d.), 4:560; al-Zamakhsharī, *al-Kashshāf 'an ḥaqā'iq al-tanzīl* (Cairo: al-Bābī al-Ḥalabī, 1977), 2:139; Ibn al-'Arabī, *Aḥkām al-Qur'ān* (Beirut: Dār al-Fikr, 1988), 2:795; Ibn al-Jawzī, *Zād al-masīr fī 'ilm al-tafsīr* (Beirut: al-Maktab al-Islāmī, 1984), 3:274; Fakhr al-Dīn al-Rāzī, *al-Tafsīr al-kabīr* (Beirut: Dār al-Fikr, 1981), 8:27; al-Qurṭubī, *al-Jāmi' li-aḥkām al-Qur'ān* (Beirut: Dār al-Kutub al-'Ilmiyya, 1987), 7:300.

35 See also Q 2:286 and 3:81, which carry the same lexical ambiguity, and Ibn Isḥāq's incorporation of the latter (*Sīra* 1:150 [Alfred Guillaume, *The Life of Muhammad: A Translation of Ibn Isḥāq's Sīrat Rasūl Allāh* (Oxford: Oxford University Press, 1955), 104]).

confirmation and predication. Jesus functions as a pivotal link between the revelation to the Jews and that which will supersede his own:

> When Jesus, son of Mary, said, "O Banū Isrā'īl, I am the messenger of God to you, the one who confirms the Tawrāt which is before me [*bayna yadayya*][36] and the one who announces a messenger who comes after me, whose name is Aḥmad/more praiseworthy."[37] When he brought them clarifications they said, "This is an evident magic."

Q 33:45, which conveys a divine announcement of Muḥammad ("truly We have sent you as a witness, an announcer of good tidings and a warner"[38]), echoes the functions as messenger, confirmer, and announcer that Jesus performs in the present verse, further underscoring the connection between Muḥammad and Jesus.

Al-Ṭabarī's exegesis of this verse is very brief. His only citation repeats the variant of a transmission from 'Irbāḍ ibn Sāriyya that he used in the exegesis of Q 2:129, but adding the section that his *Ta'rīkh* includes in its account of the angelic cleansing of Muḥammad's heart: "Thus do the mothers of prophets dream. Truly she saw at the time when she bore me that a light went out from her by which the fortresses of Syria were illuminated for her."[39] It is more interesting, however, to note what al-Ṭabarī does not mention here. Noticeably lacking is any reference to the so-called "paraclete" passages of the Gospel of John that were eventually to occupy a prominent position in the exegesis of this verse, especially in the polemical literature.

References to Jesus in the *Ta'rīkh*

With al-Ṭabarī's *Tafsīr* treatment of these three qur'ānic prediction passages in mind, it will be instructive to turn now to his *Ta'rīkh* and ask

---

36 Some classical commentators have captured this stance of Jesus simultaneously facing the Torah and announcing the advent of a future prophet in a gloss that has Jesus stating emphatically that his religion entails belief in all the books and prophets of God, both those that preceded him and those that came after. Note al-Zamakhsharī, *Kashshāf*, 6:109, and repeated in al-Rāzī, *al-Tafsīr al-kabīr*, 29:314; see also al-Ṭūsī, *Tibyān*, 9:593.

37 Muslim commentaries unequivocally identify this as a reference to Muḥammad based on the root structure common to these two names. Further to this, see McAuliffe, "Qur'ānic Context," 151.

38 *innā arsalnāka shāhidan wa-mubashshiran wa-nadhīran.*

39 Al-Ṭabarī, *Jāmi' al-bayān*, 28:87. Since the connection here is not, of course, with Abraham's prayer but with Jesus' designation as *mubashshir*, it is difficult to understand why al-Ṭabarī chose to include the full version of this *ḥadīth* rather than the truncated one that he previously used.

how the notions of prediction and prefiguration operate within the quite different structure and orientation of that work. The whole spectrum of prophets and patriarchs depicted in al-Ṭabarī's *Ta'rīkh* are potential targets for such analysis, but I will concentrate on the penultimate prophet before Muḥammad, 'Īsā ibn Maryam, namely, Jesus.

In the *Ta'rīkh*, al-Ṭabarī's first mention of Jesus occurs long before the section devoted specifically to him. It occurs in this author's introductory reflection on the total span of world time, a decidedly chronological context. He contrasts the prophetic declaration transmitted on the authority of Ibn 'Abbās that the world's total duration is seven thousand years, of which about 6,500 have lapsed, with Jewish, Christian, and Zoroastrian estimates.[40] In counting from Adam to the *hijra*, the Jews calculate 4,642 years "according to what is clearly stated in their Torah, the one which is in their hands today."[41] The Christians, however, "according to their view of the sequence in the Torah that they possess," put the figure at 5,992 years and some months.[42] F. Rosenthal notes that "the source for al-Ṭabarī's figures remains to be found."[43] In al-Ṭabarī's estimation, the discrepancy of 1,350 years results from the Jewish refusal to include Jesus in their prophet list calculations.[44] He repeats the computations in abbreviated form at the conclusion of his treatment of Sasanian history.[45] These initial and concluding reflections on the total time spans provide a frame for his consideration of pre-Islamic material and a fulfillment prelude to the Prophet's biography.

What is interesting about this first mention of Jesus is that it occurs in combination with the interrelated issues of the textual accuracy of prior scriptures and their predictive function. Al-Ṭabarī's interjectory references to the Jewish source as "the Torah which is in their hands *today*" and "to the Torah that they (i.e. the Christians) possess" are allusions to the polemical charge of *taḥrīf*, the accusation mentioned earlier that the

---

[40] Al-Ṭabarī, *Ta'rīkh*, 1:8–18.

[41] *wa-dhālika l-tawrātu llatī hiya fī aydīhim al-yawma* (al-Ṭabarī, *Ta'rīkh*, 1:16; *History* [trans. Rosenthal], 1:185).

[42] *mā 'indahum fī l-tawrāti llatī hiya fī aydīhim* (al-Ṭabarī, *Ta'rīkh*, 1:16; *History* [trans. Rosenthal], 1:185).

[43] Rosenthal, *History*, 1:184 n. 147.

[44] Al-Ṭabarī, *Ta'rīkh*, 1:16–17.

[45] Al-Ṭabarī, *Ta'rīkh*, 1:1067–68. While the Jewish and Christian figures are the same, that attributed to the Magians is different. In the earlier account the figure is 3,139, while here it is 4,182 plus ten months and nineteen days. This includes the time between the *hijra* and the death of Yazdagard, which is noted as thirty years, two months, and fifteen days.

original revelation to Moses has been deliberately or inadvertently corrupted. In his later repetition of these figures, al-Ṭabarī designates the Jewish and Christian sources as *al-Tawrāt al-ṣūra* and *al-Tawrāt al-yū nāniyya*[46] respectively, another possible allusion to textual multiplicity and thus corruption. Yet his explanation of the chronological discrepancy between the Christians and the Jews (which is not offered with the second set of references) depends upon his acknowledging the Jewish expectation of one whose "description and the time of his being sent are firmly established in the Tawrāt" (*idh kānat ṣifatuhu wa-waqtu mab'athihi muthbatatan fī l-tawrāti*), an explanation that accepts the possibility of reliable scriptural prediction.[47]

Aside from the actual chapter on his life, most subsequent mentions of the figure of Jesus in the pre-Muḥammad section of the *Ta'rīkh* serve a chronological or identification function. For al-Ṭabarī, Jesus functions principally as a time marker or a point of placement. For example, pre-Islamic world history is divided into time periods that conclude with the interval from the mission of Jesus to the sending of the Messenger of God.[48] Or Moses is counted as the first prophet of the Israelites and Jesus as the last.[49] Or God sent Isaiah to King Zedekiah (*sic*) before "the time of Jesus, Zechariah, and John the Baptist."[50] Or the "Companions of the Cave" (*aṣḥāb al-kahf*) are identified as followers of the faith of Jesus.[51] Only three mentions provide nonchronological or nonplacement information. Two credit Jesus with reviving the dead,[52] and a third mentions him as one of the four who spoke in infancy.[53]

---

[46] Al-Ṭabarī, *Ta'rīkh*, 1:1068. The Leiden editor notes the former as Syriac for *universus bibliorum textus.*

[47] Al-Ṭabarī, *Ta'rīkh*, 1:16; *History* (trans. Rosenthal), 1:185.

[48] Al-Ṭabarī, *Ta'rīkh*, 1:200–201. For further chronological marking see 1:703–4, 705–13, 741–44.

[49] Al-Ṭabarī, *Ta'rīkh*, 1:528.

[50] Al-Ṭabarī, *Ta'rīkh*, 1:638.

[51] Al-Ṭabarī, *Ta'rīkh*, 1:777–79. For additional use of Jesus as a point of identification, see 1:762, 791.

[52] Al-Ṭabarī, *Ta'rīkh*, 1:187–88 records the story, on the authority of Ibn 'Abbās, of Jesus' revivification of Noah's son Ham for the edification of his apostles; ibid. 1:538 gives ʿUmar ibn al-Khaṭṭāb's response to some Jewish assertions about Ezekiel's bringing the dead back to life: "We do not find Ezekiel in our book, and no one but 'Īsā ibn Maryam revived the dead by God's permission."

[53] Al-Ṭabarī, *Ta'rīkh*, 1:383; *History* (trans. Brinner), 2:158: "There were four who spoke when they were small, and they were the son of the Pharaoh's daughter Māshaṭa, the witness of Joseph, the companion of Jurayj, and Jesus, the son of Mary."

THE BIOGRAPHICAL CONNECTIONS

Just as Jewish and Christian influence on the Qur'ān has long been a subject of study,[54] it has often been suggested that the classical biographical material on Muḥammad was shaped by Jewish and Christian precedents.[55] Proposed models of transmission vary but generally include some assumption about the filtering function of generations of early storytellers (*quṣṣāṣ*). Al-Ṭabarī's text itself prompts a comparative reading of his biographies of Jesus and Muḥammad. At least twice he calls attention to Jesus' status as the last Israelite prophet before the interval preceding the coming of Muḥammad.[56] This allusion to the so-called *fatra* is reinforced by the pre-Muḥammadan ruler lists that record the tally "from the elevating of the Messiah to the time of the prophet Muḥammad."[57] The chronological segmentation noted earlier provides further evidence that al-Ṭabarī builds toward the biography of Muḥammad by delineating a series of discrete stages, with that of Jesus as the penultimate.[58]

This penultimate presentation, the *Ta'rīkh*'s account of Jesus and his mother Mary, occupies less than eighteen pages of the standard Leiden edition. Al-Ṭabarī's first step, following the pattern established with his previous prophet biographies, is to set forth the lineage. As with his treatment of Moses, he provides two genealogical accounts for Jesus. Much of the subsequent material, reflecting the qur'ānic emphases in its portrayal

---

[54] Some influential contributions are Abraham Geiger, *Was hat Muhammed aus dem Judentum aufgenommen?* (Bonn: Baaden, 1833); Richard Bell, *The Origin of Islam in Its Christian Environment* (London: Macmillan, 1926); Karl Ahrens, *Muhammad als Religionsstifter* (Leipzig: Brockhaus, 1935); H. Speyer, *Die biblischen Erzählungen im Qoran* (Hildesheim: Olms, 1961). For additional bibliographical assessment, see Erwin Gräf, "Zu den christlichen Einflüssen im Koran," in *Al-Bāḥit: Festschrift Joseph Henninger* (St. Augustin bei Bonn: Verlag des Anthropos-Instituts, 1976), 111–44; Tryggve Kronholm, "Dependence and Prophetic Originality in the Koran," *Orientalia Suecana* 31–32 (1982–83): 47–70; and the essay by Reuven Firestone in the present volume.

[55] Examples include Rudolf Sellheim, "Prophet, Chalif und Geschichte," *Oriens* 18–19 (1965–66): 33–91; F. E. Peters, "The Quest of the Historical Muhammad," *International Journal of Middle East Studies* 23 (1991): 291–315; and especially Rubin, *Eye of the Beholder*.

[56] Al-Ṭabarī, *Ta'rīkh*, 1:353, 528.

[57] Al-Ṭabarī, *Ta'rīkh*, 1:741, 744.

[58] Al-Ṭabarī, *Ta'rīkh*, 1:200–201, with the last era marked as "from the dispatch of Jesus to the sending of Muḥammad," and ibid. 1:1069–72, which repeats in abbreviated form the earlier world duration calculations and collects transmitted accounts (*akhbār*) that calculate the eras from Adam to Muḥammad.

of Jesus, then treats the birth events and childhood of Jesus. His role as scriptural conveyor is touched only in the most oblique fashion, a self-annunciation from the cradle that "God had given him the book" (*kitāb*).[59] There is no explicit mention of the Injīl.[60]

To create this account, al-Ṭabarī has taken a narrative segment from Wahb ibn Munabbih (d. ca. 110/728) with a bifurcated chain of transmission and interjected a second strand from Ibn Mas'ūd (d. 32/652–53) and "one of the Prophet's companions." Postresurrection material, chiefly from Ibn Isḥāq, concludes the presentation. While the individual episodes that make up this constructed narration are not without interest—and have been the subject of various source-critical searches—of equal significance is the way this entire account is framed. The immediately preceding context is the story of John the Baptist, which al-Ṭabarī introduces by tracing the lineages of both Jesus and John. These pages also fulfill his promise (which al-Ṭabarī made almost four hundred pages earlier in the Leiden edition when concluding his depiction of Abraham) to mention the reason for the vanishing of prophecy from among the Banū Isrā'īl.[61]

He then fulfills this intratextual promise in the pages that immediately precede the Jesus story, that is, those that recount the death of John the Baptist. After the slaying of John, the Israelites suffer a violent siege and blood boils in the temple until they finally admit that they have killed their prophet, one whose foretelling and guidance they have chosen to ignore.[62] Although al-Ṭabarī cites authorities who place the death of John both

---

59 Al-Ṭabarī, *Ta'rīkh*, 1:734. For a convenient summary of the parallel material on Jesus' birth, infancy, and childhood miracles that can be found in the apocryphal gospels, see W. M. Thackston's final note to his translation of al-Kisā'ī's *Qiṣaṣ al-anbiyā': The Tales of the Prophets* (Boston: Twayne, 1978), 354–60.

60 Scriptural association is given greater prominence in later hagiographical material. For example, al-Tha'labī (d. 427/1035) recounts that Jesus used to recite both the Torah and Gospel from memory because, as per *sūrat al-mā'ida* (Q 5:110), God taught him to do so (*'Arā'is al-majālis* [Cairo: Dār Iḥyā' al-Kutub al-'Arabiyya, 1960], 352).

61 Al-Ṭabarī, *Ta'rīkh*, 1:353; *History* (trans. Brinner), 2:133. As he concludes his depiction of Abraham, al-Ṭabarī states: "Prophecy and kingship continued in an unbroken succession in Syria and its environs among the children of Israel son of Isaac, until those things vanished from among them with the coming of the Persians and Byzantines after John son of Zacharias and after Jesus son of Mary. When we reach the story of John and Jesus, God willing, we will mention the reason for the vanishing of prophecy from among them."

62 For the rabbinic background to this and its connection with Nebuchadnezzar's destruction of the First Temple, see D. Sidersky, *Les origines des légendes musulmans* (Paris: Geuthner, 1933), 139–40.

before and after the ascension of Jesus, a later reference to the *fatra* firmly situates that interval between Jesus and Muḥammad only.[63] Al-Ṭabarī thus leads into the story of Jesus with a double play on the prediction and prefiguration motif. John's story embodies it, and al-Ṭabarī's own textual strategy highlights its importance.

The concluding frame for the *Ta'rīkh*'s biography of Jesus presents what can be called a prelude chronology as al-Ṭabarī lists the rulers who reigned between Jesus' ascension and the coming of Muḥammad and computes the time between the ascension and the *hijra* as 585 years and some months.[64]

Once again, following his previous practice, al-Ṭabarī introduces Muḥammad's biography with a prolonged consideration of lineage, a far lengthier treatment than that accorded to Jesus. Within this lineage examination he deals explicitly with the testimony of previous scriptures. At the point of tracing 'Adnān's descent from Ismā'īl, Ibrāhīm, and Ādam, al-Ṭabarī cites a genealogy from Ibn Sa'd on the authority of Hishām ibn Muḥammad al-Kalbī[65] (d. ca. 206/822). The latter found confirmation in the testimony of an educated Jewish convert from Palmyra who affirmed that his lineage list was well known among the learned Jews (*aḥbār*) of the People of the Book (*ahl al-kitāb*) and fixed in their writings (*muthbatun fī asfārihim*). Any discrepancies, he observes, may be the consequence of the names having been translated from the Hebrew.[66] The single longest genealogy that al-Ṭabarī cites is his concluding submission, one that was dictated to him by "a certain genealogist" (*ba'ḍ al-nussāb*) who had collated his Arab sources with those of the *ahl al-kitāb,* finding agreement in the number of names on this list but difference in their wording.[67]

---

63 Al-Ṭabarī, *Ta'rīkh*, 1:778.

64 Al-Ṭabarī, *Ta'rīkh*, 1:741–44.

65 *EI*^{2} *s.v.* al-Kalbī; Sezgin, *GAS* 1:34. In some sources ancestors in the genealogies are credited with predictions of Muḥammad that draw upon Jewish and Christian sources. For those attributed to Ka'b ibn Lu'ayy, see al-Ya'qūbī, *Ta'rīkh* (Beirut: Dār Ṣadir, 1379/1960), 1:236; al-Balādhurī, *Ansāb al-ashrāf* (ed. Muḥammad Ḥamidullāh; Cairo: Ma'had al-Makhṭūṭāt bi-Jāmi'at al-Duwal al-'Arabiyya, 1959), 1:41.

66 *li-anna hādhihi l-asmā'a turjimat min al-'ibrāniyya* (al-Ṭabarī, *Ta'rīkh*, 1:115–16; Ibn Sa'd, *Ṭabaqāt*, 1:57). Geo Widengren has done comparative analysis of narrative construction in Ibn Sa'd, Ibn Isḥāq, and al-Ṭabarī in his "Oral Tradition and Written Literature among the Hebrews in the Light of Arabic Evidence, with Special Regard to Prose Narratives," *AcOr* 23 (1959): 244–62.

67 *fa-wajada l-'adada muttafiqan wa-l-lafẓa mukhtalifan* (al-Ṭabarī, *Ta'rīkh*, 1:1118).

Muḥammad himself then steps onto the pages of the chronicle with the scene in which he is recognized and announced by the Christian monk Baḥīrā, a scene of which al-Ṭabarī provides two renditions. These are interesting for their echoes of the infancy narratives associated with Jesus, such as mention of miraculous trees and of journeys forced by fear of death.[68] Although this episode with the Christian monk would seem an obvious place to cite the qur'ānic prediction passages, al-Ṭabarī does not explicitly do so. Arguably, however, allusions to them can be found in the references to a book passed from generation to generation (*'an kitābin fīmā yaz'umūna yatawāthарūnahu kābiran 'an kābirin*)[69] and to Baḥīrā's fear that the Jews or the Byzantines could recognize Muḥammad by his description and kill him.[70] In fact, the phrase that occurs repeatedly, "with them in their pages (of scripture)" (*'indahu min ṣifatihi*),[71] echoes the most common gloss for the phrase "written with them in the Torah and the Gospel" (*maktūban 'indahum fī l-tawrāti wa-l-injīl*) in Q 7:157.[72] In the short section devoted specifically to predictions of Muḥammad's coming, there is a louder echo. The words *wa-smuhu aḥmad*, the key phrase in Q 61:6, emerge in the midst of a description by the monotheist (*ḥanīf*) Zayd ibn 'Amr ibn Nufayl.[73]

More generally, the thematic parallels between the two biographies are unmistakable. Among the most noteworthy I would include—in addition to the lineage attention—the following: (1) the sacrificial vow made by Muḥammad's grandfather and his cultic service and the temple service of Mary's guardian Zechariah and of Mary and Joseph; (2) the miracles associated with the conceptions of Jesus and of Muḥammad; (3) the visitation

---

68 Dates fall in the winter to nourish Mary's winter birth; trees bend to shade the youthful Muḥammad; God sends Mary and Joseph to Egypt; Baḥīrā pleads with Abū Ṭālib to get Muḥammad away from (1) the Jews and (2) the Byzantine scouts.

69 Al-Ṭabarī, *Ta'rīkh*, 1:1124.

70 *fa-inna l-rūm in ra'awhu 'arafūhu bi-l-ṣifati fa-qatalūhu* (al-Ṭabarī, *Ta'rīkh*, 1:1126).

71 *wa-yanuru ilā ashyā'a min jasadihi qad kāna yajiduhā 'indahu min ṣifatihi; fa-yajiduhā bi-khayran muwāfiqatan limā 'indahu min ṣifatihi* (al-Ṭabarī, *Ta'rīkh*, 1:1124).

72 Al-Ṭabarī, *Jāmi' al-bayān* (ed. Shākir), 13:164: *akhbirnī 'an ṣifati rasūli llāh. innahu la mawṣūfun fī l-tawrāti ka-ṣifatihi fī l-qur'ān. Isnād:* Ibn al-Muthannā—'Uthmān ibn 'Umar—Fulayḥ—Hilāl ibn 'Alī—'Aṭā' ibn Yasār. But cf. ibid. 13:165: Bishr—Yazīd—Sa'īd—Qatāda, with *na'tihi*.

73 Further to Zayd, see Ibn Isḥāq, *Sīra*, 1:143–49. The *sīra* recension of Ibn Bukayr explicitly cites both Q 7:157 and Q 61:6 in the section on predictions rendered by the Jews and Christians (*Kitāb al-siyar wa-l-maghāzī*, 83).

and recognition scenes of Elizabeth and Baḥīrā, respectively; and (4) episodes of messengers and magi seeking a prophet. Additionally, but beyond the scope of this chapter, it would be worth exploring some of the parallels between the stories of Mary and Muḥammad: (1) their fathers' deaths while their mothers were pregnant with them; (2) their withdrawal for worship within caves; (3) their reception of angelic interventions by Gabriel, and so forth.[74]

Concluding Reflections

Stepping back now from this discussion of al-Ṭabarī as commentator on the Qur'ān and as universal historian, it is time to ask some analytical and comparative questions. To begin, what inferences can be drawn from al-Ṭabarī's exegetical remarks on the three verses that I have presented as key qur'ānic texts? Certainly, their predictive function is reinforced. The *rasūlan minhum*, the *ummī* prophet found *maktūban 'indahum fī l-tawrāti wa-l-injīl* and the *rasūl* subsequent to Jesus, *ismuhu aḥmad*, are unequivocally Muḥammad. Al-Ṭabarī admits of no deviation from the complete exegetical consensus on this point. What about the prophetical prototypes to Muḥammad, namely, Abraham, Moses, and Jesus? What roles does al-Ṭabarī allow them to play? Fundamentally, each is decontextualized, their particular "historical" circumstances being either de-emphasized or ignored. As al-Ṭabarī elaborates these key qur'ānic passages, the figures of Abraham, Moses, and Jesus are flattened so that the consummative posture of Muḥammad can be more vividly foregrounded. Each stands as an *āya,* a sign or prototype of Muḥammad, their primary purpose to predict or prefigure, to operate as living proof texts for the annunciation of the final prophet.

Given the exegesis of these three prediction loci in the *Tafsīr* and the operation of these three prophetical prototypes, it is worth turning to the discussion of *Ta'rīkh* material to see if al-Ṭabarī uses these qur'ānic motifs in constructing his biography of the Prophet. How would the qur'ānic claim for prediction of the Prophet in prior scriptures be constructed within the genre of annalistic chronology? Any or all of the three passages just discussed, as exegetically amplified by al-Ṭabarī, would seem to be obvious buttressing for the biography's annunciation episodes. What, then, does he

---

74 Further to this, with a specifically qur'ānic focus, see Neal Robinson, "Jesus and Mary in the Qur'ān: Some Neglected Affinities," *Religion* 20 (1990): 161–75. Through the juxtaposition of various verses Robinson argues (p. 171) that "the qur'ānic story of Jesus serves to authenticate the prophetic ministry of Muḥammad and to emphasise the authority of the message of which he is the mediator."

do, if anything, with these qur'ānic prediction verses and with the prior prophets, Abraham, Moses, and Jesus, to whom they are exegetically tied?

The answer is straightforward: the search for explicit inclusion of the qur'ānic prediction passages within apposite sections of the Prophet's biography remains unrewarded. Despite incorporating into the *Ta'rīkh* the *topos* of prior attestation to Muḥammad's prophethood, al-Ṭabarī simply did not see these passages as providing it with historical verification. We find the encounter with Baḥīrā and the description of Zayd ibn 'Amr but not the prayer of Abraham, the promise to Moses, or the annunciation by Jesus.

More generally, we find scant use of direct biblical material in those sections of the *Ta'rīkh* where it might reasonably be expected. It is not entirely absent. For example, one scholar has noted that the two genealogies that introduce the Jesus biography seem to be remarkably faithful to listings in both Matthew and the books of Kings and Chronicles.[75] In his recent article in the *Journal asiatique,* Claude Gilliot drew attention to an echo of Jer 1:5 in al-Ṭabarī's commentary on *sūrat al-baqara* (Q 2:259).[76] Yet precedents for more extensive use are certainly available. Early evidence of the knowledge of biblical traditions can be seen in the works of such as Abū 'Ubayd al-Qāsim ibn Sallām's (d. 224/839) *Kitāb al-khuṭab wa-l-mawā'id,*[77] with its many paraphrases of biblical citations. Among al-Ṭabarī's other predecessors, both Ibn Qutayba (d. 276/889) and al-Ya'qūbī (d. 284/897) incorporate material directly from the biblical texts.[78] In his *Ma'ārif,* for example, the former

---

75 André Ferré, "La vie de Jésus d'après les *Annales* de Ṭabarī," *Islamochristiana* 5 (1979): 27. Ferré provides a well-annotated French translation of *Ta'rīkh,* 1:724–41, citing many possible parallels with Christian apocrypha. Although there is no mention of this article in M. Perlmann's bibliography for his English translation (*The History of al-Ṭabarī,* vol. 4, *The Ancient Kingdoms* [Albany: State University of New York Press, 1987]), Ferré can profitably be read in tandem with Perlmann's annotations.

76 "Mythe, récit, histoire du salut dans le commentaire coranique de Tabari," *JA* 282 (1994): 249. Elsewhere in this article Gilliot speaks of the profound unity between Ṭabarī as commentator and as historian, finding in his cross-over employment of *āthār* segments a major unifying force.

77 Edited by Ramaḍān 'Abd al-Tawwāb (Cairo: Maktabat al-Thaqāfa l-Dīniyya, 1406/1986).

78 Direct citation was, however, less common than undifferentiated reference to widely circulated Jewish and Christian material simply identified as, for example, "written in the books" (*maktūb fī l-kutub*) or "in the book of God" (*fī kitābi llāh*). Further to this point see Ignaz Goldziher, "Über Bibelcitate in muhammedanischen Schriften," *ZAW* 13 (1893): 315–16; and M. J. Kister, "*Ḥaddithū 'an banī isrā'īla wa-lā ḥaraja*: A Study of an Early Tradition," *IOS* 2 (1972): 215–39.

set transmitted accounts (*akhbār*) from Wahb ibn Munabbih in contrast with explicit biblical citations.[79]

One explanation for this absence is suggested by the contentions of Franz Rosenthal and Uri Rubin. As noted earlier, the latter has published a carefully detailed study of some of the predictive descriptions of Muḥammad. In emulation of his teacher, M. J. Kister,[80] he hauls in an awe-inspiring catch of citations for analysis and discovers that an early willingness to attribute the description to a biblical source and to such tradents as Ka'b al-Aḥbār and Wahb ibn Munabbih gives way, by the time of the formation of the canonical *ḥadīth* collections, to a full Islamicization of both source and attribution. To quote Rubin: "This means that the representatives of the mainstream Islamic thinking were reluctant to acknowledge the merit of the scriptures of the People of the Book as sources of attestation, and were therefore inclined to dismiss traditions in which total reliance on those scriptures was implied, even though some of the *isnāds* could be regarded as 'sound' (*ṣaḥīḥ*)."[81] As a further step in what he calls the "downgrading of the Bible as a document of attestation," Rubin finds evidence of transmutation of the "biblical" to the "historical" so that what was first encountered as a biblical prophecy about the Prophet becomes a historical account of his actual conduct. This process of transmutation may have had long-term consequences. Forty years ago Franz Rosenthal suggested

---

[79] Ibn Qutayba, *al-Ma'ārif* (ed. Tharwat 'Ukkāsha; Cairo: Dār al-Ma'ārif, 1969); see especially the early sections on creation and on Adam and the rest of the messengers and prophets. On the question of Arabic translations of the Hebrew Bible and New Testament, see Lazarus-Yafeh, *Intertwined Worlds*, 111–29; G. Lecomte, "Les citations de l'ancien et du nouveau testament dans l'oeuvre d'Ibn Qutayba," *Arabica* 5 (1958): 24–46; S. H. Griffith, "The Gospel in Arabic," *OrChr* 69 (1985): 126–67, who notes (p. 131) that actual manuscript evidence of Arabic versions of the four Gospels dates only from the ninth century; S. M. Stern, "Quotations from Apocryphal Gospels in 'Abd al-Jabbār," *JTS* 18 (1967): 34–57; S. Pines, "Gospel Quotations and Cognate Topics in 'Abd al-Jabbār's *Tathbīt* in Relation to Early Christian and Judaeo-Christian Readings and Traditions," *JSAI* 9 (1987): 195–278.

[80] The best justification for the comprehensive approach adopted by Kister and his students has recently been given by Michael Lecker, who in writing about 'Abdallāh ibn 'Abd al-Muṭṭalib's death notes (pp. 12–13) that in addition to searching the obvious *sīra, maghāzī*, and *ta'rīkh* genres, one should examine "a variety of other texts because the evidence we are looking for could have wandered about everywhere in the Islamic literature." See his "The Death of the Prophet Muḥammad's Father: Did Wāqidī Invent Some of the Evidence?" *ZDMG* 145 (1995): 9–27.

[81] Rubin, *Eye of the Beholder*, 32. Rubin has continued to explore these processes of Islamicization in his latest book *Between Bible and Qur'ān: The Children of Israel and the Islamic Self-Image* (Princeton: Darwin, 1999).

that al-Ṭabarī's failure to incorporate more biblical material and his choice to rely instead on traditional Muslim material had a stultifying influence on subsequent historiography: "His vast influence may be suspected to have tipped the scales in favour of that material, and against greater respect for the original sources, among most later historians."[82]

Is al-Ṭabarī, by neglecting to use in his *Ta'rīkh* qur'ānic citations that point to prior scriptures, acting within this pattern of the demotion or neglect of "biblical" material? Have the qur'ānic figures of Abraham, Moses, and Jesus—at least in their prefiguring function—been infected with these attitudes? In this instance that judgment would be unwarranted. Rather, I would argue that the answer is to be found in matters of genre and theological expectation. In the first place, the qur'ānic prediction verses do not transfer easily to the *Ta'rīkh* because their exegesis lacks narrative formulation. For none of the three does the *Tafsīr* offer a "historical" vignette, a contextualization of the figure of Abraham, Moses, or Jesus in the act of predicting the Prophet. In this case we are not presented with the results of that redactory redundancy that inform so much of al-Ṭabarī's *Tafsīr*. More fundamentally, al-Ṭabarī is operating within the logic of Islam as a religion of restoration, a reversion to prior instances of revelation in their primordial purity. (The prominence of the Islamic dispensation as restoration is undercut if developed theological constructs such as "seal of the prophets" and general abrogation are construed linearly.) But as his *taḥrīf* allusions indicate, al-Ṭabarī views the contemporary biblical conveyance of that revelation as corrupted. There is no point then in seeking textual congruence. Why search a tainted source for specific attestations? Yet a powerful sense of biblical presence persists. The first part of the *Ta'rīkh* is redolent with it, and al-Ṭabarī clearly uses biblical models, broadly construed, to construct his biography of Muḥammad. The prefacing genealogy, the *topos* of prediction, the maternity, birth, and infancy narrative, among other elements, all attest to this. Further, I would argue that the biography

---

82 "The Influence of the Biblical Tradition on Muslim Historiography," in *Historians of the Middle East* (ed. B. Lewis and P. M. Holt; London: Oxford University Press, 1962), 42. Stephen Humphreys has questioned Rosenthal's negative assessment from the related perspective of the metastructure of Islamic historiography, which Humphreys finds in a recurrent motif of covenant-betrayal-redemption ("Qur'ānic Myth and Narrative Structure in Early Islamic Historiography," in *Tradition and Innovation in Late Antiquity* [ed. F. M. Clover and R. S. Humphreys; Madison: University of Wisconsin Press, 1989], 271–90). Similarly, Tarif Khalidi discovers in the pre-Islamic portion of Ṭabarī's *Ta'rīkh* a continuous interplay of the Adamic (sin-repentance-ultimate reconciliation with God) and Satanic (unrepentant disobedience) fates (*Arabic Historical Thought in the Classical Period* [Cambridge: Cambridge University Press, 1994], 79).

of Jesus, Muḥammad's immediate prophetic predecessor, is shaped to segue into that of Muḥammad. Thus while the prediction verses, and their association with textual biblical attestations, are absent, the more comprehensive prefiguration provided by Abraham, Moses, and Jesus remains in al-Ṭabarī's *Ta'rīkh*-shaped prelude to the Prophet.

The Gospel, the Qur'ān, and the Presentation of Jesus in al-Ya'qūbī's *Ta'rīkh*

Sidney H. Griffith
The Catholic University of America

Jesus, the son of Mary, has always been a popular figure among Muslims,[1] and the Gospel, like the Torah, is presented in the Qur'ān as a scripture sent down from God (e.g., in Q 5:68). Nevertheless, neither the Qur'ān itself nor Muslim scholars over the centuries have paid much attention to the actual texts of the canonical Gospels and the portrait of Jesus they present. Rather, in the course of time what Tarif Khalidi calls a "Muslim Gospel" has emerged. As Khalidi so aptly puts it, in the Islamic view "Jesus is a controversial prophet. He is the only prophet in the Qur'an who is deliberately made to distance himself from the doctrines that his community is said to hold of him."[2] One of the exceptions to the general neglect of the text of the canonical Gospels on the part of Muslim scholars is to be found in the work of the ninth-century Muslim historian Aḥmad al-Ya'qūbī (d. 897). In his *Ta'rīkh*, or *History*, al-Ya'qūbī offers a portrait of Jesus that is based in large part on quotations from the four Gospels or paraphrases and interpretations of their texts as they were read in the early Christian communities. His work therefore offers an ideal place to study an early, if ultimately superseded, Islamic understanding of the Gospel, the Qur'ān, and the presentation of Jesus in the Islamic milieu. Accordingly, the present study will unfold under the following headings: Jesus, the Gospel, and the Qur'ān; al-Ya'qūbī's *Ta'rīkh* and "Bible History"; and al-Ya'qūbī's presentation of Jesus.

Jesus, the Gospel, and the Qur'ān

According to the Qur'ān, the Torah, the Gospel, and the Qur'ān itself are on a par as records of divine revelation (Q 9:111). But also according

[1] See Tarif Khalidi, *The Muslim Jesus: Sayings and Stories in Islamic Literature* (Cambridge: Harvard University Press, 2001).

[2] Ibid., 12.

to the Qur'ān, the "People of the Book,"[3] that is, the Jews and the Christians, have distorted their scriptures (Q 2:75; 3:78).[4] Nevertheless, the Qur'ān says, "Let the 'People of the Gospel' judge by what God has sent down in it" (Q 5:47). And to the Muslims their holy scripture says, "If you are in doubt about what We have sent down to you, ask those who were reading scripture before you" (Q 10:94). It is clear, then, that the Qur'ān presumes in its audience a familiarity with the narratives of the Torah and the Gospel and other books of the Bible as well. One might almost think of the Qur'ān as in part a commentary or a *scholion* on the earlier scriptures. It seldom quotes from them, but it often alludes to their narratives, paraphrases them, or puts them into a new interpretive scheme.

Often in the Qur'ān's presentation of biblical characters, there are elements in the recounting of their stories that reflect early Jewish or Christian extracanonical, apocryphal, or exegetical lore.[5] It is frequently the case that the nonbiblical elements in the Qur'ān's accounts of biblical characters are found only in the Islamic scripture. This latter phenomenon in particular reminds one of the "intertextual"[6] character of the biblical and qur'ānic

---

[3] On the dynamic sense of this expression, see Daniel A. Madigan, *The Qur'ân's Self-Image: Writing and Authority in Islam's Scripture* (Princeton: Princeton University Press, 2001), esp. the appendix, "The People of the *Kitâb*," 193–213.

[4] On this topic see especially Jean-Marie Gaudeul and Robert Caspar, "Textes de la tradition musulmane concernant le *Taḥrīf* (falsification) des Ecritures," *Islamochristiana* 6 (1980): 61–104.

[5] For Jewish materials, see, e.g., Abraham I. Katsh, *Judaism and the Koran: Biblical and Talmudic Backgrounds of the Koran and Its Commentaries* (New York: Barnes, 1962). Among the more recent studies one might cite by way of example Reuven Firestone, *Journeys in Holy Lands: The Evolution of the Abraham-Ishmael Legends in Islamic Exegesis* (Albany: State University of New York Press, 1990); Jacob Lassner, *Demonizing the Queen of Sheba: Boundaries of Gender and Culture in Postbiblical Judaism and Medieval Islam* (Chicago: University of Chicago Press, 1993); Brannon M. Wheeler, *Moses in the Quran and Islamic Exegesis* (Richmond, Surrey: Curzon, 2002). For Christian materials, see Tor Andrae, *Der Ursprung des Islams und das Christentum* (Uppsala: Almqvist & Wiksells, 1926); Richard Bell, *The Origin of Islam in Its Christian Environment* (London: Cass, 1926); K. Ahrens, "Christliches in Qoran," *ZDMG* 84 (1930): 15–68, 148–90. Among more recent studies one might cite by way of example Christoph Luxenberg, *Die syro-aramäische Lesart des Koran: Ein Beitrag zur Entschlüsselung der Koransprache* (Berlin: Das arabische Buch, 2000).

[6] The adjective "intertextual" is understood here in the sense examined in Thais E. Morgan, "Is There an Intertext in This Text? Literary and Interdisciplinary Approaches to Intertextuality," *American Journal of Semiotics* 3 (1985): 1–40. For a discussion of the phenomenon in the study of the Qur'ān *avant le lettre*, see Marilyn R. Waldman, "New Approaches to 'Biblical' Materials in the Qur'an," *MW* 75

narratives. That is to say, the stories of the Bible's main characters as they function in the several religious communities are not narratively complete either in the Bible or in the Qur'ān. The Qur'ān, as well as the earlier apocryphal, midrashic, or other extracanonical, traditional accounts, are part of the fuller narratives. Often in Islamic tradition the biblical characters have a narrative life of their own, seemingly with little or no relation to the biblical stories. The literary genres in which they circulated most prominently in the Islamic world are two: the "Stories of the Prophets" (*Qiṣaṣ al-anbiyā'*)[7] and the so-called *Isrā'īliyyāt*,[8] allegedly Jewish lore about the patriarchs and prophets, along with the collections of biographical traditions about the prophet Muḥammad.[9]

The Gospel, with its central focus on presenting Jesus Christ and his teaching, is the subject of special mention in the Qur'ān. In Arabic it is called *al-injīl*, from the Greek εὐαγγέλιον probably through the influence of the Ethiopic term *wangēl*.[10] The Gospel is mentioned a dozen times in the Qur'ān (in nine of them it occurs in conjunction with the mention of the Torah) as a scripture sent down by God. According to the Islamic view, just as the Torah is a scripture sent down from God to Moses, so the Gospel was sent down to Jesus. The Qur'ān says in reference to Jesus, "We gave him the Gospel; in it is guidance and light, and it is a confirmation of the Ṭorah that was before it" (Q 5:17).

Jesus, to whom according to the Qur'ān God gave the Gospel, is God's messenger (Q 5:75). As such he is not God (Q 5:17), but he is, by God's permission, a miracle worker (Q 5:110; 19:30–33). He is the Messiah, and he is God's Word that God cast into Mary, and a Spirit from God (Q 4:171).

(1985): 1–16. See also in the same vein M. Arkoun, "The Notion of Revelation: From *ahl al-kitāb* to the Societies of the Book," *WI* 28 (1988): 62–89.

[7] See Tilman Nagel, *Die Qiṣaṣ al-Anbiyā': Ein Beitrag zur arabischen Literaturgeschichte* (Bonn: Rheinische Friedrich-Wilhelm-Universität, 1967); Roberto Tottoli, *I profeti biblici nella tradizione islamica* (Brescia: Paideia, 1999); Brannon M. Wheeler, *Prophets in the Quran: An Introduction to the Quran and Muslim Exegesis* (London: Continuum, 2002). One of the most popular texts in this genre has an English translation; see Wheeler M. Thackston Jr., *The Tales of the Prophets of al-Kisa'ī* (Boston: Twayne, 1978).

[8] See Jane Dammen McAuliffe, "Assessing the *Isra'iliyyat*: An Exegetical Conundrum," in *Story-Telling in the Framework of Non-Fictional Arabic Literature* (ed. S. Leder; Wiesbaden: Harrassowitz, 1998), 345–69; Roberto Tottoli, "Origin and Use of the Term *Isra'iliyyāt* in Muslim Literature," *Arabica* 46 (1999): 193–210.

[9] See Uri Rubin, *The Eye of the Beholder: The Life of Muhammad As Viewed by the Early Muslims* (Princeton: Darwin, 1995).

[10] See Arthur Jeffery, *The Foreign Vocabulary of the Qur'an* (Baroda: Oriental Institute, 1938), 71–72.

But he is a man like Adam (Q 3:59), a messenger who was one of a series of messengers, like Moses before him and Muḥammad after him. Jesus announced the coming of Aḥmad/Muḥammad (Q 61:6). According to the Qur'ān, the Jews neither killed nor crucified Jesus; God took him up to himself (Q 4:157/8).[11]

There are no direct quotations from the Gospel in the Qur'ān, but there are reminiscences of and allusions to the Gospel narratives as they are found written in the canonical texts, as well as in some apocryphal Gospels. The most striking instance is surely the report of the annunciation to Mary as one finds it in two places in the Qur'ān: *Maryam* (19) 16–35, and *'Al-'Imrān* (3) 42–47. While there is little or no similarity in wording between the Gospel accounts and the Qur'ān passages, there are striking narrative parallels. In the first case, the Qur'ān account (Q 19:16–35) closely follows the narrative sequence as it is also found in Luke 1:26–38; in the second instance the Qur'ān account (Q 3:42–47) shows close parallels with the narrative in the apocryphal *Protoevangelium of James*. Accompanying stories in the Qur'ān narratives find further parallels in other apocryphal Christian texts such as the *Gospel of Pseudo-Matthew* or the *Infancy Story of Thomas*.[12] What these parallels imply is not so much that the Qur'ān has a textual familiarity with the canonical Gospels or with the early apocryphal Gospels. Rather, the parallels suggest that the Qur'ān presumes in its audience a familiarity with the Christian narrative of the annunciation to Mary as it circulated in the largely oral, intertextual, Christian kerygma as it was preached in Arabia in the late sixth and early seventh centuries.[13]

---

[11] There have been numerous studies of the Islamic view of Jesus Christ based on qur'ānic teaching. Some of the most important ones, in addition to Khalidi, *The Muslim Jesus*, cited above, are Michel Hayek, *Le Christ de l'Islam* (Paris: Éditions du Seuil, 1959); Geoffrey Parrinder, *Jesus in the Qur'an* (New York: Oxford University Press, 1977); Roger Arnaldez, *Jesus, fils de Marie, prophète de l'Islam* (Paris: Desclée, 1980); Kenneth Cragg, *Jesus and the Muslim: An Exploration* (London: Allen & Unwin, 1985); Neal Robinson, *Christ in Islam and Christianity: The Representation of Jesus in the Qur'an and the Classical Muslim Commentaries* (Albany: State University of New York Press, 1991). See also "Jesus" in Wheeler, *Prophets in the Quran*, 297–320.

[12] See most recently the study of Suleiman A. Mourad, "On the Qur'anic Stories about Mary and Jesus," *Bulletin of the Royal Institute for Inter-Faith Studies* 1 (1999): 13–24. The texts of the relevant portions of the apocryphal works mentioned here are available in English translation in Willis Barnstone, *The Other Bible: Jewish Pseudepigrapha, Christian Apocrypha, Gnostic Scriptures, Kabbalah, Dead Sea Scrolls* (San Francisco: Harper, 1984), 383–403.

[13] See François Nau, *Les arabes chrétiens de Mésopotamie et de Syrie* (Paris: Imprimerie nationale, 1933); Andrae, *Ursprung*; C. Robin and J. Beaucamp, "Le

So far no convincing evidence has come to light to suggest that there was a pre-Islamic translation of the Gospel into Arabic, or indeed of any portion of the Christian Bible, in a way that would have made it textually available in Muḥammad's milieu.[14]

There is in the Qur'ān a phrase that echoes a phrase that also appears in the Gospel. The Qur'ān says of those who deny the truth of God's "signs" that "they will not enter the Garden until the camel passes through the eye of the needle" (Q 7:40). The Christian reader thinks immediately of Jesus' saying in the Gospel, "It is easier for a camel to go through the eye of a needle than for a rich man to enter the kingdom of God" (Mark 10:25). But there is no evidence that the Qur'ān has the Gospel passage in view; the saying is not attributed to Jesus, and indeed the context is very different in the two cases. What is interesting is that in the interpretive tradition of both Christianity and Islam there is the record of the double decipherment possible with the Arabic term *jamal* and the Greek terms for "camel" and "rope" respectively.[15] The coincidence suggests more an intertextual context of shared biblical language and lore than it does any textual familiarity with the Gospel.

The Qur'ān's familiarity with other aspects of Christian discourse is also apparent. A striking example is the story of those known in the Qur'ān as the "Companions of the Cave" (Q 18:9–31), who in the Christian hagiographical tradition are called the "Seven Sleepers of Ephesus."[16]

---

christianisme dans la péninsule arabique d'après l'épigraphie et l'archéologie," *Travaux et Mémoires* 8 (1981): 45–61; J. Spencer Trimingham, *Christianity among the Arabs in Pre-Islamic Times* (London: Longman, 1979); Robert G. Hoyland, *Arabia and the Arabs: From the Bronze Age to the Coming of Islam* (London: Routledge, 2001). Without a doubt the most comprehensive study of Christianity in the Arabic-speaking milieu prior to the rise of Islam is to be found in the works of Irfan Shahid, *Byzantium and the Arabs in the Fourth Century* (Washington, D.C.: Dumbarton Oaks, 1984); idem, *Byzantium and the Arabs in the Fifth Century* (Washington, D.C.: Dumbarton Oaks, 1989); idem, *Byzantium and the Arabs in the Sixth Century* (vol. 1, parts 1 and 2; Washington, D.C.: Dumbarton Oaks, 1995); idem, *Byzantium and the Arabs in the Sixth Century* (vol. 2, part 1; Washington: Dumbarton Oaks, 2002).

14 See Sidney H. Griffith, "The Gospel in Arabic: An Inquiry into Its Appearance in the First Abbasid Century," *OrChr* 69 (1985): 126–67.

15 See Régis Blachère, "Regards sur un passage parallèle des Évangiles et du Coran," in *Mélanges d'Islamologie: Volume dédié à la mémoire de Armand Abel par ses collègues, ses élèves et ses amis* (ed. P. Salmon; Leiden: Brill, 1974), 69–73.

16 See Louis Massignon, "Les sept dormants apocalypse de l'Islam," *AnBoll* 68 (1950): 245–60; François Jourdan, *La tradition des Sept Dormants: Une rencontre entre chrétiens et musulmans* (Paris: Maisonneuve et Larose, 2001).

Indeed, the Qur'ān's account of their adventures is best read as a commentary on their story as it circulated orally in the Syriac-speaking communities of the Christians, whose monks and merchants had carried their faith and their hagiographical legends deep into the Arabic-speaking world in which Islam was born. This legend, like the Gospel narrative, while it is not significantly textually present in the Qur'ān in the way in which it circulated among the Christians, was nevertheless narratively present in the milieu of the earliest Islam. For this reason the Qur'ān could take the story of the Seven Sleepers for granted as part of the religious consciousness of its audience and allude to their exploits as the "Companions of the Cave."

In the Islamic milieu the Qur'ān itself became the ultimate arbiter of the interpretation of the earlier scriptural narratives it echoed.[17] But the significant presence of Gospel narratives in the subtext of the Qur'ān was nevertheless sufficient to draw the attention of early Muslim scholars to the Christian texts that they thought lay behind them. A particularly striking early example of this interest appears in the *Sīrah,* or "biography," of Muḥammad by Ibn Isḥāq (d. ca. 767), as it is preserved in the later work of the same genre by Ibn Hishām (d. 834).[18] It was doubtless for apologetical or even polemical reasons that Ibn Isḥāq searched for a Gospel passage that in his judgment foretold the coming of the prophet Muḥammad.[19] In the Qur'ān Jesus is quoted as having said, "I am the messenger of God to you, confirming what was before me of the Torah, and announcing a messenger who will come after me, whose name is Aḥmad" (Q 61:6). And in another place the Qur'ān says of Muḥammad that "the unlettered prophet" (*an-nabī al-'ummī*) is to be found mentioned "in the Torah and the Gospel" (Q 7:157). In confirmation of the Qur'ān's claim, Ibn Isḥāq quoted the "Paraclete" passage from John 15:23–16:1.[20] He introduced the quotation with these words:

---

[17] See Andrew Rippin, "Interpreting the Bible through the Qur'an," in *Approaches to the Qur'ān* (ed. G. R. Hawting and Abdul-Kader A. Shareef; New York: Routledge, 1993), 249–59; Jane Dammen McAuliffe, "The Qur'ānic Context of Muslim Biblical Scholarship," *Islam and Christian-Muslim Relations* 7 (1996): 141–58.

[18] Abū Muḥammad 'Abd al-Malik Ibn Hishām, *Sīratu n-nabī* (4 vols.; ed. Muḥammad Muhi d-Din Abd al-Hamid; Cairo: Matba'ah Hijazi, 1356/1936). See the English translation by Alfred Guillaume, *The Life of Muhammad: A Translation of Ibn Isḥāq's Sīrat Rasūl Allāh* (Oxford: Oxford University Press, 1955).

[19] On the apologetical dimensions of the *Sīrah* literature, see the insightful study of John E. Wansbrough, *The Sectarian Milieu: Content and Composition of Islamic Salvation History* (London Oriental Series 34; Oxford: Oxford University Press, 1978).

[20] Later Muslim scholars would follow Ibn Isḥāq's lead. See McAuliffe, "The Qur'ānic Context," 151.

> Here is what has come down to me about the description of God's messenger, God's prayer and peace be upon him, in what Jesus, son of Mary, set down in the Gospel, for the people of the Gospel, which came to him from God, as Yuhannis the apostle established it for them when he copied the Gospel for them at the commission of Jesus, son of Mary, peace be upon him.[21]

One readily recognizes Ibn Isḥāq's expression of the Islamic view of the Gospel in this paragraph, including his estimation of the role of John the Evangelist in producing it. In the quotation of the verses that follows this introductory statement it becomes clear that he is quoting a form of the Gospel text that in the early Islamic period was current in the so-called "Palestinian Syriac Lectionary."[22] But it is also clear that in the quotation he has "Islamicized" the text. Here is the quotation from John 15:23–16:1:

> Whoever has hated me, has hated the Lord. Had I not performed in their presence such works as no one has performed before me, they would have no sin. But now they have become proud and they think they will find fault with me and even with the Lord. However, it is inevitable that the saying concerning *an-Namūs* will be fulfilled, "They have hated me for nought." Had *al-Munaḥḥamānā,* he whom God will send, already come to you from the Lord, and the spirit of truth, he who comes from God, he would have been a witness for me, and you too, because you have been with me from the beginning. I have said this to you so that you may not be in doubt.[23]

At the conclusion of the quotation Ibn Isḥāq says, "*Al-Munaḥḥamānā* in Syriac is Muḥammad, and in Greek it is *al-Baraqliṭis.*"[24] In context in the *Sīrah,* Ibn Isḥāq quotes this passage from the Gospel according to John at the end of the first part of the first book, just prior to his accounts of the first revelations to Muḥammad. It is one of a number of other testimonies

---

21 Ibn Hishām, *Sīratu n-nabī,* 1:215.

22 See A. Baumstark, "Eine altarabische Evangelienübersetzung aus dem Christlich-Palästinensischen," *ZS* 8 (1932): 201–9; Alfred Guillaume, "The Version of the Gospels Used in Medina c. A.D. 700," *Al-Andalus* 15 (1950): 289–96. For the Christian Palestinian Aramaic text of the passage under discussion, see Agnes Smith Lewis and Margaret Dunlop Gibson, *The Palestinian Syriac Lectionary of the Gospels* (London: Clay, 1899), 24, 187. For the situation of Christian Palestinian Aramaic (also called "Palestinian Syriac") in the early Islamic period, see Sidney H. Griffith, "From Aramaic to Arabic: The Languages of the Monasteries of Palestine in the Byzantine and Early Islamic Periods," *DOP* 51 (1997): 11–31.

23 Ibn Hishām, *Sīratu n-nabī,* 1:215.

24 Ibid.

he cites from Jews and Christians to Muḥammad's prophethood. The "Islamicization" of the text of the quotation is evident most obviously in the alteration of the phrase "my Father" in the three places in the passage as it appears in Christian Bibles to "the Lord," an appellation for God justified by the Qur'ān. There are also other, less obvious modifications to the text as it circulated among Christians, but all of them have a resonance with the Qur'ān and its teachings.[25] Ibn Isḥāq must have been convinced that the Christian version of the text in John's Gospel had been altered from its original form, if not deliberately distorted by Christians, as the Qur'ān suggested (Q 2:75; 3:78) and as the upholders of the later, Islamic doctrine of *at-taḥrīf* stoutly maintained.[26] Ibn Isḥāq's purpose in citing the Gospel passage in the first place must have been part of his overall plan in the *Sīrah,* as Tarif Khalidi has put it, "to organize prophetic history in a historical continuum within the non-historical (or perhaps meta-historical) framework provided by the Qur'ān."[27]

Ibn Isḥāq was in fact one of the first Muslim scholars on record to search out passages from the canonical Christian Gospels for the purpose of defending the veracity of Islamic religious claims. It seems unlikely that he would personally have consulted the Christian Palestinian Aramaic text of the Syro-Palestinian Lectionary, from which modern scholars have shown that his quotation ultimately derives.[28] There are no known instances of a Muslim scholar in early Islamic times learning Syriac or any other dialect of Aramaic for the purpose of consulting the Christian Bible.[29] And while the earliest dated Arabic translations of the Gospels are also clearly related to the same text family that is in the Syro-Palestinian

---

[25] See the detailed study of Ibn Isḥāq's quotation in Griffith, "The Gospel in Arabic," esp. 137–43. An enhanced version of this study is in Sidney H. Griffith, "Arguing from Scripture: The Bible in the Christian/Muslim Encounter in the Middle Ages," to appear in the published proceedings of the MARCO Symposium, "The Study of the Bible in the Sectarian Worlds of the Middle Ages and the Renaissance," 21–22 February 2002, University of Tennessee, Knoxville, Tennessee.

[26] See Gaudeul and Caspar, "Textes de la tradition musulmane concernant le *taḥrīf.*"

[27] Tarif Khalidi, *Arabic Historical Thought in the Classical Period* (Cambridge Studies in Islamic Civilization; Cambridge: Cambridge University Press, 1994), 35.

[28] See the studies cited in note 22 above.

[29] There is a report in the *Fihrist* of Ibn an-Nadīm that one Aḥmad ibn 'Abd Allāh ibn Salām translated the Torah, the Gospel, and the books of the prophets and disciples into Arabic from Hebrew, Greek, and Sabaean in the time of the caliph Hārūn ar-Rashīd (786–809) and that it was available in the library of the caliph al-Ma'mūn. See Bayard Dodge, *The Fihrist of al-Nadīm: A Tenth-Century Survey of Muslim Culture* (2 vols.; New York: Columbia University Press, 1970), 1:42; 2:945.

Lectionary,[30] there does not seem to be any textual relationship between Ibn Isḥāq's Arabic quotation of John 15:23–16:1 and the texts of these earliest Arab Christian translations from the eighth and ninth centuries in Palestine. Given the close textual fidelity of Ibn Isḥāq's quotation to the actual, canonical Gospel according to Saint John, albeit with the alterations he saw fit to make in light of his Islamic convictions, it seems most reasonable to suppose that he had the text from a Christian informant or possibly from a Christian convert to Islam.[31]

Other Muslim writers in the early Islamic period after the time of Ibn Isḥāq, such as Ibn Qutaybah (d. 889)[32] and al-Ya'qūbī (d. 897),[33] quoted from the canonical Gospels to reinforce the distinctive Islamic prophetology that was in the process of elaboration in their days. In the interreligious controversies between Muslims and Christians, some Muslim writers quoted from the Gospels with the intention of disproving what they regarded as Christian errors or to authenticate the "signs of prophecy" (*dalā'il an-nubuwwah*) that they put forward to testify to Muḥammad's status as a prophet and messenger from God, even as the "seal of the prophets" (Q 33:40).[34] In this connection one might mention the work of the Christian convert to Islam, Rabban aṭ-Ṭabarī (d. ca. 850), who quoted liberally from the Bible to prove the authenticity of Muḥammad's prophethood and the veracity of Islamic teachings.[35] Similarly, the

---

30 See Griffith, "The Gospel in Arabic," 154–57. For the general context of these early translations of the Gospel, see Sidney H. Griffith, "The Monks of Palestine and the Growth of Christian Literature in Arabic," *MW* 78 (1988): 1–28.

31 For some thoughts on converts to Islam as a source of biblical knowledge among the Muslims, see R. G. Khoury, "Quelques réflexions sur la première ou les premières Bibles arabes," in *L'Arabie préislamique et son environnement historique et culturel: Actes du Colloque de Strasbourg 24–27 juin* 1987 (ed. T. Fahd; Leiden: Brill, 1989), 549–61.

32 See G. Lecomte, "Les citations de l'Ancien et du Nouveau Testament dans l'oeuvre d'Ibn Qutayba," *Arabica* 5 (1958): 34–46; S. Karoui, *Die Rezeption der Bibel in der frühislamischen Literatur: Am Beispiel der Hauptwerke von Ibn Qutayba (gest. 276/889)* (Heidelberg: Seminar für Sprachen und Kulturen des Vorderen Orients, 1997).

33 See André Ferré, "L'historien al-Ya'qūbī et les évangiles," *Islamochristiana* 3 (1977): 65–83.

34 See David Thomas, "The Bible in Early Muslim Anti-Christian Polemic," *Islam and Christian-Muslim Relations* 7 (1996): 29–38.

35 See Alphonse Mingana, ed. and trans., *The Book of Religion and Empire* (Manchester: Manchester University Press, 1923); idem, *Kitāb ad-dīn wad-dawlah* (Manchester: Manchester University Press, 1923). On the controversies over the authenticity of this work, see David Thomas, "Tabari's Book of Religion and Empire," *BJRL* 69 (1986): 1–7.

Zaydī theologian al-Qāsim ibn Ibrahīm (d. 860) in his *Refutation of the Christians* quoted extensively from the Gospels to refute Christian doctrinal claims.[36] Likewise, the Mu'tazilī theologian 'Abd al-Jabbār (d. 1025) in his *Tathbīt dalā'il an-nubuwwah* quoted from both the apocryphal and the canonical Gospels in the course of his long work legitimating Muḥammad's claims to authentic prophethood.[37]

From the eleventh century, if not earlier,[38] Muslim scholars seem to have lost confidence in the probative value of the text of the Gospels as it is found in Christian Bibles. Rather, they turned their attention increasingly to the issue of the corruption of the scriptures at the hands of the Christians and the other "People of the Book."[39] Ibn Ḥazm (994–1064), for example, was concerned to refute the religious claims of Jews and Christians by demonstrating in great detail the unreliability of the texts of their scriptures.[40] Al-Ghazālī (1058–1111), in whose work Jesus enjoys a high profile as an ascetic figure, shows no interest at all in the canonical Gospels in the form in which the Christians actually have them.[41] In the

---

36 See G. Vajda, "Observations sur quelques citations bibliques chez Ibn Qotayba," *REJ* 99 (1935): 68–80; I. Di Matteo, "Confutazione contro I Cristiani dello Zaydita al-Qasim b. Ibrahim," *RSO* 9 (1921–22): 301–64. See also W. Madelung, "Al-Qāsim ibn Ibrahim and Christian Theology," *ARAM* 3 (1991): 35–44.

37 S. M. Stern, "Quotations from Apocryphal Gospels in 'Abd al-Jabbār," *JTS* NS 18 (1967): 34–57; idem, "Abd al-Jabbār's Account of How Christ's Religion Was Falsified by the Adoption of Roman Customs," *JTS* NS 19 (1968): 128–85; S. Pines, "Gospel Quotations and Cognate Topics in 'Abd al-Jabbār's *Tathbīt*," *JSAI* 9 (1987): 195–278.

38 The historian aṭ-Ṭabarī (839–923) managed to tell the story of Jesus in his *Annals* without paying much attention to the canonical Gospels. See André Ferré, "La vie de Jésus d'après les *Annales* de Tabarī," *Islamochristiana* 5 (1979): 1–29.

39 See Hava Lazarus-Yafeh, *Intertwined Worlds: Medieval Islam and Bible Criticism* (Princeton: Princeton University Press, 1992); Camilla Adang, *Muslim Writers on Judaism and the Hebrew Bible: From Ibn Rabban to Ibn Hazm* (Leiden: Brill, 1996).

40 See Theodore Pulcini, *Exegesis As Polemical Discourse: Ibn Ḥazm on Jewish and Christian Scriptures* (Atlanta: Scholars Press, 1998).

41 See Jacques Jomier, "Jesus tel que Ghazali le presente dans *al-Iḥya'*," *MIDEO* 18 (1988): 45–82. A refutation of the Christian doctrine of the divinity of Christ based on extensive quotations from the Gospels is attributed to al-Ghazālī. See R. Chidiac, ed. and trans., *Al-Ghazali: Réfutation excellente de la divinité de Jésus-Christ d'après les Évangiles* (Paris: Leroux, 1939). The authenticity of the work is disproved in Hava Lazarus-Yafeh, *Studies in Al-Ghazzālī* (Jerusalem: Magnes, 1975), 458–87, who says (473), "Nowhere in al-Ghazzālī's authentic books is there any exact citation of a verse from the Bible, and mention of the name of a book in either the Old or the New Testaments, or trace of any Christian terminology."

twelfth century, the historian of Damascus Ibn 'Asākir (d. 1176) wrote a biography of Jesus that has no connection at all with the canonical Gospels.[42] After the time of Ibn Taymiyyah (1263–1328),[43] and for the rest of the Middle Ages, Muslim scholars seem never to have read the Christian Bible or to have consulted it. Presumably by then they had lost all interest in any authoritative or probative value its text may have had in the eyes of their earlier ancestors in the ninth and tenth centuries, due no doubt to the conviction, by then widely received, that its text was hopelessly corrupt.

In the early eighteenth century a hitherto unknown *Gospel of Barnabas* was discovered in an Italian manuscript in Amsterdam. The text affirms the unity of God, includes a testimony from Jesus that he was only a prophet, foretells the coming of a prophet from among the descendants of Ishmael, and says that Judas Iscariot was crucified instead of Jesus. Modern scholarship has shown that in all likelihood the *Gospel of Barnabas* was composed in the western Mediterranean world, probably Spain, in the sixteenth century.[44] It was translated into Arabic in the early twentieth century and has been widely acclaimed by some Muslims as a more authentic record of Jesus' life than is offered by the four canonical Gospels or by any other text emanating from Christian circles.

For all practical purposes, it was only in the early Islamic period that Muslim scholars were actively concerned with the text of the Gospel as the Christians actually had it. The historian al-Ya'qūbī in the ninth century relied on all four canonical Gospels, as well as on some early Christian exegetical traditions, in his presentation of the life and teachings of Jesus. It is to his work that we now turn our attention.

AL-YA'QŪBĪ'S *TA'RĪKH* AND BIBLE HISTORY

While Ibn Isḥāq, the biographer of Muḥammad whose quotation from the Gospel according to Saint John we studied above, may have originally put his account of the Muslim prophet into the context of the stories of the

42 See Suleiman A. Mourad, "A Twelfth-Century Muslim Biography of Jesus," *Islam and Christian-Muslim Relations* 7 (1996): 39–45.

43 See Thomas F. Michel, *A Muslim Theologian's Response to Christianity: Ibn Taymiyya's al-Jawāb al-sahîh* (Delmar, N.Y.: Caravan, 1984).

44 See Lonsdale and Laura Ragg, *The Gospel of Barnabas* (Oxford: Oxford University Press, 1907); J. Slomp, "The Gospel in Dispute," *Islamochristiana* 4 (1977): 67–112; M. De Epalza, "Le milieu hispano-moresque de l'Évangile islamisant de Barnabe," *Islamochristiana* 8 (1982): 159–83; R. Stichel, "Bemerkungen zum Barnabas-Evangelium," *Byzantinoslavica* 43 (1982): 189–201; David Sox, *The Gospel of Barnabas* (London: Allen & Unwin, 1984).

earlier biblical and nonbiblical prophets, that part of his work has been lost. Ibn Hishām left it out of his later digest of Ibn Isḥāq's *Sīrah*. Modern scholars have attempted to reconstruct the first part of Ibn Isḥāq's biography, the so-called *Kitāb al-mubtada'*, or "Book of the Beginnings," largely on the basis of quotations from it in the works of the historian aṭ-Ṭabarī and other early Muslim writers.[45] The work is presented as opening with an account of the creation of the world and going on to present stories of the biblical prophets as well as the nonbiblical prophets mentioned in the Qur'ān and in Islamic tradition. Its purpose would have been to provide a context in world history for the coming of the prophet Muḥammad. As such, the *Kitāb al-mubtada'* would have been the first effort at universal history produced in the Islamic world, with the largely religious and apologetical purpose of commending the verisimilitude of the claims of prophethood for Muḥammad to the earlier "Peoples of the Book," that is, the Jews and Christians. In the reconstruction of it from the texts of aṭ-Ṭabarī and the others there is a notable lack of quotations from the Bible or of paraphrases of biblical narratives. Biblical history is conveyed with reference to Islamic authorities, and although it can be shown to have affinities with much Jewish and Christian lore, the neglect of reference to non-Islamic written sources, particularly the canonical scriptures, is striking.

The opposite is the case in the earliest[46] still-surviving world history in Arabic, called simply *Ta'rīkh*, or "History," written by al-Ya'qūbī in the third quarter of the ninth century.[47] The work is arranged in two major parts, with the first part being devoted to pre-Islamic history, including cameo presentations of the major figures of biblical history from Adam to Jesus, along with accounts of the other peoples of the then-known world, their rulers, institutions, and principal cultural accomplishments. The second part of the *History* presents the story of Muḥammad and his companions, followed by an account of the successive caliphs and their accomplishments down to the

---

[45] See especially the work of Gordon D. Newby, *The Making of the Last Prophet: A Reconstruction of the Earliest Biography of Muhammad* (Columbia: University of South Carolina Press, 1989).

[46] See C. Pellat, "Les encyclopédies dans le monde arabe," *Journal of World History* 9 (1966): 644. In another place the author presents al-Ya'qūbī as more of an *adīb* than a "historian." See C. Pellat, "Was al-Mas'ûdî a Historian or an *Adīb*?" *Journal of the Pakistan Historical Society* 9 (1961): 233.

[47] Al-Ya'qūbī's *Ta'rīkh* is published in Arabic in two editions: M. Th. Houtsma, ed., *Ibn-Wādhih qui dicitur al-Ja'qubî, Historiae* (2 vols.; Leiden: Brill, 1883); Aḥmad al-Ya'qūbī, *Ta'rīkh al-Ya'qūbī* (2 vols.; Beirut: Dār Sadir and Dār Bayrūt, 1379/1960). An English translation of the *Ta'rīkh* is in preparation by a team of scholars under the general editorship of Lawrence Conrad, Matthew Gordon, and Chase Robinson.

year 872.[48] The *Ta'rīkh* is characterized by al-Ya'qūbī's close attention to the sources available to him, including, as we shall see, the canonical scriptures. This attention to the biblical narrative is one of the features that allows al-Ya'qūbī's work to stand out among the works of Muslim scholars in the early Islamic period. While his reading of the Bible is guided by the Qur'ān, he nevertheless is almost unique among his coreligionists in allowing the canonical biblical text to speak for itself; he quotes from it and paraphrases it liberally in the section of the *Ta'rīkh* devoted to "biblical history."

Not much is known of the biography of al-Ya'qūbī. He was born in Baghdad of Arab stock early in the ninth century. His full name is Aḥmad ibn Abī Ya'qūb ibn Ja'far ibn Wahb ibn Wāḍīḥ al-Kātib al-'Abbāsī al-Ya'qūbī; sometimes called Ibn Wāḍīḥ, he is most often known simply as al-Ya'qūbī. Politically, he and his family were of 'Alid sympathies. As a young man he lived in Armenia and in Khurāsān, where he was in the service of the Ṭāhirid emirs (821–73). Later, after the fall of the Ṭāhirids, he took up residence in Egypt, where he died in 897, or possibly as late as 902 or even 905.[49] He wrote the *Ta'rīkh* during his years in Khurāsān. In Egypt al-Ya'qūbī wrote the other major work that is credited to him, the *Kitāb al-buldān*,[50] a

---

[48] No major study of the *Ta'rīkh* has yet appeared, but general discussions of the work's major characteristics may be found in studies of Islamic historiography. See, e.g., Franz Rosenthal, *A History of Muslim Historiography* (Leiden: Brill, 1952), 114–16; D. M. Dunlop, *Arab Civilization to AD 1500* (Arab Background Series; London: Longman; Beirut: Librairie du Liban, 1971), 87–88; Yves Marquet, "Le shi'isme au IXe siècle à travers l'histoire de Ya'qūbī," *Arabica* 19 (1972): 1–45, 101–38; A. A. Duri, *The Rise of Historical Writing among the Arabs* (ed. and trans. L. I. Conrad; Princeton: Princeton University Press, 1983), 64–67; M. J. L. Young et al., eds., *Religion, Learning and Science in the 'Abbasid Period* (Cambridge: Cambridge University Press, 1990), 184–201; Bernd Radtke, *Weltgeschichte und Weltbeschreibung im mittelalterlichen Islam* (Beiruter Texte und Studien 51; Beirut and Stuttgart: Steiner, 1992), 11–15; Khalidi, *Arabic Historical Thought*, 115–32; Fred M. Donner, *Narratives of Islamic Origins: The Beginnings of Islamic Historical Writing* (Princeton: Darwin, 1998), 134.

[49] See C. Brockelmann, "al-Ya'kûbî," in M. Th. Houtsma et al., eds., *E. J. Brill's First Encyclopaedia of Islam, 1913–1936* (repr., Leiden: Brill, 1993), 8:1152–53; Adang, *Muslim Writers on Judaism*, 36–39. Most often al-Ya'qūbī is said to have died in 897; some scholars have proposed a later date. See, e.g., Dunlop, *Arab Civilization*, 103 n. 221; Tarif Khalidi, *Classical Arab Islam: The Culture and Heritage of the Golden Age* (Princeton: Darwin, 1985), 64; Adang, *Muslim Writers on Judaism*, 37, esp. n. 100.

[50] See M. J. de Goeje, ed., *Kitāb al-boldān auctore Ahmed ibn Abi Ja'kûbî Wādhih al-Kātib al-Ja'kûbî* (Bibliotheca Geographorum Arabicum 7; Leiden: Brill, 1892). See the French translation in G. Wiet, *Les pays* (Textes et traductions d'auteurs orientaux 1; Cairo: Institut Français d'Archéologie Orientale, 1937).

geographical essay in which he included the wealth of information he had acquired during his wide travels within the caliphate and perhaps even beyond its borders. Late in life he also produced a short historical essay on how men adapt to their times, illustrated by a discussion of the caliphs from Abū Bakr (632–34) to al-Muʿtaḍid (892–902).[51]

"Biblical history" constitutes a major part of al-Yaʿqūbī's *Taʾrīkh;* as it remains to us, the narrative begins with the story of Adam and Eve and, in the biblical history section of the work, extends to the story of "The Messiah, Jesus, son of Mary."[52] Originally the narrative began with an account of creation, according to al-Yaʿqūbī's own testimony. Later in the book he says he had included in the first part of it an abbreviated account of the "beginning of the coming to be of this world and reports of the most important ancient peoples, of the various kingdoms, and of their manifold affairs."[53] Now the account of creation is lost. In what is left of the text, the biblical material is presented under the names of the principal figures in "Bible History": Adam, the descendants of Adam, Noah, the descendants of Noah, Abraham, Isaac, Jacob, the descendants of Jacob, Moses, the prophets after Moses, David, Solomon, the kings after Solomon up to the destruction of Jerusalem,[54] and finally Jesus.[55] Just after the account of the destruction of Jerusalem at the hands of Nebuchadnezzar, there is a brief excursus on the survival of the Torah (due to the efforts of Zerubbabel, according to al-Yaʿqūbī) and on the laws, the feasts, and the religious practices of the

---

51 See William G. Millward, "The Adaptation of Men to Their Time: An Historical Essay by al-Ya'qûbî," *JAOS* 84 (1964): 329–44.

52 A Dutch translation of the "Bible History" section of the *Taʾrīkh* is available in G. Smit, *"Bijbel en Legende" bij den arabischen Schrijver Ja'qubi, 9th Eeuw na Christus* (Leiden: Brill, 1907). A French translation of the entire "Bible History" section of the *Taʾrīkh,* with the Arabic text on the facing page, is available in André Ferré, *L'histoire des prophètes d'après al-Yaʿqûbî: D'Adam à Jésus* (Rome: Pontificio Istituto di Studi Arabi e d'Islamistica, 2000).

53 Al-Yaʿqūbī, *Taʾrīkh,* 2:5; Houtsma, *Historiae,* 2:2.

54 An English translation of the section dealing with the kings after Moses up to the excursus on the laws and practices of the Jews is available in R. Y. Ebied and L. R. Wickham, "Al-Ya'kûbî's Account of the Israelite Prophets and Kings," *JNES* 29 (1970): 80–98.

55 An English translation of the section on Jesus is available in Dwight M. Donaldson, "Al-Ya'qûbî's Chapter about Jesus Christ," in *The Macdonald Presentation Volume* (ed. W. G. Shellabear et al.; Princeton: Princeton University Press, 1933), 88–105. A French translation of the Jesus section is available in André Ferré, "L'historien al-Ya'qûbî et les évangiles," *Islamochristiana* 3 (1977): 61–83, as well as in Ferré, *L'histoire des prophètes,* 90–110, in a somewhat revised version.

Israelites.[56] In the section that is devoted to the kings after Solomon, as part of the story of Ahaz, there is a brief excursus on the Samaritans.[57]

Very soon after the publication of the text of al-Ya'qūbī's *Ta'rīkh* in Houtsma's edition, scholars were quick to recognize the debt he owed to the Syriac *Spelunca Thesaurorum* or *Cave of Treasures*[58] and other works in the Syriac exegetical tradition. They also noted the close parallels between his version of the scriptural passages he quoted and the Syriac Peshitta.[59] These observations immediately raise the question of al-Ya'qūbī's sources. Did he learn Syriac and consult the *Cave of Treasures* in the original language?[60] Was an early Arabic translation available to him?[61]

---

56 See Martin Schreiner, "Al-Jaḳubî über den Glauben und die Sitten der Juden," *MGWJ* 34 (1885): 135–39. See also Adang, *Muslim Writers on Judaism,* 71–76, 117–20, 226–27.

57 Concerning the excurses on the Samaritans and the laws, feasts, and practices of the Israelites, see the translations of selected passages and the discussion in Adang, *Muslim Writers on Judaism,* 71–76.

58 See in particular Smit, *Bijbel en Legende,* 111–14, 128–34; A. Götze, "Die Nachwirkung der Schatzhöle," *ZS* 3 (1924): 60–71 ("6. Al-Ja'qûbî").

59 See the table of equivalencies in Smit, *Bijbel en Legende,* 115–27. Smit (p. 127) gives it as his opinion that in the Old Testament narratives al-Ya'qūbī followed a revision of the Peshitta text done with an eye to the Greek Septuagint by Jacob of Edessa (ca. 633–708).

60 It is interesting to read that al-Ya'qūbī says under the entry for Peleg, son of Eber, that Syriac (*Siryānī*) was the language of the Nabateans and that "it was the language of Adam." See al-Ya'qūbī, *Ta'rīkh,* 1:19; Houtsma, *Historiae,* 1:17.

61 André Ferré points out that in his *Annales,* Eutychius of Alexandria (877–940) makes use of many of the same sections of the *Cave of Treasures* for his account of the history of the patriarchs up to Abraham as did al-Ya'qūbī. He says, "la similitude entre les textes des deux auteurs est suffisamment obvie pour qu'on puisse conclure à l'utilisation d'une source commune. On peut même préciser qu'ils ont une affinité évidente avec la version dite 'syriaque orientale'" (Ferré, *L'histoire des prophètes,* xii). The implication is that there was a common Arabic version available to the two historians. In point of fact there was an early Arabic version, conserved in Sinai Arabic MS 508, dated paleographically to the ninth century. See M. D. Gibson, *Kitāb al-Mājāll, or The Book of the Rolls, Apocrypha Arabica* (Studia Sinaitica 8; London: Clay, 1901), 1–48 (Arabic), 1–58 (English). See now the edition of A. Battista and B. Bagatti, eds., *La Caverna dei Tesori: Testo arabo con traduzione italiana e commento* (Studium Biblicum Franciscanum Collectio Minor 26; Jerusalem: Franciscan Printing Press, 1979). This version of the *Cave of Treasures* seems to have circulated in Egypt. See Andreas Su-Min Ri, *Commentaire de la Caverne des Trésors: Étude sur l'histoire du texte et de ses sources* (CSCO 581; Leuven: Peeters, 2000), 63–66. Whether or not al-Ya'qūbī could have had access to it remains an open question.

Did he read the Peshitta in Syriac? Or did he make use of the services of Syriac-speaking Christian informants, who may have orally translated immediately from the texts for him? Al-Ya'qūbī's accounts often stay close to the biblical text, but they just as often also paraphrase it. We may gain some guidance for an answer to these questions by consulting al-Ya'qūbī's own remarks on how he dealt with his sources.

At the beginning of the second part of the *Ta'rīkh,* the section of the work that deals with Muḥammad and early Islamic history, al-Ya'qūbī makes a few introductory remarks about his methods and sources. He begins by speaking of the just-finished first part of the book, where, he says,

> We have given an abbreviated account of the coming to be of this world and of the reports of the most important ancient peoples, of the various kingdoms, and of their manifold affairs. We composed this book of ours according to what the ancient authorities have related, the scholars, the transmitters, and the authors of biographies, annals, and histories.[62]

In the preface to his *Kitāb al-buldān,* written many years after the *Ta'rīkh* in Egypt, al-Ya'qūbī has more to say about his sources and methods in composing that book. He says,

> I have traveled since I was a youngster. My travels have continued and as long as my foreign sojourns have lasted. I have, whenever I have met anyone from these countries, asked him about his homeland and its metropolis.... I would ask about their clothing ... their religions, and their doctrines.... Then I verified everything anyone whose truthfulness I could trust would report to me. I would appeal with questions to more and more people until I had questioned many knowledgeable individuals, in season and out of season, easterners and westerners, and I wrote down their reports, and transmitted their stories.... I continued to write down these reports, and to compose this book for a long time.... And we made this book an abbreviated account of the reports of the countries.[63]

Unfortunately, there is no surviving preface of this sort for the first part of the *Ta'rīkh;* the beginning of the book has not been preserved. But there is every reason to believe that al-Ya'qūbī would there have followed the same methodology *mutatis mutandis.* In both of the surviving prefaces he speaks of offering "an abbreviated account" (*mukhtaṣar*) of the

---

[62] Al-Ya'qūbī, *Ta'rīkh,* 2:5; Houtsma, *Historiae,* 2:2.

[63] De Goeje, *Kitāb al-boldān,* 232–33.

material at hand, which is clearly the case in the "Bible History" section of the work. In the course of the narrative he occasionally speaks of the varying opinions of the "People of the Book"[64] or "the evangelists" (*aṣḥāb al-injīl*),[65] whom he quotes by name. At one place he speaks of what the "Christians" (i.e., *an-naṣārā*) say.[66] Given his attested method of making use of informants and then writing down what they have told him, it makes sense to suppose that al-Ya'qūbī consulted the Peshitta and other Syriac biblical and exegetical texts through the good offices of Christian or Jewish informants. They may well have dictated to him with text in hand. Some of it he copied almost verbatim; some of it he paraphrased. Of course it is possible that he learned Hebrew, Syriac, or Greek for purposes of consulting the Bible on his own, but it seems unlikely, and he gives no hint of it in the text. Similarly, he could have used Arabic translations,[67] but few of them were widely available in the ninth century, and again al-Ya'qūbī makes no mention of them.

It is clear that al-Ya'qūbī approaches "Bible History" from the perspective of the Qur'ān. He does not name it in this section of the *Ta'rīkh,* but he quotes from it several times in the narrative and often refers to it by some such phrase as "God says" or, in reference to a person he names, as one "whom God, exalted be He, has mentioned."[68] He often uses the Qur'ān's names for biblical characters where they exist, as in speaking of Moses as "son of 'Imrān."[69] He folds the names of prophets known only from the Qur'ān, such as Hūd and Sāliḥ (Q 7:65–72; 73–79), into the fabric of "Bible History" by including them among the Noachites in the story of Nahor, son of Serug.[70] He sometimes corrects what the Bible says or the "People of the Book" maintain by citing the qur'ānic or Islamic traditions. For example, in the account of Noah's ark, al-Ya'qūbī says that "the vessel traveled over all the earth until it came to Mecca, and it circumambulated the house [*al-bayt;* i.e., the Ka'bah] seven times."[71] As for the ark's final resting place, al-Ya'qūbī, following the Qur'ān, says that "it came to rest on al-Jūdī" (Q 11:44).[72] But he notes that the "People of the Book" differ with

---

[64] See, e.g., al-Ya'qūbī, *Ta'rīkh,* 1:15; Houtsma, *Historiae,* 1:12.

[65] See, e.g., al-Ya'qūbī, *Ta'rīkh,* 1:68; Houtsma, *Historiae,* 1:74.

[66] See, e.g., al-Ya'qūbī, *Ta'rīkh,* 1:78; Houtsma, *Historiae,* 1:87.

[67] See Griffith, "The Gospel in Arabic"; idem, "The Monks of Palestine." See also note 61 above.

[68] See, e.g., al-Ya'qūbī, *Ta'rīkh,* 1:79, 48; Houtsma, *Historiae,* 1:88, 50.

[69] See, e.g., al-Ya'qūbī, *Ta'rīkh,* 1:47; Houtsma, *Historiae,* 1:48.

[70] See al-Ya'qūbī, *Ta'rīkh,* 1:22; Houtsma, *Historiae,* 1:19–20.

[71] Al-Ya'qūbī, *Ta'rīkh,* 1:14; Houtsma, *Historiae,* 1:12.

[72] Al-Ya'qūbī, *Ta'rīkh,* 1:14–15; Houtsma, *Historiae,* 1:12.

this view. He goes on to say that they say that al-Jūdī "is a mountain in the neighborhood of Mosul."[73] Similarly, in the matter of the Gospels' reports of Christ's death on the cross, al-Ya'qūbī, quoting the Qur'ān, says, "God, mighty and exalted be He, said, 'They did not kill him, and they did not crucify him, but it seemed so to them' (Q 4:157)."[74]

The Qur'ān's prophetology doubtless played a role in al-Ya'qūbī's decision to present "Bible History" by way of the sequence of the Bible's main *dramatis personae,* Adam to Jesus, paying close attention to the genealogies of Genesis and the sequence of prophets and kings up to the Babylonian exile. At that point he gives a quick summary of the laws, feasts, and religious practices of the "sons of Israel."[75] Then he turns immediately to the story of Jesus. This is the scheme of the Qur'ān, where there is scant interest in postexilic Israelite history from the exile until the time of Jesus.

Of all the Muslim scholars who have made use of the Bible in the spirit of the Qur'ān's admonition to the Muslims to "ask those who were reading scripture before you" (Q 10:94), al-Ya'qūbī is one of the few of them who dealt with the biblical text as the "People of the Book" actually have it. Nowhere in his *Ta'rīkh* is this more evident than in his approach to the Gospel text, in his presentation of Jesus, where Matthew, Mark, Luke, and John are allowed to speak for themselves in the passages al-Ya'qūbī chooses to quote.

Al-Ya'qūbī's Presentation of Jesus

Unlike Ibn Isḥāq, who already in the eighth century, as we have seen, was prepared to adjust the Gospel text he quoted to satisfy Islamic ideas about its proper formulation, al-Ya'qūbī took the text more or less as he found it in the hands of his Christian informants. He did not "Islamicize" it, but he did set the testimony of the Christian documents about Jesus Christ within the framework of the Qur'ān's view of him.[76] Essentially, al-Ya'qūbī uses the Gospels, and what he chooses to report of Christian tradition, to supplement what can be learned about Jesus from the Qur'ān.[77] Again, in his effort to provide a fuller picture, it is as if he were

---

[73] Al-Ya'qūbī, *Ta'rīkh,* 1:15; Houtsma, *Historiae,* 1:12.

[74] Al-Ya'qūbī, *Ta'rīkh,* 1:79; Houtsma, *Historiae,* 1:88.

[75] Al-Ya'qūbī, *Ta'rīkh,* 1:66–68; Houtsma, *Historiae,* 1:71–73.

[76] It was certainly not the case, as we shall see, that al-Ya'qūbī "was baffled by contradictions that he found between the accounts of Jesus in the Gospels and what he had read from the Qur'an" (Donaldson, "Al-Ya'qûbî's Chapter," 89).

[77] See Martin Klamroth, "Der Auszug aus den Evangelien bei dem arabischen Historiker Ja'qûbî," in *Festschrift zur Einweihung des Wilhelm-Gymnasiums in*

heeding the Qur'ān's dictum, "If you are in doubt about what We have sent down to you, ask those who were reading scripture before you" (Q 10:94). This is a dimension of al-Ya'qūbī's presentation of Jesus that it is important to emphasize because earlier commentators and translators of this section of the *Ta'rīkh* have not called attention to it, having been preoccupied more with al-Ya'qūbī's sources and the degree of his fidelity to them. But it is important also not to lose sight of his own purposes as they are revealed in the literary structure and contents of his narrative.

The presentation of Jesus, the Messiah, consists of two main parts,[78] framed between two paragraphs that provide reference points from the Qur'ān, one at the beginning and the other at the end of the main narrative. A short introductory paragraph provides Jesus' horoscope; a brief appendix gives an account of Peter and Paul and earliest Christianity. Al-Ya'qūbī himself, as we shall see, provides names for the headings of the two main sections of his narrative. The following diagram outlines this structure:

A. A Descendant of 'Imrān
   1. Jesus' Horoscope
   2. The Evangelists' Accounts
      a. Genealogy (*an-nisbah*)
      b. Reports (*al-akhbār*)
B. God Raised Him Up to Himself
C. Peter and Paul

It will yield the most clarity to discuss the narrative under the outline's main headings. At the outset it should be said that while al-Ya'qūbī stays close to the Evangelists' accounts for the parts of their narratives that most interest him, whether he quotes or paraphrases them, he often employs distinctly Islamic or qur'ānic words or phrases. This feature of his Arabic diction reminds the reader that fellow Muslims were al-Ya'qūbī's intended audience. The *Ta'rīkh* as a whole may also have had an apologetic, even a polemical dimension to it, after the manner of other texts by Muslim writers that played an important role in the elaboration of a distinctly Islamic

Hamburg am 21. Mai 1885 (Hamburg: Meissner, 1885), 117–28. This article has been the basic study utilized by all later commentators on al-Ya'qūbī's presentation of Jesus; it demonstrates his dependence on the Peshitta and suggests that he may have used Syriac-speaking informants, if not an Arabic translation of the New Testament based on the Peshitta (p. 126).

[78] Klamroth, "Der Auszug aus den Evangelien," 119, was the first to point out the two main parts in al-Ya'qūbī's narrative, including his concern for the "genealogy" (*nasab*) of the Messiah.

religious discourse in the multicultural and interreligious milieu of early Abbāsid times.[79]

A. A DESCENDANT OF 'IMRĀN

What Christians call the annunciation to Mary of her coming pregnancy with Jesus Christ is first mentioned in the Qur'ān in the third *sūra,* which carries the title *Family of 'Imrān.* A prominent feature of this *sūra* is the evocation of the annunciation scene in the Gospel of Luke, along with lore that can also be found in such apocryphal texts as the *Protoevangelium of James* and the *Gospel of Pseudo-Matthew* (Q 3:45–51).[80] Al-Ya'qūbī recalls these Qur'ān passages by opening his account of Jesus the Messiah with the mention of Hannah, the wife of 'Imrān, who gave her daughter Mary, destined to be the mother of Christ, into the care of Zachary, a priest in the temple (Q 3:31).[81] He assumes his readers' familiarity with the Qur'ān's narrative by referring to it here simply as what "God has narrated," or what "God has said," and of what God "has described."[82]

1. *Jesus' Horoscope*

After supplying the information that Christ was born in Bethlehem in Palestine on the twenty-fourth of Kanūn I (December),[83] al-Ya'qūbī gives

---

[79] In this connection see especially the studies of John E. Wansbrough, *The Sectarian Milieu: Content and Composition of Islamic Salvation History* (London Oriental Series 34; Oxford: Oxford University Press, 1978).

[80] See note 12 above.

[81] The Qur'ān speaks only of the "wife of 'Imrān." Al-Ya'qūbī has gotten the name Hannah/Anna either from earlier Muslim commentators such as Ibn Isḥāq or from his Christian informants; it is recorded in the *Protoevangelium of James.* But there is another anomaly here, from the Christian perspective. In the Qur'ān, Mary is the sister of Aaron (Q 19:26–27) and the daughter of 'Imrān (Q 66:14). It follows that Mary's mother Hannah/Anna was 'Imrān's wife. 'Imrān is also the father of Moses and Aaron, according to the Qur'ān. 'Imrān is the biblical 'Amram (Exod 11:20). The seeming confusion of Mary, mother of Jesus, with Miriam, the biblical sister of Aaron (and Moses) (Q 19:26–27) is an old *crux interpretum* in the Qur'ān. Al-Ya'qūbī does not attempt to solve it. For some indication of the variety of suggestions made by the *mufassirūn* over the centuries, see Nilo Geagea, *Mary of the Koran: A Meeting Point between Christianity and Islam* (trans. L. T. Fares; New York: Philosophical Library, 1984), esp. 60–64; Aliah Schleifer, *Mary, the Blessed Virgin of Islam* (Louisville: Fons Vitae, 1998), 36–38.

[82] See al-Ya'qūbī, *Ta'rīkh,* 1:68; Houtsma, *Historiae,* 1:74.

[83] In the *Ta'rīkh,* al-Ya'qūbī generally uses the "Syrian" names of the months.

his horoscope according to the calculations of the famed Jewish astronomer Māshā' Allah of Basrah, who flourished during the first half of the first Abbāsid century.[84] Al-Ya'qūbī wrote:

> Māshā' Allah, the astrologer, said, "The rising [of the moon] for the year in which the Messiah was born was in Libra eighteen degrees; Jupiter was in Virgo thirty-one minutes returning; Saturn was in Capricorn sixteen degrees and eighteen minutes. The sun was in Aries one minute. Venus was in Taurus fourteen degrees. Mars was in Gemini twenty-one degrees and forty-four minutes. Mercury was in Aries four degrees and seventeen minutes."[85]

2. *The Evangelists' Accounts*

At the beginning of this section, al-Ya'qūbī briefly gives the facts about Jesus' birth and infancy, noting the Qur'ān's contribution to the story, and he states how he has corroborated the accounts of the apostles. He says,

> As for the evangelists [*aṣḥāb al-injīl*], they do not say that he spoke in the cradle (cf. Q 3:46). They do say that Mary was named for a man called Joseph, of the offspring of David. She became pregnant and when her pregnancy came to term, he took her to Bethlehem. When she had given birth, he brought her back to Nazareth, by the mountain of Galilee. On the eighth day, according to the *sunnah* of Moses ibn 'Imrān, he circumcised him. The apostles [*al-ḥawwāriyyūn*][86] have given descriptive reports of the Messiah, and they have recalled his circumstances. We have corroborated what each one of them has had to say, and how they have described him.[87]

Al-Ya'qūbī then gives a list of the apostles and he goes on to say, "There were four who wrote the Gospel: Matthew, Mark, Luke and John. Two of them were of the twelve and two were not."[88] It is from this

---

84 See J. Samsó, "Māshā' Allāh," *EI*^{2} 6:710–12. Al-Ya'qūbī paid close attention to astrological calculations in his *Ta'rīkh*. He cited "the calculators" (*aṣḥāb al-ḥisāb*) for the position of the planets at the time of the flood. See al-Ya'qūbī, *Ta'rīkh,* 1:14; Houtsma, *Historiae,* 1:11. Later in the book he gave horoscopes for Muḥammad and all the caliphs after him whose reigns he discussed.

85 Al-Ya'qūbī, *Ta'rīkh,* 1:68; Houtsma, *Historiae,* 1:74.

86 This is the Qur'ān's term for "the apostles" (see, e.g., Q 3:52); it occurs five times in the Qur'ān.

87 Al-Ya'qūbī, *Ta'rīkh,* 1:68; Houtsma, *Historiae,* 1:74–75.

88 Al-Ya'qūbī, *Ta'rīkh,* 1:68; Houtsma, *Historiae,* 1:75.

point that he begins his account of the origins of Christ according to the four Evangelists.

a. Genealogy (*an-nisbah*)[89]

This section begins the main body of al-Ya'qūbī's presentation of Jesus. He gives an account of Jesus' origins and of the beginning of his ministry. He paraphrases and quotes from each one of the four Gospels under the headings of the names of the four Evangelists in their canonical order. It seems clear that al-Ya'qūbī intended this section of his work, with its long quotations, to supplement the meager information given about the origins of Jesus' life and ministry in the Qur'ān. It makes up the major part of his presentation of Jesus in the *Ta'rīkh,* taking up almost two-thirds of the number of pages devoted to him.

A striking feature of al-Ya'qūbī's presentation of Jesus in these pages is that he almost always calls him simply "Christ" or "the Messiah"; he never uses his proper name as it appears in the Qur'ān, that is, 'Īsā.[90] When he does use Jesus' proper name, he quotes it in the Christian Syriac form, transliterated into the Arabic script as *'īsū'*.[91] This usage can be

---

[89] This terminology comes from al-Ya'qūbī himself. At the end of this section he says: "This is what the four disciples, the evangelists, said about the genealogy [*nisbah*] of Christ. Then after that they recounted the reports of him [*akhbār*]." Cited from al-Ya'qūbī, *Ta'rīkh,* 1:75; Houtsma, *Historiae,* 1:83. At the beginning of his section on the Gospel of Matthew he speaks of the "lineage" (*nasab*) of Christ. See ibid., 1:69 and 1:75.

[90] This name appears twenty-five times in the Qur'ān, usually in the phrase 'Īsā ibn Maryam; i.e., "Jesus, son of Mary." The derivation of the name 'Īsā is uncertain; most authorities think that it comes ultimately from the east Syrian form of the name, Ishō'. See Arthur Jeffery, *The Foreign Vocabulary of the Qur'ān* (Baroda: Oriental Institute, 1938), 218–20; G.C. Anawati, "'Īsā," *EI*² 4:81–86, esp. 81. Donaldson introduced the name 'Īsā into the text, where it does not appear in the Arabic, at Donaldson, "Al-Ya'qûbî's Chapter," 91.

[91] Al-Ya'qūbī, *Ta'rīkh,* 1:69; Houtsma, *Historiae,* 1:75. This transcription reflects the east Syrian *Ishō';* in Arabic, the *sh* becomes *s,* and the *ō* becomes *ū,* according to the customary sound shifts from Northwest Semitic to South Semitic sound patterns. Al-Ya'qūbī's transliteration into Arabic script of the east Syrian form of the name even includes a prosthetic *aleph,* no doubt added to the usual Syriac consonants *y-sh-w-'* of Jesus' name to facilitate the east Syrian pronunciation. See Theodor Nöldeke, *Compendious Syriac Grammar* (trans. J. A. Crichton; 2d ed.; Winona Lake, Ind.: Eisenbrauns, 2001), 27. The transliteration thus suggests that al-Ya'qūbī's informant was an "east Syrian," perhaps a member of the "Church of the East," the so-called "Nestorians," as one would expect for a work composed in Khorasan. There would seem to be no philological grounds for supposing that

seen as a testimony to al-Ya'qūbī's fidelity to his sources—not even in this easy instance does he "Islamicize" the language of his report. But in less significant instances he does not hesitate to follow customary Islamic usage, employing words and phrases such as the devotional blessing "mighty and exalted be He" (*'azza wajalla*) after the mention of God (*Allāh*)[92] or speaking of the revelatory language (*al-waḥy*) Christ used in addressing his disciples.[93]

For the rest, in this section al-Ya'qūbī follows closely what the Evangelists have to say about Christ's origins and his ministry. He quotes extensively, and fairly literally, from the Sermon on the Mount in Matthew.[94] He mentions the fate of John the Baptist as reported in the same Gospel, no doubt because of the mention of him in the Qur'ān (Q 3:39).[95] From Mark he mentions John again and gives a report of Jesus' baptism, complete with the quotation of the voice from heaven saying, "You are my beloved son; I am delighted in you" (Mark 1:11).[96] He mentions the choosing of the apostles Simon and Andrew, including Christ's saying, "I will make you fishers of men" (Mark 1:17).[97] From Luke he dwells on chapters 1 and 2 and the accounts of Zachary, Elizabeth his wife, and Mary and Joseph and the birth of Christ, including the mention of Christ's genealogy traced from Joseph back to Adam. He mentions the beginning of Christ's ministry and how, when he expounded on a text from Isaiah, people were astounded and said, "Is this not Joseph's son?" (Luke 4:22).[98] From John he stresses genealogy again and highlights the prologue's words about the word of God (John 1:1–18). He quotes the statement that "Whereas the Torah was sent down by the hand of Moses, as for truth and grace, it is in Jesus the Messiah (John 1:17)," who was, al-Ya'qūbī adds, "the word [*al-kalimah*][99] that was unceasingly in the breast of its (i.e., the word's) father."[100] It seems that in the thinking of al-Ya'qūbī

---

al-Ya'qūbī's transliteration reflects a pronunciation *Aisū'*, as found in Donaldson, "Al-Ya'qûbî's Chapter," 92.

92 Al-Ya'qūbī, *Ta'rīkh,* 1:69; Houtsma, *Historiae,* 1:76.

93 Al-Ya'qūbī, *Ta'rīkh,* 1:69; Houtsma, *Historiae,* 1:76.

94 Al-Ya'qūbī, *Ta'rīkh,* 1:69–71; Houtsma, *Historiae,* 1:75–78.

95 Al-Ya'qūbī, *Ta'rīkh,* 1:71; Houtsma, *Historiae,* 1:78–79.

96 Al-Ya'qūbī, *Ta'rīkh,* 1:72; Houtsma, *Historiae,* 1:79.

97 Al-Ya'qūbī, *Ta'rīkh,* 1:72; Houtsma, *Historiae,* 1:79.

98 Al-Ya'qūbī, *Ta'rīkh,* 1:75; Houtsma, *Historiae,* 1:82.

99 In the Qur'ān, Jesus is the Word (*al-kalimah*) of Allah that He cast into Mary. See Q 4:171.

100 Al-Ya'qūbī, *Ta'rīkh,* 1:75; Houtsma, *Historiae,* 1:83.

these paraphrases and quotations from the initial chapters of the four Gospels furnish a supplementary account of how the Messiah fits within the family of ʿImrān, the framework within which he is presented in the Qur'ān.

b. Reports *(al-akhbār)*[101]

Having supplemented the Qur'ān's account of the origins of Jesus and the beginnings of his ministry from the Gospels, al-Yaʿqūbī goes on to cite from the same sources reports of other episodes in Christ's life that are of particular interest to Muslims because of their qur'ānic connections. In the first place are Jesus' miracles. The Qur'ān mentions that Jesus healed the blind and cured the lepers and even raised the dead, by God's permission (Q 5:110–111).[102] Al-Yaʿqūbī mentions these feats and then in this connection recounts more fully the raising of Lazarus, quoting liberally from John 11:1–44.[103]

Skipping much else that is in the Gospels, including any mention of the parables and other aspects of Jesus' teaching, al-Yaʿqūbī passes on to the accounts of Jesus' passion, death, and resurrection. As he says, he relies for the most part on John's Gospel, adding details from those of Matthew, Mark, and Luke.[104] He highlights aspects of the narratives that are of particular interest to Muslims or that have a special relevance to the Qur'ān's concerns. First among these matters are the Paraclete passages in John. Here al-Yaʿqūbī reports what Jesus has to say in a way that clearly reflects the construction Muslims such as Ibn Isḥāq had put upon these passages, but he does so subtly, without so obviously "Islamicizing" the text. Paraphrasing Jesus' words in John 15:26, al-Yaʿqūbī gives them a distinctly Islamic reading. He has Jesus say, "The Paraclete [*al-faraqlīṭ*] will come to you; he will be a prophet [*nabiyyan*] with you. When the Paraclete brings you the Spirit of truth and sincerity, he will be the one to give testimony about me."[105] Any Muslim reader of these words would of course think immediately of Muḥammad and of the Qur'ān sent down to him, in which

---

101 See note 89 above.

102 This same passage in the Qur'ān also mentions the miracles of Jesus' infancy and childhood, viz., his speaking from the cradle and his "blowing life" into clay birds. The latter miracle, while not recorded in the Gospel, is mentioned in early Christian apocryphal texts. See note 12 above. Al-Yaʿqūbī mentions the former miracle earlier in the *Ta'rīkh*. See the text quoted at note 87 above.

103 Al-Yaʿqūbī, *Ta'rīkh,* 1:75–76; Houtsma, *Historiae,* 1:84.

104 See al-Yaʿqūbī's statement in al-Yaʿqūbī, *Ta'rīkh,* 1:78; Houtsma, *Historiae,* 1:86.

105 Al-Yaʿqūbī, *Ta'rīkh,* 1:76; Houtsma, *Historiae,* 1:84.

there is in fact much testimony about Jesus the Messiah, the son of Mary. In the text just paraphrased from the Gospel of John, al-Ya'qūbī gives voice to the Islamic conviction that the passage is in fact Jesus' announcement, attested in the Qur'ān, of a "messenger" (*rasūl*), that is, "a prophet"[106] who would come after him, whose name will be Aḥmad (Q 61:6).

Al-Ya'qūbī turns next to the accounts of the passion, death, and resurrection of Jesus. He first paraphrases the passion narrative in the Gospel of John, then adds details in paraphrases of the passion narratives in the other Gospels. Here and there, as the narrative requires or his own interest dictates, he quotes directly from the Gospel text, usually sayings of Jesus. What most immediately strikes the reader is the accuracy of the paraphrases and quotations, given the fact that in the matter of Jesus' crucifixion and death there is a marked qur'ānic dissent from what the Christian texts report. In fact, at the end of his account of the Gospel "reports" (*al-akhbār*), al-Ya'qūbī will quote this dissent in full. In the meantime he presents the contents of the Christian texts faithfully, as the Christians actually have them. This fidelity is unusual in early Islamic accounts of the Gospels.

There are a number of small interesting points in the narrative. For example, al-Ya'qūbī reports that when Simon Peter unsheathed his sword at Jesus' arrest, "he struck the slave of the high priest, and cut off his right hand."[107] John 18:10 says that he "cut off his right ear." André Ferré somewhat implausibly suggested that in the Syriac source there could be an easy confusion between *'ydh* (hand) and *'dnh* (ear).[108] No textual variants to support this reading are to be found in the manuscript tradition of the Gospel, nor are there any extant grounds for it in the apocryphal texts. It may simply be al-Ya'qūbī's or his informant's mistake. At the end of the report of John's passion narrative, al-Ya'qūbī, without comment, reflecting his fidelity to reporting the narrative, says, "They took the Messiah out and made him carry the piece of wood on which they crucified him."[109] There is no remark here about the contradiction to the Qur'ān's teaching, as one might expect from a Muslim author; it will come later. Similarly, al-Ya'qūbī accurately reports the resurrection and ascension narratives from the Synoptic Gospels, adding only the qualifier "according to what the Christians say."[110]

---

[106] In the Qur'ān, Muḥammad, like Jesus, is normally called "the messenger of God" (*rasūl Allāh*), but he is also called "the seal of the prophets" (*khātim an-nabiyyīn*) in Q 33:40, and the text sometimes alludes to him as "the prophet" (*an-nabī*), as in Q 5:81.

[107] Al-Ya'qūbī, *Ta'rīkh,* 1:77; Houtsma, *Historiae,* 1:85.

[108] See Ferré, "Al-Ya'qûbî et les Évangiles," 79.

[109] Al-Ya'qūbī, *Ta'rīkh,* 1:77; Houtsma, *Historiae,* 1:86.

[110] Al-Ya'qūbī, *Ta'rīkh,* 1:78; Houtsma, *Historiae,* 1:87.

In this context, it is interesting to note also that al-Ya'qūbī quotes what Jesus said to Mary Magdalene after his resurrection according to John 20:17, again, without any textual alteration. He quotes, "Do not come near me, because I have not ascended to my Father.... But go off to my brothers, and say to them, 'I am going to ascend to my Father and to your father, to my God and your God.'"[111] What is interesting about this verse is that it was the most often quoted verse from the Bible in the Christian/Muslim apologetical and polemical literature of the early Islamic period. It was often cited by Muslim writers, appropriately corrected from an Islamic perspective, and used to discredit the Christian doctrine of the incarnation. Christian writers for their part often quoted it to answer the Islamic interpretation, in the process changing the emphasis of the traditional Christian exegesis to reflect the new hermeneutical circumstances provided by Islam.[112] Al-Ya'qūbī makes no mention of these matters, once again displaying his fidelity to the text he is reporting. It is only in the next section of his presentation of Jesus that al-Ya'qūbī summarily puts the whole matter into perspective from his own Islamic point of view.

B. God Raised Him Up to Himself

Al-Ya'qūbī is brief in his estimation of the Gospel reports he has so accurately presented. He quotes from the Qur'ān:

> This is what the Evangelists say, and they are at variance with one another about all the meanings [*al-ma'ānī*]. God, mighty and exalted be He, said, "They did not kill him, and they did not crucify him, but it seemed so to them. Those who are at variance about it are in doubt about something of which they have no knowledge, except for the following of opinion. They certainly did not kill him. Rather, God took him up to Himself" (Q 4:157–158).[113]

C. Peter and Paul

The last section of al-Ya'qūbī's presentation of Jesus in the *Ta'rīkh* is actually a narrative sketch of the contents of the canonical Acts of the

---

111 Al-Ya'qūbī, *Ta'rīkh,* 1:78; Houtsma, *Historiae,* 1:87.

112 See Martin Accad, "Did the Later Syriac Fathers Take into Consideration Their Islamic Context When Reinterpreting the New Testament?" *ParOr* 23 (1998): 13–32. Look for the forthcoming publication of Accad's Oxford D. Phil. thesis on the scriptures in the Muslim/Christian discourse of the early Islamic period, where this verse is studied in some detail.

113 Al-Ya'qūbī, *Ta'rīkh,* 1:79; Houtsma, *Historiae,* 1:88.

Apostles, with Peter and Paul and their missions as the focal points.[114] Paraphrase and some direct quotations characterize the accounts, with fidelity to the story as it appears in the Christian Bible being the hallmark of al-Ya'qūbī's method of composition. The most notable detail in the narrative that catches the reader's eye is an unusual exegesis that al-Ya'qūbī suggests in connection with the name "Peter," that is, "the rock." In his account of the beginning of Simon Peter's address to the assembled disciples in Jerusalem just after the ascension of Jesus, al-Ya'qūbī writes: "Simon stood up on the rock [*al-ḥajar*] and said, 'O assembly of brothers, it was necessary that the scripture be fulfilled, in which the Holy Spirit foretold...'" (cf. Acts 1:15).[115] In Greek, the name "Peter" (*Petros*) recalls "rock" (*petra*), a wordplay invoked already in the Gospels, most famously in Matt 16:18, "You are Peter [Πέτρος], and on this rock [πέτρᾳ] I will build my church." In the Peshitta version of this passage, the Syriac word *kēpā/kīpā* "rock" appears in both instances. Not infrequently in the Gospels the name of the apostle is given as Simon Peter, or in Syriac, Shem'ūn Kēpā/Kīpā, often transliterated as Cephas in English (see Κηφᾶς in John 1:42). In three instances earlier in the text, al-Ya'qūbī reflected this usage, but it is somewhat camouflaged behind an anomalous reading.[116] Here he offers an exegetical comment on the significance of Simon "the Rock's" nickname; he says that he stood on the rock (*al-ḥajar*) to deliver his first authoritative address. Al-Ya'qūbī must have gotten this nonbiblical detail from his Christian informants, but so far it has not been found in any known Christian text.

Concluding Reflection

Al-Ya'qūbī was a historian who took his sources seriously. While there was a perfectly good Islamic reason to quote the Gospel as Ibn Isḥāq quoted John 15:23–16:1, in an "Islamicizing" version that corrected what

---

114 Al-Ya'qūbī, *Ta'rīkh,* 1:79–80; Houtsma, *Historiae,* 1:88–89.

115 Al-Ya'qūbī, *Ta'rīkh,* 1:79; Houtsma, *Historiae,* 1:88.

116 See al-Ya'qūbī, *Ta'rīkh,* 1:77, 78; Houtsma, *Historiae,* 1:85, 87. In all three instances in which the double name occurs, the second element is given in Arabic in the printed editions of the text as *aṣ-ṣafā,* a seemingly impossible reading. All the translators of the text have passed over it without comment, translating simply Simon Peter, apparently assuming that *aṣ-ṣafā* is meant to reflect Cephas. But this is an impossible reading; *ṣ* cannot transliterate an original *k.* Perhaps the original text featured a transliteration of the Syriac *kēpā/kīpā* into Arabic script as *al-kīfā,* which was then misread as *aṣ-ṣafā.* In Arabic handwriting it may have been easy for a copyist to misread *ky* (كي) for *ṣ* (ص), especially in a word that would have been meaningless to him.

was considered to be a flawed text, al-Ya'qūbī chose another alternative. He presented the Gospel narratives as he found them in Christian hands, but he presented them in a context that allowed him to provide an Islamic corrective at appropriate junctures. That context was the Islamic, even the qur'ānic, structure of his presentation of Jesus in the *Ta'rīkh,* using the extended paraphrases and quotations from the Gospels to supplement the Qur'ān's own presentation of Jesus' prophetic career. There is never any doubt in the discourse about the fact that for al-Ya'qūbī the Qur'ān's point of view was authoritative. Where al-Ya'qūbī differed from other Muslim scholarly writers in the classical period, even other historians, was his willingness to present Jesus in the light of the Gospel texts as the Christians of his day actually had them. He did not give an account of Jesus on the basis of corrected versions of the Gospels or in a way that dispensed with the canonical Gospel texts altogether. One knows of no other Muslim scholar after al-Ya'qūbī who adopted his methodology. Perhaps by then the intellectual pressures of the "sectarian milieu" would have made it theologically undesirable to pay so much attention to the Gospels, or perhaps they simply became irrelevant to the by-then well-developed Islamic kerygma.

It would not be until the time of Ibn Ḥazm (994–1064) that the Gospel texts would receive as much scholarly attention from a Muslim writer as al-Ya'qūbī paid to them. But Ibn Ḥazm's purposes were very different; he was determined to show their utter unreliability.[117] It is true that a later writer, using the name of al-Ghazālī,[118] quoted liberally from the Gospels, but he was in all likelihood a Christian convert to Islam, writing as much for his former coreligionists as for Muslims; his work certainly never entered the Islamic mainstream. In the end it was as Hava Lazarus-Yafeh has said, that in the world of Islam, biblical "exegesis never became a literary genre on its own, nor did it ever play an important role in Muslim medieval theology."[119] That certainly was the case with the Gospels, but it never was the case with the Muslim Jesus. As Tarif Khalidi and others have shown, from the very beginning Jesus himself has loomed large in Islamic thought. Al-Ya'qūbī's presentation of Jesus, albeit somewhat singular in its method, does nevertheless present the Messiah, Jesus, son of Mary, from the classical Islamic perspective.

---

117 See Pulcini, *Exegesis As Polemical Discourse,* esp. 98–128.

118 See the bibliographical citations in note 41 above.

119 Lazarus-Yafeh, *Intertwined Worlds,* 97.

Abraham's Test: Islamic Male Circumcision As Anti/Ante-Covenantal Practice

Kathryn Kueny
Lawrence University

Male circumcision posed a number of challenges that demanded the development of an appropriate rhetorical response that could readily assimilate the practice into the repertoire of recommended Islamic rituals. What were those rhetorical difficulties confronted by early Muslim exegetes? First of all, circumcision, which appeared in a variety of geographically, culturally, and ethnically specific forms, was a pre-Islamic practice that was gradually absorbed by the Islamic legal tradition. To give the ritual a unique Islamic identity, early exegetes faced the question of how to interpret a practice also performed by Jews, Arabs, Ethiopians, and polytheists. Circumcision posed an even further problem to the rhetorical ingenuity of the early tradition because of its strong associations with the Jewish covenant. How did the early Islamic tradition make the practice of circumcision continuous with a common Abrahamic past while disassociating it from its strong associations with Jewish identity? Circumcision gradually evolved into a distinctively Islamic practice only through the development of new rhetorical tropes that could simultaneously retain continuity with an Abrahamic past while distancing that past from its associations with the Jewish covenant and privilege a customary practice that became, by later definition, an Islamic practice even prior to the coming of both Islam *and* Judaism.

Circumcision (*khitān*) can be found nowhere in the Qur'ān, yet it is recognized as legal to varying degrees by the schools of law. The four major legal schools differ as to whether the practice should be understood as legally obligatory (*wājib*), recommendable (*mustaḥabb*), or permissible (*jā'iz*). For example, Shāfi'ī jurists consider the practice legally obligatory for both males and females, while Ḥanafī scholars assert that circumcision on the seventh day after birth for males only is strongly recommended.[1] Mālikī and Ḥanbalī schools assume male circumcision to

[1] A. J. Wensinck, "Khitān," *EI*² 5:20–22.

be legally permissible. Despite these somewhat ambivalent views about its legal status, many jurists claim that male circumcision is necessary for participation in vital religious practices such as prayer, inheritance, or conversion to Islam.[2] Despite the legal ambivalence towards this practice, and for that matter, the lack of extensive commentary detailing its legitimacy as a distinctly Islamic ritual—there is relatively little discussion about the practice in any legal text—in popular imagination it becomes inextricably linked in various ways with one's identity as a Muslim.

For example, while one may or may not have to be circumcised in order to call himself a Muslim, circumcision is still considered by many to be a requirement for the pilgrimage (*ḥajj*),[3] one of the five pillars of Islam. The link between circumcision and the *ḥajj* was so strong that one fraudulent Western (uncircumcised) pilgrim in the nineteenth century writes in great depth about his fear of detection as he is forced to wash his body in public. He notes that his status as a nonbeliever would be exposed if his excess foreskin were revealed:

> Had anyone noticed? What happened afterwards gave me reason to think someone had, even though I had taken all possible precautions since I was terrified at the prospect of the tortures that a fanatic and barbarous mob would inflict on me if they recognized that I was a Christian.[4]

Obviously one's identity as a Muslim or non-Muslim hinged upon the mark of circumcision.

While nonqur'ānic in origin, circumcision appears to have been a cultural practice that predates Islam, as suggested by both traditional and nontraditional sources. The first-century Jewish philosopher Philo notes how both male and female circumcision were practiced in Egypt. He states that:

> the Egyptians, in accordance with the national customs of their country, in the fourteenth year of their age, when the male begins to have the power of propagating his species, and when the female arrives at the edge of puberty, circumcise both bride and bridegroom.[5]

---

[2] Earle H. Waugh, "Circumcision," *The Oxford Encyclopedia of the Modern Islamic World* (ed. J. L. Esposito; 4 vols.; Oxford: Oxford University Press, 1995), 1:290.

[3] Laleh Bakhtiar, *Encyclopedia of Islamic Law: A Compendium of the Views of the Major Schools* (Chicago: ABC International Group, 1998), 191.

[4] Léon Roches, *Dix ans a travers l'Islam, 1834–1844* (3d ed.; Paris: Perrin, 1904), 337. Quoted by F. E. Peters, *The Hajj: The Muslim Pilgrimage to Mecca and the Holy Places* (Princeton: Princeton University Press, 1994), 251.

[5] *QG* 3.47. Quotation is taken from *The Works of Philo: Complete and Unabridged* (trans. C. D. Yonge; Peabody, Mass.: Hendrickson, 1993), 857.

In this example, circumcision clearly served as a rite of passage for males and females who faced the often uncertain transition from children to adults. As Philo further deliberates on some of the reasons why male circumcision is observed, he notes how certain ethnic groups tended to adhere to the practice, as well as groups confined to a particular geographical region. He notes the following:

> Here it was thought fit that man should be circumcised out of a provident care for his mind ... since not the Jews alone, but also the Egyptians, and Arabians, and Ethiopians, and nearly all the nations who live in the southern parts of the world, down to the torrid zone are circumcised.[6]

Josephus, the first-century C.E. Jewish historian, comments on how the Arabs "circumcise after the thirteenth year because Ishmael, the founder of their nation, who was born to Abraham of the concubine, was circumcised at that age."[7] Already by Josephus's time, Ishmael was set up as a paradigmatic model for the Arabs. To what extent Ishmael served in this capacity for the Arabs living in the Ḥijāz around the time of Muḥammad is yet to be debated.

Apparently people living in the Ḥijāz prior to Islam embraced the practice of circumcision, although little rationale for the practice can be found in any extant text. In his early biography of the prophet (*Al-Sīra al-nabawīya*), Ibn Isḥāq makes some mention of how in pre-Islamic times members of the Quraysh would bring their sons, along with a hundred dirhams and a slaughter camel, to Hubal, the central idol of the Ka'ba, before they were to be circumcised.[8] Moreover, at the time the *Sīra* was compiled sometime in the eighth century, a vocabulary already seems to be in place for the uncircumcised as well as the circumcised. The term *uncircumcised* is used pejoratively in connection with Jews and Christians, who are chastised for rejecting the Torah that was given to Moses and the Gospel that was presented to Jesus, son of Mary. When God reproved these men and women for not believing in the words of his messengers, they purportedly stated, "*qulūbunā ghulfun*," or literally, "our hearts are uncircumcised."[9]

Further connotations of the root *gh-l-f* denote a sense of being covered, concealed, or even uncivilized. The use of the term here is obviously

---

6 *QG* 3.48 (ibid., 858).

7 Josephus, *Ant.* 1.214; quoted by Peters, *The Hajj*, 41.

8 Muḥammad ibn Isḥāq, *Sīrat rasūl Allāh*, in the recension of 'Abd al-Mālik b. Hishām's *al-Sīra al-nabawīya* (4 vols.; Dār al-Kutub al-Miṣrīya, n.d.). Translated by Alfred Guillaume, *The Life of Muhammad: A Translation of Ibn Isḥāq's Sīrat Rasūl Allāh* (Oxford: Oxford University Press, 1955), 67.

9 Ibn Isḥāq, *Sīra,* 1:541; Guillaume, *Life*, 254.

metaphorical, not unlike the biblical usage of circumcision/uncircumcision to signify belief/unbelief or civilized/uncivilized. In similar fashion to the *Sīra* reference, Deut 30:6 states that "The LORD your God will circumcise [*mul*] your heart and the heart of your descendants, so that you will love the LORD your God with all your heart," while Jeremiah concedes that Israel's actual circumcision holds little value, given that Israel is uncircumcised in the heart. Jeremiah 4:4 explicitly commands Israel to "circumcise yourselves to the LORD, and remove the foreskins of your heart." These statements obviously are not to be taken literally but figuratively, relying on an established symbolic vocabulary derived from actual, normative practice.

These few concrete and metaphorical examples taken from inside and outside the Islamic tradition suggest that in all likelihood circumcision in some form was practiced or recognized prior to the sending down of the Qur'ān. The rationale behind the actual practice was based upon ethnic and social prescriptions that varied from group to group and text to text, as opposed to one single justification, such as the exemplar of Ishmael. In addition, the biblical usage of the term seems widespread before the coming of Islam among those who professed a monotheistic worldview. Although circumcision is mentioned in pre-Islamic sources, or in Islamic sources that dwell on pre-Islamic times, these references are remarkably few. One would expect much more elaborate and detailed discussions about a practice that was so widely observed by so many different groups of people who later called themselves Muslims.

BIBLICAL ROOTS

Because circumcision is a topic of great interest within Judaism and Christianity, we might anticipate its repeated presence in the Qur'ān, given this text's interest in such associated topics as covenant, prophethood, sacrifice, and the community of the faithful. However, any discussion or even passing mention of circumcision is remarkably absent from the qur'ānic context.

Both the Jewish and Christian Bibles give clear prescriptions with regard to the practice of circumcision. The book of Genesis, for example, lays out a lucid and unquestionable command to circumcise in 17:10–11: "Every male among you shall be circumcised. You shall circumcise the flesh of your foreskins, and it shall be a sign of the covenant between me and you." Much recent debate has been held over the significance of this biblical act of self-mutilation.[10] Lawrence Hoffman, for example,

---

[10] See, e.g., Lawrence A. Hoffman, *Covenant of Blood: Circumcision and Gender in Rabbinic Judaism* (Chicago: University of Chicago Press, 1996); and Nancy

argues that both a preexilic (or exilic)[11] and postexilic understanding of circumcision and its relationship to the covenant can be detected in the biblical account. The preexilic or exilic covenant was characterized by a prophetic and monarchic symbolism rooted in land and sacrifice, while the postexilic covenant was connected to the priestly emphasis on circumcision.[12] These two views are represented by Abram's sacrifice of a three-year-old heifer and ram, a turtledove, and a young pigeon in Gen 15:9 and Abraham's circumcision in Gen 17:10–14.[13] In Gen 15, the preexilic/exilic account, the Lord accepts the sacrifices of Abram and makes a covenant with him based on promises of land and numerous descendants. In Gen 17, Abraham is also pledged land and progeny, this time in return for his circumcision.

Hoffman argues that between the two rival interpretations the priestly version eventually won out and was ultimately privileged as the normative account by the later rabbinic sages. The sages, however, emphasized the importance of the practice by linking circumcision more closely with blood sacrifice. According to the rabbis, blood in the context of sacrifice or circumcision is a salvific blood, that which serves simultaneously to sever between, yet to unite humans more intimately with, the divine. In the rabbinic traditions, circumcision and the sacrifice of the paschal lamb represent the two major events that make up God's most significant acts of deliverance,[14] both achieved through the processes of separating one group of people from another and then the guaranteeing of eventual salvation to those who have distinguished themselves from the unfortunate ones surrounding them. As a result of this interpretive move, the rabbis were able to underscore circumcision as the primary commandment God demands of his people:

> [Why did God divide the Red Sea?] R. Banaah said, "Because of the merit of the deed which Abraham their father did...." Simon of Teman said, "Because of the merit of circumcision.... For it is said, 'Thus says the Lord: if not for my covenant of day and night, I would not have appointed the ordinances of heaven and earth' (Jer. 33:25). Go and see which

---

Jay, *Throughout Your Generations Forever: Sacrifice, Religion, and Paternity* (Chicago: University of Chicago Press, 1992).

[11] Hoffman states that the distinction between "preexilic" and "exilic" sources is of no consequence in the discussion of biblical circumcision, since both time periods emphasized reflections on landed status (Hoffman, *Covenant,* 29).

[12] Ibid.

[13] Ibid.

[14] Ibid., 103.

covenant obtains day and night. You can find none but the commandment of circumcision."[15]

In this short vignette, circumcision becomes the sole pivot around which the covenant revolves. Those biblical references that advocate circumcision thus become the normative reading and override those passages in which the practice is never mentioned in association with God's covenant.

Given its decided importance as a direct command from God in both the biblical and rabbinical corpora, we might expect circumcision and its link to covenantal promise to continue on in the Qur'ān's portrayal of Abraham (*Ibrāhīm*). Abraham is, after all, portrayed as the original monotheist (*ḥanīf*), the first one to submit (*muslim*) to the one true God.[16] However, the Qur'ān's discussion of Abraham never takes note of God's command for him to circumcise, nor does it discuss the biblical understanding of covenant in contractual terms; that is, if one circumcises, God will deliver land and offspring. In fact, the qur'ānic discussions of Abraham have God making the same covenant (*mīthāq*) with Abraham as he did with numerous other prophets, including Noah, Moses, and Jesus.[17] Even the covenant had no special association with Abraham.

One might also expect to find some sort of combative engagement with the practice in the Qur'ān, as is the case in the Christian biblical tradition. Like the priestly writers in the Pentateuch, Paul too looks to Abraham to justify his views on circumcision. Paul, however, elegantly wipes away any obligation to circumcise by stating in Rom 4:11 that Abraham actually "received the sign of circumcision as a seal of the righteousness that he had by faith while he was still uncircumcised." In this example, Paul stresses the faith Abraham possessed prior to his circumcision. For Paul, circumcision can be lumped under the general rubric of "law," which only served as a "disciplinarian until Christ came, so that we might be justified by faith."[18]

---

[15] Quote from *Mek. Beshalaḥ* §4 (*Mekilta de-Rabbi Ishmael* [ed. J. Z. Lauterbach; 3 vols.; 1933–35; repr., Philadelphia: Jewish Publication Society of America, 1976], 1:218), taken from Hoffman, *Covenant*, 114.

[16] Q 2:129; 3:60. Along with elaborations on Abraham's true faith, the Qur'ān also explores such quasi-biblical and nonbiblical themes as Abraham's relation to the Ka'ba (2:124–126); his dismissal of idolatry (6:23); his denial of his father's religion (26:70–83); and his scriptures (53:30–44).

[17] Q 33:7.

[18] Gal 3:24. Views on circumcision in the New Testament, however, vary radically from text to text. Note the Gospel of John, where Jesus proclaims, "Moses gave you circumcision, and you circumcise a man on the sabbath. If a man receives circumcision on the sabbath in order that the law of Moses may not be broken, are

This route toward a reinterpretation of circumcision would certainly coincide with several qur'ānic injunctions that lift many of the rules and restrictions imposed upon the Jews by the Torah, a rhetorical move that parallels the same efforts in the Christian tradition. For example, the qur'ānic revelation declares that only carrion, running blood, the flesh of swine, and flesh consecrated to idols are prohibited.[19] This truncated list stands in opposition to what was expected of other Peoples of the Book, as we note in Q 6:146: "We forbade the Jews all animals with undivided hoofs and the fat of sheep and oxen, except what is on their backs and intestines and who is mixed with their bones. Such is the penalty We imposed on them for their misdeeds." Circumcision could easily have fallen under the rubric of such punitive laws and have readily been dismissed in preference for true faith.

As all these biblical and nonbiblical examples suggest, given that Arabs embrace circumcision as a cultural or religious practice, Jews use it as an essential part of their covenant in an effort to assert an exclusive identity, Christians embrace a complex polemical discourse disassociating circumcision from that very covenant, and creating a distinct identity from Jews seems essential to the burgeoning Muslim identity, one might assume that some discussion of circumcision would be in order in the Qur'ān: either endorsement (i.e., continuity); or repudiation (i.e., difference). What appears in the Qur'ān and some of the other early sources is either a loud silence or only a variety of cursory discussions concerning the legitimacy of circumcision. As a rhetorical trope that could signify either continuity or change, circumcision is simply not exploited. Certainly circumcision was a widespread religious and cultural practice among Arabs, but oddly enough it is not featured in the early literature as the specific mark of one's identity as a believer. This discrepancy between practice and meaning persists throughout the early history of Islam prior to the tenth century.

Peculiarly, given the lack of discussion on any level about the religious or cultural validity of circumcision in these early documents, many recent scholars such as Uri Rubin and M. J. Kister have been quick to argue that circumcision was already an established part of the *sunan Ibrāhīm* that existed prior to Islam and was in fact adopted wholesale by Islam as the *sunan al-islām*.[20] As Kister states,

---

you angry with me because I healed a man's whole body on the sabbath?" (7:22–23).

19 Q 6:145.

20 See M. J. Kister, ". . . And He Was Born Circumcised . . . ," in idem, *Concepts and Ideas at the Dawn of Islam* (Brookfield, Vt.: Ashgate, 1997), 10–30; Uri Rubin, "Ḥanīfiyya and Ka'ba," *JSAI* 13 (1990): 96–112.

> [s]cholars considered [circumcision] as a mark of Islam; some of them were of the opinion that it denoted servitude of the believer and his bondage to God, a visible sign that the believer carried out God's injunction. This is reminiscent of the Jewish idea of circumcision, according to which it is a sign of the covenant between God and his people.[21]

Much of their theory that circumcision was already a part of the *sunan Ibrāhīm* comes from a rather shaky foundation: the one quote from Josephus, which traces the practice back to Ishmael but legitimizes it as an *Arab* practice; the *Sīra's* rather cryptic mention of circumcision in association with pre-Islamic polytheistic rituals surrounding the Ka'ba (which was, of course, built by Abraham, according to the Islamic tradition); and a late Umayyad Syriac source that introduces the idea of Abraham's "commandments" as being sacrifice and circumcision.[22] The Qur'ān mentions such commandments in Q 2:124 but never suggests what they were or how Abraham fulfilled them.[23] It is left to later commentaries to flesh out this information.[24] What shapes the interpretations of these recent scholars is the fact that they survey the literature composed or compiled sometime between the thirteenth and fifteenth centuries. By this late date, the association between Abraham and circumcision was already clearly asserted and projected back onto earlier sources, but not, as I will argue, for any reasons having to do with the covenant in the Jewish sense.

Even if these scholars are correct about where we end up—namely, that circumcision is intimately linked with Abrahamic example—prior to the tenth and eleventh centuries the concept and the rhetoric surrounding it were in a state of flux. What emerges after this time is not an analogue to the Jewish covenant but a sharp departure from it. Instead, it took several centuries for an appropriate type of rhetoric to evolve to accommodate this practice in such a way that it could establish certain fundamental associations with Abraham, yet reject others. Moreover, the resulting associations with Abraham are not reminiscent at all of the Jewish covenantal idea of circumcision, which as we have seen above is represented as a sole command from God who bargained land and offspring for foreskin in a kind of tit-for-tat contractual exchange.

---

21 Kister, "Born Circumcised," 30.

22 Patricia Crone and Michael Cook, *Hagarism: The Making of the Islamic World* (Cambridge: Cambridge University Press, 1977), 12.

23 The passage goes as follows: "When his Lord tested Abraham with commandments [*kalimāt*], and he fulfilled them, the Lord said, 'I have raised you as leader over the people.'"

24 See below.

Rather, the rhetoric that developed over time to link circumcision with Abraham allowed Muslims to maintain the practice's cultural priority (i.e., Arabs were circumcising long before Jews) and to privilege that impulse (i.e., those who circumcised prior to Islam in fact realized the true religion of Abraham [and thus Muḥammad], along with their true natures as God originally created them). Ultimately these rhetorical moves not only kept Islamic circumcision distinct in nature from the parallel Jewish practice but also privileged the Islamic version over and above what can be described as the more inferior type adhered to by the Jews.

Circumcision in Early Islamic Sources

As stated above, circumcision—*khitān*—never appears in the Qur'ān. Neither does the root—*kh-t-n*—appear in any form. Although circumcision does appear in some nonqur'ānic early Islamic sources, its mention is rare. In addition, its treatment varies radically from text to text. Both of these facts defy the opinion that circumcision was, from very early on, an established part of the *sunan Ibrāhīm* or that the *sunan Ibrāhīm* was imported wholesale into the early Islamic tradition.

For example, the *Sīra* mentions the practice of circumcision several times briefly and in passing but not in ways one might expect. In addition, the *Sīra* nowhere associates circumcision with the religion of Abraham, except when it describes how boys who were to be circumcised in pre-Islamic times were brought to the Quraysh's favorite idol Hubal at the Ka'ba. As I noted above, some recent scholars have suggested that circumcision may be linked cryptically with practices surrounding the Ka'ba and thus with Abraham. However, in the *Sīra*'s more elaborate discussions about the religion of Abraham, circumcision is never noted. If the link between the *sunan Ibrāhīm* and circumcision were so strong, one might expect it to crop up in the lists that articulate the practices of the *ḥanīfiya*. For example, in the *Sīra*'s discussion about Zayd b. 'Amr, we find that he

> accepted neither Judaism nor Christianity. He abandoned the religion of his people and abstained from idols, carrion, blood, and things offered to idols. He forbade the killing of infant daughters, saying that he worshipped the God of Abraham, and he publicly rebuked his people for their practices.[25]

Circumcision could easily have been added to this list of Abrahamic religious practices, but it was not. The reason for its absence may be that

[25] Guillaume, *Life,* 99.

circumcision was so strongly linked with Judaism that it was omitted from any list of practices associated with the *ḥanīfīya*. Or it could be that Zayd himself was circumcised and did not want to condemn a practice he wholeheartedly embraced. In either case, the *Sīra* does not discuss circumcision as having a consistent, normative link with Abrahamic practice.

Even the *Kitāb al-mubtada'*, the excised portion of Ibn Isḥāq's original *Sīra* that has been reconstructed in recent years, does not mention circumcision in association with Abraham. Typical themes abound in the *Kitāb al-mubtada'*, such as Abraham's rejection of idolatry, his construction of the Ka'ba, and his strident monotheism; however, there is no mention of his "command" to circumcise. Here we find a reiteration of the preexilic/exilic biblical theme of sacrifice as God tests the loyalty of Abraham by requesting he offer up his son Ishmael at God's command. In the Islamic version of this sacrificial drama, God spares Ishmael by accepting a substitution in his place.[26] Here again, circumcision readily falls into the thematic framework of tests of loyalty expressed on the part of both God and human. Nevertheless, this text is silent on the issue. Even in the *Kitāb al-mubtada'*, a work that records the early efforts of many who strove to assimilate biblical narratives into Islam,[27] circumcision is severed from its ideological roots and never discussed.

In the *Sīra*'s discussion of the Torah's depiction of God's covenant, there is also no analysis of circumcision as being a fundamental part of that contract. In the *Sīra* as well as in the Qur'ān,[28] we find lengthy lists describing Torah practice, which include the worship of one God, kindness to parents, orphans, and the poor, adherence to prayer, acknowledgment of the poor tax, and the avoidance of shedding each other's blood.[29] Circumcision is again absent from these lists, whether in reference to Abraham or in reference to Jewish practice. To mention it would have resulted in a rather uncomfortable proposition: circumcision, a ritual that was obviously observed by Arabs, would have to be recognized as a Jewish practice mandated by the Torah but not the Qur'ān. How, then, does one

---

[26] See the translation of the *Kitāb al-mubtada'* in Gordon D. Newby, *The Making of the Last Prophet: A Reconstruction of the Earliest Biography of Muhammad* (Columbia: University of South Carolina Press, 1989), 78. See also Q 37:103–107 for reference to this event.

[27] See Newby, *Making of the Last Prophet*, 10. Newby notes how many scholars were interested in transmitting Jewish and Christian works into Islam, including much rabbinic material. This biblical literature is known as the *Isrā'īlīyāt*.

[28] See Q 5:45; 3:93.

[29] Guillaume, *Life*, 252–53.

account for the fact that it would have been mentioned in prior scripture but neither confirmed nor denied by the Qur'ān?

The *Sīra* also makes no mention of Muḥammad's circumcision nor notes in passing that he was in fact circumcised. By the fourteenth century, many Islamic scholars pointed to the one passage in the *Sīra* where 'Abdu'l Muṭṭalib takes the young prophet on his shoulders and goes around the Ka'ba confiding him to God's protection and praying for him[30] and suggested that since 'Abdu'l Muṭṭalib was involved in religious activities in Mecca during the *Jāhilīya,* it was certainly he who would have circumcised Muḥammad.[31] The insistence upon the Prophet being circumcised crops up in other fourteenth- and fifteenth-century works, with many scholars like al-Maqrīzī insisting that he was, in fact, born circumcised.[32]

The Shī'ītes, most notably Ibn Bābūya al-Qummī, also record how all of the major prophets, including Abraham and Muḥammad, were born circumcised and purified, along with every Shī'ī *imām*.[33] The necessity for this in utero circumcision may be linked to the Zoroastrian fear of dead material. Circumcision was not a part of the Zoroastrian purity code that influenced Shī'ism, for the foreskin that is removed results in a severe pollutant as wasted human material.[34] As we shall see, these traditions that advocate a prebirth circumcision also go against Sunnī beliefs that Abraham endured excruciating pain during his circumcision as part of God's testing him. Moreover, they certainly suggest that normal human circumcision will always be inferior to the more purified, prophetic type, a reality that simultaneously separates and elevates prophets and *imāms* as quasi-divine figures and lowers less-worthy, impure human beings further into an already-flawed world. We will speak more on Shī'īte views of circumcision below. Getting back to the eighth century and the *Sīra,* there is no explicit suggestion that the Prophet's grandfather had a hand in his grandson's circumcision or for that matter that the Prophet was circumcised at all.

---

30 Ibid., 73.

31 Aḥmad ibn 'Alī al-Maqrīzī, *Imta'ū l-asmā'* (ed. Maḥmūd Muḥammad Shākir; Cairo, 1941), 1:5, cited by Kister, "Born Circumcised," 17.

32 Abū'l-Faraj 'Abd al-Raḥmān ibn 'Alī ibn al-Jawzī, *al-Wafā bi-aḥwāli l-muṣṭafā* (ed. Muṣṭafā 'Abd al-Wāḥid; Cairo, 1966), 97; Ismā'īl ibn 'Umar ibn Kathīr, *al-Sīra al-nabawīya* (ed. Muṣṭafā 'Abd al-Wāḥid; Cairo, 1966), 1:209, as noted by Kister, "Born Circumcised," 12.

33 Ibn Bābūya al-Qummī, *'Uyūnu akhbāri al-riḍā* (ed. Muḥammad Mahdī al-Sayyid Ḥasan al-Khurasān; Najaf, 1970), 1:169, as noted by Kister, "Born Circumcised," 13.

34 I would like to thank Professor Jamsheed Choksy for this observation. Choksy also notes that not all Zoroastrian converts to Islam underwent circumcision, for the reasons noted above.

When circumcision is mentioned in the *Sīra,* it is treated in a somewhat ambivalent fashion, in particular when associated with the female version. As noted above, only boys were brought to the Kaʿba to be circumcised in celebratory fashion. Girls, if they were circumcised, obviously participated in a less-festive, more-secluded type of ritual. In addition, those who circumcised females were relegated to a marginal social status. For example, Ḥamza, "the best helper to God's messenger,"[35] smote and killed Abū Niyār during the battle of Uḥud, Abū Niyār being the son of a female circumciser (*khattāna*).[36] There is, of course, some question as to whether this title refers to a woman who would circumcise males or a woman who would circumcise females. The question is cleared up in a later passage that recounts the moment when Ḥamza calls out to Abū Niyār before he kills him. Ḥamza cries, "*ya, ibn muqaṭṭiʿit al-buẓūr,*" quite literally, "you son of a clitoris cutter."[37]

Coming away from the *Sīra,* one would have the sense that Arabs practiced circumcision but would have no idea why or how circumcision may possibly be included into the corpus of Islamic rituals, mandatory or otherwise. Certainly we find no clear links between circumcision and the *sunan Ibrāhīm.* Ironically as well, we come away from the *Sīra* with the sense too that Jews never embraced circumcision (their hearts were, after all, uncircumcised) or that circumcision would have any associations with the covenantal promises articulated in the Torah or the Qur'ān. Circumcision is conceived of as a polytheistic, cultural practice involving both males and females that is also linked to such undesirable activities as idol worship.

Circumcision in the *Ḥadīth*

Circumcision plays a much more prominent role in the *ḥadīth,* although its mention is quite minimal when compared with other ritual behaviors such as prayer or pilgrimage or with grooming practices such as the brushing of one's teeth or the combing of one's hair. Here circumcision is tied to dress, purity, and, more vaguely, Abrahamic example. Questions as to whether or not both males and females should be circumcised, or at what age one should undergo the practice, or whether it is a requirement for participation in certain rituals, are never definitively answered. Unlike the *Sīra,* the *ḥadīth* collections suggest that circumcision ought to be practiced, but the *ḥadīth* leave much room for interpretation on how, why, or where.

---

[35] Guillaume, *Life,* 425.

[36] Ibid., 375.

[37] Ibn Isḥāq, *Sīra,* 3:70.

The canonical collections of Sunnī and Shī'īte *ḥadīth,* most of which were compiled from the ninth to the eleventh centuries, rarely mention circumcision in association with Abraham, and when they do, they simply state when that circumcision took place, what tool was used, and that indeed Abraham was the first to be circumcised. For example, in Bukhārī's collection, we find the following tradition reported by Abū Hurayra: "The Messenger of God said, 'Abraham performed his circumcision with a pickax when he was eighty years old.'"[38]

In the *ḥadīth* collections, much controversy prevails as to whether females should be circumcised or not. As Abū Dāwūd's collection reveals: "A woman used to perform circumcision in Medina. The Prophet said to her, 'Do not cut too severely, for it is better for a woman, and more desirable for a husband.'"[39] Most of the *ḥadīth* that condone female circumcision are attached with some sort of disclaimer. In addition, Ṭabarī's great *History* (*Ta'rīkh al-rusul wa'l-mulūk*) also casts female circumcision in a negative light. He relays the narrative that when Sarah became angry with Hagar because she was jealous of Ishmael, she swore to cut something off of her. She said, "I shall cut off her nose, I shall cut off her ear—but no, that would deform her. I will circumcise her instead."[40] Interestingly enough, Ṭabarī's successor al-Tha'labī when relaying the same narrative notes that Sarah had both Hagar's ears pierced, as well as having her circumcised.[41] Here female circumcision is presented negatively in that it appears only as a form of punishment, a product of a jealous and irrational impulse. Obviously female circumcision would not have generated the same type of rhetorical concern as male circumcision, since (1) it was not a Jewish practice, and (2) female anatomy makes it impossible for circumcision to serve as a visual mark of a believer.

We find the most *ḥadīth* references concerning circumcision not in association with Abraham but in association with purity and a concept

---

[38] Abū 'Abdallāh Muḥammad b. Ismā'īl b. Ibrāhīm al-Bukhārī, "Kitāb al-anbiyā'," in *al-Jāmi' al-ṣaḥīḥ* (Cairo: Dār al-Fikr, 1981), no. 575. See also no. 576 for the same tradition.

[39] Abū Dāwūd Sulaymān b. Ash'ath al-Sijistānī, "Kitāb al-adab," in *Sunan Abī Dāwūd* (ed. Muḥammad Muḥyī'l-Dīn 'Abd al-Ḥamīd; Cairo: Maṭba'at Muṣṭafā Muḥammad, 1935), no. 5251.

[40] Abū Ja'far Muḥammad b. Jarīr al-Ṭabarī, *The History of al-Ṭabarī,* vol. 2, *Prophets and Patriarchs* (trans. W. M. Brinner; Albany: State University of New York Press, 1991), 72.

[41] Aḥmad b. Muḥammad al-Tha'labī, *Qiṣaṣ al-anbiyā'* (Beirut: al-Maṭba'a al-Thaqafīya, n.d.), 71.

known as *fiṭra*. These references take on the pattern of a list, either fivefold, tenfold, or threefold. The fivefold version is the most prevalent permutation. For example, Bukhārī records: "The Messenger of God said, 'Five practices are characteristic of the *fiṭra:* circumcision, shaving the pubic region, plucking the armpit hair, clipping the nails, and cutting the mustache short.'"[42] The list as it appears in the collections of Bukhārī, Abū Dāwūd, Mālik, Muslim, al-Nasā'ī, al-Tirmidhī, and Aḥmad ibn Ḥanbal remains stable throughout; that is, there are no substitutions for this list of five, though often the order changes.[43]

The list also comes in tenfold fashion, and here the components vary wildly. Sometimes circumcision is noted as an essential characteristic of the *fiṭra,* and sometimes it is not. As Abū Dāwūd records: "Ten practices are characteristic of the *fiṭra:* trimming the mustache, letting the beard grow, using the tooth-stick, cutting the nails, washing the finger joints, plucking the hair under the armpits, shaving the pubic hair, and cleansing one's private parts with water. The narrator said, I have forgotten the tenth, but it may have been rinsing the mouth."[44] One might expect circumcision to appear on this list, given its association with the *fiṭra* and its standard appearance in the fivefold purity lists, but again it is treated in no particular way. Other tenfold lists do mention circumcision, however. According to Abū Dāwūd's collection, 'Ammār b. Yāsir recounts a similar tradition but substituted circumcision for letting the beard grow.[45] Another reported by Ibrāhīm al-Nakha'ī in that same collection mentioned wearing the beard and circumcision.[46]

This list appears in abbreviated threefold form as well, without mention of circumcision. Bukhārī records: "To shave the pubic hair, to clip the nails, and to cut short the mustaches are practices characteristic of the

---

[42] Bukhārī, "Kitāb al-libās," nos. 777, 779.

[43] See also Abū Dāwūd, "Kitāb al-tarajjul," no. 418; Aḥmad b. Muḥammad ibn Ḥanbal, *al-Musnad* (ed. Aḥmad Muḥammad Shākir; Cairo: Dār al-Ma'ārif, 1946–49), 2:229, 239, 283, 410, 489; 4:264; Mālik b. Anas, "Sīfat al-nabī," in *Al-Muwaṭṭa'* (ed. Fārūq Sa'd; Beirut: Dār al-Āfāq al-Jadīda, 1981), 3:3; Muslim al-Ḥajjāj al-Qushayrī, "Kitāb al-ṭahāra," in *Ṣaḥīḥ Muslim* (ed. Muḥammad Fū'ād 'Abd al-Bāqī; Beirut: Dār al-Iḥyā' al-Turāth, 1956–72), nos. 495, 496; Aḥmad b. Shu'ayb al-Nasā'ī, "Kitāb al-zīna," in *Sunan* (Cairo: Al-Maṭba'a al-Miṣrīya, 1930), 1:75; Abū 'Īsā Muḥammad b. 'Īsā al-Tirmidhī, "Abwāb al-adab," in *Ṣaḥīḥ* (ed. Aḥmad Muḥammad Shākir; Cairo: Al-Maṭba'a al-Miṣrīya, 1931–34), 14.

[44] Abū Dāwūd, "Kitāb al-ṭahāra," no. 52. See also Muslim, "Kitāb al-ṭahāra," nos. 502, 503. In each version, the narrator notes that he has forgotten the tenth!

[45] Abū Dāwūd, "Kitāb al-ṭahāra," no. 53.

[46] Ibid.

fiṭra."[47] As is highly characteristic of many *ḥadīth*, there are no accompanying explanations why some practices ought to be included in the list and others not, nor are we given any rationale as to what holds this list together. If we examine carefully some of the list's individual components, we may be able to generalize the logic behind these practices, including circumcision.

For example, a close examination of those passages that discuss facial hair lend some insight into the underlying justification for the practice of trimming the mustache. According to Muslim's collection, "[t]he Messenger of God said, 'Act against the polytheists: cut short the mustache, and grow the beard.'"[48] Obviously trimmed mustaches served as a mark to identify believers from unbelievers.

Fingernails, another element on the three-, five-, and tenfold lists, appear to attract impurities and therefore should be kept trimmed.[49] Nicely enough, unlike other aspects of our being, if something nasty accumulates under the nails, we can simply cut them off. In the *ḥadīth*, we find that fingernails not only collect impurities but also can be used to scrape off unclean substances. According to Muslim's collection, 'Ā'isha stated, "In case I found semen on the garment of the Prophet dried up, I scraped it off with my nails."[50] So as not to remain in a potentially unclean state by what accumulates under the fingernails, nails should be kept short.

The Shī'ītes are even more suspicious of what might be lurking beneath those lengthy nails and mustaches and give more intricate reasons as to why someone should cut them. For example, Kulaynī records, "Do not grow your mustache long, for it is as if Satan took it as a hiding place, and concealed himself in it."[51] One Shī'īte *ḥadīth* even goes so far as to

---

[47] Bukhārī, "Kitāb al-libās," no. 778. See also his "Kitāb al-isti'thān," no. 312; Muslim, "Kitāb al-ṭahāra," nos. 495, 496.

[48] Ibid., nos. 500, 501.

[49] Oddly enough, perhaps, the cutting of nails and hair is not permissible in sacred time or space but should be reserved for ordinary time. For example, according to Muslim, those who intend to sacrifice an animal after the beginning of the month of the *ḥajj* should not cut nails or hair ("Kitāb al-aḍāḥī," nos. 4869, 4870, 4871, 4872). In like fashion, Mālik states that no one in *iḥrām* should pluck out hair or shave it or cut it until he has left *iḥrām* ("Kitāb al-ḥajj," 73.248). It could be that the remnants of what has been cut violate both that sacred space and time. By analogy the foreskin could also be thought of as a kind of excess appendage whose sole purpose is to collect impurities. Like fingernails and gratuitous hair, it should be removed to maintain a pure state of being, though not in sacred time or space.

[50] Muslim, "Kitāb al-ṭahāra," no. 578.

[51] Abū Ja'far Muḥammad al-Kulaynī, "Kitāb al-ziyy wa'l-tajammul wa'l-murū'a," in *Furū' min al-kāfī* (ed. 'Alī Akbar al-Ghaffārī; Tehrān: Maktabat al-Ṣadūq, 1957), 489 no. 11.

suggest that a dangerous substance rests under the fingernails, that which Satan claims.[52] The Shī'ītes also suggest that long fingernails or mustache hairs may collect various diseases underneath them, which can then spread to food and contaminate it.[53] Disease in general can be avoided when excess hair and nails are cut short: "Trim your mustaches and fingernails every Friday to protect you from leprosy and madness."[54] Clipping mustaches and nails ensures that one remains in a state of purification until the next Friday.[55]

While the Sunnī collections of *ḥadīth* do link the treatment of nails, mustaches, beards, pubic hair, and armpit hair with circumcision, the Shī'īte collections do not. In all their discussions of grooming and purity, circumcision is notably absent. Certainly in their non-*ḥadīth* corpora, many of these same prominent Shī'īte jurists supported the practice.[56] However, there is no extended discussion of the practice in the primary Shī'īte *ḥadīth* collections. Whether this is the result of a lingering fear for those dead parts of the body that now pollute the earth is unclear. As one Shī'īte *ḥadīth* instructs, "Bury hair and fingernails!"[57] Perhaps the difference between hair and fingernails and foreskin is that hair and fingernails grow, while foreskin does not. Why have an excess of impure matter in a world that is already cluttered with rotting human remains? A concern for such impurities most certainly influenced the Shī'īte claim that an *imām* must be born circumcised. This belief does suggest, however, that those born uncircumcised (whose worldly circumcision in fact further pollutes an already faulty world) may never reach a state of perfected belief.

As the Sunnī examples suggest, what may link the seemingly random items of the different lists appears to be a concern for purity, a keen interest in removing what lies beneath the recesses of excess hair, nails, teeth, or, by analogy, skin, which suggests by implication (and also explicit connection, in the case of mustaches) a strong desire for the separation of those who believe from those who do not. These notions of purity and separation will become clearer as we examine the other component of these *ḥadīth* statements: that these practices are characteristic of the *fiṭra*.

---

52 Ibid, no. 7.

53 Ibid., 488 nos. 1, 2.

54 Ibid., 490 no. 4.

55 Ibid., no. 8.

56 Kister talks about how Ibn Bābūya al-Qummī claimed that every Shī'īte *imām* is born circumcised and purified ("Born Circumcised," 13).

57 Kulaynī, "Kitāb al-ziyy wa'l-tajammul wa'l-murū'a," 493 no. 1.

On the Concept of *Fiṭra*[58]

Unlike *khitān,* the root *f-ṭ-r* appears frequently in the Qur'ān. Generally speaking, the qur'ānic context links it to two separate and distinct meanings. The first of these has to do with creation, or the originary moment. The Qur'ān uses the word *fiṭra* directly to refer to the original faith that God created and that is instilled in all humans. Q 30:30 states the following: "Set your face to the religion as one with primordial faith—the *fiṭra* of God according to which He brought people forth. There is no changing the creation of God. That is the right religion, but most people do not know." In addition to its connections with creation, the root *f-ṭ-r* also implies splitting or cleaving. Here the root in various forms appears in those sections that deal specifically with the final hour. As Q 73:18 claims, that devastating time will come "when heaven shall be split [*munfaṭir*], and its promise shall be performed."

When mentioned with the five or ten purity practices discussed above, the word *fiṭra* is more closely aligned with the latter definition, that is, splitting or cleaving.[59] Purity rituals can be understood as rites of separation, that is, "splitting" the clean from the unclean or, as is the case in many of the Shī'īte examples, "cleaving" the good from the evil. The literal sense of separating oneself from one's impure bodily excesses is captured in many of the lists mentioned above. Purity and cleanliness may keep one in good standing with God, but essentially that translates into what differentiates believer from nonbeliever, what splits believers away from undesirables.

Given that it arises nowhere in the threefold version and in only some of the tenfold versions, circumcision appears to be a late addition to an already-established chain of purity practices. Unlike the priestly or rabbinic understanding of circumcision, nowhere does it stand alone in the early Islamic context as a practice that can accomplish purity and separation; it becomes meaningful only when practiced in conjunction with the other items on the list. It is the clustered group that serves to define the pure believer from everyone else. Neither circumcision alone nor cutting the nails alone is enough to distinguish believer from idolater, Jew from Muslim. Rather, it is the observance of the entire group of items on the list, whether that list be made up of three, five, or ten, that serves to separate. Two men may be circumcised, but in order to tell the true believer from

---

[58] For an excellent study of the concept of *fiṭra,* in particular as how Ibn Ḥazm understood the term, see Camille Adang, "Islam As the Inborn Religion of Mankind: The Concept of *Fiṭra* in the works of Ibn Ḥazm," *Al-Qanṭara* 21 (2000): 393–408.

[59] I would like to thank Professor William Shepard for this insightful observation.

the false, one must check his nails, beard, teeth, and mustache as well. The cumulative effect of these purity practices makes one easily identifiable as a believer. It also, however, lessens the importance of any one practice standing as the sole mark of a believer. Now so inextricably linked with other non-Jewish practices, circumcision becomes no more important than nail clipping. In this way, then, Jewish covenantal overtones that privilege circumcision over and above all other practices have been effaced.

The second definition of *fiṭra;* that is, what has to do with creation (in particular as it refers to a person of faith), also appears in the *ḥadīth* collections, but it is not directly associated with the practices mentioned above. In Muslim's collection, *fiṭra* is described as the nature made by God in which he created man.[60] The idea that *fiṭra* is a kind of natural religion appears also in this example from Mālik's collection, which states "every child is born on the *fiṭra* and it is his parents who make him a Jew or a Christian. Just as a camel is born whole—do you see any difference?"[61] This understanding of *fiṭra* as kind of an originary religion, a religion that is coexistent with one's created nature as God fashioned it at that primordial moment, and its association with these purity practices (i.e., practices linked to an understanding of *fiṭra* as cleaving or splitting) is most clearly articulated in Ṭabarī's treatment of the figure of Abraham. The two are not rhetorically linked prior to the time of Ṭabarī, again suggesting that circumcision as part of the *sunan Ibrāhīm* was a late rather than an early development and that it was dependent upon this essential merging of the two concepts of *fiṭra* within this one figure.

Ṭabarī's Great History

Ṭabarī directly links Abraham's circumcision to the Qur'ān itself. Ṭabarī embeds his discussion of circumcision within Q 2:124, which states "and remember when his Lord tried Abraham with certain commands which he fulfilled."[62] These commandments have been the source of much speculation (as the Umayyad Syriac passage noted above might suggest), and Ṭabarī presents a number of opinions about what they might be. Ṭabarī reports that "some say that the commands were thirty portions, that is to say, the laws of Islam" or the duties of the *fiṭra*.[63] He goes on to record the various interpretations of this injunction. According to one tradition, the commands given to Abraham referred to the acts of ritual purification,

---

60 Muslim, "Kitāb al-qadar," nos. 6425, 6426, 6427, 6428, 6429.

61 Mālik, "Kitāb al-janā'iz," 16.54.

62 Ṭabarī (trans. Brinner), 97.

63 Ibid.

five in the head and five in the body. Those in the head are trimming the mustache, rinsing the mouth, cleaning the nostrils with water, using the tooth-stick, and parting the hair; those in the body are clipping the nails, shaving the pubic hair, circumcision, plucking the armpit, and washing off traces of feces and urine with water.[64] Another tradition Ṭabarī includes declares that six of God's "commands" to Abraham are in the person and four are in the cultic stations. Those in the person are shaving the pubic hair, circumcision, plucking the armpit, paring the nails, trimming the mustache, and bathing on Friday. The four in the cultic stations are walking around the Ka'ba, running between al-Ṣafā and al-Marwa, stoning the pillars, and hurrying.[65] As these examples illustrate, the items on the various tenfold lists change,[66] but in each of the cases concerning ritual purification, circumcision is always mentioned. This stress on circumcision stands in sharp contrast with the *ḥadīth* collections, which often leave it out of the equation.

Ṭabarī also reports that others have noted that the commands had nothing to do with purification practices but rather were six tests: the star, the moon, the sun, the fire, emigration, and circumcision.[67] In other accounts, the test of fire, emigration, circumcision, and the sacrificing of his son is used to demonstrate how Abraham remained unflinchingly steadfast in his faith.[68] These tests serve to demonstrate the powerful strength of Abraham's commitment and seemingly stand in sharp contrast with the demonstrations of his ability to observe daily purification rituals. After all, is the willingness to sacrifice one's son really on par with trimming one's nails? However, the act of Abraham's circumcision—here presented as both purificatory ritual and test, a test overlaid with sacrificial overtones—combines the two elements into one rhetorical trope. That is, Abraham's commitment to God is achieved through a willingness to sacrifice a part of himself, a sacrifice that both stems from yet embodies (along with other practices) the purity of his nature.

When these passages from Ṭabarī are taken as a whole, we find that circumcision becomes firmly established as an essential and non-exchangeable part of the *fiṭra,* which in turn is linked with the original

---

[64] Ibid., 99.

[65] Ibid., 100.

[66] Ibid., 99–100. For example, another list in this same section includes rinsing the mouth, cleansing the nostrils with water, trimming the mustache, using the tooth-stick, plucking the armpit, clipping the nails, washing the finger-joints, circumcision, shaving the pubic hair, and washing the rear and the vulva.

[67] Ibid., 103.

[68] Ibid., 104.

religion of Abraham (*ḥanīfīya*), whom we know from the Qur'ān was neither Jew nor Christian. The tenfold list of purity rituals no longer serves exclusively as an essential characteristic of the *fiṭra;* it now becomes inextricable from the difficult commands God bestowed upon Abraham, who fulfilled them. It is this essential grounding of the concept of the *fiṭra,* along with its ahistorical purity prescriptions, within the historical exemplar of Abraham, whom the Qur'ān describes again and again as a "man of pure faith" (*ḥanīf*),[69] that allowed circumcision to become linked with Abraham (as it is in Judaism) while challenging circumcision's covenantal overtones of Jewish exclusivity.

Conclusion

So what does this mean? How is Ṭabarī's association between circumcision and Abraham different from the Jewish idea that circumcision is a "sign of the covenant between God and his people," as M. J. Kister has suggested? Circumcision may still reflect a sign of the covenant between God and his people in the Islamic context, but what that sign now signifies has completely changed from the Jewish context. In other words, circumcision still signifies a relationship between God and his true followers, but the Jewish covenant is no longer the normative context for understanding circumcision as such a sign.

First of all, by Ṭabarī's time (d. 923 C.E.) circumcision becomes part of a larger list of activities a true believer is to perform. It does not stand as a single mark of allegiance; it takes on a significance only through its association with other types of non-Jewish practices, all of which serve to establish believer from unbeliever or, for that matter, Jew from Muslim. Circumcision may have tested Abraham's steadfastness, but so too did the emigration and bathing on Fridays. In this way, circumcision becomes less the determining mark of one who is part of the covenant but rather one of many signs indicating an individual's status as a true believer, prior to the qur'ānic or biblical revelations.

Second, Abraham's success is not based solely upon a mark but upon his willingness to submit to his true, created nature and to succumb ultimately to the source of that creation. Adherence to the purity practices of the *fiṭra* serve as a kind of test that transforms Abraham into a pristine, ideal type to which all can aspire. Some clarification of the word *all* must be given, however. There is some question as to what extent the linking of Abraham with circumcision makes the practice an exclusively male purification rite, one that is off limits to females. The three-, five-, and tenfold lists

[69] See Q 2:135; 3:67, 95; 4:125; 6:79, 161; 10:105; 16:120, 123.

mentioned above seemingly include practices applicable to *both* males and females. Obviously, some are specifically geared toward male purification (e.g., trimming the mustache, growing long the beard), while others are gender neutral (e.g., trimming the nails, using the tooth-stick) and therefore apply to both. However, a few seem completely ambiguous (e.g., plucking the armpit hair, shaving the pubic region, and circumcision). Given that some schools of law have determined that an activity such as plucking the armpit hair and shaving the pubic region is *sunna* for both males and females,[70] it could be that early on in the tradition the rite of circumcision may have been incumbent upon both males and females (as is underscored by pre-Islamic as well as early Islamic sources), a position that the Shāfiʿī school maintains. With the evolution of its association with Abraham, the male and female purification ritual gradually may have given way to the more exclusionary male practice embraced by Judaism with its covenantal promises of land passed along through righteous descendants who bore the mark of circumcision. To what extent the link between Abraham and the purity laws of the *fiṭra* excludes women from realizing their "true natures" has yet to be debated.

Abraham's ability to suffer through his various tests and endure their pains, however, becomes a characteristic all emulators must struggle to achieve, mainly by enduring the pain as well as by staying clean. Again, circumcision is not the mark of God's chosen people as it is in the Jewish context but rather serves as a painful test all male believers must endure to realize the pure faith as God created it.

Third, Abraham becomes the one who has realized the tenets of Islam before they have been revealed to him. Here the concept of *fiṭra* is key. As we recall, *fiṭra* takes on the meaning of cleaving or separating but also that of an originary creation. By welding the two meanings together into a single figure, the tradition developed a type of rhetoric that in fact privileges the Islamic version of circumcision over and above the same practice embraced by other people. As one of the essential characteristics of the *fiṭra,* circumcision is no longer a practice that has been adopted by any one tradition or ethnic group but stands as an essential part of the creation itself, the way life is, the way God wants humans to be. Jews may circumcise, but only for corrupted reasons, for Judaism itself is a corruption or perversion of the original, natural religion realized by Abraham. Those who were circumcised prior to the coming of Islam (like Abraham and others who presumably were not Jews) were therefore privileged over and above those who may have viewed their circumcision as a sign of covenantal protection.

---

[70] The Mālikī jurists, for example, suggest that removing the underarm hair and shaving the pubic region is *sunna* for both men and women.

Does this mean that the Islamic version of circumcision is less exclusionary in nature than the Jewish version? This answer is no. As part of the *fiṭra,* which is then linked to the original religion of Abraham, the practice in fact excises those who do not look upon it correctly as a test of faith or perform it along with other equally important purity injunctions that are also characteristic of the *fiṭra.* Interestingly enough, the early Islamic tradition has in many ways captured both the Jewish and Christian verdicts on circumcision by claiming that it cannot stand as a substitute for faith, yet recognizing that faith can be realized through this and other practices. This is perhaps why Ṭabarī himself reported that Muḥammad ruled circumcision unnecessary for conversion.

According to Ṭabarī, circumcision stands as only one of many characteristics of the *fiṭra.* Ironically, however, we can say the observance of male circumcision carries even more weight as part of the *fiṭra* than it does in the Jewish tradition when it stands alone as a sign of the covenant. Here, in the Islamic context, it becomes an essential part of the universal fabric created by God himself, a fabric that can be realized by anyone no matter what his geographical, ethnic, or cultural status may be. By undergoing the test of circumcision, like Abraham, one in fact realizes his own true nature in its original, divinely intended form. By undergoing circumcision for any other reason, one has missed the point. By privileging circumcision over and above the other characteristics of the *fiṭra,* one has also missed the point. In this way, circumcision takes on a universal status at the same time it becomes exclusionary. Linking circumcision with the *fiṭra,* and ultimately with Abraham, rhetorically was a way to assert cultural priority and then to elevate that cultural practice to a normative religious injunction that ultimately privileged those who adhered to it for the right reasons long before they knew why.

Within the early Islamic context, circumcision was observed as a cultural practice adhered to for many reasons. However, the practice introduced a conceptual conundrum for a tradition simultaneously asserting continuity and distinction for its definitive completion. So the rhetorical tropes that are developed to address these underlying concerns while endorsing the *realia* of cultural practice take on an ingeniously quixotic form. Abraham circumcises, not as a sign of covenantal exclusion, but rather to ratify his status as a universal member of the *fiṭra.* Once so transformed, Abraham as *fiṭra* becomes an avenue by which the Islamic exegete can assert change through continuity, a most striking conceptual twist as Islam asserted a dual identity as consistent yet complete.

Depaganizing Death: Aspects of Mourning in Rabbinic Judaism and Early Islam

Fred Astren
San Francisco State University

The ideological systems of Judaism, Christianity, and Islam often depend upon setting up an Other against whom identity is constructed. In this process, these traditions are not only engaged with each other as competing monotheisms but share a direct concern with the nonmonotheistic category of "pagan," a particularly threatening Other. One way to get at this category of pagan is to examine how Judaism and Islam, traditions with a legal orientation, define certain aspects of mortuary, funerary, and mourning practice, thereby constructing the boundaries between monotheism and what they perceive to be nonmonotheistic, pagan death practice.

It is axiomatic that religious traditions offer normative guidelines for death ritual. Traditions such as Judaism and Islam are orthopraxic—they emphasize "correct practice" or outward behavior, which is often understood to be emblematic of belief and inner experience. In these traditions the construction of liturgical, ritual, and mortuary praxis is known from authoritative literary sources, thereby assigning to the Jew or Muslim what to do or what not to do around the time of death. The legal constructions made by Jewish and Muslim jurisprudents in connection with death rituals develop practical, mostly procedural prescriptions in the contexts of Jewish and Muslim religious law (halakah and *sharīʿah*, respectively). The choices embedded in these constructions indicate fully conceived and thoughtful agendas, embodying theological principles and social transformation. These agendas create boundaries between the old and the new, the acceptable and the reprehensible.

In Islam and Judaism anything having to do with cults of the dead is understood to be nonmonotheistic, that is, idolatrous and pagan. In Muslim and Jewish worldviews, attributing to the dead power or honor or seeking some type of communion with the departed are ways of belief and behavior that are to be reserved solely for God. If the dead are feared, given undue honor, consulted, or concretized into daily life, then the awe, honor, knowledge, and presence of God can be compromised. The immanence of the dead in the cult of the dead stands in stark contrast to the transcendence of God in these monotheisms. This essay will focus on two areas that in this regard are of some concern in both traditions: excessive expression of mourning, and religious activity at the grave. That these practices could be perceived as idolatrous and pagan informs their treatment by Jewish and Muslim religious authorities, the rabbis and the *'ulamā'*.

How do these monotheists imagine idolatry and paganism? Antipagan concern identifies both the theological terrain of monotheism as well as the sociological boundaries of each community in late antiquity and the early Middle Ages. For Judaism, an explicit definition of paganism is found in the expression "the way of the Amorite," a phrase that uses an ethnic identification to presume nonmonotheistic practice. For Islam a similar function appears when the term *jāhiliyyah* is mobilized to create distance from certain types of non-Islamic practice. The ethnic monotheism of Judaism uses an ethnic designation while universalist Islam uses a temporal designation, both drawing boundaries that differentiate between paganism and monotheism.

Excessive Expression of Grief in Judaism

For Jews, prohibition against the excessive expression of grief has scriptural bases. Self-mutilation as a mourning rite is attested to as a practice in ancient Israel in Jer 41:4–6:

> The second day after Gedaliah was killed, when no one yet knew about it, eighty men came from Shechem, Shiloh, and Samaria, their beards shaved, their garments torn, and their bodies gashed, carrying meal offerings and frankincense to present at the House of the Lord.

Alternately, in both Leviticus[1] and Deuteronomy[2] self-mutilation is forbidden, indicating that during the middle of the first millennium B.C.E. boundaries were already being established for keeping at bay Canaanite and other Near Eastern practices associated with the cult of the dead. Biblical prohibitions against various types of necromancy are also to be

---

[1] Lev 19:28: "You shall not make gashes in your flesh for the dead, or incise any marks on yourselves: I am the Lord." Translations from the Hebrew Bible are taken from *Tanakh: A New Translation of the Holy Scriptures according to the Traditional Hebrew Text* (Philadelphia: Jewish Publication Society, 1985).

[2] Deut 14:1: "You are the children of the Lord your God. You shall not gash yourselves or shave the front of your heads because of the dead."

understood in this context.[3] Centuries later, the rabbis inherited biblical attitudes and specific regulations with which to consider and prohibit the cult of the dead, so that their attention was thereby freed for other matters in regard to death ritual. When we examine definitive rabbinic legal texts from late antiquity, such as the Mishnah and Talmud, in regard to death ritual, we find the central problematic of rabbinic regulation is centered on the laws of purity (*tum'ah*).[4]

The rabbis were concerned with the presence or absence of death-originated impurity, its differential effects on individuals of varying status, and its effects in time, that is, its effects on days of varying status in the ritual calendar. Excessive weeping, wailing, and self-mutilation are marginal to the rabbinic discourse because the boundary that separates them out from sanctioned practice is a priori delineated explicitly in the Torah, the Five Books of Moses. As a result, such matters are given only cursory attention in Mishnah and Talmud.

Patricia Robinson suggested that the rabbis were no longer motivated to defend against the cult of the dead because assumptions about the power or holiness of the dead had become obsolete under the influence of Hellenism, with its new ideas of immortality and the separation of body and soul at death.[5] This would seem to be supported by the fact that little of the sixth-century Babylonian Talmud is specifically concerned with death. However, in spite of pagan practice seeming to be of slight concern to the rabbis, we find explicit references to it in the appendant medieval minor tractate of the Talmud, *Evel Rabbati* ("Great Mourning").[6] It states in 8:4 that at a funeral: "Pipes may be made to flow with wine and with oil before brides and grooms, without fear that this smacks of the ways of *the Amorite*," that is, of superstitious or pagan practice.[7] In the same chapter, it is permissible to erect a canopy over the bier for a dead bridal couple and to suspend various foods from it and to scatter foodstuffs before the

---

[3] See Lev 19:31; 20:6, 27; Deut 18:11. Cf. 1 Sam 28; Isa 8:19–22.

[4] See Emanuel Feldman, *Biblical and Post-Biblical Defilement and Mourning: Law As Theology* (New York: Yeshiva University Press, 1977).

[5] Patricia Anne Robinson, "The Conception of Death in Judaism in the Hellenistic and Early Roman Period" (Ph.D. diss., University of Wisconsin, 1978).

[6] Also known later as *Semaḥot* (translated as "Rejoicings," but meaning "Mourning"). See *The Tractate "Mourning" (Śĕmaḥot): Regulations Relating to Death, Burial and Mourning* (trans. D. Zlotnick; New Haven: Yale University Press, 1966). This is a late collection of halakot (laws), dating perhaps to the eighth century, but it undoubtedly includes many traditions that are much older.

[7] Translation from Zlotnick, *The Tractate "Mourning."* On the "ways of the Amorite" (*darkhei ha-'emori*), see *t. Šabb.* 6–7. Cf. *b. Šabb.* 67a and following.

procession of the dead bridal couple.[8] Clustered among other passages that deal with the ways of the Amorite, or pagan practice, the descriptions of these rituals are reminiscent of fertility offerings associated with the cult of the dead. The rabbis transform these practices by locating them within the boundaries of sanctioned activity through the establishing of rules for determining what foods are appropriate for these uses. Thus, the practice is "rabbinized" through regulation, and by specifying that these foods may not be eaten, the sacred meal associated with the cult of the dead is prohibited.[9] Similarly, garments that have been rent for mourning purposes and that may not be mended according to halakah may not be sold to non-Jews.[10] Thus, these garments cannot be used for pagan purpose.

In another instance, a groom's inkwell and reed pen may be placed by his side on the bier "without fear that this smacks of pagan practice."[11] In these ways, the rabbis rationalized and sanctioned practices that were undoubtedly questionable but that had currency in contemporary late antique Jewish and Near Eastern practice, perhaps preserving deep psychological and cultural structures, whose roots are to be found in premonotheistic practice and belief.[12]

The rabbinic process of regulation and reformulation also characterizes the treatment of excessive mourning. In the second century, *m. Moʾed Qaṭ.* 2:9 reads: "Women may raise a wail during the festival [week], but not clap [their hands in grief]; R. Ishmael says, those that are close to the bier clap [their hands in grief]. On the days of the New Moon, Hanukkah, and of Purim they may raise a wail and clap [their hands in grief]" and so forth.[13] In the sixth-century, *b. Moʾed Qaṭ.* 27b specifies further regulation by limiting the number of days for weeping and for lamenting, and rules are given regarding striking the breast, tapping the foot, and clapping.[14] It should be noted that here the application of detailed, precise

---

8 *Evel Rabbati* 8:2, 3.

9 In fact, the eating of anything associated with death rituals is generally prohibited. For example, see the treatment of an animal that has been hamstrung after the death of its powerful owner, such as a king, in *Evel Rabbati* 8:5.

10 *Evel Rabbati* 9:20.

11 *Evel Rabbati* 8:7.

12 On rooting "seemingly heathen customs" in reason, see Zlotnick, *The Tractate "Mourning,"* 17.

13 Translations from the Mishnah are taken from *The Mishnah* (trans. H. Danby; Oxford: Oxford University Press, 1933).

14 See the translation of *Mo'ed Katan* by H. M. Lazarus in *The Babylonian Talmud* (ed. I. Epstein; London: Soncino, 1938).

regulations covers the entire range of death ritual in the context of the problematic of impurity and personal status and is not specifically tied to the context of excessive grief. But by imposing the general halakic methodology of regulation upon questionable practices, these practices are folded into the halakic legal norm without explicitly taking recourse to antipagan prohibitions.

Excessive mourning is reformulated to a place within the Jewish ideological system in a haggadah, or legend, from *b. Mo'ed Qaṭ.* 27b, aptly selected by Dov Zlotnick in the introduction to his modern edition of the tractate *Evel Rabbati.* It frames the concern for excessive mourning in terms that are divorced from any notion of the cult of the dead.

> Rab Judah said, as citing Rab: Whoever indulges in grief to excess over his dead will weep for another. There was a certain woman that lived in the neighborhood of R. Huna; she had seven sons one of whom died [and] she wept for him rather excessively. R. Huna sent [word] to her: "Act not thus." She heeded him not [and] he sent to her: If you heed my word it is well; but if not, are you anxious to make provision for yet another? He [the next son] died and they all died. In the end he said to her, Are you fumbling with provision for yourself? And she died.

In this narrative, we see that excessive mourning is a problem in terms of consequences for the mourner. In fact, we find a folkloristic symmetry of consequence that echoes biblical symmetry in relation to divine reward and punishment. "If you do thus, then correspondingly thus will occur unto you." The Talmud further limits excessive mourning by stating that after three days of weeping, seven days of mourning, and thirty days of other proscriptions "the Holy One, blessed be He, says, 'You are not more compassionate towards him [the departed] than I.'"[15] Here we see that the psychological response to death is of primary concern, and the human value of compassion is the basis for limitation. Mourning through fear of the dead, honor to the dead, or communion with the dead is replaced by a compassionate yet pragmatic concern for the continuation of human life after fulfilling proper mourning practice. This principle is mirrored in a time when death and destruction affected all of Israel—when the rabbis forbade excessive mourning for Zion after the destruction of Jerusalem and the temple in 70 C.E. They understood that the ascetic and mournful practices of the so-called *Avelei Tsiyon,* the "Mourners for Zion," such as refraining from drinking wine and eating meat, were not conducive to building a working society or carrying on a fruitful and meaningful existence, nor did they fit with the rabbis' own

---

15 *b. Mo'ed Qaṭ.* 27b.

ideological assumptions about God's providence.[16] So too with the individual in Israel.

EXCESSIVE EXPRESSION OF GRIEF IN ISLAM

When we turn to Islam, we see that the Qur'ān has no regulations regarding death and only a brief narrative which teaches that burial is the proper way to handle death.[17] The vast bulk of literary material pertaining to death is found in the *ḥadīth,* the traditions of the Prophet Muḥammad, collected and compiled in the eighth and ninth centuries, and in other later writings.[18] One finds that much attention is given to the problem of excessive expression in mourning over the dead. The *ḥadīth* exemplifies this type of behavior—tearing the clothes, slapping the cheeks, throwing ashes on one's head, and, above all, wailing—as the hallmarks of idolatrous behavior.[19] These prohibited practices are associated with the *jāhiliyyah,* or "Days of Ignorance," which preceded the advent of Islam among the

---

[16] See *Pesiq. Rab.* 34.1–2; also *b. B. Bat.* 60b. Compare the talmudic treatment of naziritism, which is seen as excessively ascetic: *b. Ned.* 10a and 77b; *b. Naz.* 19a; *b. Taᶜan.* 11a.

[17] See Q 5:31, following the murder of Abel at the hands of his brother Cain: "Then God sent a raven scratching up the ground, to show him how to hide his brother's naked corpse." Translation is based on *The Meaning of the Glorious Koran* (trans. Mohammed Marmaduke Pickthall; New York: Mentor, n.d.).

[18] In al-Bukhārī, the appropriate section is in some manuscripts entitled *Kitāb al-janā'iz*. See *Ṣaḥīḥ al-Bukhārī* (Cairo, 1967), 2:348–435; *Kitāb al-janā'iz* in *Ṣaḥīḥ Muslim bi-sharḥ al-Nawāwī* (Cairo, 1929), 6:219–38, 7:2–47; *Kitāb al-janā'iz* in Ibn Mājah, *Sunan* (1952), 1:461–524; *Kitāb al-janā'iz* in al-Khāṭib al-Tibrīzī, *Mishkāt al-masābīh* (Beirut, 1961), 1:485–556; and other *ḥadīth* collections. Other sources for the death ritual are found in the descriptions of Muḥammad's death in the *sīrah* literature. See Ibn Sa'd, *Kitāb al-ṭabaqāt al-kabīr* (ed. F. Schwally; Leiden: Brill, 1912), 1:11–89; Alfred Guillaume, *The Life of Muhammad: A Translation of Ibn Isḥāq's Sīrat Rasūl Allāh* (Oxford: Oxford University Press, 1955), 678–90; Ibn Abū al-Hajj, *Madhkhal* (1929); others. The collections of al-Bukhārī and Muslim include few traditions relating directly to Muḥammad's death, whereas Ibn Mājah has specific sections on the washing and shrouding of the Prophet (nos. 1466–71; 1:471–72). In addition, Ibn Mājah concludes his *Kitāb al-janā'iz* with a lengthy section on the Prophet's illness and death (nos. 1618–37; 1:517–24). See al-Jazīrī, *Kitāb al-fiqh 'ala madhāhib al-arba'ah* (Cairo, n.d.); and al-Sayyid Sābiq, *Fiqh al-sunnah* (Beirut, 1969).

[19] See al-Bukhārī, nos. 1160, 1162–67, 1169, 1171–74, 1178–80; 2:370–85; Muslim, nos. 2007–10, 2015–38; 6:224–38; especially Ibn Mājah, nos. 1579–95; 1:503–9, which has examples of many kinds of idolatrous practice.

Arabs in the time of Muḥammad in the seventh century. The new instructions for mourning and grieving create a boundary in time between the *jāhiliyyah* and the time of Islam.

One of the five reprehensible things that occur at the *jināzah,* or burial, is raising of the voice.[20] The prohibition against wailing seems to have taken an early form in the proverb attributed to the Prophet: "the dead is punished by the crying of his relatives over him."[21] By delineating a behavioral break from idolatry, this prophetic expression posits a negative result for those who engage in this practice. This break with the past was so important that it was a stipulated condition placed upon women at the time of giving the pledge of allegiance to the Prophet[22] and in the so-called Covenant of ʻUmar made with the tolerated non-Muslim *dhimmī* communities.[23]

Rules for Muslim death rituals are more directly engaged with the cult of the dead than those of Judaism. As mentioned above, Judaism's need to distinguish itself from pagan practice, and the cult of the dead, was no longer central to Jewish identity in the rabbinic period. In Islam, the break with idolatry is remembered as a signal definitive characteristic of the religion, both historically and in the life of the individual. It marks a watershed in historical time, identifying a caesura in history, separating the *jāhiliyyah* from the epoch of Islam. In the Qur'ān and in Muḥammad's life this point is emphasized repeatedly. In the life of the individual, the essential step in becoming a Muslim is the abandonment of *shirk* (the association of any other worship with God, that is, idolatry). Only God is to be worshiped. This principle, constituting a break in time, is evident in the structure of the rules for the *jināzah.*

A more subtle and, at the same time, more profound differentiation between the ways of life of the *jāhiliyyah* and Islam is embodied in a change of attitudes toward death, a change that identifies Muslim morality and Islam's ideological system. The prohibition against wailing instructs a new reaction to the shock of loss due to death. If the old ostentatious expression of excessive grief is no longer considered appropriate, then a new psychology is required to take its place. Included in the *jināzah*

---

[20] There is a strong aversion to this in the legal texts. An excessive expression of grief is reminiscent of pagan practice. See Sābiq, *Fiqh al-sunnah,* 538, for a discussion of the problem, including the views of many legal authorities.

[21] Cited in many *ḥadīth*. See Muslim, nos. 2015–38; 6:228–38; Ibn Mājah, nos. 1579–83; 1:503–4.

[22] Al-Bukhārī, no. 1180; 2:485.

[23] For a version of the Covenant of ʻUmar, see al-Ṭurṭūshī, *Sirāj al-mulūk* (Cairo, 1872), 229–30.

materials are many traditions that could be categorized as *ta'ziyyah*, or "consolation," having to do with *sabr* and *'iḥtisāb,* simply defined as "patience" and "submission to God's will."[24] These attributes, well known to the pre-Islamic Arabs, are endowed with new significance in the Islamic context. *Sabr* and *'iḥtisāb* are transformed from the simple masculine virtues of a bedouin warrior into important psychological guides for the individual in a relationship with the divine and within the community of believers.

In both traditions, railing against the vicissitudes of misfortune and denial of the ultimate fate of humankind are ideas now jettisoned and replaced by a knowledge that the world was created and exists as part of a plan and that a continued existence awaits the believers in the next world. Knowing this, the believer can endure hardship and carry hope for those who have died. God's plan is tempered by compassion and mercy, and the hopelessness of an unknown fate is eliminated.

Cult Activity at the Grave in Islam

Cult activity at the grave was well established among the pre-Islamic Arabs and therefore was of great immediate concern for Muslim jurisprudents. This activity was most prominently manifest by the erection of some kind of monument or marker at the gravesite. The pre-Islamic Arabs installed cult objects called *'anṣāb* or *nuṣub* over honored graves. These were often distinguished from the surrounding environment by the creation of a sacred area called a *ḥimā,* dedicated both to the deceased and to the gods and acting as a kind of sanctuary.[25] Islamic prohibitions seem to stem from practices associated with these sites.

A classical Islamic view of paganism is gleaned from a modern Muslim jurisprudential work that is based upon early collections of *ḥadīth*. It characterizes these graveside practices as manifestations of the beliefs of the *jāhiliyyah*. The sacred areas acted as honored sanctuaries where people sought the gratification of their needs through the intercession of the dead by means of many types of ritual behavior. Horrible mutilations and sacrifices were performed. In addition, the tribes engaged in violence while seeking to destroy or defame the graves of their adversaries. This text presents a dramatic description of a wide range of cultic activities that stand in opposition to the ideals of Islam.[26]

---

[24] On *ta'ziyyah*, see Sābiq, *Fiqh al-sunnah*, 562, and al-Jazīrī, *Kitāb al-fiqh*, 504.

[25] See Ignaz Goldziher, "On the Veneration of the Dead in Paganism and Islam," in idem, *Muslim Studies* (ed. S. M. Stern; 2 vols.; London: Allen & Unwin, 1966), 2:209–38.

[26] See Sābiq, *Fiqh al-sunnah*, 548ff.

Consequently, both the sacrifice of animals[27] and the erection over the grave of a tent or a permanent structure are forbidden.[28] The idea here is dissociation of legitimate prayer from the grave. Though it is not an absolute principle, it seems that too much activity at the gravesite might resemble the pagan practices of the cult of the dead.

The dissociation of legitimate religious activity from what had previously been the cult of the dead is emphasized by the ambiguous manner in which the proper place for the funeral prayer is determined. There is a tradition that specifies as the appropriate place the *muṣallā*, or open public place of worship, usually located outside of a town.[29] However, a slightly different approach to the question is found elsewhere. Questions emerged regarding the appropriateness of both the mosque and the cemetery as a place for the funeral prayer. The performance of the *ṣalāt al-jināzah*, or funeral service, at the cemetery might be regarded as questionable because the pagan death rituals formerly took place there. On the other hand, it could be considered prudent to divorce the death rites from the mosque, lest any pagan practice occur there in error. The performance of the *ṣalāt al-jināzah* is not prohibited for either locus, but "strict" prohibitive interpretations are found for both of these arguments in the literature. An intermediate position emerged resulting in the *ṣalāt al-jināzah* being performed in the immediate environs of the mosque. The fear of pagan rites being performed at either the grave or the mosque would thus be alleviated.[30]

The prohibition against building a place of prayer over a grave continues the dissociation of the normative place of prayer from the death rites. In the definitive collection of *ḥadīth* by Muḥammad ibn Ismāʿīl al-Bukhārī, this issue is first embedded within the traditions describing the

---

27 On the prohibition of sacrifices, see Sābiq, *Fiqh al-sunnah*, 553; al-Jazīrī, *Kitāb al-fiqh*, 505. In pagan understanding, the sacrifice was performed as an act of redemption (*fedū*) for either the deceased or the living or both. It was also understood as a kind of feeding of the gods or of the deceased. The prohibition obviates any theological association with these ideas.

28 See Sābiq, *Fiqh al-sunnah*, 546, 548ff., which state that these practices are of the *jāhiliyyah* and the unbelievers. See also T. Leisten, "Between Orthodoxy and Exegesis: Some Aspects of Attitudes in the Shariʿa toward Funerary Architecture," *Muqarnas* 7 (1990): 12–22.

29 Al-Bukhārī, no. 1199; 2:394. In Muslim, nos. 2123–25; 7:38–39, it is permissible for these rites to be performed in the mosque. See also nos. 2084–89; 7:24–26, where the graveside service is given precedence. See also Ibn Mājah, nos. 1517–18; 1:486 (in the mosque); nos. 1527–33; 1:489–90 (at the grave).

30 See Sābiq, *Fiqh al-sunnah*, 535ff., where opposing positions are presented for both loci in regard to the *ṣalāt al-jināzah*.

funeral service. In its first instance, Muḥammad's wife, 'Ā'isha, denounces the Jews and Christians for utilizing the graves of their prophets as places of prayer. As the *ḥadīth* states: "Had it not been for that, the grave of the Prophet would have been prominent."[31] Bukhārī precedes this tradition with an anecdote in his chapter heading, a common literary device. The uselessness of making much of a gravesite by erecting a tent is told of the wife of al-Ḥasan ibn al-Ḥasan ibn 'Alī, the great-grandson of the Prophet. "It remained for one year and then was demolished. They heard a voice saying, 'Have they found what they lost?' A second voice replied, 'No, they returned in despair.'"[32] Clearly, a place of prayer over a grave is of no use for bringing back the dead or alleviating grief.

In the second instance this problem appears with the traditions regarding burial itself, wherein the Prophet denounces the Christians of Ethiopia who would make a place of worship at a grave and "then they make those pictures in it."[33] Here, places of prayer at graves are associated with the prohibited and reprehensible use of images for worship. Another context for this prohibition in al-Bukhārī is among traditions relating to theological concepts, including intercession. In the heading for a chapter is an anecdote about 'Abdullāh ibn 'Umar, companion of the Prophet, one of the most important transmitters of *ḥadīth,* and son of the second caliph. He "saw a tent made of goat hair over the grave of 'Abd al-Rahmān, and said, 'Oh, boy! Remove it from the grave for his deeds will shade him.'"[34] In this

---

[31] Al-Bukhārī, no. 1201; 2:394ff. In this *ḥadīth* Islam is portrayed as a religion that would not suffer the cult of the saints; that is, graves of important people would not become the focus of religious activity. It makes a distinction from the Jews and Christians who follow such practices. See also Sābiq, *Fiqh al-sunnah,* 551, which also prohibits burning lamps on the graves as do the Jews and Christians, who treat their graves' markers like idols; and 548, which states that if a structure is built over a grave, "Islam cries over it." See also Ibn Mājah, no. 1487; 1:477, on burning incense; al-Jazīrī, *Kitāb al-fiqh,* 502, on standing and sitting on graves.

[32] See al-Bukhārī, no. 1201; 2:394ff. and its chapter heading. A stronger injunction appears in Muslim, no. 2115; 7:36–37, prescribing the destruction of such graves.

[33] Al-Bukhārī, no. 1212; 2:400ff. The theme reemerges in al-Bukhārī in the chapter on the graves of Muḥammad, Abū Bakr, and 'Umar, nos. 1256–58; 2:431ff. These *ḥadīth* emphasize that the graves of these important people were not exceptional and were not to be considered the objects of worship. Note the discussion in al-Jazīrī, *Kitāb al-fiqh,* 501ff.

[34] See al-Bukhārī, in the heading preceding no. 1230; 2:413ff., where pagan practice is denounced. The only "cover" or "protection" for the grave and its occupant is provided either by one's deeds in life (in the scheme of reward and punishment) or by intercession with God. A tent will offer no refuge for the departed soul.

case, the moral value of the Muslim ideological system literally overshadows the *jāhiliyyah* values.

Cult Activity at the Grave in Judaism

Graveside activity also gives cause for concern in rabbinic texts. *Evel Rabbati* 8:1 states, "One may go out to the cemetery for thirty days to inspect the dead for signs of life, without fear that this smacks of the ways of the Amorite." It seems well known to the rabbis that people go to graves for pagan practice, although it does not tell what that practice is. But it goes on, "For it happened that a man was inspected after thirty days, and he went on to live twenty-five years; still another went on to have five children and died later." This apparent gloss to the rule offers a practical explanation for graveside visitation, deflecting the explicit concern with paganism.

To understand the danger of pagan graveside activity in the Jewish context we can return to the theme of food, already mentioned above as decoration on a bier. In the Hebrew Bible, graveside meals or food offerings are attested in Jeremiah,[35] and they explain a section of the solemn declaration of a landowner that accompanied the third year's tithe in Deut 26:14: "I have not eaten of it [the tithe] while in mourning, I have not cleared out any of it while I was unclean, and I have not deposited any of it with the dead." The nexus of corpse uncleanness, as mentioned above, with the cult of the dead is clear.

More importantly, graveside meals or food offerings are alluded to in Second Temple literature, such as Ben Sira[36] and Tobit.[37] *Jubilees* 22:17 denounces those who would engage in such practices in some detail: "They offer their sacrifices to the dead, and they worship evil spirits, and they eat over the graves, and all their works are vanity and nothingness."[38]

Confirming these literary allusions to graveside activity are many Hellenistic and Roman period burials found in the land of Israel containing

---

[35] Jer 16:6–7: "Great and small alike shall die in this land, they shall not be buried; men shall not lament them, nor gash and tonsure themselves for them. They shall not break bread for a mourner to comfort him for a bereavement, nor offer one cup of consolation for the loss of his father or mother."

[36] Sir 30:18: "Good things poured out before a mouth that is closed are as messes of meat laid upon a grave." Cited from William O. E. Oesterley, "Sirach," *APOT* 1:415.

[37] Tob 4:17: "Pour out thy bread and thy wine on the tomb of the just, and give not to sinners." Cited from David C. Simpson, "The Book of Tobit," *APOT* 1:212–13.

[38] As translated by Robinson (see n. 5 above). See also O. S. Wintermute, "Jubilees," *OTP* 2:98: "They slaughter their sacrifices to the dead, and to the demons they bow down. And they eat in tombs. And all their deeds are worthless and vain."

remains of food offerings. The most significant of these are the tombs of the Sanhedrin at Bet She'arim and Jason's Tomb in Jerusalem, where soot was found on the bottoms of pots that had been placed in the *kukh*, or burial chamber.[39] More important, by the late Hellenistic and early Roman periods the architecture of important graves and mausoleums included benches around a forecourt, and sometimes a cistern, suggesting a setting for graveside activity.

With these pagan dangers awaiting Jews at the graveside, it is not surprising to see that the rabbis embraced the tradition of the mourner's meal, which transformed what had been a sacrifice and meal *with* the dead into a meal with family and clan—the representatives of Israel, the communal entity that had been so grievously disrupted by the death of one of its loved ones. Thus the rabbis co-opted remnants of pagan practice by incorporating it into the mourner's meal, bringing Torah to the table, so to speak. This strategy is aptly illustrated in *m. ʾAbot* 3:3:

> R. Simeon said: Three who have eaten at one table and have not said over it words of Torah, lo, they are as if they had eaten sacrifices of the dead, as it is said: "For all tables are full of vomit and filthiness without God" (Isa 28:8). But if three have eaten at one table and have spoken over it words of Torah, it is as if they had eaten from the table of God, for it is written, "And he said unto me, this is the table that is before the Lord" (Ezek 44:22).

Death Rituals and the Construction of Early Medieval Muslim and Jewish Identity

While phenomenological comparisons of aspects of mourning in Islam and Judaism yield insight into ethnic and universalist constructs of the boundaries of identity and into Jewish and Muslim notions of idolatry and associated practices, the literatures also demand historical analysis.[40] What kind of historical model for early Islam can offer explanation for locating the development of a Muslim funerary practice in the eighth- and ninth-century project of collecting and compiling *ḥadīth*? Correspondingly, why do the rabbis compile their own handbook for mourning and funerary practice at precisely the same time?

---

[39] See Julius Jotham-Rothschild, "The Tombs of the Sanhedria," *PEQ* (1952): 38; and L. Y. Rahmani, "Jason's Tomb," *IEJ* (1967): 96. These are cited in Robinson's 1978 dissertation; see note 5 above.

[40] Thanks to Roger Brooks, who, after hearing an early version of this material presented as a conference paper, suggested this section be added.

The outlines of Islam in its first century are hardly clear. Contrary to the image of the past in Muslim tradition, it is reasonable to assume that, like other historical religious movements, it did not emerge fully matured in its first decades during the life of its founder Muḥammad. With the creation of the caliphate, both intra-Muslim discourse and the ensuing encounter with Jews, Christians, Zoroastrians, and others required a Muslim identity marked by social, ritual, moral, and theological distinction. By the mid-eighth century, movement away from Arab ethnic particularity was accelerated by the advent of the ʿAbbāsids. When Muslim social boundaries that had been specific to Arab identity gave way to a new transethnic Muslim identity, universalist moral and theological notions began to inform the social structure and ritual life. By the end of the ninth century caliphal decline was marked by political anarchy at the new capital of Samarrā in Iraq (861–70), the growth of Ṣaffārid power emerging from Sīstān in eastern Iran, and the decline of the Ṭāhirids, the caliphate's military prop. A lack of confidence in the political institution and religious leadership of the caliphate was felt widely.

In contrast, the period also witnessed development of Muslim institutions that offered a noncaliphal vision of Muslim society. The old imperial-caliphal monopoly on legitimacy was undermined by mosques, as centers of the community, by the administration of Muslim law by religious clerics instead of government officials and by the symbolic appropriation of the land by way of holy men and holy places. New Muslim elites, detached from imperial power, rose to lead new institutions and constituencies. Identified by Marshall G. S. Hodgson as the "sharīʿah-minded," the *ʿulamāʾ*, along with early *ṣūfī*-mystic leaders, became the definers of Muslim religious and social life.[41]

Coming out of a time when Arab identity and Muslim identity were equivalent and when the caliphate represented an overarching Muslim commonality but often lacked Muslim values, the *sharīʿah*-minded traditionists began to imagine a "completely Muslim" nonethnically specific social and ritual world whose dependence on the caliphate was minimal. Whereas previously, specific belief and less specific notions of tradition held sway, the *sharīʿah*-minded sought to structure ritual life with uniformity and imbue it with true Muslim meaning. Old Arab and local practices were transformed into something wholly Muslim, in part, by focusing on the details of ritual life. In this arena social, moral, and theological identity could be shaped through the careful construction of praxis-based *sharīʿah*.

---

[41] Marshall G. S. Hodgson, *The Venture of Islam* (3 vols.; Chicago: University of Chicago Press, 1974), 1:238, 345–50, and *s.v.* "sharīʿah-minded" in index.

Among the *sharī'ah*-minded, the traditionist effort to build an Islam that was normative was not merely the result of sincere Muslim questioning of hierarchy, belief, and behaviors but was also needed to respond to increasing internal pressure from the escalating success of Islamization. Islamization occurred through a slow process that spanned centuries in the Middle East and North Africa. First individuals became Muslim, and then Muslim identity was taken on by families, clans, and other small-scale social units. In the process, many practices and social values from outside of Islam were introduced into Muslim society.[42] Correspondingly, individuals, portions of families, and whole families might be characterized by intermediate identities that could be both Muslim and non-Muslim at the same time. Intermediacy of identity, which combines social and religious behaviors, created a world in which a multiplicity of religious phenomena abounded.[43] The danger of such hybridism and the influx of questionable practices led traditionists to define carefully Muslim social and ritual behavior.

Part of the traditionist *sharī'ah* project mobilized the notion of the *jāhiliyyah* to transform the qur'ānic rhetoric of idolatry into a practical concern that governed the construction of law. Given the theological and praxis-oriented concerns of the traditionists, the *jāhiliyyah* as portrayed in

---

[42] It may be a sociological postulate that beliefs and practices centered around death are among the most tenaciously preserved in environments marked by cultural and religious change. Accordingly, changes in death rituals can mark definitive transformations of identity. See Alain Dierkins and Patrick Périn, "Death and Burial in Gaul and Germania, Fourth–Eighth Century," in *The Transformation of the Roman World, AD 400–900* (ed. L. Webster and M. Brown; London: British Museum Press, 1997), 79–95; and Friederike Naumann-Steckner, "Death on the Rhine: Changing Burial Customs in Cologne, Third–Seventh Century," in Webster and Brown, *Transformation of the Roman World*, 143–58.

[43] Recent work on Christianization in late antiquity calls into question the existence of clearly polarized religious identities, especially during centuries of religious elaboration and identity formation. The existence of hybrid identities that were both Jewish and Christian seems to have lasted until at least the fourth century and perhaps to the sixth. See Daniel Boyarin, *Dying for God: Martyrdom and the Making of Christianity and Judaism* (Stanford, Calif.: Stanford University Press, 1999), esp. 22–41. Christian-Muslim 'Ibādī identity has been located in ninth-century North Africa. See Elizabeth Savage, *A Gateway to Hell, A Gateway to Paradise: The North African Response to the Arab Conquest* (Princeton: Darwin, 1997), esp. 89–105. Mazdakite-Muslim hybrids are well known in early Islamic Iran; see Wilferd Madelung, *Religious Trends in Early Islamic Iran* (Albany: Bibliotheca Persica, 1988), 1–12.

the *ḥadīth* is of dubious historical value.[44] Nonetheless, its rhetorical and "shariatic" uses reveal social and religious issues of the eighth and ninth centuries, when traditionists sought to make clear the boundaries of the community of believers and establish within the interior of those boundaries normative visions of morality and belief. Concern with excessive expression of grief and cult activity at the grave in the many *kutub al-janā'iz* in *ḥadīth* collections are emblematic of this process.[45]

It is in the Islamic world of the same era that we locate the rabbinic compilation of *Evel Rabbati*. By and large, the text repeats much material already known from *baraitot* (tannaitic material not found in the Mishnah) and from the Mishnah and Babylonian Talmud.[46] It does not lay out much new halakic territory in terms of practice or belief, nor is it a systematic handbook for mourning and funerary practice. Nonetheless, its compilation into a single text represents a response on the part of the rabbis of Iraq (called by the Jews "Babylonia") to eighth-century concerns cognate to those faced by the emergent *'ulamā'*.

As Islamic society became dominant with a historical finality and as Islam as a religion moved toward defining its boundaries and behaviors, the rabbis were forced to respond in kind. The unification of the vast majority of world Jewry under the caliphate had brought many different types of Judaism into contact with each other, many of which may have been non-rabbinic. Just as Islamization had introduced a variety of practices and beliefs into Islam, so Jews were faced with a multiplicity of Judaisms. The rabbis responded by seeking to establish their practices and attitudes as normative but also worked to enlarge the domain of their particular type of Judaism and to expand their hegemony as preservers and interpreters of text and law. The problem of establishing a normative Judaism was further exacerbated by the successes of Islamization, which generated hybrids that

---

44 See G. R. Hawting, *The Idea of Idolatry and the Emergence of Islam: From Polemic to History* (Cambridge: Cambridge University Press, 1999).

45 Archaeological evidence indicates changes in Muslim funerary practice in this period. Before the ninth century, funerary monuments were rare. Tombs could be marked by a pile of stones or were often left unmarked. See Leisten, "Between Orthodoxy and Exegesis," 12–13. Those grave inscriptions that are known from the first two Muslim centuries use formulas that differ from those of the following period. See Solange Ory, *Cimitières et inscriptions du Ḥawrān et du Ǧabal al-Durūz* (Paris: Éditions Recherche sur les Civilisations, 1989), 57–59. Cf. C. Gébara, "Les inscriptions funéraires arabes de la ville de Der'ā en Syrie" (thesis, Aix-en-Provence, 1980). In fact, uniformity in Muslim burial practice is widespread after the ninth century. See Timothy Insoll, *The Archaeology of Islam* (Oxford: Blackwell, 1999), 169.

46 The largest section replicates material from *m. Mo'ed Qaṭ.* ch. 3.

threatened the rabbis as much as they threatened the *'ulamā'*. Individuals and groups could proclaim Islam while maintaining Judaic practices and affiliations.[47] Such defiance of traditional constructions of identity required strict constructions of praxis in response.

More specifically, as Muslim mourning and funerary practice was rendered more precise, Jews took recourse in their own tradition in an effort to circumscribe community boundaries by reestablishing firm definitions of their own mourning and funerary practices. In some instances in *Evel Rabbati* the rabbis incorporate an old Judaic polemical theme, mirroring contemporary eighth-century antipaganism in Islam but maintaining an ethnic context. Jewish identity is thereby magnified and juxtaposed against the imagined Other of the ancient and no longer extant Amorites. In a way, *Evel Rabbati* is a Jewish *kitāb al-janā'iz*.

Conclusion

It is evident that the Jewish and Muslim architects of halakah and *sharī'ah* consciously used the avoidance of paganism to advance their own social and religious agendas. Whereas the Hebrew Bible defines the cultural permeability that generates religious syncretism as a backsliding from monotheism, the rabbis were aware of questionable late antique death rituals and established norms to accommodate to them or keep them at bay. In the early Islamic Middle Ages, the rabbis redeployed traditions associated with death rituals to make firm Jewish identity in the face of Islam and intermediacy of identity. In the *ḥadīth*, memory of the pre-Islamic era gave the issue of pagan practice much more significance as individuals in mourning sought a path that was defined as a new turning away from idolatry toward Islam. Both Jews and Muslims mobilized strong attitudes against paganism in an era when nonmonotheistic religion was uncommon and was more properly to be associated with antiquity. By making the

[47] Such a strategy is described by the Muslim jurist Muḥammad ibn al-Ḥasan al-Shaybānī (d. 804), who states "today the Jews in the areas of Iraq recognize that there is no god but God and Muḥammad is the Prophet of God, but they claim that he was sent as a prophet only to the Arabs, and not to the Jews." Cited and translated by Steven M. Wasserstrom, *Between Muslim and Jew: The Problem of Symbiosis under Early Islam* (Princeton: Princeton University Press, 1995), 78. As late as the mid-tenth century, the Karaite Jew Salmon ben Yeruḥim reports: "I have learned that the Jews of Samarqand and the region, when they say 'God is One,' [people who hear it] testify that by [saying] so they have become Muslims." Cited in Haggai Ben-Shammai, "The Attitude of Some Early Karaites towards Islam," in *Studies in Medieval Jewish History and Literature* (ed. I. Twersky; 2 vols.; Cambridge: Harvard University Press, 1984), 2:10.

archaic threat of paganism a pragmatic concern in ritual life, the early medieval rabbis and the *'ulamā'* addressed social, moral, and religious issues of their own communities in their own times. The pagan idolatrous Other of text and memory stood for other more complex Others of the day.

Select Bibliography of Works Cited

Abbott, Nabia. *Studies in Arabic Literary Papyri I: Historical Texts*. Chicago: University of Chicago Press, 1957.

Abū Dāwūd. *Sunan Abī Dāwūd*. 4 vols. Edited by Muḥammad Muḥyī al-Dīn ʻAbd al-Ḥamīd. Cairo: Maṭbaʻat Muṣṭafaa Muḥammad, 1935.

Abū ʻUbayd al-Qāsim b. Sallām. *Kitāb al-khuṭab wa'l-mawāʻid*. Edited by Ramaḍan ʻAbd al-Tawwāb. Cairo: Maktabat al-Thaqāfa al-Dīniyya, 1986.

Accad, Martin. "Did the Later Syriac Fathers Take into Consideration Their Islamic Context When Reinterpreting the New Testament?" *ParOr* 23 (1998): 13–32.

Adang, Camilla. "Islam As the Inborn Religion of Mankind: The Concept of Fiṭra in the Works of Ibn Ḥazm." *Al-Qanṭara* 21 (2000): 393–408.

———. *Muslim Writers on Judaism and the Hebrew Bible: From Ibn Rabban to Ibn Hazm*. Leiden: Brill, 1996.

Ahrens, Karl. "Christliches in Qoran: Eine Nachlese." *ZDMG* 84 (1930): 15–68, 148–90.

———. *Muhammad als Religionsstifter*. Leipzig: Brockhaus, 1935.

Albeck, Ḥanokh, ed. *Midrash Bereshit Rabbati*. Jerusalem: Mekize Nirdamim, 1940.

Alexander, Philip S. "Jewish Tradition in Early Islam: The Case of Enoch/Idrīs." Pages 11–29 in *Studies in Islamic and Middle Eastern Texts and Traditions in Memory of Norman Calder*. Edited by G. R. Hawting, J. A. Mojaddedi, and A. Samely. Oxford: Oxford University Press, 2000.

Alter, Robert. *The Art of Biblical Narrative*. New York: Basic Books, 1981.

———. *The Art of Biblical Poetry*. New York: Basic Books, 1985.

Alter, Robert and Frank Kermode, eds. *The Literary Guide to the Bible*. Cambridge: Harvard University Press, 1987.

Anawati, Georges C. "ʻĪsā." *EI*² 4:81–86.

Anderson, Gary A. "The Garments of Skin in Apocryphal Narrative and Biblical Commentary." Pages 101–43 in *Studies in Ancient Midrash*. Edited by James L. Kugel. Cambridge: Harvard University Center for Jewish Studies, 2001.

Anderson, Gary A. and Michael E. Stone, eds. *A Synopsis of the Books of Adam and Eve*. 2d ed. SBLEJL 17. Atlanta: Scholars Press, 1999.

Andrae, Tor. *Der Ursprung des Islams und das Christentum*. Uppsala: Almqvist & Wiksell, 1926.

Arkoun, Mohammed. "The Notion of Revelation: From *ahl al-kitāb* to the Societies of the Book." *Die Welt des Islams* 28 (1988): 62–89.

———. *The Unthought in Contemporary Islamic Thought*. London: Saqi, 2002.

Arnaldez, Roger. *Jesus, fils de Marie, prophète de l'Islam*. Paris: Desclée, 1980.

Attridge, H. W., T. Elgvin, J. Milik, S. Olyan, J. Strugnell, E. Tov, J. VanderKam, and S. White, in consultation with J. C. VanderKam. *Qumran Cave 4.VIII: Parabiblical Texts, Part I*. DJD 13. Oxford: Clarendon, 1994.

Ayoub, Mahmoud. *The Qur'an and Its Interpreters*. 2 vols. to date. Albany: State University of New York Press, 1984–.

Aziza, Claude. *Tertullien et le judaïsme*. Paris: Belles Lettres, 1977.

al-Balādhurī. *Ansāb al-ashrāf*. Edited by Muhammad Ḥamidullaah. Cairo: Ma'had al-Makhṭūṭāt bi-Jāmi'at al-Duwal al-'Arabiyya, 1959.

Bar Hebraeus. *Chronicon Syriacum*. Edited by Paul Bedjan. Paris: Maisonneuve, 1890.

Barker, Eileen. *New Religious Movements: A Perspective for Understanding Society*. London: HMSO, 1989.

Barnard, L. W. *Studies in the Apostolic Fathers and Their Background*. Oxford: Blackwell, 1966.

Barnstone, Willis, ed. *The Other Bible: Jewish Pseudepigrapha, Christian Apocrypha, Gnostic Scriptures, Kabbalah, Dead Sea Scrolls*. San Francisco: Harper & Row, 1984.

Battista, Antonio, and Bellarmino Bagatti. *La Caverna dei Tesori: Testo arabo con traduzione italiana e commento*. Jerusalem: Franciscan Printing Press, 1980.

Baumstark, Anton. "Eine altarabische Evangeliumübersetzung aus dem Christlich-Palästinensischen." *ZS* 8 (1932): 201–9.

Beardslee, William A. *Literary Criticism of the New Testament*. Philadelphia: Fortress, 1970.

Bell, Richard. *A Commentary on the Qur'an*. Edited by C. E. Bosworth and M. E. J. Richardson. 2 vols. Manchester: Manchester University Press, 1991.

———. "Muhammad and Previous Messengers." *MW* 24 (1934): 330–40.

———. *The Origin of Islam in Its Christian Environment: The Gunning Lectures, Edinburgh University 1925*. London: Macmillan, 1926. Repr., London: Cass, 1968.

———. *The Qur'an Translated, with a Critical Rearrangement of the Surahs*. 2 vols. Edinburgh: T&T Clark, 1937–39.

Bezold, Carl. *Die Schatzhöhle »Mĕ'ārath Gazzee«*. 1883–88. Repr., Amsterdam: Philo Press, 1981.

Blachère, Régis. "Regards sur un passage parallèle des Évangiles et du Coran." Pages 69–73 in *Mélanges d'Islamologie: Volume dédié à la mémoire de Armand Abel par ses collègues, ses élèves et ses amis*. Edited by Pierre Salmon. Leiden: Brill, 1974.

Bori, Pier Cesare. *The Golden Calf and the Origins of the Anti-Jewish Controversy*. Translated by David Ward. Atlanta: Scholars Press, 1990.

Bosworth, C.E. "al-Ṭabarıi. *EI*² 10:11–15.

Boullata, Issa J. Review of John Wansbrough, *Quranic Studies*. *MW* 47 (1977): 306–7.

Boyarin, Daniel. *Dying for God: Martyrdom and the Making of Christianity and Judaism*. Stanford, Calif.: Stanford University Press, 1999.

Brown, Norman O. *Apocalypse and/or Metamorphosis*. Berkeley and Los Angeles: University of California Press, 1991.

Brueggemann, Walter. *Theology of the Old Testament: Testimony, Dispute, Advocacy*. Minneapolis: Fortress, 1997.

Bukhārī. *Ṣaḥīḥ*. 9 vols. New Delhi: Kitāb Bhavan, 1987.

Busse, Heribert. "Cain and Abel." *EncQur* 1:270–72.

Calder, Norman. "From Midrash to Scripture: The Sacrifice of Abraham in Early Islamic Tradition." *Mus* 101 (1988): 375–402.

Casanova, Paul. "Idrîs et 'Ouzaïr." *JA* 205 (1924): 356–60.

Chabot, Jean-Baptiste, ed. *Anonymi auctoris Chronicon ad annum Christi 1234 pertinens*. 2 vols. CSCO 81–82. Paris: Reipublicae, 1916–20.

———, ed. *Chronique de Michel le Syrien, patriarche jacobite d'Antioche, 1166–1199*. 4 vols. 1899–1910. Repr., Brussels: Culture et Civilisation, 1963.

Chapira, Bernard. "Légendes bibliques attribuées à Ka'b al-Ahbar." *REJ* 69 (1919): 86–107; 70 (1920): 37–43.

Charles, R.H., *Maṣḥafa Kufālē, or the Ethiopic Version of the Hebrew Book of Jubilees*. Anecdota Oxoniensia. Oxford: Clarendon, 1895.

Chidiac, Robert, ed. *Al-Ghazali: Réfutation excellente de la divinité de Jésus-Christ d'après les Évangiles*. Paris: Leroux, 1939.

Childs, Brevard S. *The Book of Exodus: A Critical, Theological Commentary*. OTL. Philadelphia: Westminster, 1974.

Coats, George W. *Rebellion in the Wilderness*. Nashville: Abingdon, 1968.

Cohen, Gerson D. "Esau As Symbol in Early Medieval Thought." Pages 243-69 in idem, *Studies in the Variety of Rabbinic Cultures*. Philadelphia: Jewish Publication Society, 1991.

Collins, Adela Yarbro. "Revelation, Book of." *ABD* 5:694–708.

Cragg, Kenneth. *Jesus and the Muslim: An Exploration*. London: Allen & Unwin, 1985.

Crone, Patricia, and Michael Cook. *Hagarism: The Making of the Islamic World*. Cambridge: Cambridge University Press, 1977.

Dan, Joseph. *Sefer ha-Yashar*. Jerusalem: Mosad ha-Bialik, 1986.

Danby, Herbert, trans. *The Mishnah*. Oxford: Oxford University Press, 1933.

Daniel, Norman. *Islam and the West: The Making of an Image*. Edinburgh: Edinburgh University Press, 1960. Repr., Oxford: Oneworld, 2000.

Dean, Margaret E. "The Grammar of Sound in Greek Texts: Toward a Method for Mapping the Echoes of Speech in Writing." *ABR* 44 (1996): 53–70.

Dégh, Linda. *Legend and Belief: Dialectics of a Folklore Genre*. Bloomington: Indiana University Press, 2001.

al-Dhahabī, Muhammad b. Aḥmad. *Siyar a'lām al-nubalā'*. Edited by Shu'ayb al-Arna'ūṭ et al. 25 vols. Beirut: Mu'assasat al-Risāla, 1981–.

Di Matteo, Ignazio. "Confutazione contro I Cristiani dello Zaydita al-Qasim b. Ibrahim." *RSO* 9 (1921–22): 301–64.

Dierkins, Alain, and Patrick Périn. "Death and Burial in Gaul and Germania, Fourth-Eighth Century." Pages 79–95 in *The Transformation of the Roman World, AD 400–900*. Edited by Leslie Webster and Michelle Brown. London: British Museum Press, 1997.

Dimant, Devorah. "The Biography of Enoch and the Books of Enoch." *VT* 33 (1983): 14–29.

Dodge, Bayard. *The Fihrist of al-Nadīm: A Tenth-Century Survey of Muslim Culture*. 2 vols. New York: Columbia University Press, 1970.

Donaldson, Dwight M. "Al-Ya'qūbī's Chapter about Jesus Christ." Pages 88–105 in *The Macdonald Presentation Volume: A Tribute to Duncan Black Macdonald*. Edited by William G. Shellabear, Edwin E. Calverley, Elbert C. Lane, and Ruth S. Mackensen. Princeton: Princeton University Press, 1933.

Donner, Fred M. *Narratives of Islamic Origins: The Beginnings of Islamic Historical Writing*. Princeton, N.J.: Darwin, 1998.

Downing, F. Gerald. "Words As Deeds and Deeds As Words." *BibInt* 3 (1995): 129–43.

Dunlop, D. M. *Arab Civilization to AD 1500.* Arab Background Series. London: Longman, 1971.

Duri, A. A. *The Rise of Historical Writing among the Arabs.* Edited and translated by Lawrence I. Conrad. Princeton: Princeton University Press, 1983.

Ebied, R. Y. and L. R. Wickham. "Al-Yaʿkūbī's Account of the Israelite Prophets and Kings." *JNES* 29 (1970): 80–98.

Eilberg-Schwartz, Howard. "The Fruitful Cut: Circumcision and Israel's Symbolic Language of Fertility, Descent, and Gender." Pages 141–76 in idem, *The Savage in Judaism: An Anthropology of Israelite Religion and Ancient Judaism.* Bloomington: Indiana University Press, 1990.

Epalza, Miguel de. "Le milieu hispano-moresque de l'Évangile islamisant de Barnabe." *Islamochristiana* 8 (1982): 159–83.

Erder, Yoram. "Idrīs." *EI*[2] 2:484–86.

———. "The Origin of the Name Idrīs in the Qur'ān: A Study of the Influence of Qumran Literature on Early Islam." *JNES* 49 (1990): 339–50.

Ess, Josef van. Review of John Wansbrough, *Quranic Studies. BO* 35 (1978): 349–53.

Feldman, Emanuel. *Biblical and Post-biblical Defilement and Mourning: Law As Theology.* New York: Yeshiva University Press and Ktav, 1977.

Ferré, André. *L'histoire des prophètes d'après al-Yaʿqûbî: D'Adam à Jésus.* Rome: Pontificio Istituto di Studi Arabi e d'Islamistica, 2000.

———. "L'historien al-Yaʿquubii et les évangiles." *Islamochristiana* 3 (1977): 61–83.

———. "La vie de Jésus d'après les Annales de Tˇabarii." *Islamochristiana* 5 (1979): 1–29.

Firestone, Reuven. "Comparative Studies in Bible and Qur'aan: A Fresh Look at Genesis 22 in Light of Sura 37." Pages 169–84 in *Judaism and Islam: Boundaries, Communications, and Interaction: Essays in Honor of William M. Brinner.* Edited by Benjamin H. Hary, John L. Hayes, and Fred Astern. Leiden: Brill, 2000.

———. *Journeys in Holy Lands: The Evolution of the Abraham-Ishmael Legends in Islamic Exegesis.* Albany: State University of New York Press, 1990.

Fishbane, Michael. *Biblical Interpretation in Ancient Israel.* Oxford: Clarendon, 1985.

Flemming, Johannes, ed. *Das Buch Henoch: Äthiopischer Text.* Leipzig: Hinrichs, 1902.

Foley, John Miles. *The Singer of Tales in Performance.* Bloomington: Indiana University Press, 1995.

———. *The Theory of Oral Composition: History and Methodology.* Bloomington: Indiana University Press, 1988.

Friedlander, Gerald, trans. *Midrash Pirke de Rabbi Eliezer.* 1916. Repr., New York: Sepher-Hermon, 1981.

Gamble, Harry Y. "Canon: New Testament." *ABD* 1:853–61.

Gaudeul, Jean-Marie and Robert Caspar. "Textes de la tradition musulmane concernant le Tah'rıif (falsification) des Écritures." *Islamochristiana* 6 (1980): 61–104.

Geagea, Nilo. *Mary of the Koran: A Meeting Point between Christianity and Islam.* Translated by L. T. Fares. New York: Philosophical Library, 1984.

Gébara, Chérine. "Les inscriptions funéraires arabes de la ville de Der'aa en Syrie." Ph.D. thesis, Aix-en-Provence, 1980.

Geiger, Abraham. *Was hat Mohammed aus dem Judenthume aufgenommen?* Bonn: Baaden, 1833. Translated into English by F .M. Young as *Judaism and Islam*. 1898. Repr., New York: Ktav, 1970.

Gibson, Margaret Dunlop. *Apocrypha Arabica: Kitāb al-Mājāll, or The Book of the Rolls*. Studia Sinaitica 8. London: Clay, 1901.

Gilliot, Claude. *Exégèse, langue, et théologie en Islam: L'exégèse coranique de Tabari (m. 310/923)*. Paris: Vrin, 1990.

———. "Mythe, récit, histoire du salut dans le commentaire coranique de Tabari." *JA* 282 (1994): 235–68.

Ginzberg, Louis. *The Legends of the Jews*. 7 vols. Philadelphia: Jewish Publication Society, 1909–38.

Ginzberg, Louis, and Israel Davidson, eds., *Ginze Schechter* (*Genizah Studies in Memory of Solomon Schechter*). 3 vols. Texts and Studies of the Jewish Theological Seminary 7–9. New York: Jewish Theological Seminary of America, 1928–29.

Goeje, M.J. de, ed. *Kitāb al-boldān auctore Ahmed ibn Abi Ja'kûbî Wādhih al-Kātib al-Ja'kûbî*. Bibliotheca Geographorum Arabicum 7. Leiden: Brill, 1892.

Götze, Albrecht. "Die Nachwirkung der Schatzhöhle." *ZS* 2 (1924): 51–94; 3 (1925): 53–71, 153–77.

Goitein, S.D. "Muhammad's Inspiration by Judaism." *JJS* 9 (1958): 149–62.

Goldman, Shalom. *The Wiles of Women/The Wiles of Men: Joseph and Potiphar's Wife in Ancient Near Eastern, Jewish, and Islamic Folklore*. Albany: State University of New York Press, 1995.

Goldziher, Ignaz. "On the Veneration of the Dead in Paganism and Islam." Pages 209–38 in volume 2 of idem, *Muslim Studies*. Edited by S. M. Stern. 2 vols. London: Allen & Unwin, 1966.

———. "Über Bibelcitate in muhammedanischen Schriften." *ZAW* 13 (1893): 315–24.

Gottheil, Richard J. H. "Abraham in Mohammedan Legend." *JE* 1:87–90.

Gräf, Erwin. "Zu den christlichen Einflüssen im Koran." Pages 111-44 in *Al-Bāḥīt: Festschrift Joseph Henninger*. St. Augustin bei Bonn: Verlag des Anthropos-Institut, 1976.

Graham, William A. Review of John Wansbrough, *Quranic Studies*. *JAOS* 100 (1980): 137–41.

Graves, Robert, and Raphael Patai. *Hebrew Myths; The Book of Genesis*. Garden City, N.Y.: Doubleday, 1964.

Griffith, Sidney H. "Arguing from Scripture: The Bible in the Christian/Muslim Encounter in the Middle Ages." Forthcoming.

———. "From Aramaic to Arabic: The Languages of the Monasteries of Palestine in the Byzantine and Early Islamic Periods." *DOP* 51 (1997): 11–31.

———. "The Gospel in Arabic: An Inquiry into Its Appearance in the First Abbasid Century." *OrChr* 69 (1985): 126–67.

———. "The Monks of Palestine and the Growth of Christian Literature in Arabic." *MW* 78 (1988): 1–28.

———. "The Qur'ān in Arab Christian Texts: The Development of an Apologetical Argument: Abū Qurrah in the Maǧlis of al-Ma'mūn." *ParOr* 24 (1999): 203–33.

Grünbaum, Max. *Gesammelte Aufsätze zur Sprach- und Sagenkunde*. Edited by Felix Perles. Berlin: Calvary, 1901.

Guillaume, Alfred. *The Life of Muhammad: A Translation of Ibn Ishaq's Sirat Rasul Allah*. 1955. Repr., Karachi: Oxford University Press, 1967.

———. "The Version of the Gospels Used in Medina c. A.D. 700." *Al-Andalus* 15 (1950): 289–96.

Günther, Sebastian. "Illiteracy." *EI*² 2:492–500.

Halperin, David J. "The Hidden Made Manifest: Muslim Traditions and the 'Latent Content' of Biblical and Rabbinic Stories." Pages 581–94 in *Pomegranates and Golden Bells: Studies in Biblical, Jewish, and Near Eastern Ritual, Law, and Literature in Honor of Jacob Milgrom*. Edited by David P. Wright, David Noel Freedman, and Avi Hurvitz. Winona Lake, Ind.: Eisenbrauns, 1995.

Hawting, G. R. *The Idea of Idolatry and the Emergence of Islam: From Polemic to History*. Cambridge: Cambridge University Press, 1999.

Hayek, Michel. *Le Christ de l'Islam*. Paris: Éditions du Seuil, 1959.

Hayman, D., and Y. Shiloni, eds. *Yalqut Shimoni*. 2 vols. Jerusalem: Mosad ha-Rav Kook, 1984.

Heller, Bern(h)ard. "La chute des anges: Schemhazai, Ouzza et Azaël." Revue des études juives 60 (1910): 202-12.

———. "La legende biblique dans l'Islam." *REJ* 98 (1934): 1–18.

Ḥiddushey Yitzḥaq be-R. Avraham mi-Narbonna: 'Al hilkhot ha-Rif mi-masekhet Ḥullin. Jerusalem: Makon Yerushalayim, 1988–89.

Hirschfeld, Hartwig. *Jüdische Elemente im Korân: Ein Beitrag zur Korânforschung*. Berlin: self-published, 1878.

Hodgson, Marshall G. S. *The Venture of Islam: Conscience and History in a World Civilization*. 3 vols. Chicago: University of Chicago Press, 1974.

Hoffman, Lawrence A. *Covenant of Blood: Circumcision and Gender in Rabbinic Judaism*. Chicago: University of Chicago Press, 1996.

Horovitz, H. S., ed. *Siphre d'be Rab Fasciculus primus: Siphre ad Numeros adjecto Siphre Zutta*. 1917. Repr., Jerusalem: Wahrmann, 1966.

Horovitz, Josef. "Jewish Proper Names and Derivatives in the Koran." *HUCA* 2 (1925): 145–227.

Horsley, Richard A., and Jonathan A. Draper. *Whoever Hears You Hears Me: Prophets, Performance, and Tradition in Q*. Harrisburg, Pa.: Trinity Press International, 1999.

Houtsma, M. T., ed. *Ibn Wādih qui dicitur al-Ja'qubi historiae*. 2 vols. Leiden: Brill, 1883.

Hoyland, Robert G. *Arabia and the Arabs: From the Bronze Age to the Coming of Islam*. London: Routledge, 2001.

Hughes, T. P. *Dictionary of Islam*. 1885. Repr., New Delhi: Cosmo Publications, 1977.

Humphreys, R. Stephen. "Qur'ānic Myth and Narrative Structure in Early Islamic Historiography." Pages 279–90 in *Tradition and Innovation in Late Antiquity*. Edited by F. M. Clover and R. Stephen Humphreys. Madison: University of Wisconsin Press, 1989.

Ibn al-'Arabī. *Aḥkām al-Qur'ān*. 4 vols. Beirut: Dār al-Fikr, 1988.

Ibn al-Athīr, 'Izz al-Dīn Abū al-Ḥasan 'Alī. *Kāmil fī al-ta'rīkh*. 12 vols. Beirut: Dār Ṣadir and Dār Bayruut, 1965.

Ibn Bābawayh al-Qummī, Muḥammad b. ʿAlī. *Tafsīr al-Qummī.* 2 vols. Qumm: Mu'assasat Dār al-Kitāb lil-Ṭibāʿa wa'l-Nashr, 1984.

———. *ʿUyūn akhbār al-riḍā.* Edited by Muḥammad Mahdī Ḥasan Khurasān. 2 vols. in 1. Najaf: Maṭbaʿah al-Ṣaydarīyah, 1970.

Ibn Ḥanbal, Aḥmad ibn Muḥammad. *Musnad.* Edited by Aḥmad Muḥammad Shākir. 15 vols. Cairo: Dār al-Maʿārif, 1946–49.

Ibn Ḥazm. *al-Iḥkām fī uṣūl al-aḥkām.* 2 vols. Beirut: Dār al-Kutub al-ʿIlmīyah, n.d.

Ibn Isḥāq, Muhammad. *Kitāb al-siyar wa'l-maghāzī.* Edited by Suhayl Zakkār. Beirut: Dār al-Fikr, 1978.

———. *Sīrat rasūl Allāh.* Recension of ʿAbd al-Malik ibn Hishām. Edited by Ferdinand Wüstenfeld. 2 vols. in 3. Göttingen: Dieterichesche Universitäts-Buchhandlung, 1858–60.

Ibn al-Jawzī, ʿAbd al-Raḥmān b. ʿAlī b. Muhammad. *Al-Wafā bi-aḥwāl al-Muṣṭafā.* Edited by Muṣṭafā ʿAbd al-Wāḥid. 2 vols. Cairo: Dār al-Kutub al-Ḥadīthah, 1966.

———. *Zād al-masīr fī ʿilm al-tafsīr.* 8 vols. Beirut: Dār al-Kutub al-ʿIlmiyya, 1994.

Ibn al-Kalbī, Hishām. *The Book of Idols: Being a Translation from the Arabic of the Kitāb al-Aṣnām.* Translated by Nabih Amin Faris. Princeton: Princeton University Press, 1952.

Ibn Kathīr, ʿImād al-Din Ismāʿīl. *Mukhtaṣar tafsīr Ibn Kathīr.* 2 vols. Beirut: Dār el-Marefah, 1999.

———. *Qiṣaṣ al-anbiyā'.* Cairo: Dār al-ʿUlūm al-ʿArabiyya, 1998.

———. *Tafsīr al-Qur'ān al-aẓīm.* Beirut: Dār al-Jīl, n.d.

Ibn Mājah, Muḥammad b. Yazīd. *Sunan.* 2 vols. Cairo: ʿĪsā al-Bābī al-Ḥalabī, 1952–54.

Ibn Manẓūr, Muhammad b. Mukarram. *Lisān al-ʿarab.* 20 vols. Beirut: Dār Ṣadir, 1955–60.

Ibn Qutayba, ʿAbd Allāh b. Muslim. *Kitāb al-maʿārif.* Edited by Tharwat ʿUkkāsha. 2d ed. Cairo: Dār al-Maʿārif, 1969.

Ibn Sa'd, Muḥammad. *Kitāb al-ṭabaqāt al-kabīr.* Edited by Eduard Sachau. 9 vols. in 15. Leiden: Brill, 1904–40.

———. *Ṭabaqāt al-kubrā.* Edited by Ihṣān ʿAbbās. Beirut: Dār Ṣadir, 1960.

Insoll, Timothy. *The Archaeology of Islam.* Oxford: Blackwell, 1999.

al-Jaṣṣāṣ, Abū Bakr. *Aḥkām al-Qur'ān.* 3 vols. Beirut: Dār al-Kitāb al-ʿArabī, n.d.

Jay, Nancy. *Throughout Your Generations Forever: Sacrifice, Religion, and Paternity.* Chicago: University of Chicago Press, 1992.

al-Jazā'irī, Sayyid Niʿmat Allāh. *Qiṣaṣ al-anbiyā'.* Edited by H. M. ʿAqil. Beirut: Dār al-Balāgha, 1991.

al-Jazīrī, ʿAbd al-Raḥmān. *Kitāb al-fiqh ʿala madhāhib al-arbaʿah.* 5 vols. Cairo: Dār al-Ḥadīth, 1990 [?].

Jeffery, Arthur. *The Foreign Vocabulary of the Qur'ān.* Baroda: Oriental Institute, 1938.

———. *The Qur'ān As Scripture.* 1952. Repr., New York: Books for Libraries, 1980.

Jellinek, Adolph, ed. *Bet ha-Midrasch: Sammlung kleiner Midraschim und vermischter Abhandlungen aus der älteren jüdischen Literatur.* 6 vols. 1853–77. Repr., Jerusalem: Bamberger & Wahrmann, 1938.

Jomier, Jacques. "Jesus tel que Ghazali le presente dans *al-Iḥya'*." *MIDEO* 18 (1988): 45–82.

Jourdan, François. *La tradition des Sept Dormants: Une rencontre entre chrétiens et musulmans.* Paris: Maisonneuve et Larose, 2001.

Justin Martyr. *Saint Justin Martyr.* Translated by Thomas B. Falls. New York: Christian Heritage, 1888.

Kadi, Wadad. "Caliph." *EncQur* 1:276–78.

Karoui, Said. *Die Rezeption der Bibel in der frühislamischen Literatur: Am Beispiel der Hauptwerke von Ibn Qutayba (gest. 276/889).* Heidelberg: Seminar für Sprachen und Kulturen des Vorderen Orients, 1997.

Katsh, Abraham I. *Judaism in Islam: Biblical and Talmudic Backgrounds of the Koran and Its Commentaries.* 2d ed. New York: Barnes, 1962.

Kelber, Werner H. "Jesus and Tradition: Words in Time, Words in Space." *Semeia* 65 (1994): 139–47.

———. *The Oral and Written Gospel.* Philadelphia: Fortress, 1983.

Khadduri, Majid. *War and Peace in the Law of Islam.* Baltimore: Johns Hopkins University Press, 1955.

Khalidi, Tarif. *Arabic Historical Thought in the Classical Period.* Cambridge: Cambridge University Press, 1994.

———. *Classical Arab Islam: The Culture and Heritage of the Golden Age.* Princeton: Darwin, 1985.

———. *The Muslim Jesus: Saying and Stories in Islamic Literature.* Cambridge: Harvard University Press, 2001.

Khoury, Raif Georges. *Les légendes prophétiques dans l'Islam depuis le Ier jusqu'au IIIe siècle de l'Hégire.* Wiesbaden: Harrassowitz, 1978.

———. "Quelques réflexions sur la première ou les premières Bibles arabes." Pages 549–61 in *L'Arabie préislamique et son environnement historique et culturel: Actes du Colloque de Strasbourg 24-27 juin 1987.* Edited by T. Fahd. Leiden: Brill, 1989.

al-Kinānī, ʿAbd al-ʿAzīz b. Yaḥya. *Kitāb al-Ḥaydah.* Damascus: n.p., 1964.

al-Kisāʾī, Muhammad b. ʿAbd Allāh. *The Tales of the Prophets of al-Kisaʾi.* Translated and annotated by W. M. Thackston Jr. Boston: Twayne, 1978.

Kister, M. J. "Ādam: A Study of Some Legends in *Tafsīr* and *Ḥadīt* Literature." Pages 113–74 in idem, *Concepts and Ideas at the Dawn of Islam.* Aldershot: Ashgate/Variorum, 1997.

———. ". . . And He Was Born Circumcised. . . ." Pages 10–30 in idem, *Concepts and Ideas at the Dawn of Islam.* Aldershot: Ashgate/Variorum, 1997.

———. "*Ḥaddithū ʿan banī isrāʾīla wa-lā ḥaraja:* A Study of an Early Tradition." *IOS* 2 (1972): 215–39.

Klamroth, Martin. "Der Auszug aus den Evangelien bei dem arabischen Historiker Jaʿqûbî." *Festschrift zur Einweihung des Wilhelm-Gymnasiums in Hamburg am 21. Mai 1885.* Hamburg: Meissner, 1885.

Kronholm, Tryggve. "Dependence and Prophetic Originality in the Koran." *Orientalia Suecana* 31–32 (1982–83): 47–70.

Kugel, James L. *The Bible As It Was.* Cambridge: Harvard University Press, 1997.

———. *In Potiphar's House: The Interpretive Life of Biblical Texts.* San Francisco: HarperCollins, 1990.

———. *Traditions of the Bible: A Guide to the Bible As It Was at the Start of the Common Era.* Cambridge: Harvard University Press, 1998.

Kugel, James L., and Rowan Greer. *Early Biblical Interpretation*. Philadelphia: Westminster, 1986.

al-Kulaynī, Abū Ja'far Muḥammad b. Ya'qūb. *Furū' min al-Kāfī*. Edited by 'Alī Akbar al-Ghaffārī. 5 vols. Tehrān: Maktabat al-Ṣadūq, 1957.

Lagarde, Paul A. de. *Materialen zur Kritik und Geschichte des Pentateuchs*. 2 vols. Leipzig: Teubner, 1867.

Lassner, Jacob. "Abraham Geiger: A Nineteenth-Century Jewish Reformer on the Origins of Islam." Pages 103–35 in *The Jewish Discovery of Islam: Studies in Honor of Bernard Lewis*. Edited by Martin Kramer. Tel Aviv: Tel Aviv University Press, 1999.

———. "The Covenant of the Prophets: Muslim Texts, Jewish Subtext." *AJSR* 15 (1990): 207–38.

———. *Demonizing the Queen of Sheba: Boundaries of Gender and Culture in Postbiblical Judaism and Medieval Islam*. Chicago: University of Chicago Press, 1993.

Lauterbach, Jacob Z., ed. *Mekilta de-Rabbi Ishmael*. 3 vols. 1933–35. Repr., Philadelphia: Jewish Publication Society, 1976.

Lazarus-Yafeh, Hava. *Intertwined Worlds: Medieval Islam and Bible Criticism*. Princeton: Princeton University Press, 1992.

———. *Studies in al-Ghazzālī*. Jerusalem: Magnes, 1975.

Lecker, Michael. "The Death of the Prophet Muḥammad's Father: Did Wāqidī Invent Some of the Evidence?" *ZDMG* 145 (1995): 9–27.

Lecomte, Gérard. "Les citations de l'ancien et du nouveau testament dans l'oeuvre d'Ibn Qutayba." *Arabica* 5 (1958): 24–46.

———. "Ibn Ḳutayba." *EI*² 3:844-46.

Leisten, Thomas. "Between Orthodoxy and Exegesis: Some Aspects of Attitudes in the Shari'a Toward Funerary Architecture." *Muqarnas* 7 (1990): 12–22.

Levenson, Jon D. *The Death and Resurrection of the Beloved Son: The Transformation of Child Sacrifice in Judaism and Christianity*. New Haven: Yale University Press, 1993.

Lewis, Agnes Smith, and Margaret Dunlop Gibson. *The Palestinian Syriac Lectionary of the Gospels*. London: Clay, 1899.

Lewis, Bernard. *Islam and the West*. New York: Oxford University Press, 1993.

———. "On That Day: A Jewish Apocalyptic Poem on the Arab Conquests." Pages 197–200 in *Mélanges d'islamologie: Volume dédié à la memoire de Armand Abel par ses collègues, ses élèves et ses amis*. Edited by P. Salmon. Leiden: Brill, 1974.

Lewis, Jack P. "Jamnia (Jabneh), Council of." *ABD* 3:634–37.

Lewy, I. "The Story of the Golden Calf Reanalyzed." *VT* 9 (1959): 318–22.

Lidzbarski, Mark. *De propheticis, quae dicuntur, legendis arabicis: Prolegomena*. Lipsiae: Drugulini, 1893.

Lundbom, Jack R. "New Covenant." *ABD* 4:1088–94.

Luxenberg, Christoph. *Die syro-aramäische Lesart des Koran: Ein Beitrag zur Entschlüsselung der Koransprache*. Berlin: Das Arabische Buch, 2000.

McAuliffe, Jane Dammen. "The Abrogation of Judaism and Christianity in Islam: A Christian Perspective." *Concilium* (1994/3): 154–63.

———. "Assessing the Isrā'īliyyāt: An Exegetical Conundrum." Pages 345–69 in *Story-Telling in the Framework of Non-fictional Arabic Literature*. Edited by Stefan Leder. Wiesbaden: Harrassowitz, 1998.

———. *Qur'anic Christians: An Analysis of Classical and Modern Exegesis*. Cambridge : Cambridge University Press, 1991.

———. "The Qur'ānic Context of Muslim Biblical Scholarship." *Islam and Christian-Muslim Relations* 7 (1996): 141–58.

———. "Text and Textuality: Q 3:7 As a Point of Intersection." Pages 56–76 in *Literary Structures of Religious Meaning in the Qur'ān*. Edited by Issa J. Boullata. London: Curzon, 2000.

Madelung, Wilferd. *Religious Trends in Early Islamic Iran*. Albany: Bibliotheca Persica, 1988.

———. "Al-Qāsim ibn Ibrāhīm and Christian Theology." *ARAM* 3 (1991): 35–44.

Madigan, Daniel A. *The Qur'ân's Self-Image: Writing and Authority in Islam's Scripture*. Princeton: Princeton University Press, 2001.

al-Majlisī, Muḥammad Bāqir b. Muḥammad Taqī. *Biḥār al-anwār*. 110 vols. to date. Tehran: Dār al-Kutub al-Islaamīyah, 1957–.

Mālik b. Anas. *Al-Muwaṭṭa'*. Edited by Fārūq Sa'd. Beirut: Dār al-Āfāq al-Jadīda, 1981.

al-Maqdisī, al-Muṭahhar b. Ṭāhir. *Kitāb al-bad' wa'l-ta'rīkh*. Edited by Cl. Huart. 6 vols. Paris: Leroux, 1899–1919.

Marcus, David. *Jephthah and His Vow*. Lubbock: Texas Tech University Press, 1986.

Marquet, Yves. "Le shi'isme au IXe siècle à travers l'histoire de Ya'qūbī." *Arabica* 19 (1972): 1–45, 101–38.

Massignon, Louis. "Les sept dormants apocalypse de l'Islam." *AnBoll* 68 (1950): 245–60.

al-Mas'ūdī, Abī al-Ḥasan 'Alī al-Ḥusayn b. 'Alī. *Murūj al-dhahab wa-ma'ādin al-jawhar: Les prairies d'or*. Edited by Charles Barbier de Meynard and Pavet de Courteille. 9 vols. Paris: Imprimerie impériale, 1861–77.

Meyer, Michael A. "Abraham Geiger's Historical Judaism." Pages 3–16 in *New Perspectives on Abraham Geiger: An HUC-JIR Symposium*. Edited by J. J. Petuchowski. Cincinnati: Hebrew Union College Press, 1975.

Michel, Thomas F. *A Muslim Theologian's Response to Christianity: Ibn Taymiyya's al-Jawāb al-sahîh*. Delmar, N.Y.: Caravan, 1984.

Millward, William G. "The Adaptation of Men to Their Time: An Historical Essay by al-Ya'qūbii." *JAOS* 84 (1964): 329–44.

Mingana, Alphonse. *The Book of Religion and Empire*. Manchester: Manchester University Press, 1923.

Morgan, Thais E. "Is There an Intertext in This Text? Literary and Interdisciplinary Approaches to Intertextuality." *American Journal of Semiotics* 3 (1985): 1–40.

Moubarac, Youakim. *Abraham dans le Coran*. Paris: Vrin, 1958.

Mourad, Suleiman A. "On the Qur'anic Stories about Mary and Jesus." *Bulletin of the Royal Institute for Inter-Faith Studies* 1 (1999): 13–24.

———. "A Twelfth-Century Muslim Biography of Jesus." *Islam and Christian-Muslim Relations* 7 (1996): 39–45.

Mulder, Martin Jan, ed. *Mikra: Text, Translation, Reading and Interpretation of the Hebrew Bible in Ancient Judaism and Early Christianity*. Assen: Van Gorcum; Philadelphia: Fortress, 1988.

Murray, Robert. *Symbols of Church and Kingdom: A Study in Early Syriac Tradition*. Cambridge: Cambridge University Press, 1975.

Muslim b. al-Ḥajjāj. *Ṣaḥīḥ Muslim*. Edited by Muḥammad Fū'ād 'Abd al-Bāqī. 5 vols. Beirut: Dār al-Iḥyā' al-Turāth, 1956–72.

Nagel, Tilman. *Die Qiṣaṣ al-Anbiyā': Ein Beitrag zur arabischen Literaturgeschichte*. Bonn: Rheinische Friedrich-Wilhelm-Universität, 1967.

al-Nasafī, 'Abd Allāh b. Aḥmad. *Tafsīr al-Qur'ān al-jalīl*. 3 vols. Cairo: al-Maṭba'ah al-Amīrīyya bi-Būlāq, 1936.

al-Nasā'ī, Aḥmad b. Shu'ayb. *Sunan al-Nasā'ī*. 8 vols. Cairo: Maṭba'a al-Miṣrīya, 1930.

Nau, François. *Les arabes chrétiens de Mésopotamie et de Syrie du VIIe au VIIIe siècle*. Paris: Imprimerie nationale, 1933.

Naumann-Steckner, Friederike. "Death on the Rhine: Changing Burial Customs in Cologne, Third-Seventh Century." Pages 143–58 in *The Transformation of the Roman World, AD 400–900*. Edited by Leslie Webster and Michelle Brown. London: British Museum Press, 1997.

Nelson, Geoffrey K. *Cults, New Religions and Religious Creativity*. London: Routledge & Kegan Paul, 1987.

Nemoy, Leon. Review of John Wansbrough, *Quranic Studies*. *JQR* 68 (1978): 182–84.

Neusner, Jacob. *Aphrahat and Judaism: The Christian-Jewish Argument in Fourth Century Iran*. Leiden: Brill, 1971.

Neuwirth, Angelika. "From the Sacred Mosque to the Remote Temple: Suurat al-Israa' Between Text and Commentary." Pages 376–407 in *With Reverence for the Word: Medieval Scriptural Exegesis in Judaism, Christianity, and Islam*. Edited by Jane Dammen McAuliffe, Barry D. Walfish, and Joseph W. Goering. Oxford: Oxford University Press, 2003.

Newby, Gordon D. *The Making of the Last Prophet: A Reconstruction of the Earliest Biography of Muhammad*. Columbia: University of South Carolina Press, 1989.

———. "Quranic Texture: A Review of Vernon Robbins' *The Tapestry of Early Christian Discourse* and *Exploring the Texture of Texts*." *JSNT* 70 (1998): 93–100.

Nöldeke, Theodor. *Compendious Syriac Grammar*. 2d ed. Translated by J. A. Crichton. Repr., Winona Lake, Ind.: Eisenbrauns, 2001.

Ong, Walter J. *Orality and Literacy: The Technologizing of the Word*. New York: Routledge, 1988.

Origen. *Homilies on Genesis and Exodus*. Translated by Ronald E. Heine. Washington, D.C.: Catholic University of America Press, 1982.

Ory, Solange. *Cimitières et inscriptions du Ḥawrān et du Ǧabal al-Durūz*. Paris: Éditions Recherche sur les Civilisations, 1989.

Paret, Rudi. "Ibraahıim." *EI*² 3:980–81.

———. Review of John Wansbrough, *Quranic Studies*. *Der Islam* 55 (1978): 354–56.

______, ed. *Der Koran*. Darmstadt: Wissenschaftliche Buchgesellschaft, 1975.

Parrinder, Geoffrey. *Jesus in the Qur'ān*. New York: Barnes & Noble, 1965.

Pauliny, Ján. "Some Remarks on the *Qiṣaṣ al-Anbiyā'* Works in Arabic Literature." Pages 313–26 in *The Qur'ān: Formative Interpretation*. Edited by Andrew Rippin. Aldershot: Ashgate, 1999.

Pellat, Charles. "Les encyclopédies dans le monde arabe." *Journal of World History* 9 (1966): 631-58.

———. "Was al-Mas'ûdî an Historian or an *Adīb*?" *Journal of the Pakistan Historical Society* 9 (1961): 231–34.

Penrice, John. *A Dictionary and Glossary of the Kor-ân*. 1873. Repr., London: Curzon, 1970.

Perles, Joseph. *R. Salomo b. Abraham b. Adereth: Sein Leben und seine Schriften*. Breslau: Schletter, 1863.

Peters, F. E. *The Hajj: The Muslim Pilgrimage to Mecca and the Holy Places*. Princeton: Princeton University Press, 1994.

———. "The Quest of the Historical Muhammad." *International Journal of Middle East Studies* 23 (1991): 291–315.

Philo. *Questions and Answers on Genesis*. Translated by Ralph Marcus. LCL. Cambridge: Harvard University Press, 1953.

———. *The Works of Philo: Complete and Unabridged*. Translated by C. D. Yonge. Repr., Peabody, Mass.: Hendrickson, 1993.

Pines, Shlomo. "Gospel Quotations and Cognate Topics in 'Abd al-Jabbār's *Tathbīt* in Relation to Early Christian and Judaeo-Christian Readings and Traditions." *Jerusalem Studies in Arabic and Islam* 9 (1987): 195–278.

Prigent, Pierre. *Les testimonia dans le christianisme primitif: L'Épître de Barnabé I–XVI et ses sources*. Paris: Gabalda, 1961.

Pulcini, Theodore. *Exegesis As Polemical Discourse: Ibn Ḥazm on Jewish and Christian Scriptures*. Atlanta: Scholars Press, 1998.

al-Qurṭubī, Abū 'Abdallāh Muḥammad b. Aḥmad. *al-Jāmi' li-aḥkām al-Qur'ān*. 20 vols. Beirut: Dār al-Kutub al-'Ilmiyya, 1987.

al-Rabghūzī. *The Stories of the Prophets: Qiṣaṣ al-Anbiyā': An Eastern Turkish Version*. Translated by H. E. Boeschoten and M. Vandamme. 2 vols. Leiden: Brill, 1995.

Rad, Gerhard von. *Genesis: A Commentary*. Revised edition. OTL. Philadelphia: Westminster, 1973.

Radtke, Bernd. *Weltgeschichte und Weltbeschreibung im mittelalterlichen Islam*. Beiruter Texte und Studien 51. Beirut and Stuttgart: Steiner, 1992.

Ragg, Lonsdale, and Laura Ragg. *The Gospel of Barnabas*. Oxford: Oxford University Press, 1907.

Rahman, Fazlur. *Major Themes of the Qur'ān*. Minneapolis: Bibliotheca Islamica, 1980.

al-Rāzī, Fakhr al-Dīn. *al-Tafsīr al-kabīr (Mafātīḥ al-ghayb)*. 32 vols. Beirut: Dār al-Fikr, 1981.

Reeves, John C. *Heralds of That Good Realm: Syro-Mesopotamian Gnosis and Jewish Traditions*. NHMS 41. Leiden: Brill, 1996.

———. *Jewish Lore in Manichaean Cosmogony: Studies in the Book of Giants Traditions*. Cincinnati: Hebrew Union College Press, 1992.

Renard, John. "Alexander." *EncQur* 1:61–62.

Ri, Su-Min. *La Caverne des Trésors: Les deux recensions syriaques*. CSCO 486; Scriptores syri 207. Leuven: Peeters, 1987.

———. *Commentaire de la Caverne des Trésors: Études sur l'histoire du texte et de ses sources*. CSCO 581. Leuven: Peeters, 2000.

Ricoeur, Paul. *Essays on Biblical Interpretation.* Philadelphia: Fortress, 1980.

Rippin, Andrew. "Interpreting the Bible through the Qur'ān." Pages 141–58 in *Approaches to the Qur'ān.* Edited by G. R. Hawting and Abdul-Kader A. Shareef. London: Routledge, 1993.

———. "Literary Analysis of *Qur'ān, Tafsīr,* and *Sīra:* The Methodologies of John Wansbrough." Pages 151–63 in *Approaches to Islam in Religious Studies.* Edited by Richard C. Martin. Tucson: University of Arizona Press, 1985.

———. "Reading the Qur'ān with Richard Bell." *JAOS* 112 (1992): 639–47.

Robbins, Vernon K. "Argumentative Textures in Socio-rhetorical Interpretation." Pages 27–65 in *Rhetorical Argumentation in Biblical Texts: Essays from the Lund 2000 Conference.* Edited by A. Eriksson, Thomas H. Olbricht, and Walter Überlacker. Harrisburg, Pa.: Trinity Press International, 2002.

———. "The Dialectical Nature of Early Christian Discourse." *Scriptura* 59 (1996): 353–62.

———. "Oral, Rhetorical, and Literary Communities: A Response." *Semeia* 65 (1994): 75–91.

———. "Where is Wuellner's Anti-hermeneutical Hermeneutic Taking Us? From Schleiermacher to Thisleton and Beyond." Forthcoming.

Robin, C., and J. Beaucamp. "Le christianisme dans la péninsule arabique d'après l'épigraphie et l'archéologie." *Travaux et mémoires* 8 (1981): 45–61.

Robinson, Neal. *Christ in Islam and Christianity: The Representation of Jesus in the Qur'an and the Classical Muslim Commentaries.* Albany: State University of New York Press, 1991.

———. "Jesus and Mary in the Qur'ān: Some Neglected Affinities." *Religion* 20 (1990): 161–75.

Robinson, Patricia Anne. "The Conception of Death in Judaism in the Hellenistic and Early Roman Period." Ph.D. diss., University of Wisconsin, 1978.

Roches, Léon. *Dix ans a travers l'Islam.* 3d ed. Paris: Perrin, 1904.

Rosenthal, Franz. *A History of Muslim Historiography.* Leiden: Brill, 1952.

———. "The Influence of the Biblical Tradition on Muslim Historiography." Pages 35–45 in *Historians of the Middle East.* Edited by Bernard Lewis and P. M. Holt. London: Oxford University Press, 1962.

Rubin, Uri. *Between Bible and Qur'aan: The Children of Israel and the Islamic Self-Image.* Princeton: Darwin, 1999.

———. *The Eye of the Beholder: The Life of Muḥammad As Viewed by the Early Muslims.* Princeton: Darwin, 1995.

———. "Ḥanīfiyya and Ka'ba." *Jerusalem Studies in Arabic and Islam* 13 (1990): 96–112.

———. "Pre-existence and Light: Aspects of the Concept of Nūr Muḥammad." *IOS* 5 (1975): 62–119.

———. "Prophets and Progenitors in the Early Shī'a Tradition." *Jerusalem Studies in Arabic and Islam* 1 (1979): 41–65.

Rudolph, Wilhelm. *Die Abhängigkeit des Qorans von Judentum und Christentum.* Stuttgart: Kohlhammer, 1922.

Sābiq, al-Sayyid. *Fiqh al-sunnah.* 5 vols. Beirut: Dār al-Kitāb al-'Arabī, 1969.

Said, Edward W. *Orientalism.* New York: Pantheon, 1978.

Samsó, Julio. "Māshā' Allaah." EI^2 6:710–12.

Sanders, James A., and Harry Y. Gamble. "Canon." *ABD* 1:837–61.

Savage, Elizabeth. *A Gateway to Hell, A Gateway to Paradise: The North African Response to the Arab Conquest*. Princeton: Darwin, 1997.

Schacht, Joseph. *An Introduction to Islamic Law*. Oxford: Clarendon, 1964.

Schapiro, Israel. *Die haggadischen Elemente im erzählenden Teil des Korans*. Leipzig: Fock, 1907.

Schleifer, Aliah. *Mary, the Blessed Virgin of Islam*. Louisville: Fons Vitae, 1998.

Schöck, Cornelia. "Adam and Eve." *EncQur* 1:22–26.

Schorsch, Ismar. *From Text to Context: The Turn to History in Modern Judaism*. Hanover, N.H.: University Press of New England, 1994.

Schreiner, Martin. "Al-Jaḳubī über den Glauben und die Sitten der Juden." *MGWJ* 34 (1885): 135–39.

Schützinger, Heinrich. *Ursprung und Entwicklung der arabischen Abraham-Nimrod Legende*. Bonn: Rheinische Friedrich-Wilhelms-Universität, 1961.

Schwarzbaum, Haim. Biblical and Extra-Biblical Legends in Islamic Folk-Literature. Beiträge zur Sprach- und Kulturgeschichte des Orients 30. Walldorf-Hessen: Verlag für Orientkunde Dr. H. Vorndran, 1982.

Scott, Bernard Brandon, and Margaret E. Dean. "A Sound Mapping of the Sermon on the Mount." Pages 311–78 in *Treasures New and Old: Recent Contributions to Matthean Studies*. Edited by D. R. Baur and M. A. Powell. SBLSymS 1. Atlanta: Scholars Press, 1996.

Séd, Nicolas. "Les hymnes sur le Paradis de Saint Ephrem et les traditions juives." *Mus* 81 (1968): 455–501.

Sellheim, Rudolf. "Prophet, Chalif und Geschichte." *Oriens* 18–19 (1965–66): 33–91.

Serjeant, R. B. Review of John Wansbrough, *Quranic Studies*. *JRAS* (1978): 76–78.

Sezgin, Fuat. *Geschichte des arabischen Schrifttums*. 12 vols. to date. Leiden: Brill, 1967–.

Shahid, Irfan. *Byzantium and the Arabs in the Fifth Century*. Washington, D.C.: Dumbarton Oaks, 1984.

———. *Byzantium and the Arabs in the Fourth Century*. Washington, D.C.: Dumbarton Oaks, 1989.

———. *Byzantium and the Arabs in the Sixth Century*. Vol. 1, parts 1 and 2. Washington, D.C.: Dumbarton Oaks, 1995.

———. *Byzantium and the Arabs in the Sixth Century*. Vol. 2, part 1. Washington, D.C.: Dumbarton Oaks, 2002.

Sidersky, David. *Les origines des légendes musulmanes dans le Coran et dans les vies des prophètes*. Paris: Librairie Orientaliste Paul Geuthner, 1933.

Slomp, Jan. "The Gospel in Dispute." *Islamochristiana* 4 (1977): 67–112.

Smit, G. *"Bijbel en Legende" bij den arabischen Schrijver Ja'qubi, 9th Eeuw na Christus*. Leiden: Brill, 1907.

Smolar, Leivy, and Moshe Aberbach. "The Golden Calf Episode in Postbiblical Literature." *HUCA* 39 (1968): 91–116.

Sox, David. *The Gospel of Barnabas*. London: Allen & Unwin, 1984.

Speyer, Heinrich. *Die biblischen Erzählungen im Qoran*. 1961. Repr., Hildesheim: Olms, 1988.

Stark, Rodney. "How New Religions Succeed: A Theoretical Model." Pages 11–29 in *The Future of New Religious Movements*. Edited by David G. Bromley and Phillip E. Hammond. Macon, Ga.: Mercer University Press, 1987.

Stark, Rodney, and William Simms Bainbridge. *The Future of Religion: Secularization, Revival, and Cult Formation*. Berkeley and Los Angeles: University of California Press, 1985.

———. *A Theory of Religion*. New Brunswick, N.J.: Rutgers University Press, 1996.

Stern, S. M. "Abd al-Jabbār's Account of How Christ's Religion Was Falsified by the Adoption of Roman Customs." *JTS* NS 19 (1968): 128–85.

———. "Quotations from Apocryphal Gospels in 'Abd al-Jabbār." *JTS* NS 18 (1967): 34–57.

Sternberg, Meir. *The Poetics of Biblical Narrative: Ideological Literature and the Drama of Reading*. Bloomington: Indiana University Press, 1985.

Stewart, Devin J. "Saj' in the Qur'ān: Prosody and Structure." *Journal of Arabic Literature* 21 (1990): 101–39.

Stichel, Rainer. "Bemerkungen zum Barnabas-Evangelium." *Byzantinoslavica* 43 (1982): 189–201.

Stillman, Norman A. "The Story of Cain and Abel in the Qur'an and the Muslim Commentators: Some Observations." *JSS* 19 (1974): 231–39.

al-Suyūṭī, Jalāl al-Dīn. *Al-Itqān fī 'ulūm al-Qur'ān*. Beirut: n.p., n.d.

al-Ṭabarī, Abū Ja'far Muḥammad b. Jarīr. *The Ancient Kingdoms*. Vol. 4 of *The History of al-Ṭabarī*. Translated by Moshe Perlmann. Albany: State University of New York Press, 1987.

———. *The Commentary on the Qur'ān: Being an Abridged Translation of Jāmi' al-bayān 'an ta'wīl āy al-Qur'ān*. Edited by J. Cooper, W. F. Madelung, and A. Jones. Oxford: Oxford University Press, 1987.

———. *General Introduction and From the Creation to the Flood*. Vol. 1 of *The History of al-Ṭabarī*. Translated by Franz Rosenthal. Albany: State University of New York Press, 1989.

———. *Jāmi' al-bayān 'an ta'wīl āy al-Qur'ān*. 16 vols. Edited by Maḥmūd Muḥammad Shākir et al. Cairo: Dār al-Ma'ārif, 1954–68.

———. *Jāmi' al-bayān 'an ta'wīl āy al-Qur'ān*. 30 vols. Edited by Aḥmad Sā'īd 'Alī et al. Cairo, 1954–57. Repr., Beirut: Dār al-Fikr, 1984.

———. *Prophets and Patriarchs*. Vol. 2 of *The History of al-Ṭabarī*. Translated and annotated by William M. Brinner. Albany: State University of New York Press, 1987.

———. *Ta'rīkh al-rusul wa-l-mulūk*. 15 vols. Edited by M. J. de Goeje et al. Leiden: Brill, 1879–1901.

Thackeray, Henry St. John. *Josephus: Jewish Antiquities, Books I–IV*. LCL. Cambridge: Harvard University Press; London: Heinemann, 1930.

al-Tha'labī, Aḥmad b. Muhammad b. Ibrāhīm. *Qiṣaṣ al-anbiyā'*. Beirut: Dār al-Kutub 'Ilmiyya, 1994.

Thomas, David. "The Bible in Early Muslim Anti-Christian Polemic." *Islam and Christian-Muslim Relations* 7 (1996): 29–38.

———. "Tabari's Book of Religion and Empire." *BJRL* 69 (1986): 1–7.

Thompson, Stith. *Motif-Index of Folk-Literature*. 6 vols. Bloomington: Indiana University Press, 1932–36.

al-Tirmidhī, Abū ʿĪsaa Muḥammad b. ʿĪsā. *al-Jamīʿ al-Ṣaḥīḥ*. 5 vols. Edited by Aḥmad Muḥammad Shākir. Cairo: Maṭbaʿa al-Miṣrīya, 1931–34.

Tottoli, Roberto. "Origin and Use of the Term *Isrā'īliyyāt* in Muslim Literature." *Arabica* 46 (1999): 193–210.

———. *I profeti biblici nella tradizione islamica*. Brescia: Paideia Editrice, 1999.

Tracy, David. *Plurality and Ambiguity: Hermeneutics, Religion, Hope*. San Francisco: Harper & Row, 1987.

Trimingham, J. Spencer. *Christianity among the Arabs in Pre-Islamic Times*. London: Longman, 1979.

Ṭurṭūshī, Muḥammad b. al-Walīd. *Sirāj al-mulūk*. Cairo: Būlāq, 1872.

al-Ṭūsī, Muhammad b. al-Ḥasan. *Tibyān fī tafsīr al-Qur'ān*. Beirut: Dār Iḥyā' al-Turāth al-ʿArabī, n.d.

Tvedtnes, John A., Brian M. Hauglid, and John Gee, eds. *Traditions about the Early Life of Abraham*. Provo, Utah: Foundation for Ancient Research and Mormon Studies and Brigham Young University, 2001.

Twersky, Isadore, ed. *Studies in Medieval Jewish History and Literature*. 3 vols. Cambridge: Harvard University Press, 1979–2000.

Ullendorf, Edward. Review of John Wansbrough, *Quranic Studies*. *BSOAS* 40 (1977): 609–12.

Vajda, Georges. "Hārūt wa-Mārūt." *EI*[2] 3:236–37.

———. "Idrīs." *EI*[2] 3:1030–31.

———. "Observations sur quelques citations bibliques chez Ibn Qotayba." *REJ* 99 (1935): 68–80.

VanderKam, James C. *Enoch: A Man for All Generations*. Columbia: University of South Carolina Press, 1995.

al-Wāḥidī, Abū al-Ḥasan ʿAlī b. Aḥmad. *Asbāb al-nuzūl*. Beirut: al-Maktabah al-Thaqāfīyah, 1410.

Waldman, Marilyn R. "New Approaches to 'Biblical' Materials in the Qur'ān." *MW* 75 (1985): 1–16.

———. "Nubuuwah." *ER* 11:1–7.

Wansbrough, John. *Quranic Studies: Sources and Methods of Scriptural Interpretation*. Oxford: Oxford University Press, 1977.

———. *The Sectarian Milieu: Content and Composition of Islamic Salvation History*. London Oriental Series 34. Oxford: Oxford University Press, 1978.

Wasserstrom, Steven M. *Between Muslim and Jew: The Problem of Symbiosis under Early Islam*. Princeton: Princeton University Press, 1995.

Watt, William Montgomery. "Iskandar." *EI*[2] 4:127.

Welch, Alfred T. "al-Ḳur'ān." *EI*[2] 5:400–429.

Wengst, Klaus. *Tradition und Theologie des Barnabasbriefes*. Berlin: de Gruyter, 1971.

Wensinck, A.J. "Khitaan." *EI*[2] 5:20–22.

West, Gerald O. *Biblical Hermeneutics of Liberation: Modes of Reading the Bible in the South African Context*. 2d ed. Maryknoll, N.Y.: Orbis, 1995.

Wheeler, Brannon M. *Moses in the Quran and Islamic Exegesis*. Richmond, Surrey: Curzon, 2000.

———. *Prophets in the Quran: An Introduction to the Quran and Muslim Exegesis*. London: Continuum, 2002.

Widengren, Geo. *Muhammad, the Apostle of God, and His Ascension*. Uppsala: Lundequistska Bokhandeln, 1955.

———. "Oral Tradition and Written Literature among the Hebrews in the Light of Arabic Evidence, with Special Regard to Prose Narratives." *AcOr* 23 (1959): 244–62.

Wiet, Gaston. *Les pays*. Textes et traductions d'auteurs orientaux 1. Cairo: Institut Français d'Archéologie Orientale, 1937.

Wild, Stefan. "The Self-Referentiality of the Qur'ān: Sūra 3:7 As an Exegetical Challenge." Pages 422–36 in *With Reverence for the Word: Medieval Scriptural Exegesis in Judaism, Christianity, and Islam*. Edited by Jane Dammen McAuliffe, Barry D. Walfish, and Joseph W. Goering. Oxford: Oxford University Press, 2003.

Wuellner, Wilhelm H. "Hermeneutics and Rhetorics: From 'Truth and Method' to 'Truth and Power.'" *Scriptura* special issue 3 (1989): 1–54.

———. "Toposforschung und Torahinterpretation bei Paulus und Jesus." *NTS* 24 (1978): 463–83.

al-Ya'qūbī. *Ta'rīkh*. 2 vols. Beirut: Dār Ṣadir, 1960.

Yarshater, Ehsan, ed. *The History of al-Ṭabarī*. 39 vols. Albany: State University of New York Press, 1987–98.

Yassif, Eli, ed. *Sefer Zikkronot hu' Divrey ha-Yamim le-Yeraḥme'el*. Tel Aviv: Tel Aviv University Press, 2001.

Young, M. J. L., J. D. Latham, and R. B. Serjeant, eds. *Religion, Learning and Science in the 'Abbasid Period*. The Cambridge History of Arabic Literature. Cambridge: Cambridge University Press, 1990.

al-Zamakhsharī, Abū al-Qāsim Maḥmūd b. 'Umar. *al-Kashshāf ḥaqā'iq al-tanzīl wa 'uyūn al-aqāwīl fī wujūh al-ta'wīl*. 4 vols. Cairo: Muṣṭafā al-Bābī al-Ḥalabī, 1966–68.

al-Zarkashī, Badr al-Dīn. *al-Burhān fī 'ulūm al-Qur'ān*. Edited by Yusūf 'Abd al-Raḥmān al-Mar'ashlī et al. Beirut: Dār al-Ma'arifah, 1415.

al-Ziriklī, Khayr al-Dīn. *A'lām*. 8 vols. Beirut: Dār al-'Ilm lil-Malāyīn, 1992.

Zlotnick, Dov, ed. *The Tractate "Mourning" (Śĕmaḥot): Regulations Relating to Death, Burial and Mourning*. Yale Judaica Series 17. New Haven: Yale University Press, 1966.

Zucker, Moshe. *Saadya's Commentary on Genesis*. New York: Jewish Theological Seminary of America, 1984.

al-Zuḥaylī, Wahba Mustafa. *Athar al-Ḥarb fil-Fiqh al-Islami*. Beirut: Dār al-Fikr, n.d.

Index to Citations of Bible, Jewish and Christian Parascriptural Sources, and Qurān

1. Hebrew Bible

2. New Testament

3. Jewish Apocrypha and Pseudepigrapha

4. Greco-Jewish Authors

5. Rabbinic Literature

6. Christian Parascriptural Sources

7. Qur'ān

4:93 41
4:97 41
4:104 37
4:109 40
4:111 37
4:115 41
4:121 41
4:122 40
4:125 180
4:127 37
4:134 38
4:136 40
4:140 41
4:141 40
4:145 41
4:147 37
4:148 37
4:153 34
4:155 33
4:157 33, 36, 150
4:157–158 136, 158
4:158 36
4:159 40
4:160 61, 62, 73, 74, 78, 80, 83, 84
4:162 40
4:163 36
4:163–164 39
4:165 33, 36
4:169 41
4:170 37
4:171 36, 135, 155
4:176 37
5:3 76
5:7 37
5:10 41
5:12 40
5:14 21, 40
5:17 33, 36, 135
5:19 33
5:27 36, 41
5:27–32 54
5:29 41
5:31 188
5:32 34
5:36 40
5:38 33, 36
5:40 33
5:41–45 85
5:42 85
5:45 170
5:46 36
5:47 134
5:64 40
5:65 40
5:68 133
5:69 40
5:71 38
5:72 41
5:75 135
5:76 37
5:78 36
5:81 157
5:85 40
5:86 41
5:97 37
5:109 37
5:110 34, 36, 124, 135
5:110–111 156
5:112 36
5:114 36
5:116 36
5:118 33, 36
5:119 40
5:120 33
6:12 40
6:13 37
6:17 33
6:18 37
6:23 166
6:27 41
6:35 33
6:42 92
6:50 37
6:53 37
6:57 34
6:58 37
6:73 37
6:74 95, 96
6:74–82 89
6:76–78 92
6:76–79 96, 101
6:79 180
6:83 37
6:85 34, 36

Index of Scriptural/Parascriptural Characters

Index of Postscriptural Traditional Commentators and Tradents

Index of Modern Authors

Printed in the United States
1351500003B/287